NEWMARKET

NEWMARKET

From James I to the Present Day

Laura Thompson

Virgin

To my father, Andy Thompson,
who, among much else,
left me his love of horse racing
1924–1999

First published in Great Britain in 2000 by

Virgin Publishing Ltd
Thames Wharf Studios
Rainville Road
London W6 9HA

A catalogue record for this book is available
from the British Library.

ISBN 0 1852 278 536

Cover design by Button Design Company
Typeset by TW Typesetting, Plymouth, Devon
Printed and bound by
Mackays of Chatham plc, Chatham, Kent

Contents

List of Illustrations

Author's Note

For the purposes of translating the sums of money mentioned in this book into approximate present-day values, the following may be of use:

£1 in 1660 is the equivalent of £69.46
£1 in 1790 is the equivalent of £52.09
£1 in 1860 is the equivalent of £42.74
£1 in 1900 is the equivalent of £53.77
£1 in 1930 is the equivalent of £29.25
£1 in 1960 is the equivalent of £13.44

As an example, it can be estimated that Lord Hastings lost in excess of £4 million on Hermit's Derby in 1867, when £1 was equivalent to £39.69.

All figures are as of November 1999, and are kindly supplied by the Bank of England.

Acknowledgements

Many people have helped me to write this book, through conversations about racing that taught me far more than I could ever have learned for myself. But I should specifically like to thank: Mr Peter Amos and Mr John Robinson, of the Jockey Club, for their kindness in showing me round the Rooms and the Estates; Mr Kim Deshayes and Captain Nick Lees at Newmarket racecourse; Mr Eric Dunning for his generously shared knowledge of local history; the National Horseracing Museum and Palace House; Humphrey Price at Virgin Publishing; Christopher Little; and my parents, as always.

1 Beginnings

'To be Run in Perpetuity' – 61 AD–1660

I T IS NOT A BEAUTIFUL PLACE. Frankly, it is above all that. What it has is a sense of purpose – more precious nowadays than beauty – unbroken and unchanged for more than three hundred years.

When beauty comes, it comes incidentally. Driving along Six Mile Bottom on the road into the town, at the start of the racing season, with leaves glittering on the trees and newness abounding amid the familiar landmarks: Swynford Paddocks to the left, the Green Man to the right; the signs that read Bottisham Heath Stud and Lordship Stud, discreet and simple signs that contain within them who knows what possibility. The first glimpse of a horse, a lazy flicking tail or a head dropping to the grass; and then the suddenly widening road, and the sense of the Heath spread around it, and the first sight of horseboxes, and the newest landmark of them all, the tall white grandstand flying above the Rowley Mile racecourse. It is a familiar journey, but every time it brings an excitement that is almost fear: of the emotions that the thoroughbred horse can command and demand.

And then, at the top of Warren Hill, on a sunny morning in late autumn, when the Newmarket racing season is over and just one or two lone horses are out in their rugs. The town below, in that other world at the foot of the hill, lightly wrapped in deep golden chiffon; the cars, driving by just a few yards away, stunned into silence; the Heath still spread around in a patient infinity of space. Quietness hums. A dog leaps and circles in the far distance like a brindled leaf. There is the sense, the knowledge, that this piece of ground, with its resilient and peculiarly taxing turf, has what almost nothing in the modern world is allowed to have – a future that is the same as its past.

How has it got away with it? The world today has no time for dedication of purpose. It loves change, makeovers, radical rethinks. So how is it that Newmarket Heath feels, not vulnerable, but strong and serene in its lack of beauty, its plain and featureless landscape? How is it that this little town – a perfectly normal place, like any other – is ruled by the law of the Heath, and that a self-regarding twit in a souped-up Nissan, who elsewhere would brush the toe-caps of jaywalking pensioners as he powers his way to a sales conference, here will stop respectfully for a string of thoroughbreds to cross the road, and get a comradely thrill from their trainer's nod of acknowledgement? How is it that the whole thing has not been turned into an open-air museum, a Stratford-upon-Avon with horses instead of hey-nonny-nos, and that there is no sign pointing to 'Newmarket's Historic Heath', just the businesslike white board, terse to the point of impenetrability, that reads: 'GALLOPS OPEN: BURY HILL; LONG HILL; SIDE HILL WOODCHIP; PEAT MOSS GALLOPS; BACK OF THE FLAT; THE FLAT'? How has it kept this fixity, this continuity?

Because Newmarket is supported by love, an apparently limitless quantity of it, and has been ever since it evolved from an ordinary market town into the home of the racehorse, the story of Newmarket is the story of love over logic. Vast, unstoppable waves of people have hurled themselves against the Heath – which, like all the best love objects, looks on with indifference – in the hope of meeting its remorseless challenge. Fabulous amounts of money have been won and lost; countless numbers of races have been run; hope has been defeated over and over and over again; and still people have come back for more, compelled by a vision of triumph, a dream of conquest which is supremely, magnificently, idiotically romantic.

Yet the most wonderful thing about Newmarket is that it is not romantic at all, just as it is not beautiful. Again, it does not have to be. It is far too busy getting on with the job. That is why it can never be an open-air museum; because it is alive whereas Stratford, by definition, is dead. And so it does not have to strive after emotion, to strain for tears in front of a little sixteenth-century Warwickshire house; because it has a constantly renewable natural source of it.

If, incidentally, the sight of horses at exercise in the early morning is so exquisite that it makes some silly owner want to cry, then that is fine; that, of course, is what is keeping the silly owner hooked. At the same time, it is the brisk acceptance of this innate romance – too deeply absorbed to require comment – that gives the silly owner an even greater buzz. One can stand on Newmarket Heath, just as owners have stood there for more than three hundred years, and yet one is just standing there. It is magical, a symbol of past and future; and it is happening in the here and now. The closer one gets to Newmarket, the more mysterious it becomes. This is not because it is striving for mystery; quite the opposite. And this is its eternal paradox, something that has kept people hooked for the last three and a half centuries.

In high summer, the sun at seven o'clock in the morning will make Warren Hill look like a pencil drawing by Peter Tillemans – who sketched the Heath in the early eighteenth century – suddenly flooded with colour. At a distance, the strings of horses coil and stretch against the flat East Anglian sky, nothing to pick them out except the rugs that they wear with their trainers' initials: HRAC, LMC, MS. One of them may appear to be flying, another labouring, but the names that anchor them to knowledge are submerged in the wider picture. It is casual, rhythmic and hypnotic, yet it is always informed by that sense of purpose, of living in the present, of racing glasses held tensely to the eyes.

A massed string, breathing and steaming like furnaces, stands like a bunch of schoolchildren at the side of the road, waiting to cross and make its languid way home. And then there is a sudden break: a horse dances sideways in a quick shock of nameless fear, eyes on fire, head and quarters seeming to whirl. Chaos briefly threatens – there are five loose horses on the Heath in an average day – but with a small, neat flourish the work rider brings his mount back into line, without fuss, without the cigarette in his mouth even moving. These riders – who are jockeys without the fanfare, although of course jockeys also work ride – compel with their thin, exhausted faces and their laconic amiability. They are so adult, so matter-of-fact, so manly, even when they are seventeen year olds, even when they are female. For Newmarket is a wholly masculine town. If the modern world has become feminised, to the extent that maleness has become a 'concept' rather than a simple fact, then here – where concepts do not really exist, there being far too much else to think about – it is the old, male, discredited virtues that hold sway: stoicism, self-discipline, courage, unfussiness, cheerfulness in the face of hardship. This is not a place where jockeys go for counselling when they crave a chocolate bar. In fact, much of what has disappeared from the modern world – for better or worse – is still here, in Newmarket. Maybe other towns held a similar sense of purpose when they had their industries and crafts, and before the shopping mall became a community temple.

So how can Newmarket not feel different from any other town, when over half of its working population – around 3,500 out of 6,500 people – is connected in one way or another with the same industry: be they trainers, trainers' wives (who tend to be smiling heroines, and do a lot of the work), jockeys, stable hands, saddlers, blacksmiths, vets, stud workers, bloodstock agents, racecourse officials, grounds-men, Jockey Club members? When skinny, bow-legged types, in whom life burns with a fierce pulse, stride along the High Street in between the slower people, and skim the aisles of Waitrose with their empty trolleys? When at the side of every road is a stable or stud full of many thousands of pounds' worth of horse? When the town is constantly descended upon by monarchs, celebrities, aristocrats, people of unimaginable wealth? When almost everyone who works there, whether they admit it or not, is head over heels in love with this wondrous other world that they inhabit, beyond which lies the exile of dread normality? When what seems like a town hermetically sealed from 'real life' is, in fact, real in a way that nowhere else begins to be?

And when, all around, for people to pass as they go to work, or to the pub, or out for a bike ride, is the Heath:

the source of this fixity, this continuity, this strong and indifferent serenity. It is forbidding; it is awesome. Yet at the same time it is open to anyone. One can park one's car by the side of the road at seven, nine or eleven o'clock in the morning, stand there and watch horses at exercise; although an invisible film lies between spectator and spectacle, through which only a very brave soul indeed would burst. There are more fences around the Heath now than there were ten years ago – white posts everywhere to separate town and thoroughbred – and so fewer accidents and *contretemps*. Yet the accessibility of the place, the public nature of something regarded as sacred, is – to someone who first encountered it on the day of the Two Thousand Guineas – still shocking, as if picnic hampers were being unpacked on the pitch at Lord's after a Test Match. Down at the winning post to the Rowley Mile – the longest piece of straight turf on any racecourse in the world – on a Sunday afternoon out of season, one can stare down that broad, plain, silent stretch of ground to the point where the start for the Guineas meets the sky. There is, again, nothing to see. No hooves are heard, no dead Guineas winners thunder up the straight. They are all there, nevertheless. Then in amongst them a dog will bound joyfully across the turf – by the two furlong pole, where Celtic Swing took the lead in 1995 before being caught by Pennekamp; and it is not exactly *lèse majesté*. It is proof, in fact, that true majesty has no need to protect itself.

As well as the two racecourses – the Rowley Mile and the July – there are 2,800 acres of training grounds on the Heath. These are split into two sides: Racecourse and Bury. Racecourse Side is flat and open and runs alongside the Cambridge Road. Bury Side is more decorative with its trees and its slopes: here are Warren Hill, Side Hill, Long Hill, Bury Hill, the famous gallops set between the roads that lead eastwards out of Newmarket. A little further up are the Limekilns, including the curve around which horses can work in reverse, left-handed, as preparation for the Epsom Derby. In all there are forty miles of turf gallops, seventeen miles of artificial gallops and, perhaps surprisingly, 300 acres of training grounds for National Hunt

5

horses.[1] A strip of turf ground used on a particular day will not, thereafter, be used for at least two years, in order that the grass may recover that strange, elastic spring (which, according to an 1863 history of racing, 'is said to arise from the nightly working of the earthworms'). There is a gallop for every horse in Newmarket, whatever age, whatever level of fitness, whatever race is being targeted. The provision is extraordinary but then it has to be, what with having around 2,500 horses to cope with. The number varies, of course, but for 1999 one can assume 28 per cent of the British total, winning 38 per cent of British races.

All this land is the property of the Jockey Club Estates, which owns a good deal else in Newmarket: an additional 1,700 acres, 74 residential properties (which house former and current workers), commercial properties including two Happy Eater restaurants (of which the Club takes 1.5 per cent of annual turnover), the Jockey Club Rooms on the High Street, Newmarket cemetery, the Hamilton Estate on which stand several training yards, and three stud farms including the National Stud, next door to the July Course, which pays a peppercorn rent. The Jockey Club is racing's ruling body and Newmarket's chief landlord. Again, this is not the modern way. One could have a field day on the subject of anti-democratic oligarchies, but it would rather miss the point. The fact is that the Jockey Club is efficient, and looking after the Heath is not a job for people who abide by EU working time directives. Just twelve men are currently employed on each side of the gallops, while there were twice as many in the 1950s. Obviously, equipment has improved but, even so, this is impressive. Keeping that turf in peak condition is one hell of a job. It costs the Jockey Club around £1.25 million a year, to which owners contribute by paying the Heath Tax of £75 per month for each horse. Without it,

---

[1] There is, of course, no jumps racing in Newmarket, and few NH horses are trained there although a surprising number of trainers hold dual licences. Yet there was a NH course in the town at the end of the nineteenth century, by The Links on the Cambridge Road, laid out by a hugely rich owner named Colonel Harry McCalmont (who lived at the beautiful Cheveley Park stud, where his best horse, Isinglass, stood as a stallion). The course was closed down in 1907. It had not been helped by the fact that 'spectators' could watch the racing from the side of the road without paying to enter.

Newmarket would be nothing, for if the Heath no longer turned out that 38 per cent of winners – including, in 1999, the winners of all five of the classic races[2] – then Newmarket might as well throw in its lot with the shopping mall brigade.

It is because the Heath is, and always has been, unparalleled galloping ground that we are all here at the end of October, as the twentieth century slides away, on the last day of racing staged by Newmarket in the 1999 season. Because of the building of the new Rowley Mile grandstand, we are still on the July Course, which usually stages only summer racing and is in a state of shock. Its tall trees are shivering like lanky girls in an under-heated dance hall; sodden leaves lie between the pages of everyone's racecard; the wind that thrusts unchecked between Siberia and Suffolk is pushing like a gatecrasher into the racecourse bars.

It couldn't matter less. This is Newmarket as it is supposed to be, even though it is the wrong course at the wrong time of year. Autumn suits the place. Other racecourses need sunshine to give them glamour, to weave a semi-blinding spell, unifying spectators and horses in a beneficent haze. Royal Ascot in the rain falls apart completely, because so few people there give a toss about racing, but Newmarket at the end of the season, when the fair-weather friends have returned to their lairs, when the big race day crowds have gone to the hypermarket, the football or the pub instead, has the brisk earthiness of a National Hunt meeting. The bars smell, thickly, of red wine and beer and fags; the spume of champagne has subsided for the year. Clothes are brown, tweedy, sporting. The *Racing Post* and *Timeform* are carried like a sword and buckler. A robust camaraderie pervades the racecourse. One feels like a member of the *cognoscenti*, even if one is no such thing. Hell, one *wants* to feel like it. Two young women stand by the paddock before the last race of that last meeting, not dressed in all the brown – dressed, in fact, in a way that seems to say that they are not there for the racing, they are there on the pull, flapping their dank

---

[2] Henry Cecil trained the winners of the Derby (Oath), the Oaks (Ramruma) and the One Thousand Guineas (Wince). In the Two Thousand Guineas and St Leger he finished second to the Godolphin-owned, Saeed bin Suroor-trained horses, Island Sands and Mutafaweq respectively.

racecards like fans and giggling as they fish leaves from out of the fronts of their shirts. How wonderfully wrong racing's judgements can be! Their conversation was a delighted, serious complexity of working out the form, of getting to grips with something unusual and fascinating, of expressing the equation of soft ground minus top weight equals plus Kieren Fallon to the power of three, and was that the solution? These women did not want to be patronised and indulged and bought drinks by some silly man. Nor, on this day, with its casual, elegaic magic, did silly men particularly want to buy drinks for women. They wanted to read the form and look at horses and lose themselves in what they were doing. They were there, like the women, to become part of this other, mysterious world, the one that they did not normally inhabit, whose spell was somehow blooming in the cold and the rain.

The charm of this racecourse is, in fact, indestructible, even when the place is overrun with drunks at evening meetings and when relaxation, the defining note of the July Course, begins to look like carelessness. It is the prettiest racecourse in the country: all rich earth and massed flowers and green velvet turf. Everything in it is reduced to a state of homely simplicity. The winners' enclosure looks like nothing so much as the back garden of a thatched cottage, roughly divided into four. The grandstand, built in the 1930s, is a bare wooden structure. The pre-parade ring, shadowy and secretive even on the sunniest of days, is shrouded by trees as tall as in a forest (planted, the story has it, by prisoners from the Napoleonic war) among which the horses tread as if in a rustic fairytale, their whinnies sliding up through the branches and shivering in the air.

It is an idyll – even during the July week meeting, when the crowds swell to 9,000 or so. There is always something clubbable about it, with that intimate little winners' enclosure which gives spectators the sense that they can just lean in and chat to trainers, jockeys, owners. There is still that closeness to the horses, as they stroll easily between pre-parade ring and paddock, on what is for so many of them their home ground. The racing is important in July week – the Princess of Wales' Stakes, the Falmouth Stakes, the sprint

July Cup, the July Stakes for two-year-olds – and still the sense persists of drifting through a garden behind which, by a stroke of magic, these miraculously engineered animals are racing up the green velvet straight.

On the Rowley Mile, things are quite different. Tension, purposefulness, the excitement that is almost fear, rise and spread across this flat and functional plain, where the deadly serious business of the Guineas, the Champion Stakes, the Dewhurst Stakes, the Cambridgeshire, the Cesarewitch must be conducted. By Newmarket standards, the July Course *is* a little feminised, a place for drinks overflowing with fruit and £2 each way on the Tote: it has a touch of the All England Tennis Club about it. But the Rowley Mile is a man's world. Bookmakers' shouts ring out clear and harsh; gamblers pace with one hand perpetually on their wallets, and the yearning for knowledge, for information, for money, for a *win* puts its hot, savoury tang into the air. The horses have slipped back behind their invisible wall; no time now for the illusion of accessibility. Christ, no, these animals are at work. Here there is no beauty, no gentrification, no rustic charm; just low brick buildings, a sweeping paddock, a stretch of unforgiving turf. Racing has been reduced to its mysterious essence. Nothing but atmosphere fills the immense spaces. Nothing more is needed.

The new grandstand, handsome though it is, as it should be for £16 million, will not change this. The Rowley Mile may move with the times, but it cannot change until the Happy Eaters have finally taken over the Heath; and let us be honest, one day this may happen, at least if the twenty-first century carries on where its ever more idiotic predecessor left off. Until then the Rowley Mile will continue to run its course from the sharp, sun-splintered newness of April's Craven Stakes through to the red-brown ripeness of the Autumn Handicap in October, at which point the spell will be suspended – not broken – but sustained by thoughts of infinite renewal: of change that does not change; of a new season in which the racegoer will be a year older and the horses in the Craven Stakes will never be more than two years of age. Not such a bad way, perhaps, to measure out one's life.

It is this sense of time accumulated and suspended that permeates the empty Rowley Mile course. All racecourses are beautiful when they are empty, but none more so than this one, proudly undecorative with its plain buildings, its as yet unfinished new grandstand and its atmosphere, which disuse does not dissipate. Like the Heath, it is accessible out of season; perhaps illegitimately, but there is nothing that actually stops one entering. Once again that dialectic between openness and forbiddingness tugs at the air.

And so there, late on a Sunday afternoon in November, when the sky hangs thick and grey, is the silent paddock; there is the tight semi-circle of the winners' enclosure; and, in the near-darkness, the connections between these arenas and the course beyond seem to be traced. Back and forth from one to the other went Brigadier Gerard, when he took possession of this place in 1971 and 1972. He is here now, looking vital and rather solitary in the centre of the shadowy pre-parade ring. His statue stands like a totem, but he seems still to be very much himself, waiting for the sound of the racing to enter once more into his sculpted ears. Closer to the centre of the racecourse, in the neat little courtyard of the Members' enclosure, there is another statue: that of Eclipse, who ran at Newmarket more than 200 years ago, and who looks totemic only, the symbol of every horse who ever made its conquest of the Heath.

But from the Devil's Dyke, it all looks rather different. From that singular standpoint, the Heath is still the home of the horse, but it is a home far older than any racecourse: a world as described in some ancient East Anglian mythology, where the sky hangs heavy and indistinguishable from the ground. The Dyke itself could be a part of this world. Without knowing, one would be very hard put to say exactly what it was, and even when one does know, there is still a good deal of mystery about it. In fact it is a man-made earthwork, a defensive barrier created out of the ground, the biggest and best-preserved of three that were built in Cambridgeshire, at some unspecified time, over a thousand years ago.

The legend is that the Devil's Dyke, or Ditch, was the work of the Iceni tribe – supervised by bare-breasted forewoman Boadicea – constructed as protection against the Romans during the revolt in 61 AD. Substance has been given to this theory by the speculation that the name 'Exning' – a village outside Newmarket – is a corruption of the word 'Iceni'. Unfortunately neither of these lovely ideas is true, although Boadicea's troops may well have trained their chariot horses on the Heath, which would have been as good then as now for the purpose. However, despite the calculation that the Devil's Dyke was, at points, wide enough to take a chariot, it does not follow that her magnificent ladyship went rolling along it, hair flying, the scythes on her hub caps slicing through the air. In fact, as was established during excavations carried out in 1973, when the Newmarket bypass cut into a slice of the earthwork, the Dyke was built at least 300 years after Boadicea killed herself. It seems quite likely that it was put up in the seventh century, at the time that the Heptarchy was created, as some sort of barrier between East Anglia and Mercia. It would have formed a defence across the Icknield Way – at that time a series of trackways between Wessex and Norfolk – which otherwise, clearly, would have given great ease of access to the enemy.

At any rate, it seems first to have been mentioned in the *Anglo-Saxon Chronicles*, whose entry for the year 903 reads: 'Aethelwald lured the East Anglian force into breaking the peace, so that they ravaged over the land of Mercia . . . Then king Edward went after them, as quickly as he could gather his army, and ravaged all their land between Devil's Dyke and Fleam Dyke and the Ouse, and everything up to the northern fens . . .' It later finds its way into the story of Hereward the Wake, who apparently crossed by it on his way from Ely.

The Dyke is an extraordinary piece of work. Obviously it needed to be enormous if it was to do the defence job properly (although there is no particular evidence of success in this respect; East Anglia was overrun by Mercia in the eighth century, and the Danes got into East Anglia from the other side, by river). However it was made in expectation of impregnability – like a chastity belt. Its three aligned stretches ran for seven and a half miles, between Reach, whose name may come from the fact that this was how far the Dyke 'reached', and Wood Ditton, just outside Newmarket, whose name meant 'the wood on the ditch'. One of these stretches ended at a site named Gallows Hill, near the village of Burwell, which was probably an execution site; something of the kind was excavated at the Bran Dyke, where a number of skeletons were found with their hands tied.

In places the Devil's Dyke is eighteen feet high and twelve feet thick. The mind frankly boggles at how it was made, which it is thought was done quickly, strip by strip. Marks of ancient spades were found in the excavations, and some sort of 'earth-shifting mechanism' seems to have been used to pile the quarried material on to the top of the Dyke. As with most of these ancient puzzles, it was probably sheer manpower, working all hours, that enabled the thing to be achieved.

It can be entered just by the July Course, where one climbs in between trees at the side of the road and finds oneself on a long, mounted, chalk path, overgrown with grass and tangles of plants, which drops vertiginously at each side down into the 'ditch'. There is something very strange about it; and not just because nothing else quite like it exists. For reasons that cannot be explained, it is sinister. The name? The thought of the execution site? The original purpose, as a static weapon in warfare? The matted darkness of trees that has grown to one side of it? It is vaguer than that: it is to do with the East Anglian landscape, which somehow always seems older than that of the rest of England, as if its flat, wide aspect had been left as it was a thousand years ago, and not tricked out with those civilising, comforting, colourful devices which break up the terror of infinite space. And this, of course, is where the Heath comes in again. The fact that it has this ancient lump running along its spine – seeming, now, neither a creation of nature nor of man, just a phenomenon unto itself – merely emphasises its mystery.

The Devil's Dyke is an essential part of the Heath. It runs between the racecourses and this is why, when one stands on top of it, they look very different – almost as if one were looking at them inside out. The two courses are not separate. For races longer than ten furlongs on the Rowley Mile Course, a mile on the July Course, they start on the same piece of turf; then they turn right-handed – cutting through the Devil's Dyke as they do so – and fork off from one another to form their straights. The Dyke actually runs between these two straights. Standing on top of it, one is looking at them both. The July Course is very close and if one toppled down the side of the ditch, and were able to climb out of it again, one would be nearly inside a drinks' tent on the edge of the racecourse. The Rowley Mile seems quite distant, as does the new grandstand, but one can make out little furlong posts and the course landmark known as The Bushes.

From this angle, slightly elevated and, despite one's nearness, infinitely remote, they just look like bushes. Their totemic quality has disappeared, as has that of the winning posts, which look like red circles in the air, and the furlong posts, which are just numbers, and the sponsorship boards, which float meaninglessly in space, and even the railings that mark out the two courses, which are merely white lines that have been ruled along the ground. From this standpoint, there is nothing but Heath – a vast unfathomable force of nature, ancient home of the horse – upon which some tiny features have been carefully drawn.

This is the beginning of the story. But at that time Newmarket did not exist, at least not in name; and, when it first made its appearance, it was in a guise that had nothing to do with the Heath. It was, in fact, as a New Market.

There is another legend to do with these early years, which is that Newmarket was 'created' when a plague in nearby Exning forced its own market to move to a new location. Like most stories to do with Exning, this is untrue.[3] Yet it *is* true that Newmarket was carved out of Exning, at the start of the thirteenth century, and then spread into Wood Ditton. This seems to have happened because the land on which the future Newmarket stood was a dowry. A Sir Robert l'Isle gave it 'in franke marriage with his daughter Cassandra unto Sir Richard de Argentein', and Argentein, in entrepreneurial spirit, then either started or developed a market on the site.

These origins help to make two important points about Newmarket. Firstly, the fact that it was cobbled together out of bits of two different villages explains the anomaly of it

---

[3] This and many other facts in this section come from Canon Peter May's authoritative *Newmarket Medieval and Tudor*.

straddling two counties: technically in Suffolk, Newmarket is surrounded by Cambridgeshire. In its early years it lay across the old Icknield Way, one of only two parishes to do so; the road went straight along what is now Palace Street, behind the High Street. In the seventeenth century a local historian wrote, in bemusement, that 'this Towne hath one side of the street standing in Cambridgeshire and the other side in Suffolk' and, according to a later map, a metal strip in the pavement outside the Post Office in the High Street was said to mark the division. The anomaly is no longer quite so pronounced. Nevertheless, when it was proposed in 1989 that Newmarket should admit what is very nearly the truth, and take Cambridgeshire as its postal address, there was uproar – it is a town that likes its oddities.

The second point about Newmarket is that, although it was a late starter, it quickly assumed a prominence that was surprising, really, for an ordinary little 'vill'. A fourteenth-century map shows Newmarket but neither Exning nor Wood Ditton, which had both been supplanted by their young bastard creation. By the fifteenth century Newmarket was, albeit in a completely different way, very much what it is today: a provincial town with an unusual buzz about it.

The Heath, meanwhile, might just as well not have existed. There was an oblique reference to it in 1313, when King Edward II issued a mandate forbidding his beloved [sic] knights 'to meet for a tournament at Newmarket on this coming Sunday'. As Cromwell was later to do, Edward may have feared the Heath quite simply because it was a good place for a big crowd to get together, and tournaments of the time often degenerated into a bit of a free-for-all.

However the life of Newmarket did not then relate to the Heath. The source of its buzz was that it was well positioned – hard to believe, this, for anyone who has tried to drive to the town from London, or indeed from anywhere west of Hitchin, but England was then much more slanted towards its eastern side, and the important London to Norwich road converged with the Icknield Way at what is now Newmarket. It was also near to Cambridge, Mildenhall, Thetford; all of which enabled it to develop its market with the brisk efficiency which still characterises the town.

The market was all it had. It had to make a success with it, hustle and trade and put itself about. Newmarket has never been agriculturally based. Despite its association with country pursuits, it does not have that self-conscious Gloucestershire-type rurality: there is, mysteriously, something innately urban about the place, now as then. Life in the Middle Ages was shaped around the little High Street, upon which there began to burgeon a cluster of businesses, providing for the constant procession of travellers who came to market: cooks selling bread (and being fined for giving short weight on loaves); women brewing beer ('John Redere's wife is a communal alewife and had 36 gallons of ale and would not sell to John Wykes, Walter Bocher, Thomas Perer, Thomas Sowtere and others, but kep them for strangers as she says . . .' – a familiar tale); and, of course, a truly staggering number of inns. In a town which, by the late fifteenth century, had a population of around 275, the account roll lists the following: The Ship, The Bear, The Maidenhead, The Sword, The Pound, The Christopher, The Bell, The Ram, The Hart, The Swan, The Bull, The Saracen's Head, The Griffin . . . This was lively, all right.

The market itself was probably very close to where Market Square stands today, behind the High Street, by the Rookery shopping centre. The Old Rookery, which may have been lively to a fault, was a warren of little shops and houses and stalls, named after its resemblance to the state of the ground beneath a gathering of great dirty birds. Sub-Hogarthian drawings from the time give a feel – exaggerated? – of what it would have been like. Animals lying open-eyed on tables waiting to be butchered; blood running over the ground; dogs running off with food from underneath the wooden stalls; peddlars hawking trays of goods; a man sitting open-mouthed on the ground, selling bread; tankards frothing; two women fighting; stall-holders haggling; a crush and bustle that is, perhaps, not so different from the scene nowadays wherever shoppers gather for bargains, but that is hard to associate with Newmarket, where the most important commodities – horses – are now traded rather differently, and desire is rarely shown honestly.

Meanwhile, around the High Street, little back alleys of tenements were growing up. The rents were paid to the

Argentein family, who were still lords of the manor (this was very much a sideline, as their centre-stage lives were rather dashing: one of them died at Bannockburn and was immortalised by Sir Walter Scott; another was said to have been killed fighting the Saracens). In the fifteenth century, when the Argenteins were replaced through marriage by the Alington family (one of whom – not to be outdone – died at Bosworth), there seem to have been fifty or so holdings down either side of the High Street. The area around St Mary's Church – built originally as a chapel, in the late thirteenth century – was strongly residential, with a block of tenements on Black Bear Lane, Fitzroy Street and Church Lane: the shape of all of this can still be identified. The street pattern of Newmarket has hardly changed, although very few old buildings survive. They were probably ugly as sin, but curiosity would still love to be satisfied by something.

What is perhaps best left unimagined is the fact that in the fifteenth century the water course – which now runs underneath the Jockey Club, up towards Exeter Road – flowed freely down the High Street. This, not very surprisingly, led to a general carelessness about throwing things in the road. Records of fines show a steady procession of entrails and dung sailing down the little river, and in 1403 some men were fined for what seems like mere sense, the offence of making 'goteres'. A truly grim speculation is that a piece of land near the water course, called Frogmore, was given the name because it was hopping alive with slimy creatures. At any rate, while the water course was overground there was little chance of cleaning things up; as is shown by the fact that the View of Frankpledge, a manorial court which went in for annual enforcement of by-laws, never made any progress on the dung-dumping front. In 1621, when royalty made its first appearance at Newmarket, the court was obliged to pass this ordinance: 'No one is to allow any dung to lie in the streets or lanes for more than eight days when the king is absent, and not at all when the king is present, under penalty of 20s for each offence.'

The King was James I and, from the moment of his arrival in Newmarket, the life of the bustling, grubby, provincial market town was changed for ever, more abruptly and decisively than even a Stuart king would have believed he could achieve. Newmarket's destiny no longer lay in its Market Square or on its High Street. From now on, its horizons would widen to that mysterious, forgotten, infinitely patient space around the town, and the Heath would hold absolute sway.

James I was a man of whim, and the luck was that he had a whim for Newmarket. He treated it like any of his favourites: gave it a palace, lavished attentions upon it, forsook all others – like Parliament, for instance, which in 1621 was obliged to send twelve of its members to Newmarket with a petition, asking him to return to London.

The pattern that critics would thereafter discern, over and over, of monarchy skiving off duty in order to play on the Heath, appeared to have been set. An alternative view, however, was given just after the King's death, in a book called *The Court and Character of King James*, written by Sir Anthony Weldon, who later became a Parliamentarian. He is hilariously biased, nevertheless there may be some truth in his assertion that Sir Robert Cecil and others 'perswaded the King to leave the State affairs to them, and to betake himself to some Country recreations, which they found him addicted unto, for the City, and business did not agree with him; to that end purchased, built, and repaired at New-market, and Royston,[4] and this pleased the King's humour well ...' Sometimes there was no better place for a monarch than a great big Heath, on which he could hurt no one but himself.

It all began very simply, when early in his reign – February 1605 – it is recorded that he 'did hunt the hare with his own hounds in the fields of Fordham and did kill six near a place called Buckland; and did afterwards take his repast in the fields at a bush near the King's Park'. Fordham is a village very close to Newmarket and, on subsequent visits to the area, the King realised the potential of the Heath as good sporting ground. Weldon says that what he actually wanted was to be away from Whitehall and closeted up with his boyfriends. Not impossible – he was the worst rider in the world, and once went head-first into a frozen pond, leaving

---

[4] A Hertfordshire town some 25 miles from Newmarket.

his boots flailing above the surface – but there is plenty of testimony to the fact that he made up in zeal for what he lacked in ability. He seems to have had a genuine love for hunting and coursing, and Newmarket was of course perfect ground for it all. Warren Hill is so called because fifty brace of hares would later be released on it annually for King James' pleasure. And whatever his motives for being there – which certainly had very little to do with horse racing, as we and Newmarket were later to understand it – the point was that, for the first time in a thousand years or so, the Heath was making its presence felt in high places. For this the King must be thanked; from the attention that he brought to Newmarket, all the rest would follow.

The huge question, of course, is whether Newmarket would have realised its destiny had it not been for this near-accidental encounter with capricious royalty. For this happened at an important time in the 'history' of racing, a concept which is now so synonymous with the history of Newmarket that it is hard to realise what went on before the two got together. Of course the idea of racing horses did not begin on the Heath in the seventeenth century. The aristocratic displacement of a man's worth on to the worth of his horse had existed as a notion since Alexander tamed Bucephalus; or since a knight-farrier wrote to Emperor Frederick II (in 1250 AD) that 'no animal is more noble than a horse, since it is by horses that princes, magnates and knights are separated from lesser people'; or since the future Richard II rode his own horse against that of the Earl of Arundel in 1377 and, having lost the race, paid the equivalent of tens of thousands for the winner when he became King.

And, by the time James I came to Newmarket, the sport of public horse racing had already begun. Indeed it may well be that it first started during the Roman occupation, when Emperor Septimius Severus raced imported horses (spoils of war?) at Wetherby; or on the Knavesmire course at York whose shape is based on that of the Circus Maximus. Certainly the first recorded 'meeting' was staged at Chester in 1540, on the Roodeye course that runs – still – alongside a Roman wall: 'There were great stories from Chester of the jollifications planned there for Shrive Tuesday . . . the municipal authorities initiated a series of horse races, to be run in perpetuity . . .' There were also races on Salisbury Plain, attended by Queen Elizabeth in the 1580s (where she saw the Earl of Cumberland win 'a gold bell valued at £50 and better') and probably on Doncaster's Town Moor, where the St Leger is still run.

It did not all begin with Newmarket, absolutely not. But Newmarket was unusually well qualified to stage the sport; and it attracted the attention of King James I at a time when racing was poised to develop. Here, then, was a fortuitous meeting of place, person and circumstance. James was never really a racing man – it was said that he was bored by the sight of horses walking about – but he was the catalyst, nonetheless, for a blessed conjunction. Whether, or how, this would have happened otherwise is impossible to answer. 'Yes' and 'somehow' would probably be the guess, however.

At any rate, in his whimsical way, he had only been in Newmarket five minutes before he was renting the Griffin – one of the little old inns in the High Street – for £100 a year. Three years later he bought it for £400, and the first of Newmarket's royal palaces began to be built.

It stood, according to Canon Peter May's highly educated guess, between the High Street and All Saints' Church, to the west of where Sun Lane now runs: an unlikely site, occupied today by a toy shop called Moons Toymaster, Threshers off licence, a Wimpy bar, empty spaces. What is hard to grasp is the scope of the palace. It had a coach-house, a 'brewhouse', a 'Dogghouse', stables, kitchens, offices, a real tennis court (there is still one of these, rather surprisingly, on Fitzroy Street). Its frontage was estimated at 114 feet and a drawing by Inigo Jones exists of what this may have looked like. It has an elegant symmetry, with long windows and a scattering of small statues. Can this really have faced out on to Newmarket High Street, as the frogs danced in the water course outside the front door?

And, if it did, what on earth would people have made of it? We know, now, about the link between Newmarket and royalty, so strong that it has moved at times towards symbiosis; but in 1613, when Inigo Jones designed a replace-ment palace (the first one, completed in 1610, had collapsed, although not on top of anyone), this was an idea that had yet to be thought up. For the court, for the ministers, for the ambassadors who attended the King in Newmarket, having come all the way from Spain, Venice, Bohemia and Persia, following James up to this freezing little town must have seemed like having to go to a bad party in Docklands when one lives in Kensal Green – like madness, in fact. Did they think it would last? Would he get over it?

Meanwhile, for the town of Newmarket, it is difficult to imagine what impact this sudden show of favour must have had: a bit like having a celebrity move in next door, perhaps. One takes pride in being blasé about it, and the celebrity is never there anyway. However much it seemed that he was rarely in London, James would probably only have been in his palace for a month at a time, twice a year. Nevertheless the psychological effect must have been considerable: a celebrity may be expected to move in next door if one lives in The Bishops' Avenue, but it is more of a shake-up in Acacia Drive. And with the palace being built it must have seemed as though the whim had an underpinning of substance (second time around, at least). Did Newmarket start tidying its market stalls, shining its shoes, putting its entrails in the litter bin? Did it begin to think about a different future?

The strange thing about King James is that he did all this for Newmarket, built a dominant and possibly attractive palace, and yet his personality does not connect with the place; perhaps because his interest was not, primarily, in racing, perhaps because it is hard to form any clear idea of the man himself. One can look to Sir Anthony Weldon, of course: 'He was naturally of a timorous disposition, which was the reason of his quilted doublets . . . his tongue too large for his mouth, which ever made him drink very uncomely, as if eating his drink . . . he never washt his hands, only rub'd his fingers ends slightly, with the wet-end of a Napkin . . . his walk was ever circular, his fingers ever in that walk fidling about his cod-piece . . .'

But this is on the mean side, and not wholly to be trusted. What *does* come across, even from less-biased sources, is this vivid impression of a man of whim: of someone who refused to allow guests to come to his Twelfth Night party unless they brought £300 with which to gamble; who would not cancel his sport when the Queen died in 1619; who coveted with a madness the house at Royston, called Theobalds, owned by Robert Cecil (and in which the King eventually died, having got his wish in a way); who appointed the Duke of Buckingham as his Master of the Horse and spent days on end with him at Newmarket. It is hard, in fact, not to think that his vague leanings towards racing were strengthened by his far more certain gravitation towards Buckingham. And it was one of Buckingham's horses, Prince, that took part in – and lost – the first recorded race across Newmarket Heath: on 8 March, 1622, in a £100 match against an unnamed horse belonging to Lord Salisbury.

This was a beginning, indeed, although the handful of people present – people of the kind who were to dominate racing at Newmarket for a couple of centuries – would have been very surprised to learn just what a beginning it really was. For there was nothing to say that it would go on from there. The palace was an anchor, yes; a tie between this unlikely town and the possibilities that it was dimly perceived to hold; but whim was not enough, it needed passion to support it. Later it would get it, over and over again.

From Charles I it did not get passion, exactly, although he certainly loved the horse – a Cavalier, after all. But he seemed willing to take Newmarket seriously as an alternative to London. Too much so, perhaps. In 1630, he stayed in the palace for three weeks with the whole court and a phalanx of officers: 'The magnificent and abundant plenty of the King's Tables hath caused amazement in Foreigners,' wrote an observer, Thomas de Laune, who did not know whether to be astounded or impressed, 'and was much for the Honour of the Kingdom . . . In the reign of Charles I there were daily in his Court eighty-six Tables, well furnished each Meal.' Well-furnished indeed: 500 dishes each time. If Charles subconsciously saw Newmarket as a sanctuary, from the unease of being near to Parliament, then he was suppressing that weak feeling with all the silly grandeur of which he was capable.

But racing itself was flourishing. The spark that King James had lit, and just managed not to slobber out, had caught fire under his son, who was said to have spent £12,000 one year on his stables. Bravura again, or just plain obtuseness? There was racing in London's Hyde Park, which must have been wonderful – 'the inhabitants of London and those parts near London assembled in their thousands to watch the running horses' – and a play was staged, by James Shirley, in which the plot revolved around a race won by a character named Jockey. In Newmarket, a grandstand of some substance was built (it had windows, so must have been enclosed); regular Spring and Autumn meetings were established in 1627; a race was run for a gold cup in 1634. Distinguished visitors began to accept as a matter of course that they would visit the palace. Rubens, then an ambassador from Spain, was knighted at Newmarket in 1630. Sir William Harvey was a member of Charles' retinue, and paid £1 a week whilst staying in the palace.

Meanwhile the Royal Studs – comprising establishments at Hampton Court, Eltham, Malmesbury (once an abbey) and Tutbury (where Mary, Queen of Scots was once imprisoned) – were stocked to the brim with wonderful horses from Spain, Italy and North Africa, collected since Henry VIII had first imported them in 1514 from the Duke of Mantua, and strongly supplemented by the Duke of Buckingham: for all his shortcomings, he had been a very good Master of the Horse. These studs were not trying to breed 'racehorses' as such. That concept, the ideal of perfectibility as embodied by the thoroughbred, was still more than fifty years away. Yet the desire to possess quality blood, to have something better, or purer, than before – for a purpose as yet unidentified, an ideal as yet unclear – had been there since men had yearned to possess the horse.

Even Oliver Cromwell felt that desire. When, in 1649, he ordered an inventory at Tutbury, with the avowed intention of dispersing the stud, he first of all picked out six of the best horses for himself. He bought another six horses from Naples, longed – as the Stuart kings had done[5] – for an

---

[5] James I had acquired a horse called the Markham Arabian for £154; probably only the son of a true Arab, and a bit of a disaster. The Duke of Newcastle, who would later teach the future Charles II to ride, said of the Markham Arabian: 'When he came to Run, every Horse beat him.'

Arabian, and not long before his death acquired a horse from Aleppo, from where the most highly prized Arabs came. Later this stallion, known as the White Turk, would be mated to a mare who, at the time of the Restoration, was concealed in a cellar in Fenchurch Street so that she should not be found: the Coffin Mare. The mating was successful, and the mare and her progeny were smuggled into the north of England. However, Cromwell's horses – said to be the best in England – were confiscated, as he had earlier confiscated those of the Royal Studs.

He had done what should not be done lightly: broken a long and careful line, and for nothing more substantial than a principle to which he was not even faithful. In a way, the banning of racing in 1650 was less serious, although doubtless it would not have seemed so to those who did not know that the hell would be over in ten years. But the sport did not yet have the hold, the structure, the power that would make it an unbearable loss; it was just a light going out, leaving dullness.

And it seemed cruel that Charles should have been held captive at Newmarket in 1647, having been apprehended as he prepared to escape to Scotland. Yet he had chosen this prison over the alternatives of Oxford or Audley End in Essex. He preferred to be where the memories were short but very bright and where, as he exercised his horse on the Heath, the illusion of freedom was as painful as it was strong. The New Model Army also used the Heath once at this time; but 'none interfered when he rode abroad'.

2 Restoration

'Jolly Blades Raceing' – 1660–1683

FOR CHARLES II, Newmarket was to become a place of refuge, albeit of a strenuous kind, and when one considers the life that he led before his reign began in 1660 it is hardly surprising that he liked being there. He was condemned for frivolity during his reign, and has been ever since by commentators who seem, frankly, rather jealous of his capacity for pleasure; but these reactions are missing the point. Charles understood, better than his detractors, the unquestioning and unquestioned importance of play in the lives of Englishmen. It was a concept that he came to embody, and this was possibly his greatest legacy to both racing and Newmarket.

He had been to the town before. At the age of ten, for example, he had performed a royal visit to Cambridge during which he was criticised, in the powerfully silent way that only Oxbridge colleges can manage, for having failed to say his prayers into his hat in the undergraduate fashion. The little boy then escaped to join his father at Newmarket, and a pattern may be discerned to have been set.

The mystery is why, as King, he did not visit the place of refuge until 1666. Of course the old palace built by his grandfather was now uninhabitable, having been bought for £1,772 in 1650 by a 'consortium' of seven (one of whom had put his name to Charles I's death warrant), which proceeded to wreak havoc in the piecemeal, pointless way that consortia so often do. Parts of the palace were pulled down, apparently with no clear view as to what would replace them, as in 1667 Christopher Wren recorded that the site was now 'a vacant yard'. Nor was it just the palace that had fallen into disrepair during the interregnum. Nastily, sacrilegiously, it had been ordered that the Heath should be ploughed. The kind of patrician activity – racing, hunting, hawking – that had gone on there since the reign of James I was just what Cromwellians hated, probably not so much on ideological grounds as because it might enable Royalist types to get together and plot beneath their wigs.

Meanwhile, of course, the dispersal of the Royal Studs meant that the production of horses for racing, something which had had very little structure before 1649, now had infinitely less. Horses were all over the place and almost impossible to trace: some up North, some in Ireland, one in a cellar. The beautiful establishment at Tutbury was found, at the Restoration, to have been broken up in the same, half-hearted way as James' palace, and Eltham stud was described by John Evelyn as being 'in miserable ruins, the noble woods and park destroyed'. Thank God, really, for Cromwell's hypocrisy: the fact that he liked good horses enough to keep propagating them, and not to put an end to the breeding of potential racers, meant that what he left behind was chaos rather than catastrophe. Soon, the scattered fruits of the studs would start appearing at racecourses, and the fact that no one knew much about their provenance probably mattered as little then, to the average spectator, as it would matter today.

People could hardly wait to get cracking again with racing. The Restoration clichés of everyone tearing off their Puritan collars and running out to play seem to have been absolutely true. In 1660 racecourses were, as a contemporary source put it, 'overgrown and choked', and some of them had been turned into 'pleasure grounds', whose ghastliness one can only guess at. However the English of the Restoration clearly had better taste than their modern descendants, and they preferred a good day's purposeful sport to wandering around like distracted children in search of amusement. Croydon, Chester, Windsor, Hampton – soon such racetracks, if that is what these almost featureless expanses of turf can be called, were all up and running in their casual, vital way. The new King probably attended his first post-Restoration meeting in 1661 at Epsom Downs, that magnificent, vertiginous course, which had staged racing before the Civil War and, during it, had been used as cover for a Royalist meeting.

From the first, the health of the sport was high on the list of Charles' priorities. Just eight days after his return from exile, he appointed a Master of the Royal Stud, James D'Arcy, a sensible-sounding man who made an assessment of the dispersed stud situation, suggested for himself an annual salary of £200 and told the King that he would provide, from his own Yorkshire stud, 'twelve extraordinary good colts' every year for a fee of £800. Charles allowed himself to be put in D'Arcy's hands – one of the first examples, this, of the power of the horse expert over the apparently more powerful person. In fact the King does not seem to have been especially involved in the breeding side of the sport. The Royal Stud, which survives to this day, was probably never so feeble as when Charles – that most famous of royal racing enthusiasts, and most famous of royal studs – was on the throne. This may have been due to simple lack of money (when D'Arcy died he was owed two years' arrears). It may also have been that the precarious years of his youth had given the King a taste for living, not in some hopeful future, but in the here and now.

Certainly he loved the thing itself: the sport, the horse. During his untroubled early youth he had been given daily riding lessons by his mentor, the Earl of Newcastle, who also instructed him never to be too devout and always to be civil to women. Both of these became guiding precepts in Charles' life.

Newcastle was a terrific horseman and, apparently, made one just as good of his pupil. In 1642 the then Prince Charles was made honorary captain of his father's troop of horse guards. Dressed in gilt armour, a true Cavalier, he mounted the white horse with which he had been presented, and paced to great applause. Later that year, at the age of twelve, he was dissuaded from charging the enemy cavalry at the Battle of Edgehill. This was recklessness, but as he grew older he treated his mounts as he probably treated his mistresses, with kindness, understanding and a cool strength that did not need to try and subjugate. After the Restoration, when loyalty had won for Newcastle a dukedom, he wrote rather excitedly that 'no man makes a horse go better than I have seen some go under His Majesty the first time ever he came upon their backs.' It is, of course, in Charles that we find the first public embodiment of the idea, prevalent in this country, that those who inhabit the racing world are unusually highly sexed.

So the new King had a demonstrable love of horses and of racing, and a care for the racing breed; but still he did not go to Newmarket. The place was in his mind, nonetheless, and indeed was coming back to life despite the lack of his actual presence. By 1663 sport was re-established on the Heath, where it was immediately patronised by the nobility. It was said that the High Street resounded with the 'cursed noise, of matches, and wagers, boldly asserted with as horrible oaths', as sporting gentlemen like the Duke of Richmond and the Earl of Suffolk plunged joyfully into the pleasure, lost for too long, of pitting their horses against each other. This first recorded match race of the Restoration, in which Richmond won the then tidy sum of £100, can be seen as the point at which Newmarket's destiny became fixed – for the next twenty years, at any rate.

Meanwhile, again in 1663, Charles was giving Colonel Robert Kerr £200 with which to bring 'hounds to Newmarket for the King's disport', which rather implies that he was thinking of a visit. Then in 1664 or 1665 (accounts differ), he founded the Town Plate. This race was one of Charles' most enduring tangible legacies to Newmarket; not just because it is still contested every year by amateur riders, usually female, but because the detailed conditions that were applied to it constitute the first serious attempt by racing to regulate itself. Rules imply arbiters. It was therefore impossible for the Town Plate to be run in the wild spirit that then prevailed – somebody had to be watching and ready to lay the law down (on occasion this would later be Charles himself). It is not too fanciful to see in the Town Plate the origins of the Jockey Club, which in the following century would start to make up the rules of racing in this same *ad hoc*, empirical but overmastering way.

The original conditions for the Town Plate are contained in a manuscript owned by the Jockey Club, and they are fascinating. They begin by stating, with a nice precision, the course that the race shall take, thus: 'Item – Every horse that rides the new Round Course three times over (set out the 16th day of October, in the 17th year[1] of King Charles II) on the outside of the Ditch from Newmarket, shall leave all the posts and flags the first and last heats on the right hand, and the second on the left hand, starting and ending at the weighing post, by Cambridge-gap, called Thomond's Post.' The Round Course – the first established of the Newmarket courses – is on the July Course side of the Devil's Dyke, extending the curve of the Cesarewitch Course and circling the grounds of the National Stud. The Round Course is still used for the running of the Town Plate although, separate as it is from the July and Rowley Mile straights, it seems now to have been subsumed into the wider entity of the Heath and it is difficult, when treading its calm and silent turf, to conjure the life that spilled on to it three hundred years ago, the drums and trumpets and bright taffetas of the Restoration at its glamorous height.

The Town Plate was a race between a number of competitors and not just a match between two, as was then the norm. Because of this, and because it had rules, it is closer to the spirit of modern racing than anything that had gone before; nevertheless, everything else about it is very unfamiliar. It was, for example, run in heats, as was the racing custom until its abolition in 1772 (which even then did not apply to the Town Plate). A mere 'half an hour's time' was given between each of the three heats for the horses to be 'rubbed', and possibly given a nip of restorative booze; then the race proper, of four miles, took place. Considering that the jockeys were riding at twelve stone (and were disqualified for weighing out at more than 1½ pounds less), this is a testimony to the then strength of racehorses. It is hardly necessary to say that these were not yet 'thoroughbreds', but a mysterious mixture of the refined imported horses and stockier, speedier native animals. Indeed, the toughness of

---

[1] The convention had been established that Charles' reign dated from the death of his father, not from the Restoration.

the Town Plate was not just for the sake of spectacle, tremendous though this must have been, but in order to propagate strength within the breed.

Certain of the Town Plate rules tell the eternal tale of racing's potentially deleterious effect upon the human character. 'Item – Every rider that layeth hold on, or striketh any of the riders, shall win no plate or prize' has a familiar ring to those who have seen jockeys in their more manic state. 'Item – Whosoever doth stop or stay any of the horses that rideth for this plate or prize; if he be either owner, servant, party or bettor, and it appears to be willingly done, he shall win no plate, prize, or bets' speaks of something even more recognisable. It will be seen that the judges of the race had the same task as faces stewards nowadays: how to know when devilment is going on. That tricky little clause, *'appears to be willingly done'*, reminds us of the deep waters that lie beneath the problems of proof – something which plagues racing today and has clearly plagued it from the start.

How Charles could bear to contemplate the entrancing scenario conjured by the Town Plate rules, and not rush off immediately to Newmarket to see his creation being enacted, is, indeed, a mystery. But there it is, he resisted until 1666. Did he feel that he should, at first, stay at the heart of events? After all, despite the rapture with which his restoration was greeted – people were sinking to their knees in gratitude in the streets – the threat of a return to a republican state was perceived, as late as 1664, still to exist. Nipping off for a day's racing at Epsom or Windsor was all very well and in the spirit of the times. Disappearing twice a year to Newmarket, well out of reach, as Charles was later to do for weeks on end, might not then have been something that he dared to risk.

This is mere speculation, of course, as is the hunch that the fall from grace of Charles' po-faced adviser, the Earl of Clarendon, might have played its part. Clarendon had been a terrible pain to Charles ever since his youth, constantly accusing him of idleness, weakness and hedonism before he actually went in for these vices. The earl had no notion of how to handle either an exiled prince or a restored king, nor was he popular elsewhere. It was not entirely fair that he should take the rap for England's humiliation in the first

Anglo-Dutch war, but nobody felt very much inclined to protest about it. One historian, Christopher Falkus, links Clarendon's dismissal in 1667 to the 'high noon of the Restoration'. Charles had made his first visit to Newmarket the year before, somewhere between the plague and the fire, but there is no doubt that, from the late 1660s, his attitude towards the town ripened into something like romantic love; a development which the removal of the nagging wife from his shoulder can only have facilitated.

What did he find when he got to Newmarket, in his thirty-sixth year, in the spring of 1666? In essence, what there is now: an ordinary little town that holds magic at its heart. After the shock of its sudden patronage by James I and Charles I, it had almost reverted to its original aspect, becoming again no more than a busy market place and a High Street thickly fringed with inns – but not quite. The 'vacant yard' that had contained the palace was a reminder of the unlikely glory that had been visited upon it; as was, perhaps, a certain restless hope among its many tradespeople that royalty was about to return and spend a lot of money. One might imagine that it would be strange, and painful, for Charles to return to this place, at which his proud and silly family had enjoyed itself so heedlessly, were it not for the fact that he must have had these feelings wherever he went.

At any rate, he decided that the journey from London to Newmarket – which was, and remains, hideous – was worth making regularly. Having also decided that the old palace was not worth rebuilding, he began to plan a new one. Thus one finds the bizarre situation of this narrow little High Street playing host to two, almost adjacent, royal houses in the space of a few years.

So in 1668 Charles bought for £2,000 what John Evelyn called 'an old wretched house of my Lord Thomond's' (he whose eponymous post marked the end of the Town Plate). We know that this looked on to the High Street because my Lord had been fined three times under the View of Frank-pledge for erecting railings in front of it. Although the house itself did not fall under this particular jurisdiction, being in Cambridgeshire, the railings themselves did because they were in 'Newmarket'. The eternal foolishness of the petty law-maker . . .

Anyway, this house was clearly a useful property for the Earl of Thomond to have owned, as was the Greyhound Inn next door, which Charles later bought for £170 10s from a Newmarket family called Pickes. In the 1630s, a member of this family had got lost one night on the Heath, and only made it home because he heard the striking of St Mary's Church bells. Thereafter he turned philanthropist and bequests to the poor and the church abounded in his will, 'all of which Gifts are payable for ever out of his house formerly the Greyhound in this parish . . .' In other words, Charles was lumbered with making these gifts as well, as was every monarch until the property was sold by the Crown in 1816. Having acquired these two houses, the King then employed a 'gentleman' architect, William Samwell, who had worked on Felbrigg Hall in Norfolk, to deal with extending the buildings into something less wretched. In this Samwell was not considered to have succeeded.

Meanwhile Charles also used the Earl of Suffolk's genuinely commanding house at Audley End, near Saffron Walden, as his base for Newmarket. 'A cheerefull piece of Gotic [sic] building', if such a thing were possible, was how Evelyn described it, and indeed it was so grand that no King was ever able to afford it. But it was somewhere useful and not insulting into which Charles could put his Queen, Catherine of Braganza, while he was off enjoying himself, and in 1669 he took the opportunity of trying to buy it at the knock-down price of £50,000. Even that, though, he could not pay. With the words 'too large for a King' he relinquished the chance to live at this Essex Vaux-le-Vicomte, which would later revert to the Suffolk family.

So Charles was stuck with his horrible palace, not that he would probably have minded. It was these people who didn't understand the joys of Newmarket who found it so dreadful. The Duke of Tuscany, for example, wrote in his 1669 diary that when 'compared with the other country houses of England (it) does not deserve to be called a king's residence'. And John Evelyn was appalled. In July 1670 he went on a visit to Newmarket and 'alighted to see his Majesties house

31

there, now new building; the arches of the cellars beneath are well turn'd by Mr Samuel the architect, the rest meane enough, and hardly fit for a hunting house. Many of the roomes above had the chimnies in the angles and corners, a mode now introduc'd by his Majesty which I do at no hand approve of. I predict it will spoile many noble houses and roomes if followed . . .' Then he really gets into his aggrieved stride. 'Besides, this house is plac'd in a dirty streete, without any court or avenue, like a common one, whereas it might, and ought to have ben built at either end of the towne, upon the very carpet where the sports are celebrated . . .'

In this last, he certainly has a point. It is hard to understand why the two palaces are slap bang in what was even then the 'town centre', and not closer to the Heath. All one can think is that James I initially intended his house to be merely somewhere to sleep over – the tennis court and dogghouse came later – and that both men, for the sake of convenience, simply bought some relatively humble building that already existed and worked around it. Evelyn does indeed say that Charles, having bought the wretched house, had been 'persuaded to set (the palace) on that foundation'. It must of course be remembered that Charles was hardly awash with money at this time; a Versailles, which his friendly enemy Louis XIV would soon be creating for himself across the Channel, was out of the question. And very likely he *enjoyed* being in the thick of things, on the High Street, watching the action. The point of coming to Newmarket was not, for these Stuart kings, to sit aloof within a separate world; rather, it was to create a world for themselves within what already existed.

Our understanding of what Charles' palace would actually have been like is quite good, although picturing it requires some imaginative effort. Part of it still exists: facing Palace Street and parallel to the High Street, the large red-pink building which houses the Newmarket tourist information centre was once, in slightly different form, the palace's south-west pavilion. In the nineteenth century this chunk of royal residence became home to the Rothschild family, along with the Palace House stables across the road, which were used as a training establishment until 1984 and which, having housed horses belonging to Charles II, have a fair claim to being the oldest such in the world. Now they lie behind a high wall in Palace Street, their windows boarded up, plastic sheeting across their roof. Only their inaccessibility hints at the grandeur that they possessed when, inside boxes whose air was heavy with history, stood horses like Leopold de Rothschild's St Frusquin who, in 1896, won the Two Thousand Guineas and was beaten by a neck in the Derby by the Prince of Wales's Persimmon.

After the Rothschilds left Palace House, the stables continued in the family's ownership, but the house – so pretty when the family lived there, with its huge windows, its outside staircase leading to the first floor and its walls covered with ivy – had fallen into disrepair when it was acquired, in 1992, by the District Council. Work then began on its restoration. This is still going on, the laudable plan being to give some idea as to what at least part of the royal palace was like in the seventeenth century.

Imagination must, all the same, stretch itself beyond Palace House itself, which is only a small part of the original whole. It must, for example, take itself to the back of the house and extend the invisible palace right down to the High Street, ignoring the unlovely mish-mash of buildings that stands there today. It must then blink away the window of Warehouse Clearance Shops, the front door of The Stables cafe and the blue frieze of the United Reformed Church (within which remnants of seventeenth-century timber have been found), and see instead the frontage of Charles' palace, the window of the great dining room through which the King and his friends could look out on to the teeming road beneath.

This is not, now, easy to picture. Frankly there hardly seems to have been room for a palace, and indeed, as royal residences go, Charles' must have been on the scale of a suburban semi-detached. Nevertheless, the fact is that the existing Palace House was no more than a corner on the end of one arm of a vague quadrangle. In the middle of this was a 'kitchen court'. On the side was a pretty garden, which still exists beside Palace House but which formerly extended further west (part of the original wall still stands). The other, vanished, eastern side of the palace cannot have extended terribly far, as a 1787 plan of Newmarket shows that there was space for a coffee house between its boundaries and the Ram Inn, now the Rutland Arms, which is towards the end of the High Street. In fact this map makes the grounds of James I's palace look much bigger than those of Charles'.

So it was on the small side and it was badly positioned; but it probably had a certain easy, ramshackle charm and, inside what is left of it, this can still be imagined. On the ground floor of Palace House, in rooms which now contain leaflets full of tourist information, the ceilings retain the vaulted arches praised by Evelyn (this floor – 'the cellars' – was then occupied by servants). On the first floor are what would then have been the King's bedroom, a dressing room and two withdrawing rooms, in one of which can be seen Evelyn's despised corner fireplace. These rooms are in no way palatial in size, but they are attractive, and the view from their windows would surely have been a delight. Charles' bedroom overlooked the walled garden, which during his reign was designed in the formal French style that he adored. From the drawing rooms he could see his stables across the road, which is all any racehorse owner living in Newmarket has ever wanted. And could he also – as a delectable bonus – see Nell Gwyn at her own window, a few yards east of the stable block, in the little house in which she lodged and which still stands in Palace Street?

Above all, the palace that was barely deserving of the name would have been a wonderful change from Whitehall and all its attendant pomp. Charles had been welcomed back to England as a symbol of monarchy. He understood the importance of presenting himself, at the Restoration, as 'the Chiefest Ray of Lustre to all this Splendid Triumph', but a part of him must have taken an ironic view of this anti-republican fervour and, by the late 1660s, he may have longed for a respite from its demands. This he certainly got at Newmarket. There he lived both more and less publicly than in London. On the one hand, according to Sir John Reresby's contemporary account, he was freely accessible as he went about his pleasurable business. He 'let himself down from majesty to the very degree of a country gentleman . . . mixed himself amongst the crowd, allowed every man to speak to him that pleased'. On the other hand, because Newmarket permitted him to lead this illusory life – the life of a 'country gentleman', albeit a highly sophisticated one – it also released him from the obligation to play the king: a role which he must always have inhabited with a certain detachment.

By 1669, the habit was firmly in place wherein Charles would travel twice a year to the town – thus establishing the tradition, which still holds, of Spring and Autumn race meetings – and staying there for weeks at a time, surrounded by his court and visited by ambassadors, just as his father and grandfather had been. Yet the tone of Charles II's Newmarket court was very different from what had gone before.

The place was probably never so lively, so uproarious, so anarchic as during the fifteen years or so of Charles' wholehearted patronage. Into the little town piled the White-hall set, bringing with it fashion and frivolity, vice and vitality. Lord Macaulay noted: 'It was not uncommon for the whole Court and Cabinet to go down there, posting in a single day. The streets were alive with colour. Jewellers, milliners, players and fiddlers, venal wits and venal beauties . . .' Such was the crush that the High Street was often impassable; coaches simply blocked the way and achieved gridlock.

Accommodation for the sudden influx of visitors was hard to come by. Tents and pavilions had to be carted, at a cost of £8,000 a year, the sixty or so miles from London, and people who might have expected better, like the Lord Chamberlain, slept inside them. The flower of the English nobility dangled its wigs and breasts outside the windows of grubby tenements in the Rookery. Even when the palace was completed in 1671, and members of the sporting aristocracy, like the Duke of Ormonde and the Earl of Oxford, began to build houses close by, the whole business of living in Newmarket seems to have retained a makeshift, temporary air. This no doubt was part of the fun. So too was arriving after a drive through half the night, dodging the highwaymen who lurked on the approach roads. In 1669, Charles' longing to get to the Spring meeting was such that, as Pepys records, 'the King and the Duke of York went by three in the morning, and had the misfortune to be overset with the Duke of Monmouth, and the Prince Rupert, at the King's Gate in Holborne, and the

King all dirty, but not hurt. How it came to pass I know not . . .' Over-excitement, no doubt.

Imagine the vitality that was running through the Restoration court at that time, and imagine all that energy letting itself loose in those tiny lodging houses and narrow streets – it must have been intoxicating, dazzling, a life that would keep you awake all night and make sleep an irrelevance. What did people actually do there? Certainly they didn't spend all their time racing. Newmarket did not then have the dedication of purpose that has characterised it for the past 250 years. Just as, nowadays, the more fashionable race meetings attract a large and irritating number of people who are there for the booze and the schmooze, the dressing-up and the whooping-up, so in the seventeenth century Newmarket would have been packed with members of the *beau monde* who had gone because it was the thing to do. Did they ever wonder what they were up to, jogging away from London for a grim six-hour journey across grey East Anglia, bunking down in a tenement room in this chilly, comfortless, provincial town? Did they ever wish that they had been born instead at the court of France? Probably not, because the tide of fashion, when it is at its height, will carry people headlong towards almost anything.

And the surest thing is that they would have never been bored, as people perhaps were in Louis XIV's world of glittering politeness. There was plenty to do besides watch horses on the Heath. In a 1673 play by Thomas Shadwell, *A True Widow*, the character Prig ('A Coxcomb'), who is the butt of his creator's rather ponderous wit, has a speech on this very subject:

> Newmarket's a rare place . . . We make Visits to Horses, and talk with Grooms, Riders, and Cock-keepers, and saunter in the Heath all the Forenoon; then we dine, and never talk a word but of Dogs, Cocks, and Horses again, then we saunter into the Heath again; then to a Cock-Match; then to a Play in a Barn; then to Supper, and never speak a word but of Dogs, Cocks, and Horses again; then to the Groom-Porters, where you may play all night. Oh, 'tis a heavenly Life! We are never idle.

The interest of this, firstly, is that it shows a clear image of Newmarket to have permeated the wider world beyond; secondly it reminds us that horse racing was only one of many, equally important pleasures on offer. And although Shadwell seems to have exaggerated, in quest of comic effect, nevertheless a version of Prig's speech – this time taken from life, describing a day spent at Newmarket by Charles II – corresponds to it almost completely: 'Walking in the morning till ten a clock; then he went to the cock-pit till dinner time; about three he went to the hors-races [sic], at six to the cock-pit for an hour, then to the play (though the comedians were indifferent), soe to supper . . .' Then comes the pleasure that the epicene Prig has left out: '. . . next to the Duchess of Portsmouth's till bedtime . . .'

Shadwell, though aiming at satire, in fact gives rather an innocent impression of Restoration Newmarket, but the more lurid commentaries – both of the time, and later – imply that the town was a seething mass of bordellos, cockpits and gaming houses, into which Charles' court was plunged from noon to dusk to dawn, only coming up for air occasionally on the Heath. Not that there isn't a good deal of truth in this. All the same, people so much love to imagine sin of this kind that they may have over-estimated its importance in the Newmarket life of the time which, as Antonia Fraser says in her marvellous biography of Charles II, probably had a 'bucolic side' to it. Sin was certainly catered for, but the point of Newmarket was not simply to transport London to it. Certainly for Charles himself there was a sense of escape, of ease, of rules being relaxed, which went beyond the mere freedom to indulge in pleasure.

Ostensibly, though, pleasure was the name of the game. For the men, as has been shown, a lot of it took the unfortunate form of blood sports; those of us who find the character of Charles II hugely attractive have, nonetheless, to deal with the fact that he loved all of these. A story is told of how, at the age of eleven, he was out riding with his father and some of the court, when the King shot a hare and left it wounded and struggling. Charles immediately romped off on his long legs, killed the hare with his bare hands and returned roaring with laughter – the party admired him greatly for this.

Of course at the time blood sports were seen as a perfectly normal taste (as indeed, amongst the more robust racing element, they still are). John Evelyn's diaries refer not just to the 'hunting and hawking' in Newmarket but, elsewhere, to activities like 'otter hunting' and 'dog-fighting'; interestingly, though, he calls this last a 'rude and dirty pastime', which proves that not everyone is always carried away with the spirit of the time.

Cock-fighting, which the King loved to watch, was regarded as a Newmarket attraction to rival match races and the Duchesse de Mazarin's gambling den. As far afield as the *London Gazette*, advertisements were printed announcing that 'The Masters of His Majesty's Cockpit do desire all gentlemen that love the game to send in their cocks to the pit at Newmarket in such seasonable time as they may be fit to fight, they intending to begin the said Cock match on the 15th day of March and there shall be feeders ready to take care of their cocks.' There is something fairly horrible about the image of these men careering off to Newmarket with their fierce, doomed birds amongst their luggage, but so many of them did it. Chief cock owner of the time was the Earl of Thomond, who seems to have had a finger in most pies. And indeed cock-fighting was more organised at this time than racing, the birds almost certainly better trained than the horses. They actually sparred, like boxers, the little spurs that they wore in real fights covered with leather to prevent injury. Then they were put in a basket by the fire to sweat, 'to bring away his grease, and to breed breath and strength' – necessary qualities, these, during what were called 'battle royals', in which any number of birds would be put into the pit together and left until just one survived.

It is fairly certain that Charles himself would have watched fights in the cellars beneath the Bushel pub, which still stands in the Rookery. Was this 'His Majesty's Cockpit'? Perhaps, but there is another possibility. At the end of the High Street, just by the Rutland Arms, a smart little dress shop called Janes holds a murky secret: the cafe in its basement, in which every morning ladies sit drinking cappuccinos and denying themselves cake, was also once a pit. Did the King visit here too? It is thought to be the setting for a Van Dyck drawing of

Charles I at a cock-fight. So it is very likely, yes, that his son descended into this grisly cellar by means of a ladder, stooping his huge height to avoid the low ceilings, and watched one bird tear another apart as gamblers roared their feverish encouragement. When the cafe in Janes is lively with clinks and chat, it is very strange to imagine that feathers would once have cascaded, blood would once have spurted in quick red arcs, on to the floor beneath all those neatly shod feet and shopping bags. Yet there is something about the dim light and the brick arches that makes the picture live.

While the men gratified their blood lust, the women – waiting for a different lust to make its nightly appearance – apparently spent money. A cliché, of course, but we do know that Newmarket was, at the time, peculiarly endowed in suppliers of luxury goods. A list of losses sustained in the town's great fire of 1683 – of which more later – shows that among those who suffered were two mercers, two merchant tailors, two hatters, two drapers, two glovers, one haberdasher, one shoemaker and three milliners. My dear, this was Bond Street – and, let us remember, it was in a town whose native population was barely 600. Newmarket was booming, as indeed anywhere would be if *le tout Londres* descended upon it; there was also a roaring trade in food, drink and tobacco. These court people were free spenders, whether they could afford to be or not, and tradespeople must have blessed them for it.

They were also, of course, hugely disruptive. Coping with their japes must have been like trying to lead a normal life in Oxford or Cambridge when undergraduates thought it droll to rampage through the streets shouting 'oik, oik, oik' and sticking chamber-pots on lamp posts. But there was a sinister aspect to Charles' court which students couldn't even begin to emulate. Men like the Earl of Rochester and the Duke of Buckingham, for example, seem to have regarded Newmarket with a kind of rapacious contempt, as a new plaything from which they intended to get the most amusement possible, at any cost.

Rochester, who was really too clever for his own good, indeed bored by his own superior brains, dedicated his time instead to killing himself at the age of thirty-four through a life of sustained debauchery. He died instantly, without a moment's fight for life: one can only say that he snuffed it. His portrait, after Huysmans, is still disturbingly sexy, his poetry disturbingly honest and his judgement upon the King – that he 'never said a foolish thing/nor ever did a wise one' – is now close to being definitive. Buckingham, the son of James I's hapless beloved, was similarly dilettante but without the sad, destructive brilliance that characterises Rochester. Considerably older, a more robust type altogether, he was a major political player and the B in the Cabal. He may, however, be better remembered for the incident in which he fought a duel with the Earl of Shrewsbury, killed him, then fell into bed with the newly widowed countess (who had held his horse throughout) while still wearing his blood-soaked shirt.

For some, now unknown, reason, Rochester and Buckingham had both been banished from court at the same time and, like two excluded schoolboys, they determined upon a *folie à deux*. They passed themselves off as inn-keepers and took the Green Man which still stands at Six Mile Bottom. Here they would prey upon the passing trade. Trying not to sound too posh, they would hold banquets during race meetings, make the men incapably drunk and then seduce the women. This was all very well, and no doubt vastly funny, until the game suddenly turned nasty. It was a plot straight out of Wycherley: its ingredients were a miser with a pretty wife, Rochester disguised as a woman, Rochester feigning illness beneath his shawl, Rochester revealed and gratefully accepted by the wife, Rochester and the wife running off to the Green Man with all the miser's money. How they laughed! Except that this story went beyond the last act, to an epilogue in which the husband hanged himself and the wife, having been passed on to Buckingham then discarded by both men, was left to a life as a London prostitute.

Rochester and Buckingham were not really wicked – obviously they never intended such consequences – but there was an arrogant cruelty about them that Charles, cock-fighting apart, simply did not have. In this sense his court was not always representative of his character. Indeed, he himself fell foul of Rochester's peculiar sadism when, during a visit to a top-of-the-range Newmarket brothel, the earl instructed one of the girls to pick Charles' pocket. Of course the King was there incognito – rather as Louis XV was to do, he liked to go out on the pull as an 'ordinary man' – and so, when he came to pay and found that he could not, he was indeed treated as an ordinary man would be. The abuse and threats were really very nasty, and Rochester, presumably, was loving every moment of them. It was not until Charles produced a ring for pawning which a jeweller, knocked up out of his bed, recognised as royal property, that he was let off the hook. Everyone laughed, no doubt rather hysterically, at the fact that they had called the King a 'black-looking, ugly rake with no money in his pocket' and, going along with the joke, Charles asked if his credit would stretch to another bottle of wine. But he never spoke to Rochester again.

Whether Charles regretted going to the brothel at all is doubtful, as he was not a man to feel shame about that kind of escapade. He might, though, have considered that he already had – not quite simultaneously, but very nearly – a Queen at Audley End, with whom he maintained sexual relations; Nell Gwyn over the road; the delicious little French dish Louise de Querouaille in the palace; the Duchesse de Mazarin and – an old flame that just kept on smouldering – Barbara, Lady Castlemaine in their gambling dens; along with sundry other compliant beauties, all of whom were at his disposal during the years he spent at Newmarket. For a special, perverse thrill he also had Frances Stuart, the model for Britannia[2] and the prettiest woman of the age, who despite all his best efforts refused to sleep with him.

It is not, on this evidence, difficult to see how Charles has acquired a reputation for licentiousness. His mistresses have passed into the world of myth, as has the fact that his nickname, Old Rowley, commemorated in the Rowley Mile course, was originally the name of his stallion hack (nudge nudge). We remember him now for his womanising, as is our prurient wont, but even at the time his exploits were much

---

[2] The sketch for Britannia was actually made at a Newmarket race meeting by the sculptor Philip Rotier.

remarked upon, either with jokes about his sceptre being of a length with his '– – – – –' (Rochester), or with disapproval about the bad example that he was setting to his court (Evelyn).

In fact John Evelyn had a low opinion of the whole Restoration court and, furthermore, of the whole Newmarket enterprise (nor was Pepys very keen; he sometimes seems curiously uninterested in anything that doesn't involve himself). When Evelyn records his visit to the town in 1670, he fixes his criticism upon the palace, but this is obviously just the focus for a wider discontentment. For him, there is a touch of self-inflicted *lèse majesté* in the way that the King descends, with such robust eagerness, upon this plebeian little place. Evelyn does thaw, though with chilly reservations, when writing of 'the stables and fine horses, of which many were here kept at a vast expense, with all the art and tendernesse imaginable'. And he enjoys his ride 'over Newmarket Heath, the way being mostly a sweet turfe and down, like Salisbury Plaine, the jockies breathing their fine barbs and racers' (were these two distinct types?) 'and giving them their heates'.

Then, in October of the following year, he makes a return visit and his misgivings become more apparent. Without meaning to be he was in the thick of an intrigue, staying as he was at Euston Hall in Suffolk where his host, Lord Arlington (an A in the Cabal), was also entertaining members of the French court. Colbert was there, as was Louise de Querouaille, maid of honour to Charles' sister, and described by Evelyn as 'that famous beauty, but in my opinion of a childish, simple, and baby face'. Negotiations for the Secret Alliance between Charles and the exquisite thorn in his side, Louis XIV, were in progress. Louise was part of the deal and it was at Euston, during Evelyn's stay, that 'it was universaly reported that the faire Lady – – – – – was bedded one of these nights, and the stocking flung, after the manner of a married bride.'

Meanwhile, in between these shenanigans, everyone trooped off to Newmarket for the other, slightly more public, sensation of the week, the 'greate match run between Woodcock and Flatfoot, belonging to the King and to Mr Eliot of the Bed-chamber, many thousands being spectators; a more signal race had not been run for many yeares'. Evelyn omits to record that Mr Eliot won the race, nor does he state that both men rode their own horses, although perhaps this was sufficiently usual not to need comment. But the excitement that surrounded the match seems to have been remarkable. Many state papers date from Newmarket at this time and to have missed the event would clearly have been unconscionable, even to those who cared nothing for racing.

Later on at Euston, where it was really all happening:

came all the greate men from Newmarket . . . to make their court, the whole house fill'd from one end to the other with lords, ladys, and gallants; there was such a furnished table as I had seldome seene, nor anything more splendid and free, so that for fifteen days there were entertained at least 200 people, and halfe as many horses, besides servants and guards, at infinite expence. In the morning we went hunting and hawking; in the afternoone, till almost morning, to cards and dice . . .

Then, five days after this diary entry, Evelyn ventures into the lion's den and spends the night at Newmarket '. . . where I found the jolly blades raceing, dauncing, feasting, and revelling, more resembling a luxurious and abandon'd rout, than a Christian Court. The Duke of Buckingham was now in mighty favour, and had with him that impudent woman the Countess of Shrewsbury, with his band of fidlers, &c.'

No denying that this all sounds marvellous fun, if of a slightly uncontrolled kind, but Evelyn seems to see in Newmarket a place where all the latent immorality of the court can breathe freely, untrammelled by rules other than those it has made up itself. This is a jaundiced view, although it may have been true for someone like Rochester. If only, when he writes these things, Evelyn didn't remind one so much of a frustrated adolescent with his face pressed up against his sexy big brother's bedroom window! He doesn't mean to be funny when he says that Euston Hall is 'seated in a bottome between two gracefull swellings', but the sense is irresistibly created that this is his subconscious talking.

Yet his sincerity, as he wrings his hands before the louche spectacle of the court, which he had so longed to see restored, is undeniable. After Charles' death he writes at length about his 'many virtues, and many greate imperfections', and re-creates a scene that he had viewed in London a week earlier – even if it aroused other more complex emotions, it clearly also caused him sadness.

> I can never forget the inexpressible luxury and prophaneness, gaming and all dissoluteness, and as it were total forgetfullnesses of God (it being Sunday evening) which this day sen'night I was witnesse of, the King sitting and toying with his concubines, Portsmouth,[3] Cleaveland,[4] and Mazarine, &c., a French boy singing love songs, in that glorious gallery, whilst about twenty of the greate courtiers and other dissolute persons were at basset round a large table, a bank of at least two thousand in gold before them . . . Six days after was all in the dust!

In which case, one might think, thank God they all enjoyed themselves so much at the time.

What Charles *can* be accused of is that, in the pursuit of pleasure, he and his court wasted money they didn't have. Public finances at the Restoration were unhealthy – in 1661–2 there was a shortfall of about one-fifth, or £300,000, between income and outgoings – and this was before the start of the Anglo-Dutch war. The hole that Charles was in was not deep, but he never quite dug himself out of it.

With this in mind, Pepys is surely justified in attacking the Newmarket visits, at one point sounding gleeful about the fact that the weather is likely to put an end to the 'proposed great pleasure' (it didn't). Evelyn too refers constantly to the 'expence' of everything. The palace had been done on the cheap, but £10,000 had been spent on improvements to Audley End even though Charles never really used it; James D'Arcy had to be paid for providing horses even though he

---

[3] Louise de Querouaille had been created Duchess of Portsmouth.
[4] Barbara Castlemaine had been created Duchess of Cleveland.

sometimes wasn't; horses had to be fed (according to the Duke of Tuscany, on 'soaked bread and fresh eggs', which is a little hard to believe); stables, to which a 'ruinous' £800 had been assigned for immediate work as early as 1661, had to be maintained; then there was the cost of transporting a whole court, plus its £8,000 tents, two or even three times a year.

It all mounted up. Charles himself was oddly austere in some ways. In fact he had to be, as at one point he had so little ready money that, according to Pepys, the royal wardrobe contained not a single handkerchief. But because he had one very strong appetite – for women – he was drawn into extravagance on his mistresses' behalf. It was to be expected that he would buy them presents, give them accommodation, provide for their children by him and give them 'retainers' – £1,000 for Nell, £2,000 for Louise in 1675, for instance. But the real drain upon his, or the public, finances came when he was obliged to pay for their gambling. This must have been especially painful when the debts had been run up by one mistress in the gambling den of another. Indeed both Lady Castlemaine and the Duchesse de Mazarin ran gaming-houses that were directly, as well as indirectly, subsidised by public money. The duchesse in particular was a fixture at almost every Newmarket race meeting – up went her tables, in went the glamorous lemmings – and as such 'officially' recognised as an adjunct of the court.

This was a bit much, as the duchesse had been left £1,625,000 by her famous cardinal uncle, which was more than Charles' entire annual expenditure. Nevertheless it was the gentlemanly convention. It was unthinkable that the King should not support his women, whether they were daughters of a 'bawdy-house' keeper, like Nell Gwyn, or members of the French aristocracy. He himself gambled in fivers while stoically, and perhaps guiltily, underwriting their excitable plunges. On the whole it was cards that did the damage, and basset the game of choice. Pepys wrote of Barbara Castlemaine that she was 'so great a gamester as to have won £15,000 in one night, and lost £25,000 in another night, at play; and hath played £1,000 and £1,500 at a cast'. Nell Gwyn, who also liked a bet on a horse, was reported to have lost 1,400 guineas in one night *chez* Mazarine. Had this been widely known she might have been less popular with the English public. Even Charles' respectable old mother, Henrietta Maria, was irresistibly drawn to the Newmarket card tables. As at the court of France, which of course had been the Queen Mother's home, gambling was the pastime of choice, not just for the young and feckless but for those who could not, unfortunately, be condemned as hopelessly louche.

This brings us to an important point about Charles' court: it was very Frenchified. Not in every way – it was less formal, less elegant and far less rich – but it had a sophistication, an understanding, a tolerant indifference to sin, which is really not very English. But then nor was the King himself. It is surprising that he so much liked to see women dressed as boys, because he had the barest spit of native blood in him: quarter parts of Scottish, Danish, Italian and French went to make up that swarthy, sexy whole, and it was *le quartier français* that dominated. In many ways he resembled his grandfather Henri IV: in his healing pragmatism in the face of danger and in his healthy, angst-free sexual appetite. Plenty of English kings have had mistresses. Charles is the only one of them who gives the impression of actually liking the women with whom he slept.

Antonia Fraser, who completely grasps the nature of her very worldly subject, says that when considering Charles 'the clue is to concentrate not so much on the question of debauchery but on the true keynote of the King's Court after 1667: and that was laxity'. Debauchery is in fact an English person's hysterical, envious view of what the French would accept as something less criminal, more venial. Men like John Evelyn, who wanted Charles to be something other than what he was, were upset and disappointed by his apparent refusal to take his job seriously. But, because Evelyn was clever in a different way from the King, he misunderstood the King's cleverness.

He failed to understand the key to Charles' character, which was detachment. The events that destroyed his father and forced him into exile did not, as in an ideal world they would have done, turn him into a king of deep wisdom: for this he was criticised, and has been ever since. Instead his sufferings developed in him what Antonia Fraser calls 'that strange streak of vacillation, or masterly inaction, or sheer intrigue . . .' On his return to England he seems, by some instinct, to have decided that the way to play it was as if wearing a mask: the mask of a Restoration monarch.

Yes, he spent more money than he could afford but this was almost certainly a calculated move, intended to fund a PR image of kingship, as was the Anglo-Dutch war for which people – front page of the *Sun*-style – were absolutely gagging. Yes, he had mistresses, but these too were part of the image. Nell Gwyn was in fact less important in Charles' life than Louise de Querouaille, as is implied by the comparative size of their retainers, but she was good publicity – England adored the idea of the little orange-seller, the People's Prostitute, sitting on the King and twirling his lovelocks. Yes, Charles indulged himself at Newmarket but this, too, may have been semi-calculated. By propagating the notion of the Merry Monarch, he allowed a sense of reassurance, of well-being, to permeate the country. How could England be in trouble, if the King was leaving London for weeks on end, in carefree pursuit of pleasure?

These feelings may have been illusory, but then they almost always are; and they still had their effect. Rochester was not entirely right to say that Charles never did a wise thing, as wisdom is not always apparent. Evelyn may have been right to say that 'never had King more glorious opportunities to have made himselfe, his people, and all Europe happy, and prevented innumerable mischiefs, had not his too easy nature resign'd him to be manag'd by crafty men, and some abandon'd and profane wretches . . .' And doubtless when the King was riding around on the Heath, or looking at his horses out of his palace window, or watching plays in the barn at Newmarket, or cock-fighting, or seducing women, he should have been sitting in Whitehall pondering the future of his country. All of this is true. What is also true is that, after Civil War, regicide and republic, a man like Charles was what England needed: someone who allowed them to live in the present and feel that it was good.

And what of horse racing? The received opinion is that, during the reign of Charles II, Newmarket was irrevocably established as the home of the sport, and that from the time of his early visits there the town never looked back. This is not entirely accurate.

Of course racing came to life during the years that Charles patronised Newmarket. According to the principle of *reculer pour mieux sauter*, the sport got going again, after the languishing years of the Commonwealth, with a sharp burst of innovative vigour that it might never otherwise have experienced. Racing proliferated on the Heath, so much so that there must have been an abundance of horses in Newmarket throughout the 1670s. Indeed, accounts of the 1683 fire record that losses were sustained in stables owned by the Lords Sutherland, Clifton, Rochester and Clarendon (not the po-faced earl). Lord Sunderland lost not only 'his chief Saddle-Horses, but his best set of Coach-Horses', while the horses belonging to the Duchesse de Mazarin were burned alive, a horror which seems to have extinguished the sparkle of her life.

The 1671 Flatfoot–Woodcock match was just the most famous among many. Ballads on the subject were written, evoking something both remote and familiar. 'The Call to the Races at Newmarket' contains the lines 'But fie on that Jockey, I fear I have lost/With ease he had won it, had won it (if he had but run it)', variations upon which can be heard in any betting shop on any afternoon. And 'The Golden Age is Come', which was actually sung to Charles in 1684, paints an impressionistic picture of Newmarket that is by no means the saccharine eulogy usually heard by monarchs:

> . . . Each corner of the Town
> Rings with perpetual noise,
> The Oyster-bawling Clown
> Joyns with Hot Pudding-pies:
>
> Who both in Consort keep,
> To vend their stinking Ware;
> The drowzy God of Sleep,
> Has no Dominion here.
>
> Hey-boys, the Jockeys roar,
> If the Mare and Gelding run;

I'll hold ye five Guineas to four,
He'll beat her and give half a Stone.

God Dam-me cries Bully, 'tis done,
Or else I'm the Son of a Whore;
And would I could meet with a Man
Will offer it, will offer it once more.

See, see the damn'd Vice of this Town,
A Fop that was starving of late,
And scarcely could borrow a Crown,
Puts in to run for the Plate.

Another makes Racing a Trade,
And dreams of his Projects to come;
And many a crimp[5] Match has made,
By bubbing[6] another Man's Groom . . .

Embroider'd and fine as the Sun,
On Horses in Trappings of Gold,
Such a Show I shall ne'er see again,
Should I live to a hundred years old . . .

Racing then *was* a sight to behold, a spectacle in which we
find echoes today – for example in the brightly coloured
taffetas worn by jockeys, or grooms. For sheer monumental
vital chaos, however, we cannot begin to rival it. No sense of
separation existed between those who watched and those
who participated; everyone milled together in one big, sweaty
swirl. Like a call to some sort of order, drums and trumpets
would announce the start of a race. Then off the horses
would go and, when they reached the point at which the
mounted spectators were gathered, off too would go their
audience, galloping along with them all the way to the
winning post. Really it was like a circular cavalry charge,
everyone yelling and hollering, whips and wigs flailing all
over the place.

The confusion was compounded by the fact that starting a
race was, in those days – and indeed for many days to come

---

[5] Bent.
[6] To 'bub' meant to drink, so presumably this meant getting the other Man's Groom
plastered.

– a very inexact business. It is concerning this that we find a record of the King being called upon to adjudicate. Lord Conway wrote on 5 April, 1682, that 'here hapned yesterday a dispute upon the greatest point of Criticall learning that was ever known at Newmarket. A Match between a Horse of Sir Rob: Car's, and a Gelding of Sir Rob: Geeres, for a mile and a halfe only, had engaged all the Court in many thousand pounds, much depending in so short a course to haue them start fairly'. Perhaps this made the starter nervous. Having called 'go' he then, almost immediately, called 'stop'. One horse, having obeyed the first command and disobeyed the second, completed the course; the other, having done the opposite, never moved. Gamblers argued the validity of each of the starter's commands, according to prejudice, and it was thought necessary to bring in Charles. 'I suppose there will be volumes written upon this subject,' wrote Conway, ''tis all referred to his Majesty's Judgment, who hath not yet determined it.' How could he? Perhaps he suggested a re-run, which was surely the sensible thing.

On another occasion Charles acted as a judge on a match, in which he found one horse to have beaten the other by a foot and a half. Why it was necessary to listen to the evidence of the jockeys, under oath, in order to reach this decision, is a small mystery.

But it was the thing itself – riding, training, jockeyship – which excited the King. He loved to sit perched on top of Warren Hill, whose use as a training ground began at this time, in the little wooden kiosk known as the King's Chair, and watch the eternal climb of the horse. He loved to invite jockeys to dinner, along with his aristocratic friends, and chat about racing. And he loved to ride himself. Two days after the 1671 defeat on Woodcock, he was reversing placings with Mr Eliot in a race also contested by a Mr Thomas Thynne and Charles' treacherous son, the Duke of Monmouth. This victory was in 'The Plate', possibly not the Town Plate because he won it again in March 1674, and the Town Plate was meant to be run in October. By the time of this second triumph Charles was forty-three, so this was some feat, even for a man so fit that he would walk ten miles across the Heath every morning. Sir Robert Carr is at pains to tell posterity that no favours had been shown: '. . . I doe assure the King wonn by good horsemanshipp.'

So was it old age, a raging regret that he could no longer command the Heath in this way, that caused Charles to want to leave Newmarket in 1683? Was it simply that a love affair had ended, which had been conducted by a man who never, from the time of his exile, formed any truly deep attachments?

All we know is that, after the great fire, the King began to make plans to 'render Winchester the seate of his autumnal field diversions for the future' (Evelyn). Of course it seems obvious that it was the fire that turned Charles against Newmarket. It had been terrible. On the evening of 22 March, it broke out in a stable yard near the market on the St Mary's side of the town, that is to say the opposite side to the palace, possibly caused by a groom 'taking tobacco'. The 'very high winde' took possession of the blaze, and soon it had 'burnt down all that side of the street with the market place and outhouses from where it began to the further end of the Towne towards Bury excepting two or three houses'. This was bad indeed, for the area around the Rookery would have been densely populated, yet rather miraculously only three people died. But sixty-six 'Mansion houses, Barnes, Stables, heyhouses and other buildings' were destroyed, a figure which shows very clearly the extent to which Newmarket had developed during the Restoration. Total losses, including household goods and shop contents, were assessed at £20,265 4s 8d. This too tells a tale of how wealth had accrued within the town – it was a very large sum at the time.

Yet the effects of the fire were barely felt on the other side of the town. It is quite possible that those in the palace – who included the future James II and Queen Anne – saw nothing of what happened. Because of the smoke the King spent the night at Lord Suffolk's house, but he did not leave Newmarket for three or four days; no doubt there were things to be organised and possibly help to be offered (in September there would be a collection for rebuilding the town). Of course Charles had been through it all before, when he distinguished himself by directing operations to contain the Great Fire of

London. Here, though, was a pitiful dimension peculiar to Newmarket: '. . . many horses which were taken out of the Flame and let loose upon the Street, to shift for themselves upon the Heath with the People, instead of making towards the Heath, made to the stables, where they were burnt without all possibility of preventing it.'

But the fact is that, if it had not been for the fire, which caused Charles to up sticks and leave the town sooner than anticipated, then he would almost certainly have been killed by other means: the Rye House Plot. The aim of this conspiracy was to ambush both the King and the future James II on the way back to London – Rye House stood at an unusually narrow point on this road – then put the Protestant Duke of Monmouth on the throne. The plot was thwarted simply because the party had left early.

So, in a strange way, Newmarket saved Charles' life; and he then set about ending the life that he had given to Newmarket. Maybe he was unnerved by the increasingly strong Whig presence in East Anglia, but there was more to it than that. He was ready to go: '. . . his Majestie very melancholy', wrote John Evelyn. When he had been near death from fever in 1679, almost the first sign of recovery that he gave was a demand to go to Newmarket. Now, though, he had had enough: of all that rampant vitality, that thrilling discomfort, those journeys through the night and nights without sleep. His last Spring meeting – we all must have one – was in 1684. After that, throughout what was to be the final year of his life, he continued to make plans for Winchester.

It was all far more seemly than what had gone before. Evelyn thought it 'infinitely indeede preferable to Newmarket for prospects, air, pleasure and provisions', and the Wren palace was intended as a rival to Versailles, a home fit for a king at last. It is quite understandable that Charles, at the old age which fifty-three then was, should have decided upon such a change. Yet it is almost shocking to think that Newmarket and horse racing might so easily have been separated. It had happened before, in 1681, when Charles summoned Parliament to Oxford and the Spring meeting was staged at Burford; everything went off well enough, and there was a distinct possibility that the whole racing outfit could be moved to this reassuringly Royalist area. Of course there was no Warren Hill in either Oxfordshire or Hampshire, but in the seventeenth century Warren Hill had not acquired the mythical resonance that it now possesses. The irony is that it is Charles, as much as anyone, who had helped to give it that resonance, and it is he who was on the brink of taking it away again.

What, then, would have happened to Newmarket, if the King had lived longer and established Winchester more firmly? Would it have survived as a centre for racing? Would it have returned, eventually, to its former life, with the memories of its improbably glamorous past subsumed into the bustle of the market? Impossible to say. All that can be said with certainty is that the post-Restoration years were a crossroads time for the town. When, after the fire, the last traces of the court of King Charles were cleared away – all that scorched finery that no one returned to buy – what remained were the foundations of a sport which might be built upon or might be left to rot. It so happened that the first option was taken; but this was by no means inevitable.

Yet the effect Charles had upon Newmarket had been incalculably deep. Probably no one was ever, subsequently, to change the town so much. If it was only his death that prevented these changes from going into reverse, the fact is that they are still with us. Not just the concrete things: the establishment of racing stables, of Warren Hill as a training ground, of the Town Plate and its rules, of the Spring and Autumn meetings. It is something that he conjured in the atmosphere of the place, something that people have felt about it ever since, something that may well have been indestructible.

He made Newmarket seem the rightful home for the sporting Englishman, that enduring character whose image the Frenchified Charles came to symbolise. He may even have 'invented' that image. Of course men had always gone out to play, but it was Charles II who, with his instinctive and superficial genius, made of these activities a whole public way of life – a lifestyle, even – that was instantly recognisable to the wider world. Having endured so much that was serious, Charles understood the importance of what was trivial, and this became the sum of all wisdom about sport in this country. By the end of his reign, the idea that everything stopped when an Englishman was at his games – that the world might be lost while a horse race was run – was so firmly established that it could have been one of the laws of nature. It underpinned Newmarket, and it continues to do so.

Even John Evelyn could not escape by the end. The entry in his diary for 30 March, 1699, reads: 'My deceased son was buried in the vault at Wotton, according to his desire. The Duke of Devon lost £1,900 at a horse-race in Newmarket.'

3 Foundations laid

'A Country Overrun by Horse-races' – 1683–1799

W HAT WAS NEEDED NOW were institutions. They took a while to come, but during the eighteenth century such a vast deal of organisation took place that, although it happened over a period of many years, it seemed to come in one great reforming rush. What had been powerful but inchoate was given form. What might have been ephemeral was given substance and structure. And it all happened at a time when royal patronage – which had seemed so essential to the fortunes of horse racing – had drifted away into a haze of Hanoverian indifference.

In 1727 came the *Calendar: An Historical List of All the Horse-Matches run, and All Plates and Prizes run for in England and Wales (of a value of ten pounds and upwards)*. This annual publication, which cost the then considerable sum of five shillings, was not absolutely the first of its kind – as early as 1679 an advertisement in the *London Gazette* had told of a Mr John Nelson who 'doth keep a register (of match races) at the Groom Porter's Office in Newmarket' – but it was the first to do the job properly. The idea had come from a man named John Cheney, who clearly recognised that the time had come to start a record of racing; after all, according to the *Calendar*, the sport was then being staged in 112 English towns. When he died, in 1751, his creation metamorphosed into the *Sporting Kalendar*, produced by an auctioneer called John Pond; then, in 1773, came the *Racing Calendar*, published by James Weatherby, whose family name was to become synonymous with the administration of horse racing. Weatherby's nephew (also James) started the *General Stud Book* in 1791. In 1766 the firm of Tattersalls conducted its first bloodstock auction on a piece of land called the Five Fields, which lay across what is now London's Grosvenor Crescent. In around 1750 the Jockey Club was formed. All of these institutions are still in existence. They were based upon something so sure, so sound, so firmly rooted in the belief that racing had a place in the life of the nation, that they would not – could not – be dismantled. This would only happen if England were to change beyond all recognition.

In 1752, the Jockey Club took the decision to lease premises in Newmarket, and from then on the link between town and sport was also indestructibly forged. Before this, Newmarket had indeed gone into the decline that had seemed all too likely after 1683. Yet it didn't happen quite as one might have thought and the place didn't become a ghost town overnight. Pleasurable aftershocks kept Newmarket going for another thirty years or so. Maybe it was a bloodless shadow of what it had been before. Maybe some ageing rake, who had watched the match between Woodcock and Flatfoot then played basset all night with Lady Castlemaine, would have found the Newmarket of the 1690s to be a sad facsimile, looking the same but feeling quite different. Ostensibly, though, little had changed.

James II did not last long enough to do any damage – at least, not to Newmarket. He had enjoyed visiting the town during his brother's reign, and had even gone racing on a Sunday (clutching his Bible). His passion for gambling had waned, however, after the visit of the Abbé Pregnani, court astrologer to Louis XIV, who had been sent over to help with negotiations for the Secret Alliance. The abbé's credibility never recovered from the failure of the horses that he picked, by use of his psychic powers, to win at Newmarket. Charles II wrote to his sister in France that '. . . he had the ill luck to foretell three times together, and James believed him so much as he lost his money upon the same score.'

As King, James went racing just once. Interestingly, this was at Winchester, which implies that the move planned by Charles was still on the cards. However James showed no desire to finish the Wren palace, despite the fact that £20,000 had already been spent on it and that it had, according to John Evelyn, 'an incomparable prospect'. Really, James' chief pastime was going as publicly as possible to Mass. Unlike his brother, he had no genius for dissemblance, no taste for triviality – which was more the pity for him.

Yet William III, who might have been expected to care nothing for either Newmarket or horse racing, was in fact a friend to both. He seems to have been hell-bent on sticking to what had been done before. Not for him the confident gesture of uprooting a sport and taking it to a new, improved site. If English kings amused themselves watching horses on Newmarket Heath, then that was how he would amuse himself. Gamely, he and his wife Mary even installed themselves in the palace, and William brought to it a few personal touches. A Dutch-style parterre garden was created, similar to the Privy Garden at Hampton Court. An inventory taken in 1783 describes the King's bedroom as containing: 'A State Bed with furniture of Orange Colour'd Damask ... 6 pieces of Orange Colour'd Damask hangings the same as the bed ... 4 Sqr. Stools cover'd and trim'd the same as the Bed ... 2 Elbow Chairs with Cases of Orange Colour'd Serge ...' Continuing the theme, which surely nobody could have missed, even the closet had a 'Draw up Orange Colour'd Damask Window Curtain'.

Then we find Macaulay writing of how, in 1698, the French ambassador 'was invited to accompany William to Newmarket, where the largest and most splendid Spring Meeting ever known was about to assemble'. There were ten days of racing. 'The attraction must have been supposed to have been great, for the risks of the journey were not trifling ... The state of those roads, though contemporaries described it as dangerous beyond all example, did not deter men of rank and fashion from making the joyous pilgrimage to Newmarket. Half the Dukes in the Kingdom were there. Most of the chief Ministers of State swelled the crowd; nor was the Opposition unrepresented ...'

Apparently unchanged, then, from the days of Charles II; if anything, it sounds as though Newmarket in 1698 was even more popular than it had been twenty years earlier. Perhaps the respectability conferred by the character of William made attending the races rather more acceptable, for ministers of state, than when Charles' more disreputable court held sway and going to Newmarket was rather like going AWOL. Macaulay writes that it 'was then the gayest and most luxurious spot in the island', but his was a nineteenth-century perspective. It is hard to believe that William III's Newmarket gave off those same effusions of wild vitality; after all, if in 1698 it was just as it had been before, then the unpredictability had been lost.

What had not changed was the untamed nature of the place. Only venture outside those tight aristocratic circles and the ravening wolves would pounce. Presumably it was highwaymen who made the journey 'dangerous beyond all example', for there were constant rumours of coaches being held up and their occupants being stripped, trussed and slung into ditches. A band of about forty highwaymen had made little huts for themselves deep inside Epping Forest, a stopping post on the London–Newmarket road, from which they would emerge to make their raids. Of course their crimes now have a certain glamour, and sometimes highwaymen did behave with a degree of style, as when Richard Tattersall was allowed to go on his way out of respect for his honest reputation as a horse auctioneer. Nevertheless they must have been terrifying, far worse than muggers because the ordeal was so uncertain and drawn-out.

There was also at this time a vast, disconcerting camp of people who would come from miles around, congregating on Newmarket Heath whenever meetings were staged, waiting to feed upon the leavings of the London rich. This army of scavengers, predatory but rather pitiful, was in one form or another to become an established fixture of the racing scene. Rubbing up against it was part of the risk one took. Entrance to a racecourse may have been free in the eighteenth century, but the potential price was to be robbed or 'dipped' or threatened, to touch the poverty that hovered at the edge of this most patrician of sports. Later, in the nineteenth century, many small courses – such as the one that, between 1837 and 1841, stretched across the posh end of Ladbroke Grove – would be forced to close because they could not cope with all the hangers-on. Even today, at the Derby, Epsom Downs will be teeming with gypsies, touts and fake book-makers, all of them poised to beg, harangue and cheat. This is not the case at Newmarket, whose atmosphere is rather less Jonsonian; although, incidentally, gypsies did set up temporary camp on Warren Hill as recently as 1985.

William III first visited the town in 1689. Immediately he plunged into Newmarket life, racing, gambling and cock-fighting with the best of them. It is perhaps unfair to say that accounts of him doing this remind one of a metropolitan New Labour politician eating mushy peas in his Northern consti-tuency – after all, the King was trying his best – yet his behaviour never quite fitted the template created by Charles II. William did not have the soul of a sportsman. For one thing, he was a terrible loser. When he gambled into nothingness the vast sum of 4,000 guineas he may not have realised that, in order to carry the gesture through, he must act with nonchalant stoicism about it all; and not, as he did the next morning, hit someone with his whip when they rode in front of him on the racecourse. This was the kind of bad manners for which Charles had cast Sir Robert Carr into the outer darkness when, having lost around £6,000 in a single day, he 'became greatly enraged'. Unable to help himself, of course, but amongst true English sportsmen – those who understand that, if the world is lost over a horse race, then it must be lost with a shrug – this simply did not do; nor indeed does it do today.

William also committed the solecism of dragging politics into racing. He ordered the seizure of all horses worth more than £5 belonging to Roman Catholics, which was really rather petty and nasty. Families were forced to drive to church with their carriages drawn by oxen. The horses which were confiscated, Cromwell-style, the King then appropriated for himself. No doubt anti-Papist public opinion took pleasure in all of this, but the spirit of racing – which, when left to itself, is proud, careless and noble – should have been allowed to rise above such considerations.

Meanwhile the King and all his Protestant friends were running some decent horses across the Heath. The diary of the first Earl of Bristol, who rented a house near Newmarket for meetings, gives us a good idea of the sort of races that took place. Most of them were still matches, as in those days a large number of entry fees was not necessary to get together a decent stake. This was very much a private business, between gentlemen. And so on 22 April, 1691: 'I won ye Newmarkett Gold Tumbler with my horse called Davers, riding him myself at 12 stone weight.' At the famous 1698 Spring meeting: 'My Lobcock beat Looby (Duke of Devonshire's), 8 miles, 8 st. 12 lb. each I won of this 325 guineys.' And, three days earlier, Lord Bristol had watched the King win his most famous victory as an owner, when Careless, 'who had ceased to run at Newmarket merely for want of competitors' (Macaulay), was beaten.

Careless was a phenomenon, regarded as invincible. His owner, the Marquess of Wharton, had the best stud in the country at this time, at Winchendon in Buckinghamshire. He would travel any number of miles with one of his animals if, at the end, there was the prospect of beating a horse owned by a Tory. His other star was Gelding, who had been sent over to make a guest appearance at one of the earliest French race meetings, held at St Germain. There he had impressed Louis XIV so greatly that the King tried to buy him, offering either the horse's weight in gold or a thousand pistoles. Both were turned down. Later, Lord Wharton would also decline the sum of £700 for the 14-year-old Careless, instead – a charming gesture, this – giving him back to the Yorkshire-man who had bred him.

Careless should never have lost the match against the King's horse. Over a distance of five miles he was carrying nine stone and his opponent 'a feather', the lowest possible weight, which may well have been less than half as much. This was a nonsense, and because of it William III's Stiff Dick won the race. And yes, it is hard to believe some of the names that were given to horses at this time. A collection of them reads like a sketched-out scenario for a highly specialised pornographic film: not just Stiff Dick but Cream Cheeks, Broad Bottom, Spanker and Bloody Buttocks. Were people having a laugh? Almost certainly not. Early records explain, with admirable earnestness, how for example the Bloody Shouldered Arabian had been named after a 'Redish stain' across his coat; and no doubt all the rest could be similarly explained away, by someone sufficiently mature.

On 3 August, 1702, John Evelyn wrote that 'The King had a fall from his horse and broke his collar-bone, and having been much indispos'd before, and aguish, with a long cough and other weaknesse, died this Sunday morning, about four o'clock.' It was a bit rotten that William III should have died after his horse tripped over a molehill in the grounds of Hampton Court; especially as he had, in that very place, re-established an old stud originally run by the first Duke of Buckingham. Hampton Court stud was to become extremely important in the breeding of racehorses, and would help no end in reviving the collapsed institution of the Royal Studs. After Charles II's rather devil-may-care attitude to the future, William's conscientious nurturing of the horse was what was needed. In his dutiful way, this king had been very good for the sport.

His sister-in-law, too, was an enthusiast. In fact Queen Anne probably liked racing – the thing itself – as much as any English monarch before or since. Being plain and vastly fat, she felt no particular obligation to spend the day concentrated upon her own fascinating being, and could therefore lose herself in sport in a way that few women actually manage. Indeed, if this splendid creature could only see the female behaviour at Royal Ascot – the hours spent in front of mirrors, oblivious to the racing, pondering the angle of the exploding blancmange perched precariously on the head – she might wish that she had never invented this increasingly silly meeting.

However in 1711, when racing was first held there, Ascot Heath was rather more robust. It skipped one of the sport's evolutionary stages in that it held Plate races rather than matches, thus taking itself closer to something that we would recognise today. Indeed the Queen's very presence was a modernising factor, as at this time hardly any women were seen at racecourses – unless peeping coyly out of family coaches, looking in vain for their men. But Anne made up her own rules. She was a far better sportsperson than William had been. As a girl she had strolled casually into the cockpit at Westminster. When she turned up at Ascot to watch the running of the Queen's Plate, she brought with her a gorgeous maid-of-honour, Miss Forester, who was not hidden away in the modest custom, but seated on a palfrey and dressed as a man in a long white riding coat, pointed court hat bound with a gold lace and a periwig. Of this we must make what we choose.

As well as Ascot the Queen sent horses to race at York, thus creating two more *de facto* national meetings and, in a benign sense, ending Newmarket's supremacy in this regard. However she gave her attention to the town. Being a decent sort, and practical in the female way, she provided the sum of £1,000 towards the paving of the streets. Then, in 1710, she granted £50 a year 'for the setting up of 2 Schools in the Town to instruct 20 Boys and 20 Girls in reading, writing, casting Accompts, and in the Knowledge and Practice of the Christian Religion'. This school seems to have been held in a transept of St Mary's Church; in recognition of the 1710 grant, an annual donation to the church is still given today by Elizabeth II.

Anne's first visit to the Newmarket palace was at the time of the 1683 fire. When she returned as Queen, in 1705, she ordered a new little block to be built for herself, with a bedroom and dressing-room. Perhaps she disliked the colour orange. Her quarters looked on to the High Street but were set back from it, occupying the site where the United Reformed Church now stands. A drawing which is thought to represent this wing shows paved paths, fringed with a few trees, leading from the street up to a building of extreme simplicity. The 1783 inventory tells us nothing definite about Anne's rooms – the Loton landscapes mentioned might not have been hung during her reign – but it does make intriguing references to 'Garrats called the Duchess of Marlborough's'. Were these used by the Queen's favourite, Sarah Churchill?

Yet the idea of Winchester – apparently abandoned by William III – was still vaguely in the air, whether as a centre for racing or not we have no idea. We do know that Anne certainly intended to complete the palace for her husband, George of Denmark, then – same old story – ran out of money. Eventually this doomed building, which had been conceived as England's Versailles, was occupied by 5,000

French prisoners of the Seven Years War, then in 1792 by banished clergy. In 1796, the palace was turned into a barracks. The vision conjured by John Evelyn, of a setting truly fit for a king and his horses, was over. It was later to be realised in France, when Chantilly racecourse was built beside the château, and training gallops established in the forest. This *ensemble* is indeed exquisite, beautiful as a dream, almost unreal in its champagne- and dusk-coloured elegance. It is not, somehow, imaginable in England.[1]

So the royal patronage of Newmarket continued, much as before. Yet the most important force in the town at this time was not a monarch but a nasty-looking man named Tregonwell Frampton: the 'Keeper of the Running Horses', manager of the royal racing stables, and the first person to make his livelihood synonymous with Newmarket and its sport. As with an American film star it was his longevity, as much as anything, that was the secret of Frampton's success. Born in 1641, he came to Newmarket in his thirties and, although there is no record of it, possibly worked within Charles II's racing establishment. After this he kept going for so long – through the reigns of William III, Anne, George I and George II – that by the end he appeared to be indispensable.

Frampton was, in a sense, the first professional racehorse trainer. He was paid to keep the royal horses in his stable, which was almost certainly at the bottom of Warren Hill on the site of what is now Heath House. Accounts vary as to what he was paid for this: £1 a week for each of William's horses seems to have doubled by the time that Frampton was working for Anne. Whether what he did amounted to anything like 'training', we have no real idea. What he certainly did was to take control of the royal racing Establishment, and the feeling that someone was in charge was both new and presumably rather comforting. He seems to have imported fourteen Arab horses for William and Hampton Court stud. When Anne ascended the throne, he was there to organise a programme for her stable. On one occasion he

---

[1] Kelso racecourse is on the doorstep of the Roxburghe family's Floors Castle, but this does not correspond to the original idea of making Winchester a centre for racing.

produced six of her horses and with them issued a challenge to six horses belonging to the Dukes of Devonshire, Rutland and Somerset. One especially good animal of the dukes' was not allowed into this competition, which was handy. The outcome is unknown, but the impression we are given is of a man who could get things done. Anne called him 'Governor' and Frampton, for his part, did not call the Queen the names that his misogynistic tendencies might have led him to do.

It is his character, though, rather than anything particular that he achieved, which seems to have given Tregonwell Frampton his reputation for cleverness as a horseman. He was, for example, a reckless gambler – and one that knew how to lose. A contemporary account says that 'one day he lost 1,000gs., the next he won 2,000, and so alternately. He made as light of throwing away 500l. or 1,000l. at a time as other men do of their pocket-money, and was perfectly calm, cheerful, and unconcerned when he had lost a thousand pounds as when he won it.' This would have impressed. In addition he busied himself all the time organising matches – frequently with his own horses – which also gave a great appearance of astuteness. However, records do not show these to have been an unqualified success (no doubt his admirers thought he was backing the other fellow's horse). Here, for example, are three of the matches that he made against the first Earl of Bristol. In 1701 'ye odds was two to one of Frampton's side, but he was beat.' In 1710 Bristol's 'famous horse Wenn . . . won his twentieth match by beating the Whiteneck mare'. And in 1711 the earl's diary records that 'tho' Thiefcatcher was so lame that he went upon three legs, yet I ventured to run him against Thief, upon the contemptible opinion (you know) I always had of him, and beat him the last mile by dint of goodness.' Earl of Bristol 3: Tregonwell Frampton 0.

It may well have been that Frampton tried to be too clever in his dealings with racing. As the phrase has it, he couldn't lay straight in bed. He pitted horses against the Duke of Rutland's marvellous mare, Bonny Black, believing that if they carried a 'feather' then she could be beaten. Eventually he had to write to the duke, in very humble mood, saying that 'I am now throughly perswaded that no slow hors can feather such nimble ones' (which incidentally reflects well on Stiff Dick). Rather than winning a match fair and square, he seems always to have looked for a cunning way of doing so – this, no doubt, gave him more pleasure. A famous story tells of a match that he made between one of his horses, name unknown, and a decent Yorkshire animal called Old Merlin, who had been sent down to Newmarket for the race. These North–South contests always attracted a great deal of money, so Frampton suggested to Old Merlin's connections that they might try the two horses privately, before the actual race, in order that they should know where to place their own bets.

Frampton's plan was that his horse should carry seven pounds more than the race weight. He would then make his own, secret deductions from the result of the trial, which Old Merlin won by a length. But a reasonably bright child could have guessed the truth, which was that Old Merlin would also be carrying extra weight – seven pounds, in fact – and that the match would, therefore, produce almost exactly the same result as the trial. It is the weakness of racing cheats never to think about what the other side might be up to. Tregonwell Frampton, 'the cunningest jockey[2] in England', was too busy being shrewd to be sensible.

Yet this silly tale tends to be told as if he had done something terrifically droll; there is a side to racing, inexplicable and irritating, which admires this kind of man. The sport is full of polite, attractive people with a real love of the sport and the horse. Yet put together a mixture of dourness, deviousness and harshness, and racing immediately gets excited: 'a character!' goes up the cry, the sort of person who gives racing its colour, who goes beyond the sentiment, the romance and the mystery so beloved of novices, who really *understands* the sport. Tregonwell Frampton was such a 'character'. His gambling, his tricks, his toughness, his charmlessness, his disdain for personal grooming – all of these combine to make him a legend in the racing world.

And what of his cruelty? The other famous story about Frampton is neither droll nor silly. The simple facts are these: Frampton ran his best horse, Dragon, in a 1,000

---

[2] 'Jockey' at this time simply meant a person connected with horses.

guineas match race against an unnamed mare, and Dragon won. The mare's owner then announced that he would run her the following day, in a 2,000 guineas match, against any mare or gelding in England. That night, Frampton castrated his horse. The next day, still bleeding, Dragon beat the mare then collapsed and died.

Now it must be stressed that this story is not properly authenticated. The only record of it is a magazine article published around seventy years after the event. The form in which this is written is easy to mock – the conceit is that Dragon himself is telling the tale – yet it has the power to move, because something in it speaks of all the cruelty that humans inflict upon animals. 'It is true (replied the steed), I was a favourite; but what avails it to be a favourite of caprice, avarice, barbarity? My tyrant was a wretch who had gained a considerable fortune by play, but more particularly by racing. I had won him many large sums; but being at length excepted out of every match, as having no equal, he regarded even my excellence with malignity . . .' Then the alleged circumstances are recounted. The story finishes: 'Injured as I was, the love of glory was still superior to the desire of revenge. I determined to die as I had lived, without an equal; and having again won the race, I sank down at a post in an agony, which soon after put an end to my life.'

It is not known how the man who wrote this, Dr John Hawkesworth, came to hear of it. He had no connection with racing, but one may assume that it was the kind of lurid legend that might easily spread and endure. But was it true? Was this the sort of thing that went on in eighteenth-century racing? This is the opinion of John Lawrence in his *Philosophical and Practical Treatise on Horses*: 'Every sportsman I hope holds in equal detestation with myself the memory of the brutal and callous-hearted Frampton . . . I never view the portrait[3] of that savage sportsman without discovering in the hard lines of his face and the knowing leer of his eye all the treachery, cunning, and inhuman profligacy of the lowest blackguard retainer of the stable . . .' Strong stuff, and

---

[3] If the painting in the National Horseracing Museum is anything to go by, Frampton did indeed resemble a monstrous hobgoblin.

interesting, incidentally, in its ambivalent definition of the word 'sportsman'.

But Lawrence then goes on to reproduce an extract from a letter, written by a Newmarket man whose uncle knew Tregonwell Frampton and who totally refuted the possibility that the story was true. 'Farther, it may be fair to suspect that the cruel anecdote of the Father of the Turf and his horse Dragon is a pious fraud, invented by those who might think it a great merit in a religious way to cast a slander that would stick well upon the unholy exercise of horse-racing.'

Yet the conclusion, when it finally comes, is that 'the anecdote, however barbarous, is strictly probable, and may be matched in too great a number of melancholy instances'. Most racing books nowadays take the opposite, sceptical view. Yet however vivid people's imaginations may be – and, where racing is concerned, they do tend to run amok – it is a little hard to believe that the Dragon legend arose out of nothing. Ill-treatment was not unusual at this time; it was not an age of animal welfare. The stock may have been far sturdier than that with which we race now, but eight-mile matches and twelve-stone weights were still horribly harsh, especially as horses then raced so often. A history of Tattersalls[4] tells of how, before entering the sales ring, horses would have iron plugs inserted into holes drilled into their hooves, so that they would appear lively in their paces. The book also recounts the story of a horse bought for three guineas by a Quaker: 'It was old, half-blind and decrepit, but the good man paid the money down and walked the poor creature to his nearby country home, where it was destined to work the mill. Horse stealing was punished regularly by the hanging or transportation of the malefactor; cruelty – very rife in this period – was a man's private affair.'

So it is not entirely impossible that Tregonwell Frampton did, indeed, creep into his horse's box and – the thought of 2,000 guineas guiding his hand – cut off its balls. This was an age that celebrated the spectacle of birds tearing each other to death; why should a sportsman not geld his horse for the sake of a match? Whatever the truth of the Dragon story,

---

[4] By Vincent Orchard.

what is certain is that the character of Tregonwell Frampton was one around which such a myth could be woven. He was the first, but by no means the last, of the perverse heroes that racing has created for itself.

The combination of Frampton's death, in 1727, and a pair of German kings was enough to send Newmarket into the decline which had threatened for the previous forty years or so. Fashion has gathered this unlikely little town into its fickle embrace, and now it was bored. The poor old palace, starved of majesty, was in such a state of neglect that in 1721 it was rented out to the Duke of Somerset for just £30 per annum.

Yet, in this same year, as the last vestiges of Restoration glamour finally fled Newmarket, an event of vast significance took place. And this was something that would last. Watched by the usual handful of mounted spectators, there galloped across the Heath a horse named Flying Childers: 'allowed by Sportsmen to be the fleetest horse that ever ran at Newmarket, or, as generally believed, that was ever bred in the World'. Racing had had star animals before – Flatfoot, Careless, Black Bonny – but nothing like this had yet been seen. With Flying Childers came the idea of greatness in a racehorse; after him, the sport knew what it was looking for; since him, it has never stopped in its search.

Little is known of Flying Childers' career, although the impression that he left remains plain as day. Two matches are recorded: in the first, he beat the Duke of Bolton's Speedwell over four miles for 500 guineas, in the second Lord Drogheda's Chaunter over six miles for 1,000 guineas. More revealing are the trials that he ran. Details of the first were published, admittedly twenty-five years after the event, in the *Sporting Kalendar*: 'Childers won a Trial Match against Almanza and Brown Betty over the round Course at Newmarket (which measures three Miles and three Quarters) in six Minutes and forty-eight Seconds . . . though this was not the shortest Time it is imagined he could run it in, yet it is one Minute less than any Horse now in being can perform it in.' The timing of this trial cannot be completely relied upon, of course, nor the contemporary opinion that 'he had moved 82 feet and a half in one second of time, which is nearly the rate of one mile in a minute, a degree of velocity which no horse has been known to exceed.[5] He likewise ran over the Beacon Course ... and it was supposed that he covered at every bound a space of 25 feet.'

The second recorded trial was the only one ever to feature in the *General Stud Book*, although the details given were not correct. In fact Flying Childers gave a stone in weight to a horse named Fox – one of the best in the country, winner of three King's Plates – and beat him by nearly two furlongs.

This bay meteor, whose four white feet went flashing and dazzling across Newmarket Heath, was the son of a horse named the Darley Arabian. Foaled in 1700 – probably in Aleppo – he was brought to England by 'an agent in merchandise' named Thomas Darley, lived to the age of thirty, and was the single most influential import that racing has ever made. It is well-known that all modern racehorses descend, in the male line, from three foundation stallions: the Darley, the Godolphin Arabian and the Byerley Turk, none of whom ever ran. Of these the Darley Arabian transmitted by far the most powerful line. The thoroughbred – a word whose usage is first recorded in 1713, in a letter written by the Earl of Bristol – is a construct, a beautiful artifice made by breeders; but above all it is the creation of that horse.

So what did it matter if Newmarket's palace was no longer filled up with royalty, when all of this was going on: when the foundations of racing were being laid so surely, so strongly? Once the notion of the thoroughbred had been conceived, everything was possible. Records would be needed, rules would be needed, control would be needed. This development, more than anything, would give shape, purpose and unity to the sport.

Of course exotic horses had been imported for many years into England – Spanish, Italian, Barbs, Arabians, Turks – and prized, like all expensive foreign purchases, like all love objects, for their exquisite otherness. They were neither fast nor large, but they had more rarefied virtues. 'Spanish horses,' wrote Charles II's riding instructor, the Duke of

---

[5] For however brief a time, no horse can run at nearly 60 mph. In 1995 the great sprinter Lochsong covered three furlongs in 33.1 seconds, which is about as good as it gets. Those recording her thought that their stopwatches had broken.

Newcastle, 'were like princes, and Barbs like gentlemen in their kind.' Their beauty seems to have had an almost spiritual effect upon those who saw them. John Evelyn, in an enchanting passage from his diaries, describes the arrival at court in 1684 of 'three Turkish or Asian horses' taken as spoils at the siege of Vienna (which was how a lot of them came to England):

> I never beheld so delicate a creature as one of them was, of somewhat a bright bay, two white feet, a blaze; such a head, eyes, eares, neck, breast, belly, haunches, legs, pasterns, and feete, in all reguards beautifull and proportion'd to admiration; spirited, proud, nimble, making halt, turning with that swiftnesse, and in so small a compasse, as was admirable. With all this so gentle and tractable as call'd to mind what I remember Busbequius speakes of them, to the reproch of our groomes in Europe, who bring up their horses so churlishly as makes most of them retain their ill habits.
> They trotted like does, as if they did not feele the ground . . .

It was only three or four years after this, during the reign of James II, that the Byerley Turk arrived. A spoil of war again, having been captured by Captain Byerley when Buda was taken from the Turks, the horse was later ridden at the Battle of the Boyne before going to stud. One of his sons, Jigg, formed the base of a male line which can be traced down to the twentieth century.

The Godolphin Arabian is commemorated in the most successful racing operation of the late twentieth century, that of the Maktoums, ruling family of Dubai, whose horses are mostly trained in Newmarket but who – appropriately enough – send their best to spend the winter in the desert. Of the three foundation stallions, the Godolphin was the least important. Yet this is not to deny the truth of the words surrounding his portrait by Morier: 'Esteem'd one of the best Foreign Horses ever brought into England'.

The Godolphin Arabian was foaled in 1724, died on Christmas Day 1753, and has origins shrouded in mystery (the French writer, Eugene Sue, actually took the horse as a subject for one of his melodramatic tales). He may have been presented to Louis XV by the Bey of Tunis. He may have been discovered in Paris drawing a water-cart. He may have been bought by Edward Coke, who imported him to England for £3. He may have belonged at one time to a London coffee-house proprietor. He may have been a teaser[6] who fought the real stallion until he himself won the right to do the honours (the mare in question was named Roxana; an equine Cyrano, then).

What probably happened is that he was, indeed, given to the French king and sold in 1729 to Edward Coke, who later passed him on to Lord Godolphin. There, at the earl's Cambridgeshire seat, he was used as a stallion, made friends with a cat with whom he was painted, and was buried. During his long life he was examined by a vet who wrote, fascinatingly, that 'There was never a horse . . . so well entitled to get racers as the Godolphin Arabian; for, whoever has seen this horse must remember that his shoulders were deeper, and lay further into his back, than those of any horse ever yet seen . . .'

Portraits of the Godolphin convey this unusual strength and power. By contrast the Darley Arabian appears to have a refinement, a delicate liveliness of form, typical of his kind (the Byerley seems taller and altogether different, but then Turk and Arab were not synonymous terms). All three are rendered with the small, elegant, chiselled heads and wonderful crested necks that characterised the Eastern horse. And all three were prepotent, which was what English breeders wanted. But of course there was no grand plan in the idea of using these stallions. They were not used to the exclusion of other Eastern horses; the idea of 'purifying' the breed, in so far as it existed, was not articulated. It just happened that way. As is so often the case with racing, the intention became apparent after it had revealed itself.

So it was probably quite a shock to Mr Leonard Childers of Doncaster, who bred the horse named after him in 1714, then

---

[6] The teaser is the horse brought out to soften up a mare, with his kind attentions, before she is given to the real stallion.

sold him to the Duke of Devonshire, that Flying Childers should turn out to be so absurdly superior. No one would have expected the Darley Arabian to produce something so fast, so immediately. Nor would anyone have dreamed that he would propagate lines like the near-omnipotent Northern Dancer (foaled 1961) dynasty, which continues to dominate thoroughbreeding all over the world. Again, it just happened that way. The Darley – also commemorated by the Maktoum family, his name having been given to Sheikh Mohammed's breeding operation – was in fact a freak horse, with blood so good that his progeny could leave the rest of their kind behind. Thus the instant thoroughbred; glimpsed on the Newmarket Heath in 1721, moving faster than any horse had ever run; living still.

From this point on, racing began to be institutionalised: six years later came the *Calendar*, and then the men who owned horses would feel the urge to institutionalise themselves. The first recorded intimation of this was through an announce-ment in what had then become the *Sporting Kalendar*: 'There will be run for, at Newmarket, on Wednesday, April 1st, 1752, a Contribution Free Plate, by horses the property of the noblemen and gentlemen belonging to the Jockey Club at the Star and Garter in Pall Mall.'

It must be stressed that, at the start, the Jockey Club was in no way intended to be racing's regulatory body. It became that, as the need for it became apparent. If those gentlemen owners who were the club's first members – having met up with each other in the Star and Garter in Pall Mall, the Thatched Tavern in St James' Street and the Clarendon in Bond Street – had been told that they were forming an entity which was to become the sport's ultimate authority for the next 250 years and more, they would have been most surprised. What they sought was, if anything, contrary to the idea of rule-making: they simply wanted somewhere they could drink and chat and make matches and bets among their own kind. And, wonderfully for the town, this somewhere was to be in Newmarket.

Despite its then *démodé* status, it was the obvious place if one was looking outside London. It had that precious snob thing of inaccessibility, of being just a little bit too far from anywhere to be 'got at'. Open yet forbidding, the Heath lay in wait to protect Newmarket against the unwanted (still does). And it had the other, even more precious quality of authenticity. Compared with Newmarket, Ascot was *nouveau* (still is). Nowhere else was remote yet reachable; nowhere else had the history; and where else could possibly provide a better home for the thoroughbred and those who worshipped him? Thus the Jockey Club must have reasoned – or maybe it didn't even have to reason. The decision was taken to set up in Newmarket in 1752 and, since then, the logic of it has never been questioned.

A piece of land was duly leased, upon which a Coffee Room was built, this being almost certainly the site of the Coffee Room within the present Jockey Club building, which stands behind an elegant neo-Georgian façade on the High Street. Before the room was ready for use, in 1771, it is thought that the Club met in the Red Lion (now demolished) on the corner of Old Station Road.

Not much is known about its original membership, as the first official list was not published until 1835. Rather like members of the Bullingdon or Leander, they may have worn a special coat: in this case brown with lettered gilt buttons. Quite simply they would have been the sporting aristocracy of the time. If you were posh, you were in; if you weren't, you weren't. This has not changed at all (although 'trade' now counts as posh) which sends some people into a frenzy, although it is hard to see just what the Jockey Club would achieve by losing its air of exclusivity. The temptation to quote Groucho Marx on the subject of clubs should always be resisted, but what he said is never so applicable as here. If the Jockey Club were to become a body run on the lines of a Liberal Democrat council, then it might as well not exist at all, for it would no longer reflect the sport that it governs.[7] *Au fond*, antipathy to the Jockey Club equals antipathy to flat racing. Anyone who loathes élitism must, by definition, loathe a sport which takes this as its guiding principle. Also,

---

[7] In January 1993, the formation of the British Horseracing Board saw the Jockey Club concede some of its power base, as it inevitably had to do, to a more 'democratic' set-up. The Club remains racing's regulatory body – its original function.

as with common law, the rules of the Jockey Club have developed empirically: *a posteriori*, guided by the evolution of the thing that they were governing, rather than according to some pre-declared constitution. This process of accretion is clearly suitable to a sport whose chief source of strength is its traditions; although the modernising instinct, again, is to come breezing in with something clean and new, swept of all the cobwebby mysteries whose dark, delicate structures hold the essence of racing.

This is not to say that the Jockey Club doesn't rile with its attitudes, or is in any way above criticism. Yet it is essentially adaptable, like all aristocratic institutions (this is not the popular view, but just think of all those dukes merrily erecting dodgem car rides in the grounds of their stately homes), and has changed itself a good deal in the recent past, not least in sanctioning the instigation of the British Horseracing Board. And who would ever have dreamed, a century ago, that the sacred Coffee Room might now be hired out for conference use? But the Club knows, like the dukes, that survival in an antagonistic world requires this. It does its job, the job of running racing and making money for it, really rather well. And it knows that, if they are honest, every person connected with the sport in this country would die to be elected.

The great step towards becoming the Jockey Club that we know today was taken at the end of the eighteenth century, in circumstances so fascinating and peculiar that they are still impossible to fathom. That comes later. Meanwhile, back in the 1750s, the members of the new club were having a whale of a time, blissfully unaware of the responsibilities that were to fall upon them. In London their behaviour had not always been good – they had too much money and time on their hands for that – hence stories of a fight at the Star and Garter between the great-uncle of Lord Byron and a Mr Chaworth, who ended up dead, or of the offer by Lord Barrymore to find a man willing to eat a live cat for a bet. Nor were these men to become models of rectitude in Newmarket. But the open air, the sport, allowed them to rampage more freely and innocently, to get into scrapes, to behave exactly as they wished, without harming too many people, in a land ruled by themselves. The establishment of a base for racing men turned Newmarket into a great big outdoor country club. The Heath was theirs, to gallop across in their hats and cut-away coats, to make matches and bets and enjoy the sporting life in all its pure, energetic glory. The presence of women, an essential adjunct to Newmarket life in the sophisticated days of Charles II, was relegated to the near-invisibility that the English sporting gentleman frankly prefers.

The second half of the eighteenth century could, in fact, be seen as the apotheosis of flat racing, and perhaps of Newmarket. During those years, the Spring and Autumn meetings were continually augmented by new fixtures, all of which survive to this day: in 1762, the second October meeting; in 1765, the July meeting; in 1770, the Houghton; in 1771, the Craven. Here was a constant source of new delights with which the gentlemen of England could play. The world outside, with its *hoi polloi* and its commercial pressures, was somewhere beyond the Heath. Never before, and certainly never since, would racing and Newmarket be so entirely the possession of those who loved the thing itself.

The rest of life stops when racing takes over, which is why Newmarket has this heady air of being a world unto itself, and why, when one is there, living in this other world seems completely natural. Although an illusion, this is also a fact; and never more so than in the second half of the eighteenth century. When Newmarket was on, everything else simply made way for it. This had happened before, during the reign of Charles II; but now it was part of the pattern of upper-class society. This, too, had become institutionalised.

Those who were not under the spell regarded this obsession of the English ruling classes rather as, today, someone who hates football views its incomprehensible omniscience. Horace Walpole, son of the first Prime Minister, man of letters, unparalleled if sometimes rather queeny correspondent, has periodic snipes at the cult of horse racing. In 1769, when the Middlesex riots were raging in London: 'Luckily, Newmarket begins on Monday, during which holy season there is always a suspension of arms.' And in 1782: 'The recess of Parliament ... for the holidays, re-elections, and usual jaunts into the country, and the never-to-be-violated

festival of Newmarket, have dispersed many.' He was entirely proof against its charm. 'Though I . . . have been fifty times
in my life at Newmarket, and have passed through it at the
time of the races, I never before saw a complete one. I once
went from Cambridge on purpose, saw the beginning, was
tired and went away.'

The delicious tone does not, however, disguise the fact that
Walpole sees something frighteningly brainless in this wor-
shipping at the shrine of the thoroughbred. Again, the voice
is familiar: who has not heard the yelps of despair as some
twerpish little nineteen-year-old footballer is elevated to
mythical status? In a broader sense, who has not heard – or
indeed made – a lament for the death of cultured life at the
hands of vacuity? Of course those of us who love racing never
see it as vacuous: some find it infinitely intriguing, others
divine in it something poetical and romantic. But those who
don't, don't – and Horace Walpole was no trendy twentieth-
century intellectual, yearning to view sport through the eyes
of its followers and a pair of Gucci specs. To him, it was
merely pointless. People should have more civilised things to
do. England deserved better than to be: 'A country over-run
by horse-races! A gaming, robbing, wrangling, railing nation,
without principles, genius, character, or allies; the overgrown
shadow of what it was!' It sounds familiar, all right.

Thus it was an unfortunate irony that Walpole should end
up, in his cosy middle-age, having to sort out the estate of his
nephew, Lord Orford,[8] who had succumbed to madness 'in a
public inn, on the great road to Newmarket and Norfolk'.
Orford – who even before he went insane liked to drive
around in a coach drawn by stags – had dedicated his life to
sport and gambling. He made the famous bet with Lord
Rockingham, 'a match of five hundred pounds, between five
turkeys and five geese, to run from Norwich to London'.[9] The
estate of which Walpole had to dispose comprised large
numbers of horses; he was therefore obliged to immerse
himself in the world of racing, about which he had not a clue.

---

[8] The family home, Houghton Hall in Norfolk, gave its name to the Houghton meeting
held at Newmarket in mid-October.
[9] Possibly in all seriousness, the *Gentleman's Magazine* wrote that 'Both sides have begun
to train for this expedition.'

His letters are funny about it, but only just: 'I can talk of nothing but sweepstakes and forfeits ... In short, I have begun my education again. Mr Burlton (an habitué of Newmarket) comes to me three times a week to give me lectures on jockeyship; the other days I study conveyancing, mortgages, and annuities; and my head not happening to be very clear, I make sad jumbles, and confound jockeys and usurers, and t'other day asked my tutor when the match was to be run between Mr Manners and Black-and-all-black ... the application I am forced to give to what I do not understand turns my brain.'

Then he becomes pathetic, begging Lord Ossory – a racing man, but also a friend – to guide him through the labyrinth of bloodstock dispersal sales. 'Brief, may I trust Mr B? (Burlton). I am advised to let him sell Lord Orford's horses in this July meeting; and his mares, fillies, &c. in October ... He did tell Lord O's solicitor that he reckoned the whole would fetch £4,000. T'other day I got him to give me a rough sketch of the value of each, and it amounted in all but to £2,000. This frightens me ... He sold Stoic for 500 guineas, but with what he has paid, he makes a balance against us of near £300. All this is so alarming that I am afraid to go on ...'

Orford's madness, on top of his extravagance, was in fact a disaster for the Houghton estate. When Walpole inherited, on the death of his nephew, he called himself 'the poorest earl in England'. The magnificent paintings collected by Robert Walpole had to be sold for the ridiculously low sum of £40,000; although Orford was concerned about 'nothing but his dogs and horses, and the physicians themselves are afraid of telling him they are gone'.

Walpole and Newmarket should never have had to mix, and it really was comic that they ever did. The men who followed racing at this time were of a far coarser breed – Walpole has a distinct touch of the Georgie Pillsons – and they were also, on the whole, far more stupid. While he was writing letters in perfect French to Madame du Deffand, they were making bets for 1,000 guineas on whether a man could ride 2,900 miles in 29 days. He could: to spare his horses the daytime heat, the jockey John Woodcock rode his 100-mile trip every night, including a circuit of a lantern-lit Racecourse

Side. Or they were gambling on whether they could produce a four-wheeled carriage that would take a man nineteen miles in less than an hour. This wager – or dare – was carried out by the Earl of March, later Duke of Queensberry, who in 1750 made his journey, starting and ending at Six Mile Bottom, and won 1,000 guineas.

March was quite a fellow, in his way. In 1757, he rode a match on the Across the Flat course, which runs parallel to the Rowley Mile, and won 1,000 guineas again. In 1750 he had sent out a horse to win another match, after which the other side claimed that March's jockey had emptied his saddle bags beforehand and passed the weight to an accomplice. The earl challenged his accuser to a duel then backed off, grovelling, when he arrived to find a coffin inscribed with the date of his own death: that very day. Not long afterwards he became a member of the Jockey Club.

As Duke of Queensberry he was also a member of the Hell-Fire Club, and known as the wickedest man in England. Yet nothing he did seems to have been very terrible, apart from the fact that he was still insatiably lecherous in extreme old age, and drank Tokay in the rather touching hope that it would help him act out his desires. Maybe it did, as a satirical ballad written near the end of his life still flatters him with puns on the letter 'Q' (la queue). At sixty-three, in the year that the French Revolution broke out, he had his best ever season in Newmarket. In yet another one of the 'handicap' matches that took place across the Heath, Queensberry's horse Mulberry was given 35 pounds by one of the first Derby winners, Sir Peter Teazle,[10] and confirmed his odds-on starting price. After this, the duke retired to his house in Piccadilly where there was a better selection of pretty women – one hardly hears mention of a single female in Newmarket at this time – and he could sit, dressed in yellow breeches and a blue coat, a little brown hat on his head, leering to his heart's content.

He owned what Walpole calls a 'palace' at Richmond – at which poor, doomed Madame du Barry stayed in 1791 – and

---

[10] The horse was thus named because his owner, the 12th Earl of Derby, had married an actress after seeing her play Lady Teazle in Sheridan's *School for Scandal*.

perhaps the nicest house in Newmarket. It was certainly one of the best positioned: coming in to the High Street from the Cambridge Road, Queensberry House stands on the right, half-hidden by a wall and trees, at the top of the little hill that slopes down into the town. The original house was demolished – sadly, there is hardly any architecture left from this period – and rebuilt in red brick by Lord Wolverton in 1898. It is now occupied by the British Bloodstock Agency and has a very lovely garden, with a leafy, semi-secret pathway leading directly to the Tattersalls sales ring. Across the High Street is Queensberry Lodge, a now empty yard, which would be used in the late nineteenth century by the famous trainer, Mathew Dawson, when he had no more room at Heath House.

Queensberry had more freedom than he knew what to do with, like most of his kind, but the great joke is that although his wholly hedonistic life should by rights have brought him to a bad end, in fact everything turned out right for him. When he died, in 1810, at the then immense age of eighty-five, he was worth nearly a million pounds, having won nearly a quarter of a million in his lifetime and, according to Sir George Trevelyan, 'still wallowing in sin ... Amidst a great deal in the received account of his last days which may charitably be set down as fabulous, this much is clear, that he met death with well-bred indifference'. The bore about dying, of course, was that one would never know the winner of next year's Two Thousand Guineas: the race had been inaugurated in 1809.

Queensberry, though, was just rich and irresponsible and colourful. The problem, as set out by Walpole and Trevelyan and many others, came when pleasure took over the lives of those who had other things that they should be doing. The 3rd Duke of Grafton, for example, gave the fullness of his attention to racing, and was Prime Minister on the side.

Grafton owned a stable on Old Station Road, and gave his name to Grafton House on Fitzroy Street, which he acquired in 1789. He was a descendant of Charles II – the first duke had been the king's son with Lady Castlemaine – and established his powerful stud at Euston Hall, where Charles had begun his liaison with Louise de Querouaille. The omens were not good that this would be a prime minister like his predecessor, Pitt the Elder, and indeed Grafton was astonishingly cavalier about his position. He attended Newmarket and Ascot with his mistress, Nancy Parsons, whom he had apparently picked up in the street. He once sent a message to his cabinet that he would be late for a meeting as he was running a horse in a match at Newmarket; he then sent another message saying don't wait up, he would be back the following evening. 'What can one say of the Duke of Grafton, but that his whole conduct is childish, insolent, inconstant, and absurd – nay, ruinous?' wrote Walpole in a letter of 1768, regarding the way in which the government had lost a minister, Townshend, to the opposition because he could no longer stand his capricious treatment at Grafton's hands. 'Because we are not in confusion enough, he makes everything as bad as possible, neglecting on one hand, and taking no precautions on the other. I neither see how it is possible for him to remain minister, nor whom to put in his place . . . (he is) like an apprentice, thinking the world should be postponed to a whore and a horserace . . .'

Trevelyan, writing in 1899, goes even further. 'The frivolity of the last century was not confined to the youthful, the foolish, or even to the idle. There never will be a generation which cannot supply a parallel to the lads who, in order that they might the better hear the nonsense which they were talking across a tavern-table, had Pall Mall laid down with straw at the cost of fifty shillings a head for the party' (this did indeed happen). Here, though, those who should have known better were behaving even worse: '. . . men of age and standing, of strong mental powers and refined cultivation lived openly, shamelessly, and habitually, in the face of all England, as no one who had any care for his reputation would now live during a single fortnight of the year at Monaco . . .' (!)

The impression is given, in fact, that for periods at a time the country is being governed as if it were one vast Newmarket: casually, by an oligarchy intent on its own pleasure. As Walpole put it in 1782, 'It is very entertaining that two or three great families should persuade themselves that they have an hereditary and exclusive right of giving us a head without a tongue . . .' These great families – the

Graftons, the Bedfords, the Portlands, the Rockinghams – ruled England just as they ruled the turf. In both, their fortunes fluctuated – during the early reign of George III, governments came and went in the style of the French Fourth Republic – but this in no way affected their pre-eminence, nor their capacity for making up their own rules of conduct. The Duke of Grafton, for example, procured a £500-a-year pension from the Treasury for an old Newmarket friend who had squandered his fortune on racing. This was the code of the club, applied to a country.

And this was the era of clubs: as Trevelyan says, 'By the time George III was on the throne, persons of rank and position were tired of being challenged to stake their money by frequenters of public coffee houses, whose capacity to pay was doubtful.' Clubs were instituted 'with the object of providing the world of fashion with a central office for making wagers'. For this was, too, the era in which gambling rose from a cult to become a religion. 'Society was one vast casino.' Rather as with drugs nowadays, gambling seemed like something hardly worth even trying to resist: if it was there, people would do it. It was an addiction and a contagion, not just among men of rank but among servants buying lottery tickets, farmers betting at rural race meetings and respectable *bourgeoises* losing up to twenty pounds a night at faro and whist. For the aristocracy, though, who were not doing it in order to try and make money, gambling had a more obscure significance.

Obviously it went on at Newmarket, and obviously the fascination of racing for the English upper classes went a long way towards fuelling the mania. Yet racing and gambling are not, as many believe, indivisible. They never have been, and they still are not. Of course far more often than not they go together; but the passionate impulse towards watching horse races is not the passionate impulse that leads one to put money on them. One is pure, the other makes it impure. The sporting gentlemen who frolicked across the Heath were throwing money around like nobody's business, of course they were; but that was not the fundamental reason for being there. They were there for the thing itself, the heart of which beats strong and separate.

The real gambling was in London, a surreal correlative to what was going on at Newmarket. Here, neither racing nor cards were enough. The betting book at Brooks's Club records a succession of gentlemanly equivalents to the two cockroaches racing across the floor of a prison cell: '50 guineas that Mlle. Heinel does not dance at the opera house next winter ... 5 guineas down, to receive 100 if the Duke of Queensberry dies before half an hour after five in the afternoon of the 27th June, 1773 ... Lord Ossory betts Mr Charles Fox 100 guineas to 10 that Dr North is not Bishop of Durham this day two months, provided the present Bishop dies within that time.' A man who had a seizure on the club threshold was the subject of much speculation as to his prospects of survival. When it was proposed that he should be bled, those who had gambled on his death protested that the use of a lance would affect the bet.

Gambling was a compulsion without which life lost its savour and even its point. When Lord Chesterfield was sent to Bath as a convalescent, he wrote that 'were it not for the comfort of returning health, I believe I should hang myself; I am so weary of sauntering about without knowing what to do, or of playing at low play, which I hate, for the sake of avoiding high, which I love.'

But it was Charles James Fox who was to become the symbol of this compulsion: his recklessness fascinated because it seemed, in his case, so especially perverse. This was no Duke of Queensberry who had nothing to do but indulge himself; no Lord 'Cripplegate' Barrymore, who lost £300,000 in four years and killed himself at twenty-four when loading a musket; no Duke of Grafton who lacked the brains to see the interest in being prime minister. This was a man of powerful intellect and purist Whig sensibility who, nonetheless, gambled like a fiend, like the most idiotic of inbreeds. His losses were legendary, unbelievable, the stuff of street talk. When, in 1773, his father Lord Holland decided to clear his debts for him, £140,000 was found to be owing. And barely was the slate rubbed clean before he was off again: moving, as a contemporary observer put it, 'from the House of Commons to the faro table, from the faro table to Newmarket, and from Newmarket to the House of Commons'. He once lost £11,000 at faro in twenty-two hours of continuous play. By the end he had sold or mortgaged every scrap of his inheritance and half-ruined all his friends, who had given annuities as securities for him 'to the Jews'. Walpole once enumerated the things in the world most worth finding: the longitude, the philosopher's stone, the certificate of the Duchess of Kingston's first marriage, the missing books of Livy 'and all that Charles Fox had lost'.

Walpole was intrigued by Fox, who was all that he admired and deplored; indeed almost like an alter ego, a man who lived out what Walpole fearfully contemplated. Fox's charm, his insane energy, his careless brilliance flicker into life through Walpole's correspondence. In 1772, for example, after having seen him speak against Edmund Burke in Parliament, he writes that 'Fox was dissipated, dissolute, idle beyond measure. He was that very morning returned from Newmarket, where he had lost some thousand pounds the preceding day. He had stopped at Hockerel, where he had found company; had sat up drinking all night; and had not been in bed when he came to move his Bill, which he had not even drawn up. This was genius – was almost inspiration.' But another picture shows the man of quiet refinement who lived within Fox's manic exterior. A friend visited him one night when he had squandered so much at faro that suicide actually seemed a possibility. He was sitting at home, calmly reading Herodotus: 'What would you have me do?' he said. 'I have lost my last shilling.'

Fox had resigned from his various clubs when, in 1770, he accepted office under Lord North. He had also sold his horses. But soon he was back at Brooks's and Almack's, dressed in his high hat covered in flowers and ribbons, and back at Newmarket. He had his best win of £16,000, laying a favourite who was beaten a neck. It was said that 'the King's messenger' (hiding his badge of office, in shame) 'was obliged to appear on the course to seek one of the Ministers of England among the sportsmen on the Heath to deliver despatches upon which the fate of the country might have depended.'

The 1780s find Fox getting together with Lord Foley, owning a stable and a string of up to thirty horses trained by an Irishman, Richard Prince, on the approximate site of what is now Exeter House yard. At first things went well, which was probably the worst thing that could have happened. Decline inevitably followed and, like almost every owner in the history of racing, the vast proportion of whom would be far less intelligent than Fox, he was reduced to making recherché excuses. His horses were as good as anybody's, he said, but 'they would never gallop fast enough to tire themselves'.

Things were kept afloat by a win in a 1787 match race against a horse of the Duke of Queensberry's, and in 1788 in the Town Plate. On balance, however, the racing partners were not lucky for each other. Foley had entered racing with an estate of £18,000 a year and around £100,000 in ready money. By the year of his death in 1793, it was all either mortgaged or spent.

But it was London that ruined Fox, who was not *au fond* a racing man, although he brought his urgent, almost eroticised passion for gambling to Newmarket. 'When his horse ran,' wrote a contemporary observer, 'he was all eagerness and anxiety. He placed himself where the animal was to make a push, or where the race was to be most strongly contested. From this spot he eyed the horses advancing with the most immovable look; he breathed quicker as they accelerated their pace; and, when they came opposite to him, he rode in with them at full speed, whipping, spurring, and blowing, as if he would have infused his whole soul into his favourite racer. But, when the race was over, whether he won or lost seemed to be a matter of perfect indifference to him . . .'

There is something about this description that implies, not just inner emotion, but an element of display: Fox's grandiose addiction had, as it were, a PR dimension to it. As Stella Tillyard puts it in her book *Aristocrats*, one of whose subjects is Fox's mother, Lady Caroline Lennox, men like this gambled 'to indicate a way of life that had political as well as social parameters'. In every way, it showed that one was *in*. One had enough money, enough position, to be able to disdain both. And so there was a vast and heady pressure that prevented these men from breathing normal air and seeing themselves clearly. Certainly they didn't want to do so. To have stopped what they were doing would have excluded them from the charmed circle. They would have become like the man who left Brooks's with £12,000 in winnings, not realising, or not wanting to realise, that he was meant to stay and lose it; beside his name in the club book was written: 'That he may never return is the ardent wish of the members.' Or they would have been like Pitt the Younger who, having played at cards, 'perceived their increasing fascination, and soon afterwards abandoned them for ever'. How much better, how much more glamorous to say, as Fox did, that winning was the only thing more enjoyable than losing!

Yet it was Pitt's career that thrived, while Fox's – allied as it was to the causes of the Regency, reform and even republicanism – stuttered and stalled. Almack's in the 1780s may have felt like England's socio-political epicentre but, as with Cliveden nearly two hundred years later, the influence of its set crumbled quite easily. Mixing pleasure with politics can give an illusion of great solidarity, but it only works up to a point. By the end of the eighteenth centry, this particular relationship between power and gambling had played itself out, and never again would a man of Fox's stature ruin himself in quite so deliberate and public a manner. By the end of the next century, however, there would be a small graveyard full of casualties: lesser men, equally helpless in the grip of gambling.

The relationship between power and Newmarket also, inevitably, changed. The ruling classes continued to gravitate towards the place – as, indeed, they still do, except that they are no longer the ruling classes – but the days of politicians like the Duke of Grafton and the Marquis of Rockingham were numbered. Slowly, ministers were becoming more accountable. So too was racing. The gentlemanly free-for-all that had existed on the Heath had been glorious, but it could not last for ever; and ironically, it was to be the Jockey Club itself that called time on it.

As with the court of Charles II, criticism was hurled at the politicians of the late eighteenth century for their eager dereliction of duty. It does seem quite extraordinary that, at a time when France was revving itself up to revolution, the English aristocracy was sitting heedlessly astride its collective horse; but again, as with King Charles, a peculiar kind of good sense may have lain behind this apparently dense behaviour. When Horace Walpole referred to the 'suspension of arms' that Newmarket could bring about in political life, this was not intended as praise, and yet his comment could be read in that way. Similarly in 1771, when he wrote that French politics 'some way or other, must end seriously . . . Methinks, it is playing deep for the power of tyranny. Charles Fox is more moderate: he only games for an hundred thousand pounds that he had not'.

In other words, the English obsession with play – although worthy of satire – could always save the country from something more threatening. Thomas Warton, in an angry poem of 1751, was therefore missing the point when he wrote:

Meantime, no more the mimic patriots rise,
To guard Britannia's honour, warm and wise;
No more in Senates dare assert her laws,
Nor pour the bold debate in freedom's cause;
Neglect the counsels of a sinking land,
And know no Rostrum, but Newmarket's stand.

He was right, but he was wrong about England. England was charmed by Charles James Fox, not because he was clever but because he did so much that was stupid. England may have disapproved of the Duke of Grafton, but still found something reassuring about a man who would rather be on the gallops than in a cabinet meeting.

This idea is given wonderful expression in the chapter on eighteenth-century painting in Andrew Graham-Dixon's *A History of British Art*. As the author says, the ruling classes commissioned shrines to themselves from Gainsborough and Reynolds, but they 'never made the mistake of taking themselves too seriously in public': their utter assurance pervades the paintings, but attention is deflected from the subjects themselves to their country house, their garden, their animals. Oh Lord, don't look at me, I'm only the Duke of Devonshire! This is the mentality that caused Newmarket to become a sacred place to the English gentleman, who was so serenely confident of his place in the world that he could take pleasure in putting his racehorse first, in allowing it to acquire all the glory that a different type of person would want for himself. After all, the horse was about the only thing better-bred than he was. And it is still the case that the upper classes instinctively defer to the thoroughbred, something in this humility only serving to emphasise their belief in their general superiority.

The sporting genre of painting was hugely popular in the eighteenth century. Again, it was used as a validation of the English self-image, which was reflected obliquely through scenes of the hunting field or the racecourse, or through 'portraits' of the thoroughbred. The fact that some of these paintings were very bad was, as Graham-Dixon says, merely another sign of confidence in those who commissioned them. Quality was hardly the point. And so painters like Francis Sartorius (1734–1804) and James Seymour (1702–52) were heavily patronised as producers of racing art, despite the fact that neither was especially talented. Yet their very inadequacy gives their work a stark and mysterious atmosphere, which has undoubtedly shaped our image of the sport at the time. Sartorius' horses, for example, many of which race across the walls of the Card Room in the Jockey Club, are highly unrealistic – here was an exponent of the famously misguided 'all four hooves up in the air at one time' theory. But there is something about the whip-thin, outstretched necks, and the complete absence of physical individuality, which conveys the effort that horses then were forced to make and the indifference with which this was often viewed.

Seymour was more varied in his style. One of his works shows two horses on Newmarket Heath: there is literally nothing else in the landscape, only emptiness, except for this pair of rangy, hooded animals with their tails cropped to a brush[11] and their eyes masked. Yet this deserted scene conveys a feel of the Heath, and of the freedom with which the thoroughbred then ran through it. A painting of Flying Childers is better, despite the fact that he seems to be

---

[11] This cruel practice, which involved amputation of the tail bone, ended in the 1820s though it was not outlawed until 1948.

balancing like a ballerina on his points. But the wildness in the horse's eye and the dark sky behind have a look of Gericault; and the sparse composition has a strange, unconscious ability to poise the horse halfway between myth and reality, which is exactly where we put him ourselves.

Of course George Stubbs (1724–1806) was to do this a thousand times more successfully. His horses are so placed in their landscape that they become generic, symbols for all time; in the paddocks around Newmarket, living Stubbses continually compose themselves. It is impossible to look at his paintings and not to think of them, for ever afterwards, every time one sees a horse in a field. With Stubbs, one feels in his brushwork the twitch of the ears, the smooth flick of the tail, the loose and stalking tread. A frieze such as *Mares and Foals in a Landscape* transcends the 'sporting' genre with the ease of genius; a stallion portrait like *Whistlejacket*, which effortlessly dominates one of the great rooms of the National Gallery, has a fair claim to being the finest of all English paintings. To the horse's chestnut coat Stubbs gives a rich, seeming infinity of shade; but what is most striking is the contrast between Whistlejacket's bold, rearing pose and the nervous uncertainty in his eye.

So lifelike is the work, it is said that the real stallion tried to attack his painted image when confronted with it. Stubbs was the first within his genre to bring realism to the depiction of horses (and indeed of other animals). It is well known that he acquired his knowledge the hard way, dissecting horses in a shed in Lincolnshire and, in the Renaissance tradition, making a minute study of their anatomy. The fifteen tables that he then drew – showing bones, musculature, veins, nerves – are peculiarly moving, perhaps because one knows so well what he can do with his subject when the *orbicularis occuli* is shining with life and the *vena cephalica* pumping blood. His profound acquaintance with the dead horse seems to have given him a very particular respect for it: as Andrew Graham-Dixon writes, 'A horse . . . drawn by Stubbs is more poignantly alive than one drawn by anyone else.'

It was the great luck of eighteenth-century racehorse owners to have such a man to immortalise their animals for them, although they didn't necessarily appreciate this. Stubbs was commissioned by Sir Henry Vane-Tempest to paint his horse, Hambletonian, who in 1799 had contested one of the most famous matches of the century: four miles two furlongs over the Beacon Course, 3,000 guineas a side, against Diamond. Hambletonian had won over twenty races, including one of the early St Legers (this race, the first inaugurated of the classics, had been run since 1776), and was giving three pounds to Diamond who carried eight stone. He, too, was a highly regarded horse, but Hambletonian started at odds of 5/1 on.

An extraordinary, some said unprecedented, crowd arrived at Newmarket to watch this race, and it was a fight to get a bed for the night. Why, it is impossible to know; obviously the reputations of both horses went a very long way before them. And perhaps they were too well matched, too willing and too brave. Hambletonian led until the final half mile, when Diamond began to close him down; it was head to head all the way to the post, when a final push gave Hambletonian victory by half a neck; but he finished the race half dead, streaming blood from the whips and spurs. This was the kind of spectacle – tough, robust, undeniably enthralling – that racegoers wanted to see. It was the kind of triumph that owners like Vane-Tempest, who had also won a small fortune, wanted to gain. Yet George Stubbs painted Hambletonian not as a conqueror but as a magnificently bewildered victim: looming unsteadily into the foreground of the picture,[12] supported by the impassive yet sympathetic grooms, the pitiful brush of his tail standing aloft from his exertions. Vane-Tempest rejected the work. Stubbs had to go to court to get his £30 fee.

The first Earl Grosvenor, a more enlightened man, owned eleven Stubbses. It was in the paddock of his Eaton stud that the artist painted some of his mares and foals. In 1761 Horace Walpole wrote of Grosvenor that 'he is made a Lord Viscount, or Baron – I do not know which, and nor does he, for yesterday when he should have kissed hands he was gone to Newmarket to see the trial of a racehorse.' This was not

---

[12] The stance, which shows two legs on the same side off the ground at the same time, is, in fact, anatomically impossible, but artistically impeccable.

Gimcrack, who was foaled in 1760, but the marvellous little horse was to be Lord Grosvenor's best, winning 26 from 36 starts and commemorated in one of the season's most prestigious two-year-old races, the Gimcrack Stakes at York. He was painted several times by Stubbs. One of these is a simple depiction of the horse with his groom, a joyful work which puts more sun into a grey coat than one would have believed possible. But the composition which seems to have obsessed the artist, and of which he made several versions, placed Gimcrack alone in the foreground of the painting while, behind him on the Heath, one of his victories – probably from July 1765 – is distantly rendered. No crowds watch. The image of the race is oddly melancholy. It is as if the whole point of Newmarket, the reason why we are all there, has been shown to be an irrelevance, merely illusory in its enslaving glamour.

This feeling will strike sometimes, unawares – when, for example, one sees the fear in the eyes of yearlings waiting to be led into the sales ring, or the dedicated faces of stable hands, who have plaited the mane of their useless selling plater as if it were a Group winner, or the trickle of blood running down the flank of a horse who has given its all to a finish, and lost. Then the fierce pleasure that one takes in the sport of racing will ebb away, leaving behind something more fragile and unsure. It is a feeling that can be assimiliated, and usually is, but it should not be ignored or forgotten. And Stubbs – of whom Andrew Graham-Dixon rightly says that 'his realism was . . . a form of moral vision' – is its careful and compassionate guardian.

4 Jockey Club rules

'2 to 1 on Escape' – 1791–1828

T HE EVENTS WHICH LED TO THE Jockey Club assuming absolute authority within racing were strange in the extreme. They took place in 1791, and at their centre was the Prince of Wales, the future King George IV.

Prinny was a racing man, as indeed he was a man for most things in the 1780s. Although kept short of money by his father George III – who believed in abstemious living, and was heartily despised for it – he managed to do fairly well for himself in his establishment at Carlton House. One of the grooms who worked there said that from noon to night the Prince had nothing on his mind but horses, which rather begs the question of when he thought about Mrs Fitzherbert and about eating. But racing does seem to have been a passion with him.

One wonders why. The sport in those days was for rumbustious outdoor types, not dandified lovers of chinoiserie, and although George was active in his youth – he rode the 108 miles from London to Brighton in ten hours, and was painted by Stubbs on horseback – he quickly succumbed to indolence. Indeed it was said of him that he might have made a good rider if he had put up ten stone lighter. Nevertheless he was a follower of fashion, and racing was the thing to do at this time; and something about the owning and breeding of thoroughbreds may have satisfied the aesthete collector within him. He would pay anything for a horse that took his fancy, not out of a spirit of competitiveness but for the simple, childish pleasure of possessing it. As much as anything, though, he seems to have liked the conviviality of a day at the races. He was a gregarious soul, the type who enjoyed things far more when he was surrounded by people (unlike many lovers of racing, who take pleasure in the sense of solitude within the throng), and many of his friends went in for the sport – Charles James Fox, of course, whom the Prince loved and who supported the Regency cause against George III; the 5th Duke of Bedford, who won three Derbys and three Oaks in just thirty-seven years of life, in between sleeping with the Duke of Grafton's former mistress, Nancy Parsons; Sir John Lade, who was to be banged up in the King's Bench prison for debt; Lord Clermont; Lord 'Cripple-gate' Barrymore and his two equally dreadful brothers ('Hellgate' and 'Newgate'). The Prince liked nothing better than nipping down to Brighton or Lewes for days out with this diverting set of gentlemen. A contemporary observer described these as 'the gayest scenes of the year in England ... the "legs"[1] and bettors, who had arrived in shoals, used all to assemble at the Steyne at an early hour to commence their operations on the first day, and the buzz was tremendous, till Lord Foley' (Fox's partner in crime) 'and Mellish, the two great confederates of that day, would approach the ring, and then a sudden silence ensued to await the opening of their books. They would come on perhaps smiling, but mysterious-ly, without making any demonstration ... "Come, Mr Mel-lish, will you light the candle and set us a-going?" '

And he always did – because Harry Mellish, a man of great charm, was possibly dafter than the rest of them put together. Although a real racing man, who at one time had 38 horses in training and won the St Legers of 1804 and 1805, he was an even more helpless gambler than Fox. It was said that he once staked £40,000 on a single throw of the dice – and lost.

The Prince of Wales seems first to have attended Newmar-ket in 1784 when, at the second Spring meeting, his horse Hermit lost a match over the Beacon Course then, later that day, won a re-run of the same race (running upwards of eight

---

[1] Legs were the original bookmakers, who would lay just one horse in the race rather than drawing up a 'book'.

miles in one day was, of course, quite usual at this time). This match win was the first of George's many victories as an owner.

It was his uncle, the Duke of Cumberland, who had introduced him to the sport, quite possibly for the express purpose of annoying George III. The duke was a heavy gambler, as indeed who wasn't, and also a philanderer of repute whose best-known exploit involved the wife of Stubbs' great patron, the owner of Gimcrack. 'To be sure,' wrote a gleeful Horace Walpole in 1769, 'the younger Highness has had the mishap of being surprised, at least *once*, with my Lady Grosvenor, who is actually discarded by her Lord.' The earl then sued the duke for £13,000 for 'criminal conspiracy' – ! – the payment of which nearly ruined him. Walpole remarked: 'We have lived these two months upon the poor Duke of Cumberland, whom the newspapers, in so many letters, call *the Royal Idiot*' (quite an accolade, in that family).

The title had been revived for the duke after the death of a more substantial – in every sense – figure, otherwise known as the Butcher of Culloden. This Duke of Cumberland, the son of George II, had been a professional soldier who, in 1745, had suppressed the Jacobites with assiduity and whose fall from grace came twelve years later during the Seven Years war. After the defeat by the French at Hastenbeck, Cumberland had made terms with the slippery Duc de Richelieu and signed a treaty (Closter Seven) which left both men looking very shady. Back to England came the duke, booed on all sides, and gave up his army command. After this he became hugely gross, which also seems to have been a family trait. Wicked Walpole remarked that 'playing at hazard with a great heap of gold in front of him he looked like the prodigal son of the fatted calf'.

More kindly, he wrote of him at the funeral of George II: 'The real serious part was the figure of the Duke of Cumberland, heightened by a thousand melancholy circumstances ... His leg extremely bad, yet forced to stand upon it near two hours, his face bloated and distorted with his late paralytic stroke, which has affected, too, one of his eyes, and placed over the mouth of a vault, into which, in all probability, he must himself so soon descend – think how unpleasant a situation! He bore it all with a firm and unaffected countenance.' In fact this was a bit premature, for although he continued to inflate and to disintegrate, the duke lasted until 1765.

But disgrace had quenched him and racing, in which he had formerly taken an interest, was now something in which he took refuge. Although this would hardly have been his intention, he became one of the most influential breeders in the history of the sport. He was made Ranger of Windsor Great Park (Virginia Water nearby was named in honour of his position as governor of the state of Virginia), which brought him into close contact with Ascot racecourse. He was also the first member of the Royal Family to join the Jockey Club, which was a considerable boost to the club in its early years. In 1753 Walpole wrote of Newmarket, as usual in a spirit of irritable irony, that 'the Duke of Cumberland is at present making a campaign (there) with half the nobility and half the money in England attending him – they really say that not less than £100,000 has been carried thither for the hazard of this single week. The palace has been furnished for him.' After Hastenbeck, he had a good deal of freedom to use it.

Yet he is remembered, at least in the racing world, as the breeder of the greatest thoroughbred of the eighteenth century. The story of how this came about – which, as it should be, is satisfyingly full of 'what-ifs?' – began when the duke swopped foals with a Yorkshire breeder, who received an Arabian as his part of the deal. In exchange, Cumberland got Marske, a grandson of the brother of Flying Childers. Marske's sire, Squirt, had been so crippled with laminitis that he was on the point of being shot when a stud groom pleaded for his life. A moral is to be found here, if ever there was one. Had Squirt been callously despatched, there would have been no Marske, and without Marske there would have been no Eclipse: 'the fleetest horse that ever ran in England since the time of Childers'.

Marske himself was nothing special on the racecourse, although he did win the Jockey Club Plate at Newmarket, but the Duke of Cumberland decided to give him his chance as a stallion and he stood at the Royal Lodge stud at Windsor. He was mated to a mare named Spiletta who – third time lucky – was finally got in foal by him. The next year there was an eclipse; four years later, there was to be a similar eclipse of every racehorse in the country by the one who bore that name.

There is an oddly evocative story of the trial run by Eclipse before his first race, the four-mile Noblemen and Gentlemen's Plate at Epsom in 1769. The touts, as so often getting things slightly wrong, arrived too late, but found an old woman who had seen a 'whitelegged horse' (Eclipse was chestnut with one stocking) 'running away at a monstrous rate', and she was sure that 'the other horse would never catch him if he ran to the world's end'. This was the impression that Eclipse made: not of racing, but of running in a different world. The phrase 'Eclipse first ... the rest nowhere' has become legendary, and nothing could be more beautifully succinct; in fact it was conceived not as an aphorism, but as a prediction. Colonel Dennis O'Kelly, part-owner of the horse, had gambled on the result of the second heat of the Epsom race. For three miles, Eclipse galloped apparently tamely alongside his four rivals, then his jockey could hold him no longer. The horse took off, winning by the 240 yards plus which constituted 'a distance'. The rest, indeed, were nowhere.

And this was to be the result, over and over again. Eventually Eclipse had to be taken out of training, because it was getting silly: nothing could live with him. He finished his career with eleven wins and seven walkovers. It was at Newmarket that he came closest to being given a proper race: over the Beacon Course, by a horse named Bucephalus, whose career was ended by the brave and futile effort of trying to keep up with him. In the end he just pulled away, in his casually devastating style. Like Flying Childers, he had taken the thoroughbred forward with one of those mysterious, incalculable leaps that have shaped the sport. The Group One Eclipse Stakes has commemorated him at Sandown since 1886, and his exquisite little statue stands in the Members' enclosure on the Rowley Mile course, perfectly at home.

Eclipse had a lot of fire in him, and there is a legend – possibly true – that he was taken out poaching at night on

Epsom Downs to dampen him down. He was a big horse for the time – fifteen hands three inches – and, as is not uncommon among prodigious racing animals, he had a huge heart weighing around fourteen pounds. A painting by John Nost Sartorius (son of Francis) shows him tall and elegant, with a long lean head and – perhaps to emphasise his size – what looks like a toy soldier sitting on his back. George Stubbs depicts a similar conformation, but with the reality painted in. His Eclipse has a strong sloping shoulder, a low curving neck and an intent eye: he looks very much a thoroughbred, not a trace of Arab to be seen any more. But the true Eclipse is to be seen in the National Horseracing Museum in Newmarket, where his skeleton is displayed: an object of extreme fascination. One can stare for long minutes at that spare, complex, miraculous mechanism – dissected by an inquisitive Frenchman, in search of the secret of equine greatness – and try to flesh it out with the myth of the horse who, more than 200 years ago, left all the rest for dead.

Eventually Colonel Dennis O'Kelly acquired the whole of Eclipse. After the Duke of Cumberland's death, the horse was bought for 75 guineas by a shrewd Smithfield meat salesman named William Wildman, who – half-realising what he had – then bought Marske for twenty guineas. These were among the great bargains of racing history. Marske, whose value was just waiting to rocket, was subsequently sold to Lord Abingdon for 1,000 guineas, and stood at stud for the then vast fee of 100 guineas (although, of course, he never threw another star). Meanwhile, O'Kelly bought the first half of Eclipse for 650 guineas and the second for 1,100 guineas. He estimated before his death in 1788 (a year earlier than his horse) that he had earned £25,000 in stud fees; for, unlike Flying Childers, Eclipse was also a tremendous sire. He threw the winners of 862 races, including three of the early Derbys.

This was wonderfully successful dealing on the part of these clever, non-aristocratic men, and a sign of things to come. Of course O'Kelly was not allowed to join the Jockey Club, despite owning a horse for which most of the members would have renounced their peerages. This meant that Eclipse was ineligible for races like the Jockey Club Plate, although he himself did make it into the club: after death, one of his hooves was mounted in gold, and in it were placed the names of horses nominated to take part in matches. O'Kelly himself was far too rakish to get through the doors of the Coffee Rooms. Had he been an Irish peer, like the Lords Barrymore, and not an Irish adventurer who started life as a litter-bearer, this would not have mattered – as it was, colonel or not, he had no chance.

But he surely knew that he could run rings around most of those superior gentlemen and that, unlike them, he could handle his money. A story is recorded of how he accepted a bet from a posh proposer who 'inquired where lay his *estates*, to answer for the amount if he lost? "My estates!" cried O'Kelly, "oh, if that's what you *mane*, I've a map of them here," and opening his pocket book, he exhibited banknotes to ten times the sum in question, and ultimately added the inquirer's contribution to them'.

It was a bit rough on the Duke of Cumberland, dying of fatness before Eclipse achieved his supernal greatness, but he did see Herod, whom he also bred, and of whom the *Turf Register* wrote that he was 'allowed to be one of the best horses this kingdom ever produced'. In 1764 Herod took part in a match over the Beacon Course, against the Duke of Grafton's Antinous, upon which around £100,000 was allegedly gambled. He won by a short neck, and the Duke of Cumberland waddled off the racing stage in style. Afterwards Herod was sold to the breeder Sir John Moore. He stood as a stallion for a fee of ten guineas, plus five shillings to the groom – another wild misjudgement, as the horse was to throw the winners of 1,042 races.

The Herod and the Eclipse lines were the Duke of Cumberland's legacy to racing. And it was magnificent – because when the 'speedy and jady' Eclipse offspring were mated with the 'hard and stout' Herods,[2] as they were to be over and over again, the result was the classic thoroughbred: that fine equilibrium of pace and strength, which shows itself to perfection over distances between eight and fourteen furlongs; which was to develop over the next century in

---

[2] In fact Herod was a 'bleeder' – he burst blood vessels in racing – but few of his progeny inherited this.

concert with the development of the classic races; which represents the apotheosis of the breed.

Sir John Moore was later to refuse an offer of 2,000 guineas for Herod from the King of Poland. This was not for love of the horse who, at the end of his wonderfully productive life, was left to die in dirt and neglect. And it is a false comfort to dismiss cruelty as belonging to the age, because the impulse towards it does not die: how can it? But if one believes at all that civilisation follows legislation, then from the late eighteenth century onwards life would start to improve – slowly, and with a good deal of barbaric backsliding – for the average racehorse.

This was the era of Sir Charles Bunbury. Commonly called the 'first Dictator of the Turf', in 1768 he became Steward of the Jockey Club – then a sole office, although there are now seven of them – at the age of twenty-eight. He reformed and modernised the sport, turning it into something that we can recognise, taking it forward in a leap comparable with that made by Eclipse: unimaginable beforehand, yet afterwards showing itself to have been inevitable. Charles Bunbury was also the man who, in 1791, in the name of the Jockey Club, took on the Prince of Wales.

Prinny had already had problems with racing – or with money – in 1786. He was so strapped for cash, having tried and failed to live on £62,000 a year – half of which was being spent on his stable – that he closed off most of Carlton House and got rid of almost all his horses. An announcement appeared, previewing the sale: 'To be sold at AUCTION by Messrs Tattersall, near Hyde Park Corner Turnpike on Monday 24th and Tuesday 25th (July) instant at Twelve o'clock . . .' And afterwards: '. . . the famous horse, Rockingham, 1781, by Highflyer-Purity by Matchem, that cost the Prince of Wales 2,000 guineas, was bought yesterday at Tattersalls for 800 guineas by an eminent breeder.' Two colts who, a few weeks previously, had run in the Derby, were sold for 170 guineas and 75 guineas; two fillies were sold who, the following year, were to finish first and second in the Oaks. If this was economising, it was hardly economics. As the St James' Chronicle wrote, 'The Stud of HRH the Prince of Wales was not sold but given away . . .' Frankly, it was all a bit of a joke.

If it was also a gesture designed to show that George had been forced to throw away a great deal for the want of far less, then eventually it worked: Parliament voted him more money. He got £160,000 with which to clear his debts and an extra £10,000 a year from his father (who, at this time, was too mad to notice). Off went George, flinging open the doors at Carlton House and refilling his stable – which was even more of a joke, of course, except that between 1788 and 1792 he won 185 races, including the Derby, and over £30,000 in prize money. He was, in fact, one of the most successful owners in the history of the sport. Had he been more astute, or had better advisers, he could have funded a very nice life for himself with his racing. But cause and effect finances were not his style. Like the Maktoum family nowadays, he bought horses indiscriminately; unlike them, he lacked the money to do so. Indeed he was a free spender in every area of his life ('Newmarket and other extravagances more referable to profusion than essential to dignity'). Unable to resist writing cheques – though always reluctant to part with any cash, which presumably felt more like real money – four years after being bailed out by Parliament he was back in debt, to the discordant tune of more than £400,000.

But in the first flush of excited wealth he had doubled the size of his stable, acquiring around forty horses, including some that he had recently sold. One of these – the property of a Mr Franco – was a bay brother to Miss Kitty, who had run third for the Prince in the 1785 Oaks. This colt, whom George had bred and for whom he now paid £1,500, was called Escape. As a yearling, he had had an extremely close shave after catching a fetlock in his loose box, which was how he got the name. After that things went very well for him. He won the 1788 Town Plate and, in 1789, beat one of George's own horses in a match at Newmarket. Possibly this is what gave the Prince the urge to have the horse back. Later that year he won at Newmarket for George himself; but it would have been better, all the same, if he had left Escape in the hands of Mr Franco.

The subsequent story of the horse is one of the most bizarre in the history of racing. There are various theories as to the truth behind it, and it is extremely frustrating to think that this truth can never be known. One would give a great deal to find out what really happened.

These are the simple facts, as recorded in the *Racing Calendar* of 1791. On 20 October, at Newmarket, Escape ran in a sixty guinea race, two miles across the Ditch In Course. He started 1–2 favourite but finished fourth of four, behind Mr Dawson's Coriander, Lord Grosvenor's Skylark and Lord Clermont's Pipator, all of whom were regarded as considerably inferior. The following day he was out again. This time the race was over the four miles of the Beacon Course. Escape won at a price of 5–1, with Skylark behind him in third.

Now this, of course, looked bad. It is the most familiar scenario in racing: everyone knows, and presumably has always known, that it happens; everyone almost enjoys the fact that it happens; but still the front is maintained that it should *not* happen. The Newmarket crowd of 1791 was unhappy, just as it would be today, but this too is normal. They would have got over it. So why did Warwick Lake, the Prince's racing manager – who should have been on his side and tried to smooth things over – go marching up to George, saying: 'I give your Royal Highness joy, but I am sorry the horse has won. I would sooner have given a hundred guineas'? Why did he anticipate so instantly the storm that did, in fact, break? Charles James Fox was furious with Lake on this account: '. . . people will suspect,' he wrote in a letter at the time, and he was right. An irresistible sense is created that certain players in this drama actually *wanted* trouble.

For there is little doubt that those two races, dubious though they looked, would satisfy the stewards today (only of course their circumstances would never now occur). That does not mean that skulduggery hadn't gone on. It means that it could be explained away – which is what these cases come down to. Escape was known to be in-and-out in his running, and known to prefer the four miles of the Beacon Course. On 3 and 5 October he had won two races over it, beating the same horse – Grey Diomed – into second place both times. However, in June, when he had been tried in the two-mile Oatlands Stakes at Ascot – a new and very valuable handicap – he could only finish fourth.

In the light of this, the real question was why he had even been run in the 20 October race? To set up the coup? But surely there was no need to be quite so bloody obvious about it? It is, in fact, the dim-witted blatancy of what happened which makes one think that it cannot have been intentional. Also, why was Escape 5/1 in the first place? Surely no one who knew his record over four miles could have thought that a sensible price? But in racing memories can be quite alarmingly short; reputations can rise and fall with the sun; hence the sense of affront when a horse who runs badly one day runs well the next. Escape had, in effect, made fools of them all.

Yet his jockey, Samuel Chifney, had predicted exactly what would happen. According to him, Escape was not fit on the 20th; the horse was 'stuffy', he said, in need of a blowout; and he was right. But the fact of this rightness was precisely what was at issue. Had he used it for gain? Yes, in the sense that he had openly backed Escape for twenty guineas on the 21st, and not on the 20th (it was not then illegal for jockeys to gamble). This, again, could be explained away by his knowledge of the horse. But was 'knowledge', in this case, more than that? Did Chifney merely guess that Escape would not win on 20 October, or did he 'know' it? In other words, was he stopping the horse? This was the allegation, indeed assertion, being made by many people after the two Newmarket races. It was certainly the implication of Warwick Lake's remark to the Prince – which also, more seriously, carried the hint that George himself might be suspected of involvement. Even in an age which treated the Prince of Wales with the kind of contempt that the current incumbent was to suffer, exactly 200 years later, this was pretty strong and daring stuff to be hitting him with.

As for Chifney: Warwick Lake did not like him, and neither did the Prince's trainer, Francis Neale. They would both have hated the fact that he knew their job better than they knew it themselves. He had as good as said that Escape had run when in no condition to do so and, worse, had been proved correct. In fact few people did like Chifney, although George – who recognised an unusual gift when he saw it – had made him his jockey for life in 1790, giving him the then very generous retainer of £200 a year. However most thought him an arrogant little upstart. There was a snob element to this, of course – what was he, after all, but a hired horseman from Norfolk? – yet there was also a kind of fear. Chifney had the power to win races that no other rider could; he therefore had more power than any other jockey had ever had.

He was, indeed, the first professional jockey as we understand the term. The 'grooms' who had come before him, who rode those horses that their gentleman-employers were too old or knackered to get up on themselves, were a different breed altogether: faceless creatures in their black huntsmen's caps, distinguishable only by their master's liveries. These were the original 'colours', which by an early 'decree' of the Jockey Club – applicable to hardly anyone except its own members – became obligatory in 1762. An early list of them shows that the Duke of Cumberland's were purple, the Duke of Grafton's crimson, the Marquis of Rockingham's green, Lord Grosvenor's orange and the Duke of Devonshire's straw, as they still are (solid colours, like the Godolphin blue, remain the most desirable). Prinny's, however, were regally opulent, the same as the Queen's colours today: a purple waistcoat, scarlet sleeves, gold trim and black cap.

Sam Chifney would have loved wearing this outfit. From the time he entered George's circle in 1790, he caught the habit of foppishness and, at the fairly advanced age of thirty-seven, would appear on racecourses in full fig: love-locks, ruffles on his shirt, ribbons on his boots. Anyone who thinks that a jockey like Frankie Dettori is a showman should take note that he had nothing on Chifney. Having started in racing at the lowest level, as a stable apprentice, twenty years on he had evolved a self-image that was astonishingly grandiose, considering the low esteem in which jockeys had hitherto been held. In 1795 he was to publish an autobiography entitled *Genius Genuine*, which reads in parts as if it were written by Geoffrey Boycott. It sold for the immense sum of £5 – it must be said that a large number of people were prepared to pay this – and in it Chifney says: 'In 1773 I could ride horses in a better manner in a race than any other person ever known in my time.'

It was true, though; he could. He was the first to formulate a *theory* of jockeyship. The 'grooms' simply took their mounts along as best they could, while Chifney did it with artistry. He approached a race as if it were a piece of music, playing it slow and quiet until coming at the end with a beautifully modulated crescendo, swooping past his one-paced rivals in what was to become known as the 'Chifney Rush'. This finish was to change the whole concept of race-riding, and would be adopted by jockeys from Frank Buckle, who rode in the late eighteenth century, all the way through to the American Cash Asmussen, who still rides today. It is easy to get it wrong, though – Asmussen is notorious for arriving late, like a coy bride – and it was the unsuccessful waiting ride that Chifney gave to Escape in the first of the Newmarket races which helped give rise to the suspicion that he had not been trying on the horse.

But George Stubbs, who painted the 'Chifney Rush' in a picture that shows the jockey winning the Oatlands Stakes, might well have recognised a man who understood the thoroughbred. Although an undoubted twit in many ways, Chifney was an instinctive horseman. He rode with tremendous ease and relaxation, which of course relaxed his mounts, and his confidence allowed him to do things that had not been done before in races: to use a loose rein, to shift his weight in the saddle in order to lighten the load on his horses, and to treat their mouths with great care and delicacy. When pulling up a horse, wrote Chifney, 'he should be enticed to ease himself an inch at a time, as his situation will allow'. He illustrated this with a charmingly exact image: 'This should be done as if you had a silken rein as fine as a hair, and you were afraid of breaking it.'

So in his way Chifney was, yes, a genius, However, as is so often the way with sportsmen who have fame thrust upon them, success made him arrogant and arrogance made him foolhardy. He was, in fact, a sitting target for the powers-that-be within racing; just as, in a less populist age, the pert and self-publicising Dettori would have been.

At any rate, someone – Warwick Lake? – evidently tittle-tattled about Chifney to the Prince of Wales, as after the race won by Escape on 21 October he was sent for by his employer. 'I am told,' said George, refusing to say by whom, 'that you won six or seven hundred pounds the day before yesterday, when you rode Escape and were beat on him.' Furthermore: 'I am told that you won six hundred pounds yesterday when you rode Escape and won on him.' He also asked for the truth of a story that Chifney had been arrested on Ascot Heath for a debt of £300, and that this money had been paid for him by a bookmaker named Vauxhall Clark.

The jockey denied every one of these accusations; the only thing he ever admitted was the bet of twenty guineas, which he had made with Clark. Nothing too terrible about that – all the same, his lovelocks must have drooped at this point. It was surely clear, even to poor cocky Sam Chifney, that the knives were out for him. The Prince asked if he would agree to be questioned by the Jockey Club. Before Sir Charles Bunbury, and the two subsidiary stewards now appointed to conduct the ever-increasing club business, Chifney reiterated that Escape had needed the run on the 20th and that the four miles of the second race had suited him better. It was completely plausible; it seemed as though it was going to be accepted. But Bunbury was not having it. A few weeks later, he visited Carlton House and told George that 'if Chifney were suffered to ride the Prince's horses, no gentleman would start against him'. And that was that. George stood by his jockey, continuing to pay him the £200 a year retainer. He made preparations to return to Tattersalls with another load of horses to sell. In fact his absence from the sport did not last: he was a bit of a threatener and, as before, he was soon back, flourishing his poor cheque-book, winning 107 races between 1800 and 1808. He also returned to breeding, and maintained a stud at Six Mile Bottom. But he never returned to New-market.

So what on earth was going on? Impossible to say – certainly with regard to those two races, which take their place, along with all the innocent and forgotten rest, in the *Racing Calendar*, hiding their secrets inside those almost wilfully plain statements:

> H.R.H. the P. of Wales's b.h.[3] Efcape, 6 yrs – 4. (fourth)
> 2 to 1 on Efcape . . .

and, one day later,

> H.R.H. the P. of Wales's b.h. Efcape, by Highflyer, 6 yrs
> – 1. (first)
> 4 and 5 to 1 agft Efcape . . .

Ironically, what is most likely is that Escape did run honestly on these two occasions, but that Samuel Chifney was got at anyway, for what he *might* have done, or for what he had probably done in the past. Like many jockeys of the time – and indeed, of every time since – he was suspected of pulling horses on which he had gambled. There is no hard evidence of this, which is of course in the nature of the offence, and which doesn't mean that he wasn't doing it. The decision may have been taken, therefore, that as long as Chifney *looked* guilty, he could and should be pinned down for the slippery crime of crookedness. He was arrogant; he was far too powerful for a jockey, and he was almost certainly misbehaving; the question of whether he had been up to no good in this particular case was not the issue.[4]

The desire to be rid of Chifney may have come from Warwick Lake, he whose behaviour was so bizarre on the day of Escape's win. Before the race Chifney, in rather touching innocence, had actually asked Lake to place his twenty guinea bet for him! and was told: 'No, I will have nothing to do with it, there are so many unpleasant things happen.' This was most peculiar. It is easy to cast Lake in the role of scandalmonger, spreading rumours about how Escape had been held up in the 20 October race contrary to orders. At the Jockey Club inquiry he denied making any of these funny little remarks. All the same, one member of the Club – Colonel Anthony St Leger, after whom the classic race was

---

[3] Bay horse.
[4] There was a similar case recently. The 1995 Chester Cup win of a horse named Top Cees – the Escape *de nos jours* – was branded in the press as a cheat; not so much because of that particular race, as because it was seen as the tip of a very crooked iceberg. A court case ensued and the trainer of Top Cees was, quite rightly, exonerated. If skulduggery can't be proved, then it didn't happen.

named – was said to believe that Warwick Lake was behind the whole thing.

And it is not so strange, really, that a man who enjoyed his position of closeness to the Prince of Wales should have resented this common little fellow, with his £200 retainer and his superior understanding. What *is* strange – the strangest thing of all – is that the Prince should have been implicated in this sordid business. The intention may have been to make an example of Samuel Chifney, but surely it can't have been necessary also to allow stories to develop about the bets that the Prince himself had had on or against Escape, or about whether or not he had been seen giving the horse a bucket of water before the race on the 20th. Yet this is what happened; this is what was said. Was the intention also, therefore, to make an example of George?

After all, it was a hell of a thing for Bunbury to do, marching round to the Prince of Wales with an ultimatum in that peremptory way. Did he think that George would take it as a well-meant warning, against Chifney and his wicked ways; that the Prince would agree to disown his jockey, and would thereafter continue racing in a more seemly manner? Or did Bunbury, for some reason, actually *want* George out of the sport?

The two men had been linked before *l'affaire* Escape, and in a very odd way: the Prince's father, George III, had once been passionately in love with Bunbury's ex-wife, Lady Sarah Lennox, and had briefly hoped to marry her himself. Hard to imagine that this connection would not have been in Bunbury's thoughts, but equally hard to believe that it affected his judgement in any way. What resentments could he feel on that thirty-year-old score? If he was so sensitive with regard to Sarah, he would hardly have supported her nephew, Charles James Fox, with such devotion in Parliament (in his spare time, Bunbury was the not very inspired MP for Suffolk).

No – that was not motivating Bunbury. But perhaps the hardest thing of all to imagine is just what *was* going on inside that rather saturnine head. In almost all the records of this man's actions, the impression given is of impenetrability. As much as anything, *he* is the mystery here.

He had emerged as a suitor to Sarah Lennox – a daughter of the Duke of Richmond – in 1761, when she was still sore after the painful abortion of the King's attentions. She saw Bunbury as 'a marquis in a French story book', and indeed paintings do show him to have had, in youth, a rather suave and dark handsomeness. However, his laid-back, elegant manner concealed something very much like indifference. The couple married, while everyone around them wondered why they were doing it, and within days they themselves had discovered their mistake. With Sarah, it is easy to see that she had grabbed Bunbury on the rebound; but it is impossible to know what he was up to, entangling himself with a wildly romantic seventeen-year-old girl to whom he was completely unable to respond. Did he simply marry her for money?

They set up home in Suffolk, and Bunbury threw himself into the world of racing. Whether he did this because his marriage was a disaster, or whether the marriage stood no chance because he only wanted to be with horses, again it is difficult to say. At all events, Sarah eventually began to have affairs – it was around this time that Bunbury became Steward of the Jockey Club – and, in 1776, the couple divorced. Certainly Bunbury does seem to be the archetype of the English sporting gentleman, the kind who – according to the sporting artist Ben Marshall – would commission a painting of his horse for fifty guineas but think ten guineas too much for one of his wife. Yet it may have been Sarah herself – sexy, insecure, in constant need of attention and reassurance – who pushed him into inhabiting that role.

For whatever reasons, Bunbury lost himself in Newmarket life and, at only twenty-eight, found himself in charge of the Jockey Club. Of course, at this point – 1768 – the club had done very little except provide congenial surroundings for its members and tell them that their jockey must wear coloured silks. But the very fact of appointing a Steward implies some sort of impulse towards regulation. By 1770 an announcement was being made to the effect that 'the Members should meet annually at dinner on the day preceding the King's birthday' and that 'three members should be appointed Stewards' (as seen in the Escape inquiry), with full powers to conduct racing affairs at Newmarket. Then, that same year, the Jockey Club issued a rather drolly worded notice in the *Racing Calendar*: 'In order to save Mr Quick, Mr Castle, or any of the Ascott confederacy the trouble and expense of training, they are desired to take notice that none of their horses will be allowed to run for any of the above plates . . .' In other words, this bunch of likely lads was being warned off: the first time that the Jockey Club had exercised this particular power.

So the club's authority was growing, in an *ad hoc* sort of way – rules were made as and when they seemed necessary – but as racing also grew, so it became harder to contain and control. Only after the Escape affair did the Jockey Club have the strength to do this. By taking on the Prince of Wales, it had shown that the laws of racing – despite the fact that they didn't really exist – were, nonetheless, implacable. And, from 1791 onwards, the authority of the club was absolute.

Was this Bunbury's intention? Some commentators think that it was: that he was willing to make an example not just of a dodgy jockey, but of the man who employed him – all the better if this man was the heir to the throne, for what clearer way of showing that the integrity of racing came before anything?

There is also a theory, rather less elevated, that a faction within the Jockey Club was jealous of the Prince's successes, and wanted to see the great fat back of him. But perhaps most intriguing of all is the idea that Bunbury himself might have been got at: that Prime Minister Pitt, on behalf of the King, was using the Escape affair in order to force the Prince to leave the turf. This was why, when the scandal broke out, rather than hushing it up the Jockey Club allowed it to take its course – right to the ignoble end.

Implausible though this may sound, it must be remembered that George was carrying on like nobody's business at a time when, in France, people were having their heads cut off for less. A publication entitled *The Jockey Club, or a Sketch of the Manners of the Age*, shows how extremely *mal vu* the Prince's antics actually were, describing his 'chosen companions and confidential intimates' (that is to say, his racing friends) as 'the very *lees* of society . . . if a man of the most depraved, the vilest cast were, from a vicious sympathy, to choose his company, it were impossible for his choice to fix anywhere else'. Sir John Lade, a gentleman jockey who gave George advice on his horses, is especially condemned as having married 'a common prostitute' – not quite accurate, although the gorgeous Lady Letty had once been the mistress of a highwayman, Sixteen-String Jack, whose neck was broken for him at Tyburn. So Newmarket was not exactly preparing the Prince to be a sober, sensible monarch – that was hardly its role in the life of royalty. And it is not, therefore, impossible that the government was willing to countenance a temporary slur on George's – already some-what flawed – public character in order to avert permanent crisis.

If so, it didn't really work. What, in the end, were the consequences of this bizarre business? A great, if silly, jockey was forced out of racing, for no one would employ him after 1791. The Prince converted his £200 retainer into an annuity, which Chifney then sold for £1,260, no doubt believing that the money would merely launch him into a new and successful life, but of course it did not. In his autobiography he wrote, pitifully, 'if the Jockey Club will be pleased to give me 200 guineas I will make them a bridle as I believe never was', but of course they did not do so. He paid £350 to a saddler to have the bridle made anyway – and it was later used all over the world – but he could not pay the debt, was committed to the Fleet Prison, and died there at the age of fifty-three.

Meanwhile George had stood by Chifney, and by his resolve not to forgive the Jockey Club. This is always seen as evidence of the Prince's innate nobility, although it is quite possible that what looked like loyalty to his jockey was, in fact, fury at the fact that his own character had been impugned. Could he really have ditched Chifney and still have stayed in Newmarket, amongst the people who had put him in so ghastly a position? For all his weaknesses, George was not an unkind man (except to his wife), but his sympathy for Chifney was, in fact, empathy: they had both been put in the same leaky boat. Hence his remark to the jockey, when he saw him at Brighton at 1802: 'Sam Chifney, there's never been a proper apology made; they used me and you very ill. They are bad people – I'll not set foot on the ground more.'

Like all gestures of this kind, it was tricky to keep up. Horses that George had bred were, of course, trained and running at Newmarket. But he resolutely kept his own presence away from the place. And perhaps the most ludicrous aspect to this whole, overblown story was that, by 1805, the Jockey Club was begging him to return. 'May it please your Royal Highness,' began the plangent letter sent to the Prince, 'the Members of the Jockey Club, deeply regretting your absence from Newmarket, earnestly entreat the affair may be buried in oblivion; and sincerely hope that the different meetings may again be honoured by Your Royal Highness' condescending presence.' This panicky piece of obsequiousness was, above all, a recognition of the fact that the Escape affair – whatever lay behind it – had gone too far. No doubt the Jockey Club thought that the Prince would feel the same way. However, contrary to those reports which have him making a polite reply, he told the Members where they could stick their deep regret.

As for Escape: he came out of it all better than any of them. He was bought by Richard Tattersall, the bloodstock auctioneer, and spent the rest of his life as a stallion. What brave soul would have dared to buy one of his offspring?

The Jockey Club did, in the end, emerge infinitely stronger from this confrontation; its little show of *faiblesse* was really an aberration, very much out of character. It was busy doing all sorts of important things, next to which the absence of Prince of Wales from Newmarket was a minor matter.

It was during this period that the racing season began to take a regular and, to us, recognisable shape. The most obvious sign of this was the institution of the classic races: in 1776 the St Leger (1 mile 6 furlongs, for colts and fillies), in 1779 the Oaks (1 mile 4 furlongs, for fillies), in 1780 the Derby (1 mile 4 furlongs, for colts and fillies), in 1809 the Two Thousand Guineas (1 mile, for colts and fillies), and in 1814 the One Thousand Guineas (1 mile, for fillies). These were not a 'conception' as such, since there was no grandiose notion of creating five races that would last as long as the thoroughbred. As is usual with racing, the classics evolved empirically: for example, the Derby was originally run over a mile, then extended to become a 'male' counterpart to the Oaks. However the idea of seasonal races that owners and breeders actually aimed to win – that would look good, as it were, on a horse's CV – was hugely important. Henceforth there would be such a thing as a generic thoroughbred career, and the eight to fourteen furlong distance covered by the classics would mark out true thoroughbred territory.

The classics are, of course, for three-year-old horses, and it was around this time that the movement began towards encouraging precocity in the breed. As shown by the career of Eclipse, it was not unusual for a horse to start racing at the age of five or six, like a chaser today. Four-year-olds were not recorded as competing until 1727; three-year-olds in 1731; and, in 1769, a two-year-old colt named Gibscutski won a six-furlong sprint across the Rowley Course, receiving three stone from a six-year-old mare. The trend moving rather madly from one extreme to the other, there was even a brief vogue for racing yearlings in the 1770s. Those poor soft skeletons – it doesn't bear thinking about.

The first proper race for two year olds – the six-furlong July Stakes, which is still run at Newmarket – was instituted in 1786, and it was as important, in its way, as the classics. From this time onwards, the old style of horse race – the lolloping hack across Six Mile Bottom, the test of endurance over the Beacon Course – was doomed. In true modernising fashion, the emphasis was to turn to youth: young racehorses, carrying light weights, running shorter distances.

These changes would have happened anyway, because the continual refinement of the breed demanded them, but they were pushed along at a rate of knots by Sir Charles Bunbury. His was the guiding hand, shaping the natural evolution that was taking place within racing. It is said that, had he won the toss of the coin at the dinner when the Derby was conceived, the race would have been called the Bunbury instead. This is probably a nonsense, as the race was almost certainly named after the Earl of Derby because he was hosting the dinner at his Epsom house, The Oaks. But although the idea of a Bunbury being run every year is usually seen as a great joke – *The Importance of Being Earnest* has made it hard to take the name seriously – it would have been a fair tribute to the mysterious character who influenced his sport so deeply. No doubt he was happy enough that his horse, Diomed, won the first running of the race. And he is, perhaps more appropriately, commemorated in the Bunbury Mile on New-market's July Course.

Bunbury's great *aperçu* was that the thoroughbred's development depended upon the development of its speed: 'speed, more speed and yet more speed', as HH Aga Khan III, who dominated racing in the 1930s, put it. This now sounds like the supreme statement of the obvious, but in the 1770s it was not, because the races of that time required horses with stamina as opposed to pace. Only a freak, like Eclipse, could show speed in those gruelling conditions. Horses like him were the future. Rather than a miraculous one-off, he had to become the template to which the thoroughbred conformed. And in order to do this the racing season had to be constructed, designed, engineered.

The sport was becoming, gradually, more *professional*; so too was Newmarket. Not yet a business – those killjoy days were still more than a hundred years away – but no longer just a jolly romp. In the wake of Samuel Chifney, for example, came proper jockeys; and the notion that a rider, as opposed to just a horse, might win a race for an owner. Although this brought an added dimension to racing it also, in a sense, made it less pure.

On to the racing stage they came, a procession of little bow-legged starvelings: Frank Buckle, Dick Goodison, the Arnull brothers, Jem Robinson. In the years between Chifney's fall and the heyday of his son, Sam Chifney junior, the status of jockeys changed a good deal. They were still regarded as low class – and indeed on the whole they would be for many years, well into the twentieth century – but at the same time they were fêted and their services assiduously courted. In 1790, the elder Chifney's £200 retainer was viewed with astonishment. In 1820, after the younger Chifney had won some hugely lucrative races for, among others, the first Duke of Cleveland, an elegant house was built for him as a show of gratitude. This long, low piece of neo-classical symmetry on Old Station Road – now used as business premises, but still called Cleveland House – stands out a mile as one of the most attractive buildings in Newmarket.

It was Frank Buckle who was the most successful of them all: his record of 27 classic wins is surpassed only by Lester Piggott, who has 30. Buckle was born in 1766, the son of a Newmarket saddler. Unlike the flamboyant Chifneys, he was not a man for vast retainers or posh houses, being unassuming, plain-looking and possibly too stupid to seek great advancement (it was said that if he was turned round once after a race, he would forget what had happened in it; twice, and he would forget what horse he had ridden). He was, though, completely honest. Again, trickiness may have been beyond his mental powers; but in fact his clean reputation served him very well, so perhaps he was the clever one after all. His services were sought by Lord Grosvenor and by the 3rd (disreputable) and 4th (respectable) Dukes of Grafton. This patronage allowed him to build a decent solid wealth for himself. That Buckle's probity was highly unusual is shown by the words on his tombstone: 'Jockeys attend – from his example learn/The meed that honest worth is sure to earn'. John Gully, a former boxer who, in the early nineteenth century, became a rich and important owner, said that he had only ever known three incorruptible jockeys: the names are not recorded, but Buckle would certainly have been one of them.

Buckle was a gifted imitator of Sam Chifney senior and, like him, arrived late in a finish. 'If I win by the length of my arm, won't that do just as well as winning by a couple of lengths?' he once asked connections of a Yorkshire-based horse. 'Nay lad, thy fine finishes shorten a man's life.' He also rode Hambletonian in the 1799 match race against Diamond, after which the half-dead horse was painted by Stubbs. The jovial owner, Sir Henry Vane-Tempest, greeted Buckle, saying: 'I would give half my fortune, Frank, for such a nerve as yours.' Vane-Tempest thought that the race had been won because his jockey – superior and daring – had left something in reserve on Hambletonian, which he could pull out at the very end to win by that bare 'half a neck'. In fact, it was won because the horse was prepared to burst his heart open; but the notion of victory by jockeyship was taking a hold by this time, and is still an article of faith among many followers of racing.

Dick Goodison, a contemporary of Chifney, was born in Yorkshire around 1750, won the first three runnings of the Oaks and rode for the lecherous old Duke of Queensberry. He was unsubtle but effective, very different from Chifney, especially in his disgusting appearance: no ruffles and ribbons on dirty Dick. A rivalry developed which, in 1799, was sorted out by means of a boxing match, staged at Queensberry House, and won by Goodison. After this the two men – both of whom were old enough to know better – became friends for life.

Sam Arnull, who was born in around 1760, won the first Derby, on Diomed: the breeches that he wore for the ride hang inside the Jockey Club and look as though they might just fit a skinny nine-year-old. It was to become very common for families to immerse themselves, *en masse*, in racing – from the Chifneys through to the Piggotts, Dettoris and Edderys – and the three Arnull brothers won twelve Derbys between them.

Jem Robinson, who was riding at the beginning of the nineteenth century, may have been one of John Gully's three honest jockeys: he was straight, and highly talented, but he was also a bastard who – according to one of his rivals, John Day – could 'punish a horse most in the least time'. Who wouldn't rather have a kindly crook? Born in 1793, Robinson was the son of a Newmarket farm labourer. His ability caught the eye of the ageing Frank Buckle, and in 1821 the two jockeys met in one of the last, legendary Newmarket match races, which ended in a dead heat. Robinson's unnamed mount had savaged the rider a week earlier – this horse was a bit of a sod, no doubt about it, having also bitten off the thumb of his stable lad – but Robinson took a nasty, brainless revenge during the match and hit the colt without restraint. Two years later, when he was standing at the stud of his owner, Lord Exeter, Robinson was prevailed upon to enter the box of the horse, said by then to be 'as quiet as a lamb'. On catching sight of his former jockey, he went completely berserk and tried very hard – failing, unfortunately – to have another go at him.

Between 1825 and 1848, Robinson won the Two Thousand Guineas nine times, which remains a record. It was at this time that the Newmarket classics began to assume real prestige. Surprisingly, they had lagged behind the others in this regard, perhaps for the simple reason that they were established later, perhaps because they were run over the shortest distance, perhaps because Newmarket offered so much else besides. Two of Robinson's greatest Guineas winners also won extraordinary Derbys. Cadland – who is commemorated in Cadland House Stables, a very old yard at the foot of the the Heath – won a *rerun* Derby in 1828, after the first running ended in a dead heat. Jem Robinson took a phlegmatic pinch of snuff in between the two races and got on with the job. Bay Middleton, triumphant in 1836, was one of the most glamorously intractable of horses. On his first gallop under Robinson, he stamped on his lead rein, broke it and flashed off towards Cambridgeshire. Perhaps the jockey had learned the lesson of Lord Exeter's poor, angry colt; he tamed Bay Middleton – in so far as this was possible – without cruelty.

Around this time, a jockey like Robinson was earning £3 per mount and £5 per win, although this would go up to £100 to ride in a big race, and after a victory an owner would be looked upon very unfavourably if he didn't stump up £500 or so. He didn't always, however: Sir Charles Bunbury gave Tom Goodison (son of Dick) a couple of tenners after the jockey had won him the 1813 Two Thousand Guineas and Derby. However that was Bunbury's almost comically rigorous style. Most owners were only too glad to throw money at jockeys who won for them.

Jem Robinson was an idiot, though, and spent all his money living it up in London at the end of the season, when his weight would go soaring up to nearly 10 stone. His career ended when he was thrown during a match race in 1852, broke a thigh and was left with one leg four inches shorter than the other. He would certainly have finished up in the workhouse, a very pathetic figure indeed, had not kind patrons like the Dukes of Rutland and Bedford provided him with a home – less stately than Sam Chifney junior's, but pretty enough. The red brick cottage stood opposite Cleveland House, a little further down Old Station Road, and forms part of what is now Machell Place yard.

Sam Chifney junior was the acknowledged star, and was thought to be a better rider, even, than his father, who had been training him on the gallops – over a specially marked course up Warren Hill – from the age of six. From motives of loyalty, or of defiance, or possibly of simply wanting the best jockey around, in 1805 Prince George began paying him a retainer. This time, though, it was for £8 a year, which was frankly on the cautious side.

So the Escape affair did not die; and it could be said that George was determined not to let it. Nor was William Chifney, son of the disgraced jockey. He was sent to jail for six months after beating up one of the men who had called his father a cheat; the victim, George's stud manager Colonel Leigh, afterwards extended an admiring olive branch, admitting that he should not have said what he did. And William Chifney, who became a trainer, went on to thrive – for a while, at least. With his brother as stable jockey, he won the Derbys of 1818 and 1820 for owner Thomas Thornhill, a Norfolk squire. In 1825, he also won the Oaks with a filly who, two days earlier, had been claimed out of a seller and was running as a pacemaker for her stablemate.

But the Chifneys – Sam especially – had inherited some of their father's silly streak. Sam was actually suspected of stopping a horse in the Derby, which now seems beyond belief; he presumably had his money on when the filly, Manuella, then won the Oaks at 20/1. The brothers were hugely successful throughout the 1820s – between them they won ten classics – yet they, more than anyone, should have known the remorseless way in which racing glory can crumble. And, all too often, their success was founded on shifting sand: on pulling off gambling coups. While it worked, of course, it was wonderful. Off the brothers would go to the races in their top-of-the-range carriages; back they would come to entertain in their smart houses. William, urged by his wife – the daughter of none other than bookmaker Vauxhall Clark – had built a rival establishment next door to his brother. Warren House, as it was called, is now the site of a block of highly desirable flats, The Gallops. The high point of the Chifneys' fortunes came when they both backed Priam, William's magnificent 1830 Derby horse, and won something like £18,000 on the race (run in conditions of 'hail nearly the size of French beans', and after fourteen false starts).

Four years later, they were pretty well ruined when Shilelagh, whom they had backed to win the 1834 Derby, ran second to 'that great bullock' Plenipotentiary (later doped in the St Leger). The brothers had done their best to get a decent price, sending out a horse almost identical to Shilelagh, but heavily bandaged, to work badly on the Heath and start rumours that 'the Chifney Derby horse' should not be touched with a bargepole. But the Chifneys' cunning back-fired, as it so often does. Apart from anything else, everyone knew that they were having all their money on, so their attempts at deception were hardly convincing, although no doubt they kept everyone amused during the Derby build-up. Nowhere does rumour fly so free and so gaily as across Newmarket Heath.

After that, Sam – who, like many naturally gifted sports-men, though few jockeys, was lazy – rather lost the will to continue with his hectic, impossible life. He put on weight easily but felt disinclined to do as many jockeys then did, which was to sweat off pounds by taking marathon walks muffled up in a greatcoat. Instead he sat at home and watched his pet foxes playing in their pen. He turned down a retainer from Lord Chesterfield, refused rides that were a long way from Newmarket – and not many places are very near – and won only one more classic, the One Thousand Guineas in 1843 for Thomas Thornhill (whatever else might be said about them, these Chifneys do seem to have com-manded fidelity from owners). William, meanwhile, was forced to shut his yard, and moved to London. A memoir of his old age[5] describes how:

> for years before his death (he) had been in very poor circumstances, living in the model lodging-houses at Pentonville, and getting down to his dear Heath when the state of his exchequer admitted of a third-class return ticket to Newmarket. Even then he was some-times too feeble to get farther than the top of the town, where, with his back to the cemetery wall, he would watch the horses returning to the stables after the races.

---

[5] From *The Badminton Library of Sports and Pastimes: Racing*.

When it was one of his good days, he braved the blasts of the Heath in an ancient blue coat, and a hat made secure by a parti-coloured bandana . . .

Aged seventy-eight he died in 1862, eight years after his brother, in his rooms near St Pancras station.

William Chifney had been one of the most prominent trainers of the time and – as with jockeys – the status of the profession was becoming better established. Newmarket was still a long way from the days of Mathew Dawson who, late in the nineteenth century, would be able to rule owners with a rod of iron. However the trainer was now rather more than just a stableman hired to look after his lordship's horses. Robert Robson, for example, whose stable jockey was Frank Buckle and then Jem Robinson, had a considerable amount of clout and was known as the Emperor of Trainers. He was entitled to be; for between 1793 and 1828 he won 33 classics, mainly for the 3rd and 4th Dukes of Grafton. One of these was actually a walkover, received by Tontine in the 1825 One Thousand Guineas, the only instance of this occurring in a classic race.

Robson remains a shadowy figure, despite this almost embarrassing – indeed unparalleled – weight of success. What is best known about him is that, contrary to the normal practice of the time, his theory of training horses was to be easy on them. 'While the Chifneys were persistently inflicting upon their Derby horses eight-mile sweats two or three times a week, Robson won the great Epsom race in 1823 with Emilius, to whom he never gave a sweat at all, and it was a saying often on Frank Buckle's lips that in the preparation of a delicate horse Robson was seven pounds ahead of any other trainer.'[6]

Several years ahead too, it would seem. Robson's prodigious record gave substance to the idea that a trainer could make a difference to a horse; that there could be an artistry in understanding the thoroughbred, and in causing him to peak at the newly instituted seasonal climaxes. After Robson retired, in 1828, the Grafton horses ceased to dominate as

---

[6] *Ibid.*

The Fox, now in Newmarket, at his original home off Hyde Park Corner. 'Tattersalls' Horse Repository' by Rowlandson and Pugin (1800)

Above Charles II with his mistress Nell Gwynn

Right Edward VII in military mode. A portrait from the early twentieth century, around the time of Minoru's classic victories

Right The two-year-old Shergar in 1980, his white blaze hidden from view, at home with his lad in Sir Michael Stoute's Beech Hurst yard

Below Gimcrack, 'the sweetest little horse', by George Stubbs

Left Jockeys before a race in the Rowley Mile saddling enclosure, 1988

Horse and work rider on Newmarket Heath, 1992

The last Newmarket classic of the millennium. Kieren Fallon and Wince win the One Thousand Guineas on the July Course, 2 May 1999

they once had. This may have been coincidence, but it certainly would not have seemed that way. It would have been said of Robson, as it is now of Henry Cecil or Sir Michael Stoute, ah, he gets something out of them that the others don't. This doesn't mean that Robson's methods were universally adopted. Plenty of trainers stuck to the Chifney methods of galloping and sweating and keeping a horse 'as thin as a hurdle'. For some animals, of course, that method worked then and it still does now. What Robert Robson realised was that what worked for one horse would not work for another. This statement, which sounds so very simple, contains the infinitely complex sum of all wisdom about training racehorses. Robson would not have been the first to grasp this, but he was the first to give it life on Newmarket Heath. His approach influenced James Edwards, who in 1836 managed to turn Bay Middleton's ferocity outwards on to the racecourse, not in upon himself; and the highly sophisticated Dawson brothers, of whom Mathew was merely the best known. In his subtlety, Robert Robson belonged to a later age. And the forward-looking man was king – or emperor – at this time; as racing galloped ever onwards in its chase to keep up with the thoroughbred, and the ideal of perfectibility that he embodied.

Thus, in the years around the turn of the eighteenth to nineteenth centuries, racing began to be absorbed into the daily life of Newmarket. Before this, it had imposed itself in excitable bursts. People would make periodic descents upon the little town, taking lordly possession of it even as they submitted themselves to the mysterious power of the Heath; then off they would go again, leaving only the bustle of the market and, always present in the background, the rhythmic clip of thoroughbred hooves. But as training establishments like Robert Robson's turned the sport into a proper job, even an industry, so racing and Newmarket became indivisible from one another. The town was filling up with stable lads, blacksmiths, saddlers, jockeys. As it does today, when over half the working population of Newmarket is involved in the racing industry, the early nineteenth-century High Street began to swarm with tough little men, an exhausted, faraway look in their eyes, their demeanour dedicated to the point of eroticism. To the world beyond, flat racing was and – *pace* the all-weather – is a seasonal business: in Newmarket, it became and remains a constant presence.

A couple of the yards that were in use at this time are still living, working stables. There is Cadland House, parts of whose yellow walls date from the eighteenth century, and the charming little red-trimmed Sackville House Stables, which lie close to Cadland, between Sackville Street[7] and Old Station Road, and which may once have been owned by Sir Charles Bunbury, although this is uncertain. Queensberry Lodge, Albert House at the foot of Bury Road, and Palace House – where, in the late eighteenth century, the philanderer Duke of Cumberland's horses were trained – now stand empty, their unrestored façades displaying a certain indifferent grandeur. Other yards, about which little is known, have been demolished and, as with the Newmarket palace, the imagination has to work pretty hard to reconstruct them. Kingston House, for example, where Robson trained his 33 classic winners, stood within untidy, unlovely Kingston Passage off the High Street. Somewhere between here and All Saints' Church, which lies just behind, the horse Waxy – winner of Robson's first Derby in 1793 – is supposedly buried. Middleton Cottage, which may have been used by the Prince of Wales before he stormed out of town, was on Exeter Road, off Mill Hill. And Mill Hill itself was the site of Richard Prince's stables, where the horses belonging to Lord Foley and Charles James Fox were trained.

Close to the yard was the Five Bells, which is still a pub and was then an inn. In 1811 a man named Daniel Dawson lodged there. Though educated and reasonably well liked, he was earning his living as a tout, which at the time was regarded as rather worse than working as a prostitute. A tout was not, as now, seen as a disseminator of information, but as its thief, and as such was chased from the Heath by the Jockey Club; the Devil's Dyke, however, proved an excellent natural look-out post on Racecourse Side. Before the 1811 Spring meeting Dawson had been noticed hanging around

---

[7] Sackville Street was then called Shagbag, and seems to have been the site of one of Newmarket's several cockpits.

Richard Prince's yard – this was par for the course, though, as it was a heavy gambling stable.

Around this time a rumour had somehow reached Prince of a plan to nobble the water tank on the Heath from which his horses drank after a gallop. Most trainers had their own tanks, which were kept locked. For a few days Prince took notice of the warning but – as one does – he eventually decided that there was nothing to it and let the horses drink. Most of them refused to do so: they smelt danger, or something more tangible. However five of them did take a little of the water and were immediately seized so badly with griping that they could hardly get back to the yard. Two were given castor oil and recovered. The other three were kept waiting for their own vet – a disastrous piece of rectitude – and died in agony. One of them, Spaniard, had run second the day before when 1–10 favourite in the Newmarket Claret Stakes; a bare few hours later, he endured what Richard Prince's head lad said were the worst sufferings he had ever seen. The three horses were buried in a gravel pit by the Severals, the piece of open land just beyond the Clock Tower.

Daniel Dawson – spied lurking on the scene, purveyor of a despised trade, known to have fallen on hard times – was suspected almost immediately. In a touch straight out of Grand Guignol, a bottle marked 'Poison' was found by his landlady in the room that he rented at the Five Bells, and he was committed for trial in Cambridge. The chemist, Cecil Bishop, from whom he had obtained the arsenic, turned King's Evidence. Dawson had no chance after that, of course, but it should really have been obvious that he was acting under orders, in this case almost certainly those of a couple of bookmakers – the Bland brothers – who were laying against Richard Prince's horses at the Spring meeting. This is not in any way to condone what Dawson did. The idea of it is repellent beyond belief; and Cecil Bishop's evidence, as reported in *The Times*, told a horrible tale. According to him, Dawson had been provided at first with corrosive sublimate, 'to sicken horses'. However, because Richard Prince was avoiding the water tank – by a ghastly irony, it was the well-meant rumour that caused the horses such eventual suffering – Dawson 'complained that the stuff was not strong enough', and was given arsenic instead. 'On being informed if it was made strong it would kill the horses, he replied he did not mind that, the Newmarket frequenters were rogues, and if he, meaning witness, had a fortune to lose, they would plunder him of it. The prisoner afterwards informed witness he used the stuff, which was then strong enough, as it had killed a hackney and two brood mares.'

Obviously Bishop was trying to cover his own back, so what he said must be taken with a degree of scepticism. But even if he exaggerated, and if the outcome of this story did go beyond the intention, nobbling is a soulless crime. When one reads about the fate of Spaniard and the others, it is hard to care about the fact that Dawson was condemned to death (in an age which still practised great cruelty towards horses, destroying them 'maliciously' was a capital crime). To portray him as the guileless fall guy, as some accounts do, is inaccurate.

Nonetheless Dawson was the actor, not the instigator. Whether this was generally realised is not clear; but Lord Foley, who inherited after the death of Fox's friend and who, like him, had horses with Prince – one of which was affected by the poison – tried his best to get the sentence commuted. *The Times* reported on 8 August 1812 that 'Dawson, who was . . . sentenced to be executed this day, has been reprieved.' Was he told this? One can only hope not, because on 10 August the newspaper wrote:

> The report of this culprit being reprieved was unfounded; he suffered the sentence of the law on Saturday at 12 o'clock, at the top of Cambridge Castle, amidst a surrounding assemblage of at least twelve thousand persons . . . He made an unsolicited declaration of the whole poisoning business, from the time of physicking Rubens, at Brighton, to the poisoning at Newmarket, in 1811. The parting with his wife on Thursday was an affecting scene. She is a respectable woman; and the prisoner seemed more affected at the recollection of his former indifference to her, than at approaching death itself . . . In his last moments he

declared that he never meant to *kill*, but merely to prevent the horses from winning.

The degree of Dawson's guilt can be argued; what is sure is that he was guilty of crimes against the integrity of racing. And in the eyes of the Jockey Club, which had offered 500 guineas for information leading to an arrest in this case, no price was too high in such matters: a prince's patronage, a jockey's career, even a man's life. Over the last thirty years or so, the Jockey Club's right to conduct the war for the soul of its sport had been won. But the war itself was only just beginning.

5 Dirty tricks

'Dead of a Derby Favourite' – 1820–1868

A S THE SPORT OF RACING became more professional, so too did the practice of corruption. During the first half of the nineteenth century, the things that went on are enough to make one's hair stand on end. In their absolute and unrepentant crookedness they are almost comical – conducted in a cunning, prancing, Chaucerian spirit which could be nothing but English.

Newmarket had never exactly been a place for clean-living types. All the same, compared with what was to follow, the wild boys who went on the rampage throughout the mid-eighteenth century had a rather sweet and silly innocence about them – the innocence of Oxbridge dining clubs, which is really what they were, except that to them Bucephalus was the horse who raced against Eclipse across the Beacon Course. These men had inhabited a world entirely of their own making. Now, the world outside – which did not play by Jockey Club rules – was starting to encroach upon the sacred Heath.

In the early years of the Jockey Club, racing was the plaything and possession of its members. By 1791, the List of Subscribers in the *Racing Calendar* is still headed by a long succession of noble names – 148 of them – beginning with the Prince of Wales and his brother, the Duke of York, and moving in stately fashion through 'His Grace the Duke of Grafton, 2 fets' . . . 'Right Honourable the Earl of Barrymore' . . . 'Right Honourable the Earl of Cork' . . . 'Right Honourable

Charles James Fox' . . . 'Honourable Champion Dymoke' . . . 'Honourable Mr. Walpole'[1] . . . 'Sir T. Charles Bunbury' and so on. But the list also includes a huge number of less venerable titles, Esquires and plain Misters, showing the spread of the sport's appeal across a wider society, for the *Racing Calendar* was not cheap, costing 10s. 6d. for the 1791 volume, a sum that only a true *aficionado* would have spent. All the same, even down in Cornwall, 'Henry John, Efq' and 'Mr Whitaker' were clearly interested in reading about the doings of the racing world. So too was 'Mr Bodger, Land Surveyor' in Huntingdonshire and, most bizarrely, 'Mr Ifaac Newton' in Hertfordshire. In London, meanwhile, the *Racing Calendar* was taken by diverse fans of the sport, including 'Warwick Lake, Efq.', 'Mr Tattersall', 'Mr Walker, Painter and Glazier, Duke-ftreet, Grofvenor-fquare', 'Mr F. Sartorius, Horfe-Painter No.17, Gerrard-ftreet, Soho' and 'Mr Sex'. The publication would have been read extensively beyond the list of 192 individual subscribers, since establishments like the 'Piazza Coffee-houfe, Covent Garden', the 'Cocoa-tree, Pall Mall', 'Munday's Coffee-houfe, Maiden-Lane' and the 'Bell and Hare, Tottenham' all took it for the edification of their clientele.

Later still, the 'democratisation' of racing can be seen in the list of winning owners in the classic races. The Derby, the prize that everyone wanted to capture was, in its early years, firmly in the clutches of the old guard: Bunbury, Lord Grosvenor, Lord Egremont, the Dukes of Grafton and Bedford. Only clever Dennis O'Kelly managed to gatecrash the nobs' party. But by 1830 Priam – formerly owned by the Earl of Chesterfield – was winning the Derby in the name of Mr W. Chifney, and in 1832 St Giles won in that of Mr R. Ridsdale, a Yorkshire groom whose fortune had been gained by the systematic corruption of trainers, jockeys and stable lads.

The Jockey Club did not like it – who would? – but its members were realists, in their way. And in this way of theirs – arrogant, oligarchic, yet not inefficient – they set about dealing with the fact that racing was no longer the sole

---

[1] Walpole presumably was forced into taking the *Racing Calendar* when disposing of the horses of his nephew, Lord Orford, who, mad as he was, was also still subscribing to the publication.

preserve of their own kind. After the death of Sir Charles Bunbury in 1820, the man who led the Club into battle was Lord George Bentinck: the second 'Dictator of the Turf'.

If the impression given by Bunbury is of a chill impregnability, hiding who knows what, then Bentinck comes across as more obviously peculiar. Indeed, none of the three men who held the position of *de facto* head of racing – Admiral Rous comes a little later – was exactly your average bloke. They all gave off an air of solitude (indeed Bentinck never married), of extreme self-sufficiency, of disdain for popularity. It was as if a certain impersonality within their characters enabled them to give themselves over to their sport. They were not inadequates, although had they been born to a different station in life they might have been. And it is easy to see, through them, how those who *are* misfits, to a greater or lesser degree, can find a very particular kind of relief in the world of racing. The history of the sport is full of such people.

What Bunbury, Bentinck and Rous seem, above all, to have had in common is that they took racing seriously – more seriously than anything else, more seriously than one would believe possible. When Bentinck launched himself fully into his political career, he actually gave up the sport, as if it would be impossible for him to treat it as just an enjoyable sideline. These three men were unmarked by that charming streak of levity which, from Charles II onwards, has run through the English sporting gentleman. Bunbury and Bentinck appear not to have had a funny bone in their bodies, and examples of the Rous humour – he liked, for example, to do a running commentary on himself when playing billiards in the Jockey Club – are very leaden indeed. No doubt this was the secret of the three Dictators' success; but their attitudes, which frankly went beyond pomposity, must have made them fairly heavy weather.

Bentinck, especially, would have been exhausting. For a start he was extremely posh, being the third son of the 4th Duke of Portland, who owned great tranches of London W1 (all those Portland/Bentinck/Holles/Welbeck/Cavendish streets and squares), and who also sat resplendent at the very heart of the racing world. The duke had been a member of the Jockey Club from its early years. He had lent the cash with which the Club bought the freehold of the Coffee Rooms. He owned a vast amount of Newmarket Heath, as well as some surrounding land, which the Jockey Club had leased from him since 1753; this, together with its own purchases, gave it control of almost the entire area by 1819. Arguing with Lord Bentinck, therefore, would have been like arguing with Newmarket itself – not to be contemplated.

So the 4th Duke of Portland was a vitally important figure within racing, who won the 1819 Derby with Tiresias. The 6th Duke owned what was possibly the greatest horse of the nineteenth century, St Simon. The 5th, however, took no interest in the sport, preferring to live underground in the suite of rooms that he had built beneath the family seat, Welbeck Abbey. His generation was represented – and how – by Lord George: gambler, dandy, politician, despot.

There is no doubt that Bentinck did a great deal of good for racing, perhaps more than Bunbury had done, but his importance seems to have resided in his presence as much as anything, its patrician perfection striking a kind of stunned awe into those around him. The Samuel Lane portrait of him in the Jockey Club shows him to have been good-looking in an epicene, untouchable way. According to the Goodwood trainer John Kent, who seems to have been half in love with him, he was 'the beau ideal of an English nobleman. He stood over six feet in height; his figure was, beyond that of any other man of my acquaintance, stately and elegant; his features were extremely handsome and refined, his hands and feet small and beautifully shaped, his whole appearance most commanding'. There follows a panegyric to Bentinck's wardrobe, concluding: 'I must revert for a moment to his scarfs, in order to say that, although they cost nearly a pound apiece, nothing would induce him to wear them more than once. They were then put away, and many drawers were full of them when he died ...' He also wore very special breeches, made from the hides of his own stags. The *ensemble* was clearly dazzling, and the nineteenth-century racing writer 'Thormanby' said of Bentinck that he was 'the idol of the sportsmen of his own day'.[2] This, after all, was an almost

---

[2] In his *Kings of the Turf*.

wholly male society, stuffed to the gills with English public school types; it is not surprising that it chose to worship gorgeous Lord George.

So Bentinck had impeccable external credentials for running the Jockey Club, or at least for acting as a figurehead; with regard to his behaviour, though, he was really no better than he should have been. For example in 1826, at the age of twenty-four, he lost £26,000 on the running of the St Leger. Afterwards he persuaded two of his brothers to open a bank account for him, to a limit of £300,000, with which to pursue his love of racing and – just as strong with him – of gambling.

Indeed the great joke is that Bentinck was doing all the things that he was supposed to be fighting against, if with slightly more style. He was one of the heaviest gamblers of the century. In 1838, after the St Leger meeting, he wrote: 'I am just about to address myself to the weary task of making out my book, upon which I have not won a single bet. And yet – I would rather be in my position than in that of Lord Chesterfield who, with such a horse as Don Juan in his possession, has only won £1,500 upon the Leger. Had Don Juan been mine I would not have left a single card seller in Doncaster with a coat to his back.' This was rather bitchy, as the poor earl – called 'The Magnificent' when he entertained everyone on the Lucullan scale at Chesterfield House in Mayfair – was, at thirty-three, completely broke, and could afford no more than a token bet on the last decent horse he ever owned.

Where Bentinck differed from men like this – and from those like Harry Mellish and Charles James Fox – was that, after that first disastrous Leger, he became very successful in his betting. In the 1845 season, for example, he won more than £100,000, which covered the costs of his training operation – he had huge numbers of horses with John Kent – twice over. Bentinck was no glorious gentlemanly 'plunger', but a shrewd and calculating operator. Gambling financed his racing: indeed he could have made his living by it – which, had he been less intrinsically aristocratic, might have seemed rather common, a little too much like the man who left Brooks's club before losing everything that he had won.

After all, this kind of finely judged, fully informed gambling was what had launched men like John Gully on to the racing scene. Having pulled off a series of coups during his career as a 'leg', he found himself in a position to set up his own stud, and became one of the biggest owners in the country, as well as MP for Pontefract in the first Reformed Parliament. At the age of twenty-one he served time for debt in the Fleet Prison; in 1807 he fought for the boxing championship of England in a ring set up at Six Mile Bottom (winning in the 36th round); then he became a publican in Lincoln's Inn. After this he began bookmaking and made a great success, for reasons explained by 'Thormanby':

> The Turf, it must be remembered, was in a very different state then from what it is now; for although not a quarter of the number of horses were kept in training the betting on them was far heavier, and as the bookmakers were scanty in proportion, so the profits they made out of the big wagers of such notorious speculators as the Duke of Queensberry, Lord Foley, Lord Abingdon, Colonel Mellish, and others of that kidney, must have been immense ... In Gully's early days what we call 'public money' was almost unknown ... The professional bettor of the first three or four decades of the century laid the odds himself and worked commissions for the big backers. Gully soon had the commissions of the cream of the noble sportsmen.

Later he had their horses, too. There are similarities, in fact, between his story and that of Dennis O'Kelly – except that the extremes of Gully's situation were more pronounced, and the structures of nineteenth-century racing, within which he operated, were both more and less rigid. Yet he fought his way towards acceptance, and to all appearances won it. Charles Greville, a cousin of Bentinck who acted as racing manager to the then Duke of York, wrote with great condescension that although Gully was 'totally without edu-cation, he had strong sense, discretion, reserve, and a species of good taste ... and he has gradually separated himself from the rabble of bettors and blackguards of whom he was once the most conspicuous'. Greville may have been naïve in believing this, however, as in the 1830s Gully – though a decent man – was still associating with members of the racing underworld like Robert Ridsdale.

It was hard not to, if one wanted to keep one step ahead of the game. It was like trying to keep afloat in the world of asset-stripping in the 1960s, or futures-selling in the 1980s: one had to know what the other fellow was up to. And, like O'Kelly, Gully was a very bright spark indeed. He bought the 1827 Derby winner, Mameluke, from the Earl of Jersey for no less than 4,000 guineas – the earl's racing interests had, by then, put him about £400,000 out of pocket – and backed him to win £10,000 in the St Leger. Then he laid £10,000 that Mameluke would beat ten specified horses, and £10,000 that he would beat nine. These were bold bets, but Gully looked as sure as one ever could be to collect.

However, with this 1827 Leger he was in the biggest of leagues, and he fell foul of it. It seems that the starter in Mameluke's race was bribed. There were seven false starts, which drove the horse mad, and according to one account the flag was finally dropped for the off when Matilda, the eventual winner, was already seventy yards ahead and Mameluke was facing the wrong way – although the Derby winner only lost, in the end, by half a length. Unfortunately Matilda (10/1) was in both the group of ten and the group of nine that he was supposed to beat.

The man behind this piece of chicanery was believed to be William Crockford, whose name remains synonymous with gambling. At the time he ran one establishment on St James's Street, London, and another on Newmarket High Street, the site of which – pretty little Rothesay House – is now occupied by the Bradford and Bingley building society (he also built Crockford's farm, near the Links, and of course had one of the best houses in Newmarket, on the corner of the High Street and Old Station Road). Crockford had acquired for himself an appalling reputation, and was called, rather excitably, the most evil man ever known to racing. Rowlandson's cartoon of him, which presents a slumped, watchful face with a hat askew across it, was titled 'Crockford the Shark Keeper of Hell Gaming House Piccadilly'. 'His cheeks,' wrote a contemporary commentator, 'appeared whitened and flabby through constant night-work. His hands were entirely without knuckles, soft as raw veal, and as white as paper, whilst his large flexible mouth was stuffed with "dead men's bones" – his teeth all being false.'

Crockford may well have been dreadful. He was apparently assiduous in the collection of debts, but this kind of puritanical lambasting has a hypocritical ring in a society that enjoyed gambling so much. It is a bit like a tabloid newspaper editorial bemoaning the decline in moral standards (indeed the description of Crockford is rather of the demonising tabloid variety). And this was the paradox within racing in the first half of the nineteenth century. The very same things that were being condemned were – at the same time, and often by the same people, Lord George Bentinck notable amongst them – being determinedly indulged in.

There could be no racing without gambling: everyone knew as much but, as is still the case today, nobody really faced the facts. The British government still taxes betting to a ludicrous degree, not just from greed but because of some lurking sense that gambling is reprehensible, and a knowledge that cutting the duty from 6.75 per cent (at the end of 1999) would cause uproar in certain prim quarters. In the nineteenth century, similarly nervous evasions were enacted. The 1845 Gaming Act did not make the gambling contract illegal, but it did make it unenforceable through law; it existed, but at the same time it did not. Again, the 1853 Betting Act did not prohibit gambling itself, but 'provided that no house, office, room or other place should be opened, kept or used for the purpose of betting . . .' This law was useful in that it helped suppress some truly terrible gambling dens, but the definition of 'other place' became rather hazy when it came to considering whether standing at a racecourse was illegal. If a bookmaker had with him a stool and an umbrella, was he thereby setting up a little office? Judgements went either way on the issue; and this absurdity was not resolved until 1928.

So gambling bobbed and weaved its way through the nineteenth century, seducing and repelling in equal measure. It took a man of the good sense of Richard Tattersall (the bloodstock auctioneer) to speak the truth, which he did in 1844 to a Special Committee on the Gaming Laws. To the question: 'Are you of opinion that it would be desirable to legalise bets, and to make them recoverable in a court of law?' Tattersall replied: 'Yes; I am sure it would prevent an amazing deal of betting, and it would prevent a great many people being ruined, because there are a great many men that go for a stake that never mean to pay if they lose.' This good advice was not, of course, taken in the subsequent Act. But the really important point is made when Tattersall is asked: 'Do you think that if betting were put an end to entirely, it would diminish and put down the breeding of horses?' He answered: 'If betting were put an end to there would be an end of my breeding; I cannot bring a horse up to be a yearling under £120.' In other words, gambling was funding the production of horses upon which to gamble. No one could sustain a breeding or racing operation unless they gambled successfully, upon the knowledge that they had of their horses, to finance it; this, one might say, was their quid pro quo. The Earl of Jersey was not a gambler and his debts were therefore irrecoverable. Lord George Bentinck, on the other hand, did so well on his horses that he was able to keep up to forty at a time in training. Of course it was possible to lose as well as win; but at least by having a go one was, so to speak, improving the odds.

So Bentinck knew, none better, that gambling was the pungent stew off which racing fed. Yet he objected to having so gross a dish thrust under his elegant nose and, in 1835, he was confronted full on by the consequences of this paradox.

One of his horses had run at Heaton Park and beaten a colt, Rush, who was owned by a man named George Osbaldeston.[3] The next day the two horses met again, in a big handicap, and Rush won the race. The story has a very familiar ring to it; but Bentinck did not behave with quite the same lethal coolness as Bunbury had done in similar circumstances. This was because, unlike Bunbury, Bentinck himself was involved in this incident, having laid Osbaldeston's horse on the second day to the tune of £400. The affront was therefore not merely to the integrity of racing – it was personal.

---

[3] Osbaldeston was famed in Newmarket for having pulled off a £1,000 bet that he could ride 200 miles in less than ten hours; using 29 horses, he made fifty extended laps of the Round Course in eight hours and 42 minutes; then changed and went out to dinner.

Bentinck gave instructions that Osbaldeston was not to be paid the £400 that he owed on the race. At Newmarket's Craven meeting, the feisty little man confronted Bentinck outside the Jockey Club – where he was standing in his beautiful breeches – and asked for the money. Bentinck, looking down on to the top of Osbaldeston's head, replied that he was astonished to be asked 'as the whole affair was a robbery, and so the Jockey Club considered it'. All the same he did pay – 'can you count?' – in an agonising series of very small notes.

Now it was understandable that Bentinck should have been annoyed about this. He was almost certainly right to think that skulduggery had gone on in this instance; although it depends, all the same, on what one means by skulduggery. Osbaldeston had been 'cheating' the handicapper, no question, in that Rush was carrying far too low a weight when he won. But the whole point of handicaps is to get a horse 'well in' at the weights, by running it with something left in hand. In that sense, almost everyone is cheating. Also, part of Osbaldeston's motivation seems to have been a desire to prove that the handicapper, himself, was not always above suspicion. Some owners – Bentinck among them, no doubt – were being treated better at the weights than others. Osbaldeston was merely getting a bit of his own back. This was no defence, of course, in the eyes of the 'law', but what was the law of racing in these cases? As with gambling, the truth was rather less clear-cut than most people were prepared to admit. And so it was hardly a good idea for Bentinck to stand on Newmarket High Street and declaim on the subject. Apart from anything else, Osbaldeston was rather trigger-happy; indeed, within a few minutes of being told that he was a robber, he had sent Bentinck a challenge to a duel.

Everyone was galvanised by this. Osbaldeston was a terrific shot and it seemed that Bentinck, if he accepted the challenge, would soon be an exquisite corpse. He was sensitive on the subject of duels, having refused to fight one during his army career. Therefore a good deal of effort had to go into saving his life, his honour and preferably both. Really it was very serious, yet there is something deeply comic about the image of Osbaldeston strutting like a bantam-cock up to the languid Bentinck and – entirely careless of his dignity – putting him in this dreadful situation. What was to be done? Accounts differ, although it seems probable that an intermediary – the racing man George Payne – knocked some sense into Osbaldeston by saying that Bentinck had, after all, had a point in protesting against the running of Rush, and that killing him for it would be an overreaction.

All the same, the duel did go ahead, at Wormwood Scrubs. Perhaps this was only for form's sake, although one report does say that Bentinck was dressed all in black 'without a speck of white to aim at', so he may still have had his worries. Again, what happened next is disputed. It may have been that Bentinck fired into the air and Osbaldeston through Bentinck's (black) hat; or that Osbaldeston deliberately missed and Bentinck's bullet cut a hole through one of Osbaldeston's whiskers. Whatever the truth, it must have been entirely thrilling – and had no effect on either man, in that Osbaldeston was soon challenging John Gully to a duel after an argument in the Doncaster Subscription Rooms, and Bentinck continued to lay down the law of racing.

Much of what he did was very good and necessary. For example, in around 1836 he introduced the system of 'vanning', whereby horses were taken to race meetings in vans rather than on foot. It seems incredible, but this innovation was initially ridiculed; partly, perhaps, because it was Bentinck's own St Leger runner, Elis, who first benefited from it. Two years earlier, Plenipotentiary had been walked all the way from Saffron Walden to Doncaster, to contest a Leger in which, having been nobbled beforehand, he ran last. Elis was transported there in style, and won. The price was huge, too, as bookmakers had laid him like mad, believing he would not run because he was still in his box the week before the race. Another coup for Gorgeous George.

It was at race meetings themselves that Bentinck had his greatest effect, bringing them immeasurably closer to what we would recognise today. For, in the 1830s, they were not so very different from how they had been one hundred years earlier: completely chaotic. Newmarket Heath is a place in which the eye can easily lose itself at the best of times. In those days, unless one was absolutely up to speed with what was going on, watching racing would have been like being in the midst of a thundering fog: horses all over the place – thoroughbreds, hacks, carriage horses; bookmakers hollering 'lay six 50s to four', or 'the field a hundred'; everyone galloping off to different starting posts for races that never began at the time they were supposed to.

Nowadays, racing comes to the spectator, as best it can on a vast tract of land like Newmarket Heath. Then, the spectator went to the racing. There were, by this time, eighteen different 'courses' on the Heath, so races might begin anywhere: the Beacon Course, the Abingdon Course, the Ditch In Course, the Old Cambridgeshire Course, the Rowley Mile. This is still the case – obviously enough, races of different distances require different starting places – but in those days, when the start moved, the spectator moved with it. The bookmakers would up sticks, driving their carriages down to one of the various betting posts, where they would form a 'ring'. Close behind came the racegoers, the gentlemen on their hacks and the 'rabble' – as it was called – on foot. After a delay of half an hour waiting for the jockeys and stewards to appear, for the horses to line up in some sort of order, for a few false starts, the race would finally get under way. And, just as they had done in the days of Charles II, a phalanx of spectators would ride alongside it – how else, they would have asked, were they to see what happened?

They had a point, but this wild practice had to be stopped, all the same. There were sometimes as many as a thousand people on horseback on the Heath, frantically making their way towards a finish. In 1802, a spectator had fallen and brought down the man behind him, whose mount broke its neck; the rider himself was none too well after a clump of following horses had galloped over him; but the surprising thing, really, was that this kind of disaster didn't happen more often. Of course many people hugely enjoyed riding the finish, and it must have been exhilarating, but it was banned by the Jockey Club in 1838.

Around this time Lord Bentinck was introducing measures to make race meetings rather more civilised. Conditions were spartan, even for those robust times. There was almost nothing, for example, in the way of shelter or refreshments.

The more aristocratic racegoers would repair for lunch in their carriages, with their women, rather as one might nowadays picnic from the car at Royal Ascot; but, for the rest, when racing at Newmarket it was a nasty sandwich from Jarvis's booth, a stall which also sold what were called 'thumbers' – thumb-size pieces of meat that the customer himself would cut. It has to be said that catering for the average racegoer has not improved as much as all that, even now, although the idea of going to racing in order to eat is – or should be – a nonsense.

So Bentinck improved amenities – not difficult at Newmarket, a Nissen hut would have been an improvement – and was the first to introduce differently priced enclosures at racecourses. This was not universally enforced until 1875, the year that Newmarket built its first proper stand. The sliding-scale entry is now, of course, an established principle in this country: that one pays so much to go in Members', rather less for the club enclosure and less still for the 'Silver Ring'. Of course this does not take into account the mysterious areas whose doors are not opened by the flourish of a credit card, such as the Royal Enclosure at Ascot and the Jockey Club Rooms. In the first half of the nineteenth century, the impregnable parts of Newmarket racecourse were far greater; but there was the beginning of a sense that this might also be a place for other people, those who did not belong to the world of the sporting gentleman. In a way, though, racing was more honest when it did not make these efforts to embrace what it still clearly regarded as *hoi polloi*. The very notion of giving a specified enclosure to the 'ordinary' person emphasised his separation from those who were at the heart of the sport, running the show, wandering wherever they wanted. It is often said that race meetings are egalitarian: the lowliest punter can rub shoulders with a duke, goes the cry! Up to a point, Lord Bentinck.

Where Bentinck's reforms really did take effect were in his enforcement of better conduct by race officials. This, more than anything, was a way of making the sport less remote and less impenetrable. Incidentally, they also made it more centralised, as these were Jockey Club rules that came out of Newmarket and applied, in theory at least, to every racecourse.

Bentinck tackled, for example, the terrible delays during meetings, by fining clerks of the course ten shillings for every minute that a race went off late. Horses had to be saddled in a specific place, whereas before this had happened anywhere at all, so on big race days jockeys were often unable to find their mounts. Each horse was numbered on the racecard and a number board was displayed. Although this was not compulsory, horses were paraded before a race. Weighing in and out was subjected to more intense scrutiny, so that the scales could no longer be rigged. The tradition was ended of owners giving judges a present after a ruling had been made in their favour; and, perhaps most important of all, races were no longer to be started by some corrupt incompetent squawking the word 'go' (if he was able – on one magnificent occasion at Goodwood, the starter suffered from a stammer). From the 1840s onwards, until the introduction of the starting gate some fifty years later, the off was signified by the drop of a flag, held by a man – sometimes Lord George himself – standing in front of the field, in full view of every jockey.

All of this went a good way towards cleaning up some of racing's more glaring irregularities, but that was a hell of a job, because in the first half of the nineteenth century lawlessness had a real hold on the sport. The notion of integrity was so tarnished as to be almost invisible in this murky atmosphere. Almost every running of a classic race had its tale of nobbling or bribery to tell. Gambling – which, like racing itself, was becoming 'democratised' – was out of control. 'What had been more of a pastime among owners,' wrote the racing commentator known as 'The Druid', 'degenerated into a science.'

Around the start of the nineteenth century, the 'legs' who had previously taken the bets at racecourses began to evolve – if that is the term – into bookmakers. Whereas 'legs' had laid just one horse in a race, bookmakers – in their infinite sophistication – would make a 'book' of prices for the whole field. And, as their activities developed, so they became ever more powerful and omnipresent. Men like the Bland brothers (suspected of being behind the Dan Dawson poisoning affair), Robert Ridsdale, 'Crutch' Robinson, 'Ludlow' Bond, Joe and 'Facetious' Jemmy – were silly names of this kind supposed to make the species more lovable? – began to be regular fixtures at the big meetings. Their presence was felt elsewhere too.

Since 1780, the bloodstock auctioneers Tattersalls – which was then based on a plot of land at Hyde Park Corner, later to become part of Belgravia[4] – had provided Jockey Club members with a subscription room – actually the laundry in Richard Tattersall's own house. Here bets of a private, gentlemanly kind could be made.[5] However, in 1815 the new, larger Subscription Rooms were opened, as much as anything to separate the respectable horse breeders from the gamblers, who were increasing both in number and in unattractiveness. Within these expanded Rooms, the new breed of bookmakers formed themselves into a sort of union: a collective group known as the Ring which, by 1856, had 400 members.

Tattersalls was unaffected by the legal restrictions on gambling, being a 'club' which could only be used by members (of which there were around 350 in the 1840s, paying two guineas a year for the privilege of losing infinitely more). And it was there, in the Subscription Rooms, every Monday morning, that the hour of reckoning arrived. Debts run up during the previous week's racing were paid: a grim business. A painting from 1835, James Pollard's *Settling Day at Tattersall's*, shows the members of the Ring sitting like pashas at tables under the verandah, outside the rooms, while everyone else wanders around – no doubt feeling very manly and important, but looking rather the opposite – giving and receiving bills. Sometimes this could take the whole day. In 1816, after Prince Leopold's Derby win, the settling amounted to around £300,000. Twenty years later, after the glorious victory of Bay Middleton:

> hushed voices at Tattersall's . . . buzzed with rumours concerning a nobleman who, it was known, would have to face a heavy Settling Day on the 24th May. The Hon.

---

[4] A small triangle of ground within Tattersalls – by what was then known as the Knight's Bridge – was left undisturbed for many years, as legend held it to have been a burial site for victims of the 1665 plague.

[5] This function is remembered in the Tattersalls Ring – 'Tatts' – which still exists on every racecourse.

Berkeley Craven, a member of the Jockey Club, well liked and respected, was one of the gay crowd on the Downs who did not believe in the merits of the Derby favourite. He laid against him heavily and, after the race was over, returned to his house in Connaught Terrace, flung himself on a sofa, and later shot himself with a duelling pistol. His liabilities, about £8,000, were trifling. His friends would have paid them, had they known.[6]

There was something splendid about this: pitiful he may have been, but Berkeley Craven was through and through a gentleman. In this sense he represented a dying breed. For, by the time of the 'filthy forties' – as racing's most ignoble decade was known – the notion of a code of honour in gambling, as maniacally upheld by men like Charles James Fox, was laughed to scorn. Now, it seemed, there was no dishonour in dishonour and men defaulted shamelessly. On one occasion, Lord Bentinck was dining at his club when he saw such a culprit at a nearby table, and called for the man's bill: 'Before Captain —— —— orders such expensive dinners,' he announced to the room, 'he should pay his debts of honour.' This was appallingly rude, of course, and typical bitchy Bentinck, but in a sense one can see his point, for something had to be done about the disdain with which gamblers were treating their obligations. After all, Bentinck had paid Osbaldeston his £400, however much he had tried not to. 'What a humbug it all is,' wrote Charles Greville, referring to his cousin's crusade on behalf of racing, 'and if everybody knew all that I know of his tricks and artifices, what a rogue he would be thought. And yet, strange to say, I am persuaded he would not commit for anything on earth a clear undoubted act of dishonesty. He has made for himself a peculiar code of morality and honour, and what he has done, he thinks he has a right to do . . .'

And, in 1844, Bentinck had his finest hour. This was the year of perhaps the most intensely corrupt race ever run: the Derby won by Running Rein.

* * *

---

[6] From Vincent Orchard's *Tattersalls*.

First things first. The 1844 Derby winner was in fact a four-year-old horse named Maccabaeus. His owner, a respectable man named Wood, had run his colt at Epsom in all good faith, believing him to be the three-year-old Running Rein; the horse that he had, as he thought, bought from a man called Abraham Levi Goodman. This low-lifer, who was in fact a fairly successful owner, had had, in 1841, the idea of buying a yearling and a foal, with a view to eventually passing the first off as the second. To this end he dyed Maccabaeus' legs with stuff bought from a hairdresser near Regent Street.

The switch was first made in 1843 – when Maccabaeus was described by a journalist as 'the forwardest two-year-old I have ever seen' – and suspicions were instantly aroused, hardly surprisingly in the dubious climate of the time. By the time it came to examine the horse, however, Goodman had swapped him back for Running Rein. The hour of judgement had been postponed and, so Goodman must have thought, when he sold Maccabaeus to Mr Wood under the name of Running Rein, averted altogether. Off he went to back the horse for the Derby.

In May, when the Derby was then run, and when some three-year-olds have barely reached their real birth date (although of course they are assumed, for the sake of convenience, to have been born on 1 January[7]), they have almost no chance whatsoever against a four-year-old. Maccabaeus duly won the Derby. However, Lord Bentinck had had his eye on the horse since the previous season, and had in fact been waiting to pounce since the time of the Two Thousand Guineas, in which he had expected Maccabaeus to run. Sleuth-like, he had been amassing evidence, and had even tracked down the hairdresser – Mr Rossi – who had sold Goodman the dye with which Maccabaeus' legs were painted. So why did Bentinck wait until *after* the event, when presumably the horse's teeth could have been examined, and his age proved, before the start of the Derby? Perhaps because – like Sir Charles Bunbury – Bentinck knew the value of a real splash. So much more impressive to make an

---

[7] In fact 1 May was then the official thoroughbred birthday; the rule changed in 1858.

example of the actual, rather than the intended, Derby winner. After all, the Goodman dodge had been tried before, in 1832, 1833 and 1840; these Derbys were probably all won by four-year-olds, but none of them had been caught. Bentinck did not want this great slippery fish to slip the hook again.

The joke – if that is what it can be called – is that *le faux* Running Rein was not the only over-age horse in the 1844 Derby; in that sense, he can be said to have won on merit. Leander, who had been entered by a pair of dodgy Germans, may well have been as old as six; it was impossible to know, as during the race he was kicked by Maccabaeus in the fetlock and had to be destroyed. He was buried, then dug up again in an attempt to confirm the fraud. However, his head – and teeth – had been taken away.

Nor was this the end of the list of mischiefs practised upon 'the dirtiest Derby in history'. The favourite, The Ugly Buck, was pulled. And the second favourite, Ratan, who belonged to William Crockford, was nobbled – according to a contemporary report, on the morning of the race 'his coat was standing like quills' – and then pulled for good measure by his dreadful jockey, Sam Rogers, who was consequently warned off. Crockford, who had done plenty of this kind of thing in his time, nevertheless met his match in the 1844 Derby. He had backed Ratan heavily, but he had also set his sick heart on winning the classic race once before he died. On the morning of the Oaks, two days later, he was pronounced 'dead of a Derby favourite'. The story is that his friends, not wanting to forfeit his bets, propped him up in his club window so that he could be seen by passers-by; he had been said to resemble a corpse when he was alive, so the ruse may have come off.

Meanwhile, Lord Bentinck was encouraging Colonel Peel – the owner of the runner-up, Orlando (and brother of Sir Robert) – to lodge an objection to 'Running Rein', and to obtain a court order prohibiting Weatherby's from giving up the Derby stakes money until the case had been decided in a legal action. This seems to suggest that Bentinck wanted Peel to go beyond the jurisdiction of the Jockey Club, and bring the full weight of the law to bear upon the criminals – which is what they were – who were manipulating racing so ruthlessly. Of course things were not as straightforward as all that. Like a policeman with a nark, Bentinck used an underworld contact, an ex-bootblack named Harry Hill, to get the evidence he needed in making his case against that same underworld. Purity was not possible. As the judge in the case remarked, 'If gentlemen condescended to race with black-guards, they must condescend to be cheated.' But integrity was still worth the fight, and when Orlando was pronounced the winner of the 1844 Derby,[8] Bentinck was seen to have won his own particular battle.

This is not to say that corruption disappeared – as, incidentally, Abraham Levi Goodman did, very smartly in-deed – and there was a plot to nobble John Gully's Derby favourite, Old England, the very next year. But 1844 did represent a kind of awful peak, after which things could only really go one way. And Bentinck may have thought that he had done enough. In the age of Parliamentary reform, he had reformed racing practice more than perhaps any other man could have done. He had, in addition, won vast amounts of money at gambling, along with gaining two victories in the Two Thousand Guineas, three in the One Thousand Guineas and one in the Oaks. Did he think that there was no more to prove? Was he bored, feeling – like Alexander – that there were no more worlds within the turf to conquer (except, of course, the Derby, the greatest of them all)? At any rate, in his usual peculiar way, he left racing for good in 1846: '. . . apparently in a fit of petulance', as his friend Disraeli was to put it.

There is no real way of knowing what was in Bentinck's pretty head when he sold up his stable one morning, literally over breakfast, to the Honourable Edward Mostyn, who bought the whole lot for £10,000. The ostensible reason was that he did it to pursue his political career. He had been galvanised by the repeal of the Corn Laws, over which he opposed Peel: 'I keep horses in three counties,' he said, 'and

---

[8] The start of the race was painted by John Herring: his work wonderfully conveys the chaotic life that the sport then had. The notorious horses can be picked out by their colours. Leander, in the lead, is green with white sleeves; Ratan, in sixth, white with red cap; Maccabaeus, lying seventh, is – rather ironically – all in white.

they tell me I shall save £1,500 a year by free trade. I don't care for that: what I cannot bear is being *sold*.'

Supported by Disraeli, who at the time needed a posh sponsor, Bentinck became leader of the Protectionist Party, and gave up dinner – along with his horses – in order to stay awake at night during debates. It was somehow typical Bentinck that he was prepared to defend the principle of protectionism with all sincerity, while dismissing as exaggerated the reported realities of the Irish potato famine. At any rate, in 1848 he achieved a success with his resolutions within the Repeal Act, in favour of the colonial interest: 'We have saved the colonies,' he proclaimed, for all the world as if he were back on the threshold of the Jockey Club. 'It is the knell of free trade.'

Yet a few days before this, Disraeli had found Bentinck in the Commons library, in a state of black despair. Surplice, a horse that he had sold to Mostyn two years earlier, had won the Derby: 'All my life I have been waiting for this, and for what have I sacrificed it? You do not know what the Derby is.' The one world left to conquer had been taken by the man to whom Bentinck had ceded his place. Four months later – the week after Surplice won the St Leger, and at a time when he was planning his return to racing – Lord Bentinck was found dead, at the age of forty-six, in a meadow on the Welbeck estate, from 'a spasm of the heart'.

Had he, like Crockford, been propelled at speed towards death by the pain of missing out on his chance at the Derby? Of course this would be dismissed as fanciful (by those who do not know what the Derby is). Yet the character of the man makes it somehow feasible. If he really had sold his horses in some strange, inexplicable tantrum – and the suddenness with which he did it favours this theory – and found someone else reaping the glory that should have been his, this irony would have had an agonising effect upon someone who, like Bentinck, believed that the riches of the world were his to command. And who, indeed, had no sense of irony.

The further irony is that a man of such arrogance should have done so much that was 'democratic' within racing. Bentinck really did live in a world of his own, and in that sense he was supremely suited to racing, which is in its turn a world of its own. Yet Bentinck both did and did not see it in that way. The rest of the world was something that he wanted to keep out, because frankly, like Sir Robert Peel, it didn't know how to behave. At the same time, with his reforms at race meetings, his clarifications and tidyings-up, he was more instrumental than anyone before or since in bringing the rest of the world *in*. Like a lot of fabulously posh people, Bentinck had a loftily philanthropic streak. Perhaps it was all right as long as he was making the rules, and – in the time-honoured manner of the racecourse executive, smiling down from a comfortable box on the heaving, drunken masses below – not actually having to mix with any of the public.

Bentinck was also a pragmatist. After the death of the Duchess of Portland, just before the Leger meeting, he wrote to John Kent: 'As my mother will be buried before the races, the event will make no difference to the running of my horses, so take them as before arranged.' Inside that wonderfully romantic appearance was a soul of iron. Disraeli wrote of him that 'he counted his thousands after a great race as a victorious general counts his cannon and his prisoners'. (He was said, however, to be fond of his horses – 'In the stable he would . . . fondle and caress them,' wrote the envious John Kent – and for this one will forgive him anything.)

Yet his attitude to racing was, like Sir Charles Bunbury's, ruthlessly clear-eyed. He saw a future which would not be sustained by the glorious follies of England's gentlemen, and set about preparing for it. Not for him the thundering fog of Newmarket Heath; he was not susceptible to that image. Instead, his legacy was to make race meetings infinitely more accessible, infinitely closer to the spectacle – or, to be accurate, the performance – than they are today. The thing itself – the galloping horse on the Heath – was becoming ever more obscured from view.

This, of course, is an argument that would continue to rage for the rest of the century, and that rages still: how far can modernisation be taken in a sport whose strength derives, in every possible sense, from its past? It is like modernising the Royal Family: after a certain point, it becomes clear that a truly 'modern' version (whatever that means) would render the whole thing completely meaningless – which is perhaps what the real modernisers want.

Meanwhile the nineteenth-century 'democratisation' of racing, which was beginning to take effect, was producing its inevitable, unlovely consequences. This is not snobbery. It is simple acceptance of the fact that a gambling sport plus people trying to make money out of it – as opposed to people who didn't need to do so – equals trouble. Richard Tattersall said as much to the Special Committee in 1844, when he spoke of the 'little tradesmen' who approached him, begging for membership of the Subscription Rooms: 'and I have written to them that I should not let them in. My Advice is, if they have a little Money, to keep it; not to engage in Betting. Those are the Sort of People who are ruined; they have an Itching for it . . .'

Of no one was this truer than William Palmer – a doctor, rather than a little tradesman – although he was a person so singular that no advice could possibly have taken account of him. Known as the 'Rugeley Poisoner', Palmer was in the Orwellian tradition of great eccentric English murderers, a pillar of the community who owed money to a bevy of loan sharks, a respectable surgeon with a smile on his face and a bottle of strychnia in his pocket. He was also the supreme example of someone seduced, for all the wrong reasons, by the world of racing. Once in it, the only way he could keep himself there was by murder; although mad as a hatter, he was at the same time killing for very precise motives of gain.

During the 1850s, Palmer turned, with awe-inspiring abandon, to owning horses. In the normal way, he gambled completely beyond his means, at first with great success. The extent to which he was involved with the sport now seems truly incredible. After all, the average doctor nowadays would be hard put to afford half a fetlock in a thoroughbred; but this terrible man actually owned the favourite for the 1854 Oaks, Nettle, whom he had bought with part of the £13,000 life insurance obtained from the poisoning of his wife. Murder, obviously, can put one right up there with the *richissime*. In the Oaks itself, however, Nettle fell and her jockey broke his leg. The possibility arises that Palmer's trusty bottle of strychnia was also used on the horse – or even her rider – as the betting on her went suspiciously haywire the night before.

At the start, Palmer seems to have got along in racing on luck and skill. In 1851, for example, he won a £900 race at Warwick, together with £6,000 in bets. The problem came, as it inevitably does, when he had a few losses and began chasing money: backing other people's horses, running his own too often, coveting animals that were out of his league, borrowing from the wrong people. In 1853, he had a great coup when he won the Chester Cup – the finish had looked like a dead heat, which must have caused Dr Death some anguish – and took £15,000 in stakes and bets. However, he was already hugely in debt, and caught in the inescapable trap of raising cash on bills with money-lenders. In 1854 he discounted a £2,000 bill with a man named Padwick (of whom more later), having forged his mother's name as acceptor. He had also forged bills with a Mr Pratt, whom he owed £11,500 by the end of 1855.

Like Emma Bovary, Palmer used poison as a way out of the usurer's clutches; unlike her, he used it on other people. He insured his brother's life for £80,000 and – almost certainly – polished him off. Unfortunately the company made difficulties about paying the money, which meant another murder – that of a racing 'friend' of Palmer's named John Cook. Poisoner and victim had gone, most companionably, to watch Palmer's mare, Polestar, win the 1855 Shrewsbury Handicap. Cook won £2,050 on the race, which sealed his fate. Seeing a way to get his hands on some winnings, albeit not his own, Palmer then poisoned Cook in a Shrewsbury hotel, and applied to Tattersalls to collect the money. With it he intended to pay off Pratt, but he never got that far. The game was up.

Palmer was arrested and tried at the Old Bailey in 1856. The case was relayed in complete and sombre detail by *The Times*, which described how 'at a very early hour every entrance to the court was beseiged by persons of respectable appearance'. Among those desperate to watch proceedings were the Earl of Derby, Earl Grey, General Peel, Lord Lucan(!) and the Duke of Wellington. The trial was very long but the jury's deliberation very short. Palmer was, of course, convicted and – as he had more or less asked to be, by his antics – was hanged outside Stafford prison.

Palmer was born in around 1824. Had he been born more than twenty years earlier, he might still have been poisoning people for one reason or another. He seems to have enjoyed it (he may have murdered at least ten times) and quite possibly its proceeds would have funded some sort of gambling, which he also enjoyed. But he would not, before the middle decades of the nineteenth century, have been murdering in order to buy a filly good enough to win the Oaks. That possibility would not have occurred within the mind of a Staffordshire surgeon, however singular his personality. That world was then impenetrable. But Palmer, in his strange and doomed way, got into it, so much so that after his execution one of his seventeen horses was bought by the Royal Stud – a wonderfully robust irony. The surprise is that no contemporary commentators seem to have pondered this, to have lamented the effect of turf pursuits upon those who could not afford them. A Victorian homily on the Medical Man who fell from Grace at Tattersalls might have been just the thing, what with the prevailing climate within racing at the time. But no. What is sure, though, is that the case would never have become such a *cause célèbre*, especially among the 'decently dressed' set who went to watch Palmer die, had it not been for the added thrill of the racing connection. Then, as now, society was really rather stultified and bored, and at such times the image conjured by the sport – of daring, of loucheness, of fate boldly tempted to do its worst – can create one hell of a frisson within the newspaper-reading public.

By this time, the Jockey Club was in the hands of Admiral Rous, who was neither daring nor louche, and this was all to the good. After the death of Bentinck, there had been a hiatus of around ten years before his successor took control, which was dangerous, as it meant that all the good done by *l'affaire* Maccabaeus could have been dissipated. The growth of the railways[9] ('facilitating the movement of indolent roughs') and a general rise in income in the 1840s meant that there was a

---

[9] A race train first went to Newmarket in 1848. The line proper was opened in 1851.

growing public appetite for racing, as well as for gambling, for which there was apparently always an appetite. And so a load of nasty little race meetings started up at this time. Between 1845 and 1869, 186 of them were founded. Just as greyhound stadia would do, when the sport began in 1926, these new racetracks sprang up in the environs of cities, so that the working man could get to them easily. However, the working man who went dog racing before the Second World War was a good deal better behaved than the one who went to the horses before the Crimean. Frankly, one would have preferred William Palmer.

Tracks like Harrow, Kingsbury, West Drayton, Croydon and Bromley were absolutely riotous, resembling nothing so much as Millwall football ground and attracting the same type of person (it is hard to know whether it is a comfort or not, realising that hooliganism is a part of the human condition rather than a function of modern life). The point of going racing then was to get drunk – these meetings were often sponsored by publicans, so imagine the jolly free-for-all that resulted – and then to make trouble. Much as footballers are barracked nowadays, and referees threatened with lynch mobs, so jockeys in the mid-nineteenth century were liable to be confronted by nutters wielding ripped-up iron railings. That was just tough, for a lot of those little men were probably no better than the London low-lifers baying for their blood. What is unbearable is to think of the thoroughbred horse amongst all this, terrified and sweating and frothing white at the neck. He has always been too good for most of the people who watch him.

Eventually something had to be done about these race-tracks and, in 1879, the Metropolitan Racecourse Bill prohibited racing within a radius of fifteen miles of London.[10] However, they had effectively been put out of business three years earlier when the Jockey Club cunningly stipulated a minimum figure for prize money, way beyond their means. By the 1870s, only 43 of the 186 new race meetings still survived. Another enemy shot down in flames.

---

[10] This law no longer being in force, there are now plans to open a racecourse on the east side of the city. The last 'London' track was Alexandra Park, closed in 1970.

It must be said that at this time the forces of democracy were not exactly marching across Newmarket Heath waving a banner. What went on at other racecourses was their business; perhaps the poor things needed the money. Actually Newmarket could have done with some money itself, as during the reign (no other word for it) of Bentinck, revenue from Jockey Club lands came to only £3,000 a year. However – like the man himself – the place retained its noble impregnability. So it did during the reign of man who followed him: the 'Third Dictator of the Turf', the Lord High Admiral himself, Henry Rous. Rous got the land revenues up to £18,000 a year at the time of his death in 1877, as much as anything through an increase in the number of horses being trained in Newmarket – a Heath Tax of one guinea per horse was first levied in 1819, and now stands at £75 a year. He did not, however, make any money by welcoming new faces to the racecourse. Magnificent creature that he was, Rous 'resolutely set himself to keep the Newmarket meetings as select as possible, and his mode of procedure certainly proved thoroughly effective'. This, from an article written in 1895 for *Racing Illustrated*, gives a wonderful feel of what the place would have been like during the middle years of the century, when it was gleefully keeping itself free from the taint of populism.

Occasionally an unwary stranger would pay a chance visit to a Newmarket meeting, and this was the sort of experience that awaited him. On consulting his card he would discover that the first race finished at the Rowley Mile Post, and this involved a walk of nearly two miles – a considerable portion of it uphill – from the railway station. The second would end at the Top of the Town, which meant that he must retrace his steps for nearly a mile ... and so on through the card. If the visitor's pedestrian powers were only of an average quality, he probably remained quietly at one particular spot, and resigned himself, with more or less calmness, to missing about half the day's sport. If, on the other hand, he happened to be an athlete, he would settle down to his work with the grim determination of seeing everything, and would accomplish it by putting in ten miles at what the touts – we apologise, the 'men of observation', but we would call them touts in those days – would describe as a 'nice useful pace'.

In either case the stranger's first visit to headquarters was almost invariably his last, and the Admiral's little scheme to keep his beloved Heath free from invasion by the multitude proved completely successful.

This wicked writer – whom, when one thinks about those terrible afternoons spent shoving through crowds striving for a glimpse of a horse's tail, one cannot help but understand and adore – goes on:

Given fine weather, and a handy, well broken hack [which of course the Common Man did not have] and the brisk canters over the glorious Heath, coupled with the backing of a winner or two at decent prices, made up a day's enjoyment that could scarcely be beaten if you travelled all over the world in search of it. There was, however, a reverse side to the picture. With the exception of a refreshment marquee or two, and that funny little stand at the Top of the Town, there was not an atom of shelter of any sort, and, when rain does fall on Newmarket Heath, it always seems to come down with more persistence, and to soak you more thoroughly, than in any other spot in England . . .

Englishmen, however, are no feather-bed sports-men . . .

And there it is. That was what Rous inherited, and what he assiduously preserved, until very nearly the end of his life.

Admiral Rous was not quite in the mould of Bentinck – indeed, who was? – being less beautiful, less posh and more in something like the real world. Rous descended upon those who sinned against the integrity of racing, but not from so great a height. He was not an innovator, as Bentinck had been. But nor was he a hypocrite. Although not against gambling as such, which he recognised as essential to the funding of racing, Rous did not really go in for it, and thus was not applying different rules to himself from those he applied to others. He was, in fact, open to a fault. He thought gambling to excess was detrimental to the health of all concerned, including racing itself, and said so (one of his many letters to *The Times* stated that anyone winning over £30,000 on a race should forfeit it, which Bentinck wouldn't have been very happy about). He had a very low opinion of jockeys, and said so ('Any man who follows the advice of his jockey is sure to be ruined'). He loathed smoking, and said that too ('a vile and pernicious weed'). He was, frankly, a bit of an old sod; but he was also a staunch and stalwart person, unimpeachable in all the right ways, and – like Bentinck – he was an embodiment of the past at a time when racing was moving towards a sometimes alarming future. For this reason, if for none other, he was invaluable.

Born in 1795, brother of the second Earl of Stradbroke, Rous' career in the Navy ended in extraordinary circumstances when he got stuck off the coast of Labrador in 1835. He sailed the 1,500 miles home in twenty days, in a ship with a split rudder and a leak that made two feet of water every hour. This was the stamp of the man, but the Admiralty, whose behaviour towards him made the Jockey Club seem as down-to-earth and matey as the Wheeltappers' and Shunters', received him with a court-martial. He was exonerated, of course, but without warmth. The next year, Rous left the Navy.

He turned his abilities to the handicapping of horses, for which his thoroughness and innate incorruptibility fitted him well, and in 1850 drew up the definitive weight-for-age scale which is still, pretty well, in use today. When he went deaf, he was perfectly happy because he was working out weights all the time in his head. Late in life he was to say: 'It's a very odd thing, I lose my way going from the Turf Club' (in Grafton Street) 'to my house in Berkeley Square, but *I can still handicap.*' He famously handicapped the 1851 match – one of the last of its kind – between the two previous Derby winners, The Flying Dutchman (1849) and Voltigeur (1850). Carrying eight and a half pounds more, a weight which Rous had allotted after much pondering, the older horse won by half a length – a triumph of handicapping.

Rous was a constant presence on the Heath, watching the gallops – which were then an arena for public trials – to see if a horse was being pulled with a view to getting a good weight. Yet despite his shrewdness he could, like many of his kind, be oddly daft. For example, he sent someone out to exercise his hack every morning, and apparently had no idea that this man was clocking all that went on, then touting the information, until the trainer Charlie Blanton said: 'Admiral, if that old horse of yours could talk, he might tell you every trial there's been on the Heath for the last three months.'

In a strange way, though, that combination of suspiciousness and naïvety was what made Rous so perfect for his job. Over-cynicism is as destructive a force as its opposite, within those who work in racing. Rous really cared about integrity; that would be impossible if one didn't believe that it existed.

Rous became a symbol of the nineteenth-century Newmarket man, in a way that the more fey, metropolitan Bentinck had never been (he may indeed have lived on the High Street, close to The Avenue, in a house on a site now occupied – with supreme inappropriateness – by the Pegasus nightclub). Rous was a very Victorian figure, with his sternly patriarchal appearance, his profound self-assurance, his belief in standards and work and reliability, his invisible wife. And he seemed to live for Newmarket. The trainer William Day described his presence at the racecourse – in the mid-nineteenth century, it was a fixture as familiar as the Devil's Dyke – and unconsciously gives a sense of how much it would have been missed. 'His bold and manly form, erect and stately to the last, in a shooting or pea jacket, wearing black boots or leggings of the same colour, with dog-whip in hand, ready for mounting his old bay horse for the course, no matter what the weather might be, was an imposing sight. Before the start he would take his position close to the 'bushes', where he became like an equestrian statue, silent and motionless, with the reins resting on the neck of his horse . . .'

After the febrile excitements of the past decades, there must have been something very welcome about Rous' side-whiskered stolidity. Yet the greatest excitement of all was still to come.

* * *

The history of racing is composed of moments: fleeting, imperishable. The moment when Escape cruised past the Beacon Course post with five horses floundering behind him; the moment when Eclipse suddenly kicked free of his opponents on Epsom Downs; the moment when Maccabaeus cantered blithely – he didn't know that he was four, after all; he was just having an easy race – up to the line. These events are now so familiar, so legendary, that it is hard to realise that they did, indeed, happen in real time; that there was a moment when the hooves and shouts could be heard, when excitement quickened amongst the spectators like flames, when *no one knew what was going to happen next*. Hard, too, to realise that these moments – glimpsed, barely grasped, and gone for ever – can support the mythical power that devolves upon them. But this is the central, irreducible paradox of racing, this tug between the ephemeral and the enduring, which gives to the sport its remote and sometimes painful beauty.

In May 1867, there was a moment that formed the climax to one of racing's most extraordinary stories. If Hermit hadn't won the Derby that year, three lives would have been different, and a rich pattern of ironies would have disintegrated. But, with the sublime unconsciousness of the thoroughbred, he passed the post in front, creating a moment that bore a vast and heavy weight of consequence, and drawing the threads of the story together in a way that no dramatist would have dared.

Watching him do it was a racing public galvanised, as rarely before, by the knowledge of what depended on this victory. And two men above all would be affected by it: Hermit's owner, Henry Chaplin, and Chaplin's former friend, Lord Harry Hastings.

These two were close in age – Chaplin, born in 1841, was the elder by a year – and, from the first, their lives had run along similar courses which, three years before this strangest of Derbys, became thorny and intertwined. Both Chaplin and Hastings inherited large estates in their youth: Chaplin at Blankney Hall, Lincolnshire at the age of eighteen, Hastings at Donington Hall in Leicestershire at nine. Both attended Christ Church, where they behaved according to an ironic pronouncement by Thackeray: 'English gentlemen get up such a prodigious quantity of knowledge in their early life, that they leave off reading soon after they begin to shave.'[11] Chaplin spent his whole time riding to hounds and was frequently before Dean Liddell (father of Alice) for wearing hunting boots beneath his surplice in Cathedral, while Hastings learned how to set himself up for a day's inanition with a breakfast of mackerel fried in gin.

Afterwards, both plunged into racing with all the uncontrolled fervour of King John guzzling a bowl of lampreys. Chaplin caused deliciously fearful shock waves – as a big new buyer always does – when in 1865 he paid 11,000 guineas, then a truly enormous sum, for two colts, Broomielaw and Breadalbane. Although exquisitely bred, neither really repaid what had been spent on them, which merely added to everyone's excitement. Broomielaw, who had been fostered by a cart-mare when his dam died, developed a terrible temper; Breadalbane was 'done with, defeated, disgraced', when he finished eleventh in the 1865 Two Thousand Guineas behind the great French horse, Gladiateur ('the avenger of Waterloo').[12]

The question people were whispering was: had Chaplin spent so heedlessly on these two in order to forget his broken heart? The previous summer, he had fallen in love with a dinky-looking little girl named Lady Florence Paget, daughter of the Marquis of Anglesey, one of those demure types that the Victorian era – which was now at its height – so admired. 'A sugar Aphrodite,' as John Fowles described the genre in *The French Lieutenant's Woman*, 'risen from a bed of white linen.' Half London was allegedly in love with Lady Florence – such feelings are usually contagious – but it was Chaplin who got her. Among those who offered congratulations was the then Prince of Wales, who had known the lucky beau at Oxford.

Just before becoming engaged, Lady Florence had attended Royal Ascot with Lord Hastings, whom she counted among her admirers and who had – a very clever move for a would-be seducer – named a filly after her. After the

---

[11] From *Mr Brown's Letters to his Nephew*.
[12] Gladiateur's tail hangs in the National Horseracing Museum; it was preserved as his most fitting memento, being the view that all other horses had of him.

engagement, Hastings was still hanging around, for example in Chaplin's box at Covent Garden. Chaplin was either very sure of *sa belle petite*, or very dense, because he apparently saw nothing and was as surprised as everyone else at what happened next. It was, indeed, bizarre in the extreme. One Saturday in July, a couple of weeks before the marriage was due to take place, Lady Florence spent the morning twirling around in front of her father in her wedding dress. She then left home in a brougham without a servant – unusual in those days – saying that she wanted to shop for her trousseau. No doubt Lord Anglesey sent her off with a benign wave, little suspecting that the next time he saw her she would be the wife of Lord Hastings. Keeping up the fiction that she had gone out to buy ribbons, she had driven to the Vere Street door of Marshall and Snelgrove – a touch that no one could have invented, this – tittupped daintily through the shop, and met Hastings at the Oxford Street entrance. There, they had piled into a carriage and, no doubt as high on their own daring as if they had just snorted several lines of cocaine, made for St George's, Hanover Square.

Why the woman had gone through this rigmarole, God only knows. Why get engaged to Chaplin in the first place? Of course, Hastings may have taken her by surprise at the last minute, with his proposal. Yet all summer she must have been aware of his interest, so why not hold out for a formal engagement with him? Nowadays, of course, hers is the sort of stunt that people pull regularly in the hope of getting into the papers, but in 1864 it was truly scandalous. One can only assume that Lady Florence got a kick out of playing her two suitors off one another and that, within her coy exterior, there lurked 'certain buried wildnesses' (Fowles again). Nothing else could explain the perverse desire to parade gleefully in her wedding dress an hour before absconding to marry another man.

To such a girl, Harry Hastings would undoubtedly have been more attractive than Henry Chaplin. Physically, neither of the men looks up to much: Chaplin in youth resembles Lewis Carroll and Hastings a defrocked Gerard Manley Hopkins (Lady Florence, incidentally, is like a young and much prettier Bette Davis). But judging from the letters that Chaplin wrote to the woman whom he did, eventually, marry, there was something profoundly unromantic about his character. For example, he asks his wife to let him know her weight, in order that he may buy her a horse of the right size: 'Only ten stone, well! I thought it would have been eleven at least . . .' Hastings, on the other hand, gave off a languid yet intense air which, to a certain type of female – the type who, in 1864, would have been erotically bemused by the paintings of the Pre-Raphaelites – was fatally intriguing. Like Lady Florence, he had a character that was weak, but wilfully so. He had everything, and was always ready to risk it all – for love of her, she no doubt thought, and nothing could have excited her more.

In fact, rather like Sir Charles Bunbury with his equally soul-stirred bride, Hastings seems to have tired pretty quickly of his conquest. A fascinating photograph shows him lounged beside her, detached and enervated and with a look of Henry Wallis' Chatterton, while her pretty little centre-parted head is bent over some embroidery. What was going on between them? She must, inside, have been dismayed by him, for although she had written a very sickly letter to Chaplin explaining the irresistible strength of her feelings for Hastings, he was almost certainly not, for his part, in love with her. The question is whether he had been carried away by the thrill of adventure, or by a more calculated desire to score over Chaplin. To judge by his letters, there is something slightly irritating about Chaplin's cheerful complacence, and an unstable character like Hastings may have longed to disturb it. But Hastings' reasons for doing things are always obscure, an unfathomable mixture of the conscious and the involuntary. It was as though he knew his own weakness and, fascinated and helpless, allowed it free rein. For example, by virtue of his birth he held the position of Master of the Quorn, but he was a disaster – his one aim was to get home from meets as early as possible in order to play cards all afternoon. Certain hunt members wrote scathing little poems about him, and these he had reprinted and circulated, as if he himself believed what they wrote to be the truth and wanted to lacerate himself for it. He no doubt also knew that the tenants and retainers at Donington were bribed to bowl him easy balls on the cricket pitch, so that he could stagger his way to

a few runs in between calling for 'refreshment' breaks every
ten minutes. No wonder he saw in the abduction of Lady
Florence a means to manliness.

And what were Hastings' motives in *l'affaire* Hermit? This
was the next act in the drama.

Hermit, like Escape, was to acquire a huge and unwitting
notoriety and, oddly enough, he shared a name with George,
Prince of Wales' first ever winner. He was bought as a
yearling by Chaplin in 1865, the year of his great post-
Florence splurge, and cost 1,000 guineas – not a silly price,
although it would still have bought an ordinary yearling at the
1999 Tattersalls Autumn Sales in Newmarket. Hermit came
from the Middle Park stud at Eltham, Kent, where Tattersalls
conducted a hugely prestigious annual auction[13] until a
railway line was laid across the paddocks in 1882. From there
the horse went to Bedford Cottage – now Bedford House – on
Newmarket's Bury Road. Here Chaplin had recently put his
horses into the care of a shrewd operator named Captain
James Machell, of whom more later.

It was obvious from the start that Hermit was classy in the
extreme. He was not large – the same height as Eclipse,
which one hundred years on was now the average – but he
had magnificent musculature, particularly in his quarters. As
a yearling he had a four-furlong trial up Bury Hill in which
he gave 35 pounds to a filly, who would subsequently win a
good race early the following spring, and beat her by two
lengths. He ran as a two-year-old at the Newmarket first
Spring Meeting in 1866, where he finished second but showed
great promise, then went on to win five times that year.

So this was a potential Derby winner and was being
gambled on as such. Lord Derby (who may have felt a
proprietorial interest in the race) was then leader of the
Opposition – 'always at Newmarket and Doncaster, when
Europe is in the throes of immense changes', Disraeli said of
him in 1857, which has a familiar ring. At the end of 1866 he
wrote of the bet that he planned to make for the next year's
Derby: '. . . though the offer on my part is rather a rash one,

---

[13] Commemorated in the Middle Park Stakes, a prestigious two-year-old race run, since
1866, at the Newmarket Second October Meeting.

as already there is a rattling favourite in Hermit'. Yet he was not the only one prepared to lay against Chaplin's neat and graceful chestnut. 'Harry,' wrote Lady Florence Hastings, in a tone both appalled and enthralled, 'is betting against Hermit as if he were dead.'

Indeed throughout the winter of 1866 and spring of 1867, Hastings seems to have done very little else. He wagered thousands and thousands against the horse, obsessively taking every opportunity to oppose him. Not that gambling in thousands was unknown to Hastings. He spent uncontrollably, knowing very well the madness of what he was doing: 'money with me oozes away; in fact, it positively melts'. This despite the fact that his marquisate was worth only £20,000 a year – more than enough at the time, of course, but not for someone who lost £79,000 in one night at hazard.

There is a touch of the Lord Lucans about the way in which Hastings gambled – not with the fine, hilarious flourishes of a Colonel Mellish or a George Payne ('it's a pleasure to lose it, by God!') but with a lonelier, grimmer determination. Like Lucan, Hastings was a man whose life was just waiting to be enjoyed, if only the man himself had known how to do it. They were both joyless, both bored, both rather thick; both found a solution to these problems by playing the endgame of gambling what they did not have. For men of this exhaustedly privileged kind, gambling is the one challenge that really rouses them and allows them to escape themselves. Although it will take everything that they have, in a strange way it demands nothing from them.

Lord Hastings began his gambling career on a high, which, of course, is the worst thing that can happen, success being so much more treacherous than failure. In 1866 he won £75,000 when his horse, Lecturer, took the Cesarewitch. This was a coup to rank with the Marshall and Snelgrove abduction and, of course, a similar means to manliness. But the wild urges in Hastings seem to have intensified after the abortive thrill of the elopement. Obviously it didn't satisfy him, and it was as though, knowing that he had done something atrocious, he was determined to compound the sin. Illogically, yet somehow understandably, he continued to treat poor blithe Chaplin as his rival. For example, he was so determined to have a runner in the 1865 Two Thousand

Guineas, in which Breadalbane was the glamorous 'talking horse', that he paid £12,000 for Kangaroo, who was to end his racing career in minor steeplechases. Incidentally this horse was sold to him by Henry Padwick, the money-lender who ten years earlier had been tangled up with Dr Palmer, and who was to do his bit to bring Hastings, in his turn, to death and destruction.

So this backing against Hermit was done from mysterious motives, barely comprehensible – one imagines – to Hastings himself. A book[14] written by Chaplin's daughter, the Marchioness of Londonderry, naturally enough says that it was done out of malice: 'In truth, Hastings' prejudice against Hermit can only be described as malignant . . .' And it may have been that Hastings, subconsciously trying to put himself in the right, was treating Chaplin's horse as the enemy. At the same time, and even more subconsciously, he may have been longing for Hermit to win, so that he could expiate his feelings of guilt – a therapist would be pleased with that one.

Of course, putting aside such delicious psychological speculations, Hastings may simply have believed that the horse would not win the Derby. There were others around with good chances – like Vauban who, heavily backed by Hastings, was to win the Two Thousand Guineas. Hermit had beaten him the previous season, but turning the corner between two and three is a precarious manoeuvre for thoroughbreds. And indeed, ten days before the Derby, it looked very much as though Hastings had made an extremely good bet.

Hermit did not race as a three-year-old before Epsom. His preparation, as orchestrated by Captain Machell, was a very modern one, in the manner of Derby winners from the 1990s like Lammtarra and Shaamit: the idea being – get them ready on the gallops. Accordingly, Hermit had a mile and a half trial alongside the Devil's Dyke, receiving sixteen pounds from the four-year-old with whom he was galloping. For the first mile he looked magnificent. Then suddenly he coughed, blood poured from his nose and he almost collapsed in his stride.

What Chaplin thought, when the news was brought to him, one can only wonder. He must have known that Hastings was

---

[14] *Henry Chaplin: A Memoir.*

backing against Hermit 'as if he were dead', and it would have seemed as if the bet had done its evil work upon the horse, as if Hastings himself had caused the blood to burst out of Hermit's lung. Of course Chaplin's first impulse was to scratch his horse. He was dissuaded on the grounds that Machell stood to lose a good deal of money if Hermit did not at least take his chance; nevertheless Chaplin's jockey, Harry Custance, was released to ride the then Derby favourite, The Rake. Meanwhile, the story of Hermit's broken blood vessel was spreading like a disease through the racing world: out his price went to 100/1. Thus stood the potential fortunes of Chaplin and Hastings, a week before the Derby.

But Hermit, although delicate, was a formidable little beast, and on the Saturday he cantered the reverse way up the Rowley Mile without ill-effect. Off he went to Epsom, where in those days Derby horses had trial gallops before the race: a sensible idea, considering the roller-coaster nature of the course. There Custance rode out on The Rake and, on his way back, caught miraculous sight of Hermit revived like Lazarus, doing a fast canter, pulling like a demon and 'bounding over the ground like a cricket ball'. When The Rake himself bled in a gallop, efforts were made to get Custance back on Hermit; these failed and this was, perhaps, a blessing. Machell – who understood the horse very well, and whose faith in him never wavered – had seen that Hermit 'was in dread of Custance, and often trembled when the jockey approached him'. So the ride went to an inexperienced boy, John Daley, which in the eyes of the racing world did nothing for an already lost cause. No jockey name was written beside Hermit's in the Derby racecard; it was, indeed, as though he was only half-present.

And to see him, wandering round Epsom before the race, it seemed as though he should not have been there at all. Despite the joyous canter over the Downs – which was, after all, only a canter – he looked terrible. His price had come in, but only to 66/1. 'Everyone said what a brute he looked,' wrote Chaplin afterwards. The racing man Sir John Astley, a friend of Chaplin's who, like everyone except clever Captain Machell, had laid heavily against the horse, wrote[15] that he

---

[15] In his memoirs: *Fifty Years of My Life.*

saw Hermit 'walking about (quite a hour before the race) with his coat staring, and a dejected, languid look about him, as if he was more likely to die on the course than to win the great race'. This, before the Derby, when the young thoroughbred gleams with the vitality of hope, of possibility, must have been a strange sight. But then this was a very strange Derby: a race which took place in near-darkness, as snow showers fell on to the course, and which – as with Hermit's participation – seemed as though some mistake had been made and it should not really be happening.

For it is still hard to believe, that victory of Hermit's. Down at the start, jockeys and horses were kept waiting for half an hour, pelted by hailstones, as the thirty entrants attempted to put themselves into some sort of order. Among them, as well as the 6/4 favourite, Vauban, was a colt named Lord Hastings. Again, you couldn't make it up. In the grey light, it was hard to see much of what was happening but, around Tattenham Corner, it was Vauban who appeared poised to pounce then, into the straight, the Guineas third, Marksman, was being shouted the certain winner. Hastings must have been in a state of almost agonising bliss, counting the thousands he had made, the points he had scored. Yet, as if from nowhere, the 'all rose' colours of Chaplin came to challenge, fluttering like the banner of righteousness and revenge. Marksman and Hermit fought it out with such savage bravery that for some minutes it was uncertain which of them had won. Many thought Marksman, but that thinking may have been wishful. Then came the announcement: Mr Henry Chaplin's Hermit, by a neck.

Hastings had the style, if not the soul, of a gentleman, and he was the first to pat the rich red chestnut neck of the horse who had lost him £120,000. 'Hermit fairly broke my heart,' he was to say when he was dying, 'but I never showed it, did I?'

After this climactic moment, the story staggered on to its conclusion. Hastings now owed Chaplin vast amounts of money, and accounts differ as to how the situation was resolved. Chaplin, who could afford to be magnanimous, and would hardly have been human if he hadn't relished the power of patronising Hastings, sent a letter saying that the £120,000 need not be paid on the following Monday. 'I am only sorry that my success should have been so disastrous to you, but certainly nobody in the world, after what had happened, could possibly have foreseen the result of the race.' To this Hastings replied, very much in character, saying: 'I would sooner cut off my hand than ask anybody to do such a thing, but as you say it will not inconvenience you I shall take advantage of your offer for a short time . . . you know as well as I do that however well off a man may be to get £120,000 in 24 hours is rather a hard job. I am just off to Paris as I am sick of being pointed out as a man who has lost such a sum . . .'

After this, most reports say that Hastings sold his Scottish estate to the Marquis of Bute for £300,000, and settled promptly. However, the book by the Marchioness of Londonderry tells a different story, and she has the evidence to prove it. On 22 September – four months after the Derby – Hastings was writing to Chaplin apologising for not having paid up at the start of August. 'But it is not my fault, but my cursed old lawyer . . .'

Now this was very naughty of Hastings, and not gentlemanly at all, as he had won hugely at Royal Ascot that year when two of his horses – Lecturer and Lady Elizabeth – took three races between them. 'The markis – God bless him!' the bookmakers had cried, as Hastings entered the ring – a man amongst men, at last – and left it with pretty well everything he had lost on Hermit. This was Chaplin's money, of course; but Hastings, presumably, couldn't quite bear the thought of giving it to him.

Did he actually think that, if he shilly-shallied for long enough, Chaplin would waive at least part of the debt? Hard to believe – except that he may have known that his wife, the feckless Florence, was in contact with Chaplin, sending him what Lady Londonderry calls 'pathetic little notes' in doll-size, two-inch envelopes. Knowing all too well that she, like her husband, had backed the wrong horse, she was in plaintive but determined pursuit of her ex, and Chaplin, who again was only human, seems to have encouraged her rather. Quite possibly Hastings encouraged her too. Her own motivation seems to have been purely selfish, an understandable desire for attention or reassurance. While the whole post-Hermit episode was being dragged out, Chaplin was putting twee little sums on horses for her: 'I enclose you £43,' she wrote, with hilarious irony, 'which I think is what I owe you.' Yes, he must have been tempted to reply, and could your husband please send me the other £119,957? 'You know the position I am placed in, and that of course in the eyes of the world I am bound to stick to my husband.'

Hastings did pay up in the end. He was not, as the legend has it, ruined by Hermit, of whom it was said 'he destroyed a Marquess, avenged a Commoner, and attained turf immortality' – only the last two of those were strictly true. But what *was* destroyed was the uneasy balance that Hastings had maintained, up until that time, between daring and restraint. After Hermit, his nerve had gone; without nerve, a gambler has nothing; and things very quickly reached a grim conclusion.

This time, it was a horse that did not win when it should have done. Lady Elizabeth, the two-year-old who had shone so brilliantly at Royal Ascot, was regarded as the surest of things in the Middle Park[16] at Newmarket. She was an exquisite filly – 'I take my hat off to that darling,' *Punch* wrote of her. Unfortunately Hastings, helplessly chasing money, had run her far too hard all season; she finished fifth and he lost £50,000 on the race. The history of the sport is so full of these mad, bold bets that the impact inevitably becomes blunted on the reader. Not on Hastings: who, watching as his beautiful filly crumpled, 'turned pale and staggered under the crushing blow. The expression on his face was one of such appalling anguish, that Maria Marchioness of Aylesbury, most kind-hearted of women, by whose carriage he was standing, fearing a painful scene, hastily thrust her betting book into his hand, and, pretending that she was deeply agitated by her own losses, whispered: "Tell me how I stand!" In an instant the Marquis pulled himself together, ran his eye over the book, and in a perfectly calm voice replied: "You have lost £23."'[17]

Poor little Florence must have been in despair; no wonder she had a frantic flirt with Chaplin while staying with a friend

---

[16] Now only for colts, the Middle Park was for both sexes until 1870, when the Cheveley Park Stakes for two-year-old fillies was inaugurated.

[17] From Thormanby's *Kings of the Turf*.

in Maidenhead. Hastings was pawning, selling, mortgaging, borrowing from Henry Padwick – all to try and pay the East End Eumenides hovering inexorably at Tattersalls. But the bookmakers who had cheered him with such gruesome sycophancy, at Royal Ascot in 1867, now hooted him as a defaulter. By the time of the 1868 Derby, Hastings owed them £40,000 and, when the race was over, the means of paying it were forever beyond his reach.

Lady Elizabeth had run for Hastings in the Derby. She had started 7/4 favourite on the strength of her glittering two-year-old career; but the spark had gone out of her and she trailed sadly home, swamped by ungallant colts. Two days after this humiliation, Hastings ran her again in the Oaks. The Epsom crowd booed him for treating his poor, ruined filly in this way, a show of noble spirit that one would be hard put to find at a big race meeting nowadays. Yet Hastings had probably scarcely known what he was doing with Lady Elizabeth, so enmeshed was he by this time in disaster

What he should have done, in fact, was run his other Derby entrant, a colt named The Earl. Yet this fine animal was scratched the night before the race, almost certainly on the orders of Henry Padwick. Padwick had laid against The Earl with almost the same fervour that Hastings had used the year before against Hermit, and he would therefore have lost heavily had the horse won the Derby. The Earl's subsequent career – in Padwick's ownership – suggests that he would have done exactly that, as he beat the actual winner very shortly afterwards. But Hastings, impotent as never before, could do nothing but contemplate the thwarted destiny of himself and his horse.

Admiral Rous, who naturally enough loathed the drooping, unmanly marquis, was nonetheless roused in his defence, for the integrity of racing was under threat from men like Padwick, and *The Times* must be informed. 'Lord Hastings has been shamefully deceived,' wrote the admiral. 'I state that he stood to win £35,000 by The Earl and did not hedge his stake money. Then you will ask, "Why did he scratch him?" What can the poor fly demand from the spider in whose web he is enveloped?' In his reply, Hastings denied that he had scratched The Earl under pressure, saying it was done 'by my express desire and authority' – a pitiful lie, told according to his strange code of honour. Hastings' trainers, the rather dubious Day family whose yard was out at Danebury, were ready to sue Rous for his assertion that Lady Elizabeth had been hidden from her owner when he went to see her gallop: 'If he had seen her move, the bubble would have burst.'

Quite possibly a court hearing would have been the best thing. 'To hush up such a case aggravates it,' declared the *Saturday Review*. It would have exposed to public opprobrium the ghastly Padwick, who was soon to claim another victim in the Duke of Newcastle (and was almost lynched when he brazenly attended a sale at one of the duke's estates). It might have saved Hastings. But in the end Rous backed down – although he had been right in what he had written, he could have employed more discretion – and the scandal fizzled out untidily. Queen Victoria, though, had taken alarmed note of it. She wrote to the Prince of Wales, who was already showing signs of what was to become a *grande passion* for racing: 'Dearest Bertie, Now that Ascot races are approaching, I trust that you will . . . confine your visits to the Races to the two days Tuesday and Thursday . . .'

By the time of the 1868 St Leger, Lord Hastings was getting about on crutches. At the Newmarket First October meeting, the last that he attended, he was 'seated in a basket carriage, with death stamped upon his pinched features and attenuated frame'. Thormanby goes on, in his wonderful way, to describe how Hastings 'watched the beautiful Athena, once his own mare, win a race and, leaving his carriage, stepped up to pat her neck as she was being led to the weighing room. The once magnificent plunger could not now go beyond a pony, and even when he ventured that modest sum he was brutally told by the bookmaker with whom he made the bet, "Now, mind, I'm to be *paid* this."'

It is uncertain what actually killed Hastings at the age of twenty-six; he seems just to have worn out. Without doubt the final blow was delivered by Padwick, but no one except Hastings himself can be blamed for the position into which he had been placed. And he seems, somehow, to have wanted it that way. The embodiment of etiolated aristocracy, he seems to have felt that nothing was worth pursuing except the end of everything. So he stole Lady Florence Paget, knowing that he would be vilified for it; he backed like a madman against Hermit, knowing that he could lose his birthright over it; he raced Lady Elizabeth as if she were a selling plater, knowing that he would destroy his best horse in the process. And, when the end finally came, he had no resistance to it. Lying like a ghost at his home at Donington Hall, he heard the sound of a carriage outside. 'Who is coming?' asked his brother-in-law, who was sitting with him. 'It is only for me,' said Hastings; and died.

For Lady Florence, it was no doubt a relief. She married again, although her new husband, Sir George Chetwynd, also had his troubles and was involved in a court case in 1887, after bringing a libel action against the Earl of Durham. The earl had accused Chetwynd of complicity in corruption at the Newmarket stable – Chetwynd House, now known as Machell Place – where his horses were trained. The outcome was unsatisfactory. Chetwynd was cleared but awarded a farthing in damages, after which he resigned from the Jockey Club.

So what was it about this sweet little woman: was she a bad picker, or was there something tricky and insistent in her character, which impelled her men towards folly? There can be no doubt that Henry Chaplin was well out of it, especially as Florence was still writing coquettishly – 'I am going to bother you again about trying to win me some money' – twenty years after running away from him. But in 1876 he married a kind and sensible woman – another Florence – with whom he seems to have been very happy. 'The charm of Newmarket to me was excitement,' he wrote to her, 'and I have learnt now that there may be, and is, happiness greater than excitement . . .'

Chaplin was, in his way, a squanderer – although the flame of his profligacy did not burn with Hastings' sado-masochistic fire – and when he died, in 1922, it was in a suite of rooms at Londonderry House, his son-in-law's home on Park Lane. Before this, he had lived on at Blankney, to which Hermit retired in 1870. 'Lady Londonderry' – she writes of herself – 'as a child, used frequently to be lifted on to Hermit's back and ride him round his box – a kinder, better-dispositioned animal never breathed.' Harder than ever, reading that, to imagine the moment at Epsom when the horse stuck his neck out in front, and brought one of racing's great stories to its fiercely perfect climax.

Hermit never rediscovered that epiphanic form; but at stud he was a success, breeding 846 winners, including those of five classics. 'Although they are no longer mine, I am always pleased when young Hermits do well,' wrote Chaplin. The horse died, aged twenty-six, in 1890. As was then the custom with celebrated thoroughbreds, his skeleton was preserved, in the Museum of the Royal College of Veterinary Surgeons. Chaplin also had a hoof mounted for use as an inkstand, which he presented to his friend, the Prince of Wales: '. . . dear old Hermit! . . . Thanking you again for your kind remembrance of me and giving me so interesting a souvenir of your "best friend". From yours very sincerely, ALBERT EDWARD.

'P.S. – I shall always take the shoe about with me.'

6 Popularity

'The Matchless Rowley Mile' – 1852–1893

NOSTALGIA IS A FUNCTION of human nature, and nowhere more so than in the world of racing. Whatever it is like now, it is never as good as it was before. Just as many Newmarket racegoers today yearn for the paradise of thirty years ago, when the Members' enclosure was half-empty and no children perched precariously on the paddock railings, so at the end of the seventeenth century they would have lamented the wildly glamorous days of Charles II; at the end of the eighteenth century the days of the Duke of Queensberry, when racing was a private club for sporting gentlemen; and, at the end of the nineteenth, the days of Bentinck, Osbaldeston, Crockford, Rous, Hastings – people who were often dreadful in their various ways, but who disseminated an atmosphere that was felt – after the event, at least – to have been wonderfully rich and enveloping.

These vanished men were what would be called 'characters': a terrible word, which nowadays means anyone who speaks their mind or wears a hat, but in this context means people so lost in the world of racing that, like actors on a stage, they appear to take on the role of playing themselves. This is what racing can do, and why it exerts such an enduring fascination. People nowadays may not particularly take an interest in the sport itself, but they are intrigued by what it represents; as much as anything because it is so alien to the modern world. Life now is all about self, racing is about something beyond the self. It requires one to believe, not in

one's own importance, but in that of the thoroughbred horse. This belief does not have to be stated – indeed, it is best left as a secret known to everyone – and it does not necessarily go with love of the horse, more with an obsession with what he represents. But if one holds the belief, it is impossible to tire of racing; without it, it is impossible ever really to be lost in it; and, ironically, it is precisely that loss of self which brings racing people to such vivid and indestructible life.

Illusory life, in a sense. A man like Lord Hastings was really a pitiable misfit who, had he not launched himself upon racing, would have been dismissed – rather than mythologised – as such. And a man like the 5th Earl of Glasgow would have found no place except within that hermetic sphere. He was an absolute horror, but because he gave himself up to racing he got away with it. Anywhere else he would probably have been put in an institution; but the world of racing allowed him to play the part of himself and, ghastly though that was, be applauded for it.

Like Admiral Rous, Lord Glasgow was a naval man of brusque temper, but unlike him he went in for rudeness because he simply did not know what else to do. In fact he was quite pathetic, standing alone on racecourses in what 'The Druid' describes as 'low shoes a world too wide, white trowsers [sic] in which (he) could conscientiously have danced a hornpipe, and not infrequently in a blue coat with gilt buttons ... The more they jeered at his stud tribes the more he stuck by them. He cared nothing what he spent out of a reputed £60,000 a year ...'

Glasgow was stunningly unsuccessful with his racing – winning only the 1864 Two Thousand Guineas in a fifty-year turf career – although he spent hundreds of thousands in his plodding yet maniacal way. It was hardly surprising that things went so badly for him, as his one aim was to follow his own caprices. He was, for example, the only person ever known to have complained that his horse was too *low* in the handicap ('if you don't put seven pounds more on, Admiral, I'll scratch him this instant'). He priced his stallions out of the market by giving them ridiculously high stud fees, so that no one but himself would use them. He gambled with ponderous aggressiveness: 'He would lean his back ... against a post in the Stand or the Rooms,[1] rubbing his neck with his hand, apparently from some nervous habit, and ready to lay odds almost to millions when once in the vein. It was dangerous for a trainer or a jockey to advise his lordship to put £100 on a horse, as he was sure to multiply the advice by ten, or twenty, or even a hundred'[2] (let the silly old bastard get on with it, might have been the best advice of all). He would change stables continually, coming back to the old ones after he had done the round. He was also a nightmare with jockeys. In 1867 he ran a filly in the One Thousand Guineas who finished last and hopelessly outclassed. Glasgow followed her rider afterwards on his own horse, shouting 'You disobedient young gentleman, did I not tell you to make the running, eh?'

This poor animal had been raced simply as 'a roan filly', as another of Lord Glasgow's quirks was not to name horses until they had won. On one occasion he was persuaded to exercise his wit and register the following with Weatherbys: He-has-a-name; Give-him-a-name; He-isn't-worth-a-name. But usually he did not bother. As Thormanby put it, his horses 'were for the most part shot unnamed'. This is mentioned so casually that one rather blinks over it; yet it is exactly what happened. Lord Glasgow believed that a bad horse was fit for nothing but a bullet. Even if someone offered to buy one of his stock, he still preferred to shoot it. And so, although this pig of a man deserved exactly the disastrous racing career that he got, for their own sake one wishes that his horses had been better.

One Friday evening in 1852, Glasgow announced – like the old show-off that he actually was – that he would run six of his stable in match races at the following day's Houghton Meeting, and shoot every one that did not win. This was in the interim years between the rule of Bentinck and Rous. One likes to think that, had either of them been in charge of the Jockey Club at the time, they would have shamed the earl into submission; it is possible but, what with Glasgow being 'one of us', not certain.

---

[1] This presumably refers to the Subscription Rooms opened in Newmarket in 1843, for a thirty guinea entrance fee, which stood next to the Jockey Club in the building now occupied by the National Horseracing Museum.
[2] From Thormanby's *Kings of the Turf*.

Naturally enough a vast crowd turned up at Newmarket on the Saturday, and a kind of hysterical sentimentality seems to have possessed the spectators before each race – 'Goodbye, my beauty! We've seen the last of you!' – as Lord Glasgow cocked his gun. At least three of the six were regarded as certainly doomed. The almost erotic terror of the public execution gripped the crowd as the horses galloped as fast as they were able – which, in most of their cases, was not very fast – towards the scaffold. People were so galvanised that they even forgot to have a bet. Yet one by one Glasgow's horses eluded their fate: by a short head, by 100 yards after the opponent bolted, by receiving a walkover when the Duke of Bedford – perhaps out of a merciful kindness – chose to pay a forfeit rather than race against the unnamed filly. As the crowd toasted each re-prieved horse, one wonders whether it felt primarily pleasure or disappointment. As for Lord Glasgow, it is impossible to imagine what was going on inside that grim and sorry soul.

But, as was seen in the case of Tregonwell Frampton, racing all too often has a respect for this kind of terrible person. Perhaps it arises from a fear of sentimentality, which is seen as the hallmark of the ignorant outsider: its opposite is, therefore, a sign of know-how. In fact those people who work at racing's heart, who are closest to the horses, are almost always amazingly soft about them, but the idea persists that toughness is somehow 'authentic'. And so although Lord Glasgow would appear to have known almost nothing about racing – indeed, it was hardly possible to be more stupid about it – his behaviour accorded with some mad, purist ideal of the sporting gentleman. Thus 'The Druid': 'With all his foibles he was a glorious old landmark to the Turf, and while he was still among us defying the roll of the ages' (he lasted seventy-seven years, dying in 1869), 'with his quaint garb and blunt speech, some may perchance have felt his presence was a wholesome corrective to the modern spirit, which has lowered the sport of kings into a doubtful trade, a contest for honour into a lust for long odds.'

This is drivel, of course, but the point being made is clear enough. Racing will always seem to have been better in the past than it is in the present, because the past will always, by definition, be closer to the sport's original spirit: to the thing itself. Yet in what way can some wicked old weirdo in a pair of boat-shaped shoes be an embodiment of this spirit? For the simple reason, perhaps, that he *was* so peculiar. Lord Glasgow – like Lord Hastings, even like Bentinck, Bunbury and Rous – behaved in a way which would be impossible outside the world of racing; and which emphasised, therefore, racing's difference from – and superiority to – that less rarefied world beyond the Heath.

The sense that past is better than present comes down to this idea: that as the life outside of racing has progressively loomed, so the thing itself has become ever more cast into shadow. Yet the essential purity of Newmarket was – and remains – untouched, because its bond with the thorough-bred is so deep and impregnable. All the same, Admiral Rous's dream of a Heath eternally populated by sporting gentlemen came to an end, as it had to do, a couple of years before his death in 1877. It was around this time that racecourses began to take on a completely new and different aspect. Lord George Bentinck had seen ahead to this, with his pioneering of the enclosure system. So far-sighted had he been that what he envisaged actually took around thirty years to come into being, but once the principle of gate-money meetings was established, the whole ethos of racegoing was changed forever. This was consolidated by the creation of 'park' courses, which came along to replace the little hives of hooliganism in the London hinterlands: like Sandown, built in 1875 and, although fine and respectable, still alluringly close to the capital. The idea of a racecourse as a part of the landscape, which one visited on horseback and treated as a near-natural phenomenon, was being supplanted by the notion of an arena, a place of entertainment, an open-air *palais*. This, Newmarket was not.

But, as the *Racing Illustrated* essay of the last chapter – that unabashed eulogy to the Rousian paradise lost – put it:

When Sandown Park came out with its £10,000 Eclipse Stakes, and Manchester, Kempton and other places quickly followed suit with other big prizes, it soon became evident that Newmarket must move with the tide, if the headquarters of the turf was to hold its own.

It was not likely that owners would be contented to go on racing for £100 plates, when such rich stakes tempted them elsewhere, and it was speedily apparent that Newmarket, too, must launch out with its 'ten thousand pounders'.

This sort of thing cannot be done without a big revenue, so stands, rings, and enclosures of all sorts sprang up as if by magic, much of the old charm of the place was destroyed ... On the other hand the Jockey Club gained an income which enabled them to establish the Newmarket Stakes, the Princess of Wales' Stakes, the Jockey Club Stakes and other splendid prizes, so that Newmarket was once again in a position to fear no rivalry ...

Not quite true, as the 'London' tracks – Sandown, Kempton, Epsom – were naturally a great draw, and the first two of these, with their superior amenities, were still easier to cope with than Newmarket (Epsom somehow retained its entrancingly untamed quality, right up until the 1990s and the building of a new paddock and stand). But Newmarket had had no choice except to follow where the park courses were leading. Now that this *beau idéal* of convenience had emerged, a new type of racegoer had emerged with it, who had no thought of putting up with discomfort, poor viewing and nasty 'thumbers' to eat. These people had paid their money and, reasonably enough, they wanted something more. Nor were they prepared to get up on a horse and find it for themselves.

Of course it was impossible that the Heath should have continued as it was, in a state of sublime chaos, while the world around it grew ever nearer and ever more regularised. Impossible, too, that the old stand on the Rowley Mile, replaced in 1875, could have lasted much longer. When it was pulled down, it was found that it had only been kept up by the grace of God (of whom, it has been said, one must be a close friend in order to get into the Jockey Club, so perhaps He had indeed lent His support). Most of the bricks in it had been laid lengthways, with a great hollow between the inner and outer shells, filled only by rubble and chalk. For some

years the stand's upper storey had been perceived to be
unsafe – naturally this was the only place from which to get
a decent view – but it was clear, after the event, that the
whole thing could have come toppling down at any moment
on to a raft of Jockey Club heads, which might have given
pleasure to some non-members.

The new stand was the work of Sir John Astley. He was a
friend of God – a steward of the Jockey Club – and also of Henry
Chaplin; his memoirs had described Hermit as looking at death's
door before winning the Derby. Writing about the 1875 project,
which he undertook with gusto at the age of forty-seven, he
recounts hearing the familiar cry of *où sont les hippodromes
d'antan?* – 'Some of the old hands grumble at times, and declare
they "wish the new stand had never been built".' This they may
well do again now that has opened, when another new and
improved grandstand opens on the Rowley Mile.

But, continues Astley, 'as age tells on them, and they find
the expense of a hack, and the discomfort of betting in bad
weather at the old ring opposite the Bushes is saved them,
their growls grow fainter and gradually less; while all truthful
sportsmen must acknowledge, that they can get a good view
of the races from almost any part of the raised ground or
stand.' He triumphantly concludes that 'a finer investment
was never heard of, for the money that passed through my
hands for the buildings and paddocks was only some £20,000,
and now the income from the new stands and paddocks, in
the gross, is about £25,000 per annum . . .'

This, from Astley's memoirs *Fifty Years of My Life*, is
typical stuff. The book has great charm, reading as if written
by a child who spends his evenings drinking brandy and soda
at White's – but boy, is Astley pleased with himself. In fact,
nothing he ever does is wrong. Although he relates endless
stories of failed bets, of his failure to keep his seat in the 1880
General Election, of his failure to hold on to any money, it is
all told with an apparent self-deprecation which is, in fact,
quite the opposite. For example, he claims a filly called Laura
who turns out to be a bleeder, and sells her for £25. After this
she breeds 'thirteen or fourteen foals, five consecutively, of
which all could race . . . Petrarch was sold for £10,000 to Lord
Dupplin . . . That was a bit of bad luck for me, wasn't it? I

guess you will say it was bad judgment as well' (yes) 'but, you must recollect, I had no place then where I could turn a mare out . . .'

His behaviour in *l'affaire* Hermit was also rather clueless, although naturally not portrayed as such. First of all, when Hermit was ante-post favourite, Astley laid against him. Then he ignored Chaplin's offer of 12/1 with which to cover his bet. Then he laid against him again. After the race, he saw Chaplin and 'I could see his good fortune was marred by the knowledge that I had lost, and he then and there said, "Put your losings into your account on Monday to my name, and I will pay them." ' What an old nuisance Astley must have been! getting it wrong three times. He did pay Chaplin back, however, just as soon as he could: this jolly old buffer was no Lord Hastings.

Indeed Astley portrays himself, in his memoirs, as the typical nineteenth-century English sporting gentleman: less carefree than his earlier counterpart, and squirearchic rather than anarchic, but still a person who understands the profound importance of triviality. In February 1855, he makes a bet on Wild Dayrell for the Derby – 'I took 200 to 5 about him, and as he started at even money it was a pretty bet' – then is sent to the Crimea. War and destruction come and go, but the Derby is the Derby, and a certain type of person would want to know the result even if standing in a tumbril on the way to the guillotine: 'Early in June we got the news that Wild Dayrell had won . . . I rode up to the front, and lunched with the 88th Regiment – a very cheery lot of fellows, and one of the best of them was "Crow" Corbett, a very great pal of mine. Poor Corbett was detailed as one of the storming-party, and I think I never saw so sudden a change come over so brave a man. He took me on one side and said: "I feel a strong presentiment that I shall be killed this morning. Will you take care of my Derby winnings when they arrive?" '

Afterwards, Astley organises horse races on Balaclava hill: 'We got up a flat race for the Frenchmen, which was clipping fun . . .' He has a shot at boxing, whippeting, coursing, and even the dreaded cock-fighting, of which Admiral Rous was a fan – all of these were going on in and around Newmarket, in the second half of the nineteenth century. He competes in what he calls 'foot-racing', and wins a £200 match over 100 yards, after which 'those whom I had bet came clustering round me to pay their debts in nasty dirty one pound notes; so I kept my crisp monkey intact'. He even – riding at sixteen stone six – takes part in a £500 match over the Suffolk Stakes course at the July meeting. Running around in training for the race he had, he says, 'got rid of some five or six pounds of fat; but was so thirsty after it, and the pop at luncheon so beguiling, that I don't think I was an ounce lighter the next morning . . .' But his rival was unable to train at all – 'he went wrong in his feet' – and so Astley won the match on his horse, Drumhead, who was trained at Bedford Cottage. 'Good old Drumhead! . . . I once gave him some whisky before he ran at Shrewsbury, and the old boy liked the cordial so well, that he followed me round the paddock in hopes of another suck at the bottle . . . I have often sat on his quarters and smoked my baccy whilst he was lying down in his box.'

The joy that Astley takes in these pleasures – which, for so many people at Newmarket, sometimes seemed more like miseries – is a joy, in its turn, to read about. Yet for all that he seemed the epitome of openness, Astley could be a bit of an old twister. In 1876 he arranged a £200 match race over dinner with Captain Machell (matches still took place as private agreements between gentlemen, but in the wider scheme of the sport they had been supplanted). The deal was that Machell would run his older horse, Oxonian, against Astley's three-year-old home-bred, Brigg Boy, at even weights over the Ditch Mile. 'It was a queer match to make, as the old horse was past his best, and a straight mile at Newmarket was too far for my little horse . . . at last I gave way, and the match was duly drawn out, signed, and sent to Weatherbys.'

The fact that neither horse was likely to shine in the conditions meant that jockeyship could win the day. Astley's usual jockey, George Fordham, was 'unwell'[3] at the time; Machell, meanwhile, had stated over dinner that he intended Fred Archer to ride Oxonian. Fordham and Archer were far

---

[3] Almost certainly Fordham had been indulging in one of his periodic bouts of drunkenness.

superior to any other rider of this period. And so, as Astley casually writes, 'As I strolled home I bethought me it would be judicious to secure Archer'. Then on he goes with his tale, in his usual disingenuous manner: 'So next morning I stowed away my rasher of bacon and drop of tea a bit earlier than usual, and set my cob and cigar going up the Bury Hill. I soon found Archer, whom I thus accosted: "You ain't beholden to Captain Machell, are you?" '

Later that day Astley himself was accosted by Machell. ' "You're a pretty fellow!" "Right!" said I; "I thought so when I looked in the glass this morning . . ." ' A reply which must have made Machell want to call for George Osbaldeston, but he merely reminded Astley that he had had first call on Fred Archer. 'I replied, "I have a vivid recollection of all that passed last night, and undoubtedly you were keen to have Archer; but I had a fancy that way, too, and I have got him – so it's odds on 'pop' against claret for early rising, ain't it . . .?" ' Which was all very droll, of course, and certainly the behaviour of a 'character', but not, perhaps, that of a sporting gentleman, especially as Archer on Brigg Boy won the match by a short neck.

But Astley's chief delight was to gamble on the big Newmarket handicaps. These, he seems to have thought, were proper manly races, offering chances of proper coups, and this is an attitude which persists. Gamblers and gambling trainers still swoon at the thought of the Autumn double. A chance to make money, a chance to be shrewd, a chance to stuff the bookmakers.

The double was inaugurated in 1839 and its two legs, the Cambridgeshire and the Cesarewitch, are indeed a wonderfully robust pair of races, run when the Newmarket air is turning brisk, its trees red-gold and its racegoers to an image of themselves – invigorating, delusive – as wily analysts of form. Originally the Cesarewitch was run first, but in 1968 the races changed places, and the Cambridgeshire was thereafter staged at the first October Meeting. It is run over a straight mile and a furlong, and gets its name from the fact of Newmarket's strange straddling of two counties: Cambridgeshire closely surrounds the racecourse straights. A description of the race, written in 1875, still holds fundamentally true: 'There is no fear of jostling or of disappointment on the matchless Rowley Mile; and when, in the waning light of an October afternoon, forty horses thunder abreast up the Cambridgeshire hill you can see that even if the field was half as large again there would be room and to spare . . .'

The Cesarewitch, now run at the Houghton Meeting, is a true staying race over two and a quarter miles. It starts way out on the Heath, on the empty land behind the Devil's Dyke, where the world of the racecourse seems not to have penetrated. The race was named in honour of the future Russian Emperor Alexander II – the Tsarevich – who visited Newmarket and gave £300 to the Jockey Club, which was used as first prize for the race. This was a primitive form of sponsorship, a nobleman's version of the NGK Spark Plugs Handicap Stakes run, in 1999, on the same day as the Cesarewitch. Alexander continued to give his annual £300 until 1849, when the looming Crimean war made it rather embarrassing to do so. The spirit of racing was not, unfortunately, all-conquering to that extent.

These two Newmarket handicaps were important from the first. In the days before Bentinck clamped down on the practice of offering presents to the racecourse judge, winning owners would give £30 for each leg of the Autumn double and only £10 for the Two Thousand Guineas, whose day of glory had not yet come. Very early in the history of the Cesarewitch – 1841 – the race was won by the future Prime Minister Palmerston, that truly splendid man who confirmed Derby Day as a national holiday (thus giving Parliament the day off also).[4] In 1897 and 1908 the race would be won by Lillie Langtry.

Meanwhile the Cambridgeshire, especially, was not just a big gambling heat but a race of real prestige. The French horse Gladiateur ran in it after winning the 1865 Triple Crown, which is now inconceivable but was then quite logical, as there was nothing else for him to do at the end of the season. He finished unplaced, having given 52 pounds to the winner. Then in 1892 La Flèche, the winner of the fillies'

---

[4] This, of course, was before the disastrous 1995 move of Derby Day from Wednesday to Saturday – not that many of today's po-faced politicians would *want* the day off or, like Churchill, would break off in the middle of a debate to ask: 'Who won?'

Triple Crown (One Thousand Guineas, Oaks, St Leger) went on to win the Cambridgeshire. The race was displaced as a target when others, more suitable to classic horses – like the Champion Stakes, first run at Newmarket in 1877 – were introduced into the season. Yet the Cambridgeshire recently rediscovered something of its former stellar status; by default, however, rather than design. Its 1994 winner, Halling, a three-year-old carrying only eight stone eight, leapt the chasm – narrow, but unfathomably deep – which separates handicaps from Group races, and went on to become dual winner of the Eclipse Stakes, and one of the greatest mile and a quarter horses of the century.

The Cesarewitch, too – which is now often won by horses who nip between the flat and the sticks, like the 1999 winner, Top Cees[5] – was once a draw for classic winners. In 1848, for example, the favourite for the race was Surplice, the horse sold by Lord Bentinck who subsequently won the Derby. Bentinck's chilly but susceptible heart stopped before he could have the pleasure of seeing Surplice beaten in the Cesarewitch, by a horse carrying 4 stone 13 pounds. Twenty years later Blue Gown, who won the Derby for which Lord Hastings' horse, The Earl, had been scratched the night before, was also unplaced in the Cesarewitch. In 1884, however, St Gatien – who had dead-heated for the Derby – gave 38 pounds to the second in the race and won by four lengths.

All of this is now beyond belief: that a horse who had won the greatest mile and a half race in the world – a race whose prestige was at that time unquestioned and absolute – should go on to a contest a handicap, over a distance three-quarters of a mile further, humbly offering bushels of weight to insignificant little horses who could thereby skip past and thumb their nose at the Derby winner. Really, handicaps are a form of communism (although gambled upon in a highly capitalistic manner), which is perhaps a necessary counterbalance to racing's otherwise raging élitism.

Nowadays a classic or Group One winner does not know that communism exists. At least, he may have dabbled

---

[5] The horse at the centre of the 1995 Escape-style scandal had returned with a vengeance.

therein, in his earlier foolish days, but then he will, as Halling did, shake off its taint, put clear blue distance between himself and it, and move in higher circles. Sometimes it works the other way, of course, and a horse who, in his *jeunesse dorée*, has contested a classic, will come tumbling down into the rougher arena of weights and coups and nifty little dodges.

Yet the two worlds are innately separate; and this was true, even one hundred plus years ago. For all that the Autumn double could seduce and conquer horses like Gladiateur and Surplice, it has always signified a different racing ethos – not the pure quest for greatness articulated by the classics but something more earthbound. Big handicaps of this kind were the People's Races. They *involved* people, in a way that the classics can never quite do. A handicap was – is – all about opinions, each of them, in its way, as good as another. There was also the low thrill of possibly seeing a Derby winner get his come-uppance. Admiral Rous – despite his position as Public Handicapper – disliked these races on principle, but at the same time he recognised that there was nothing to be done about them. They were the way forward and, although racing was now being pushed further and faster in this direction than the purists would have wished, pragmatism was always the order of the day.

And it was only someone like Rous who could dismiss the Cambridgeshire and Cesarewitch as 'country handicaps'. The Autumn double was, and remains, very much at the top of the handicap tree; a very upmarket kind of communism. It is also *fun*, which was never really Rous's thing. The machinations which went into preparing horses for these two races were a source of extraordinary, bustling amusement to clever men like Captain Machell, and to slightly silly ones like Sir John Astley. Even when things went wrong – after all, what tends to get forgotten is that the other chap just might be planning a coup as well – they were still hugely, perversely enjoyable. This is Astley in 1876:

I kept Hopbloom for the Autumn Handicaps, and thought he was good enough to win the Cesarewitch at 6 stone 12 pounds, but poor Rossiter rode his head off.

I particularly impressed upon him not to come to the
front till he got the Bushes, but in the Bird Cage,[6] after
the race, little Charles Rayner ('The Weasel') confiden-
tially informed me, that Hopbloom would win the
Cambridgeshire; for, said he, I was on my hack at the
corner of the Ditch, and your horse was leading the lot
four lengths (so much for my orders to Rossiter!)

But Hopbloom, at 40/1, lost the Cambridgeshire – by a neck
– to Rosebery, who had also won the Cesarewitch (and was
owned by a couple of bookmakers, who took around £250,000
on the two races). 'I was riding my hack on the top side of
the course whilst the race was being run, and galloped
parallel with the running horses from the Red Post, halloaing
like a madman "Go it, Hopkins! well done, Hopkins!", and
from where I was – behind the horses – I really thought I had
won but no such luck!' And, for all that Astley must have
been in agony, he was also – like a masochist with a black
leather boot in his face – in a state of peculiar pleasure: riding
and halloaing and suffering with the big boys.

Astley's character was jovial, complacent and energetic,
neither that of a misfit nor a victim. Yet in his way he, like
so many others, was a casualty of racing. 'I think I must have
gone a bit wrong in my head,' he writes of his manic
gambling and spending in 1865. In 1881, he won 64 out of 261
races in which he had either bets, or runners, or both: 'more,
I believe, than was ever won by any man in one year ...
£16,800 in bets and £15,871 in stakes'. But as the story of Lord
Hastings has shown, success of this kind makes no difference
in the end. Astley was still 'cruel hard up ... I continued
spending when I won, and borrowing when I lost'.

The worst blow came in 1867 when he was horribly out of
funds at Goodwood, 'and Satan in the guise of two old
Austrian General Officers ... bid me £3,000 for me pet
Ostregor. Now, I owed old Padwick that very sum ...' If
anyone was Satan, it was that terrible money-lender. Astley
was forced to sell his beloved horse in order to pay him by

---

[6] The private enclosure at the side of the Rowley Mile Course; commemorated in
Birdcage Walk.

the following Monday; three days before which, Ostregor won the Chesterfield Cup and £5,000 for his owner.

> Deary me! How I hated myself, old Padwick, and the Austrian Generals! I got the two old boys together and offered them £1,000 to be off the bargain, but no bet. I then asked Tattersall to go and offer them £2,000 to let me keep my dear old horse, but they replied no money would tempt them; they had bought him for the Emperor of Austria and they must deliver him to their master . . . Good old horse! I had inscribed on that cup (and, though stony broke it reposes still on my sideboard): 'The best-looking, best-tempered, and gamest horse of his day. We shall ne'er see his like again' . . . I paid old 'Paddy' on the Monday, but to me it was the price of blood.

All the same, in 1870 he was living with his wife in Newmarket, having bought for £3,000 (quite a large sum) the pretty red cottage built for the jockey Jem Robinson, which later became Machell Place yard. 'I don't think I ever enjoyed any period of my life so much as those pleasant meetings at Newmarket; for we did the thing "proper".' But it was impossible to keep up the expense, unless Astley were to have abandoned the reason for being in the town in the first place, and eventually – the year is not specified – he is forced to sell 'the nicest little crib in Newmarket', in whose paddock he had buried his hack, Ruskie ('beneath this yer sod lies my poor old quad/He was very fond of me and I of he you see', reads the ludicrously touching plaque on a wall in Machell Place). The jockey Charlie Wood – acquisitive, talented, cunning as a monkey – bought the cottage and built the stables. For Astley, the jolly days were over.

Indeed, his book was written for the simple reason that he had no money. 'Am dead broke, shall have to live at Elsham (home) entirely, like a blooming maggot on a nut.' What he hoped, in fact, was that the sales of his memoirs would enable him to buy a horse good enough to contest the Autumn double, and so start the whole irresistible whirligig up again. Bonkers, of course – but that is what racing does to people.

Although a caricature of the time shows Astley a big and burly Victorian, bearded and side-whiskered, with a cigar screwed into his mouth and feet planted wide and confident on the Newmarket ground, racing had him by the balls right up until the end of his life in 1894 – as surely as it had had the effete Hastings.

In fact, it is hard to find many people who were not, in the end, casualties of the sport. One after another they hurled themselves against that remorseless and alluring Heath – George, Prince of Wales; the Chifney family; Harry Mellish; the Earl of Jersey; Berkeley Craven; William Crockford; Lord Glasgow; Lord Hastings; Henry Chaplin – and, to a greater or lesser extent, they were all forced to concede defeat. Yet still they kept on coming, roused by the thought of what was, to them, the ultimate challenge. There would be more casualties yet before the nineteenth century was out, including the most famous of them all.

At the same time, the Victorian era was having its effect upon Newmarket. After all, men like Rous and Astley were no reprobates, but decent citizens by almost anyone's standards (except perhaps when in the House of Commons; where Rous did nothing, and Astley was best known for making a maiden speech in 1874, in which he stood half way across the floor and called the Irish members 'forty of the most confounded rascals ever seen'). But both men treated racing as a means towards living an active life, rather than as a way of wasting it. True, Astley lost all his money – over and over again – but he compelled others to give in a good cause, such as the Astley Institute for stable lads, which still exists as the New Astley Club ('I collected about £2,500 out of the £3,000 subscribed,' he boasts in his cheery way, 'and was accorded a certain amount of kudos for the nippy way I was always alongside a rich owner as soon as his horse's number was up . . .'). He also engineered a tribute to Rous when, after the admiral's death, Astley raised money with which to build the Rous Memorial cottages on Old Station Road (formerly almshouses and a hospital, now flats for the elderly).

And the town itself was acquiring the look, at least, of respectability. Much of its architecture today comes from this prosperous period: it is not exactly beautiful, indeed often quite the opposite, but it has a solid look which fascinates, perhaps because one is thinking of what racy things might have been going on behind those firm, upstanding brick façades.

Nothing, one hopes, in the case of the churches – All Saints', for example, which was rebuilt in neo-Gothic style in 1877. It stands behind what was once the back end of King James' palace, was originally built in 1536 and was almost certainly used, without irony, by Charles II and his court, who had probably not been to bed beforehand on Saturday night. In its chancel is buried Tregonwell Frampton; and in the dark, eerie little graveyard (the betting shop across the road is a welcome sign of life) lies the jockey Nat Flatman, renowned for honesty, one of whose last intriguing requests was not to be buried in Newmarket cemetery.

This was opened in the 1840s, and stands at what was known as the Top of the Town, opposite Birdcage Walk and the slope down to the Rowley Mile course. It is a big, flat piece of land, unusually open to the wind and rain like most of Newmarket. Yet it has an unadorned dignity, and is moving rather than depressing. Rows of regular white stones commemorate the war dead, including those who – like 'Queenie Kerry, Post Office Employee' – died when the High Street suffered a direct hit in 1941. The far side looks over on to some paddocks; not, then, such a bad place to be laid in for men like Captain Machell (died 1902), although he lies in a more sombre corner, close to the road. Trainers buried in the cemetery include Charles Blanton (d. 1887) of Wroughton House; Mathew Dawson (d. 1898) and Jack Waugh (d. 1999) of Heath House; Martin Gurry (d. 1923) and Harry Wragg (d. 1985) of Abington Place; George Lambton (d. 1945) and Bernard van Cutsem (d. 1975) of Stanley House. There are also jockeys like Jem Robinson (d. 1865), Fred Archer (d. 1886) and Manny Mercer (d. 1959); and, again intriguingly, the wife and daughter of Nat Flatman.

It is the houses, though, that most give off the look of the high Victorian age. There are, for example, those large formal buildings made attractive by the fact that they stand up on the Terrace, that raised piece of ground at the top of High

Street. One of these, No. 121, was the Newmarket home of Lord Lonsdale (as in belt), and No. 125, which is now the office of Tattersalls, was once Terrace House Stables. Until as late as 1968, horses lived in the yard behind that little hill. The land there is now waste ground, giving no clue to its former use. There is something strangely pleasing about the way in which, in this town, history is so omnipresent that it can go almost arrogantly unproclaimed.

On the corner of the High Street and The Avenue is Godolphin House; again, not beautiful, but Arthur Sullivan – of all people – stayed there in 1886 and did a bit of composing (the final part of the *Golden Legend* oratorio). The little Scotch Tea Rooms on the side of the house was, as is obvious from its cavernous old fireplace, the kitchen wing. The Avenue itself, which leads to Tattersalls sales ring, was built as a road to the railway station around the end of the nineteenth century, and is lined with rather grand houses – now mostly inhabited by bloodstock agencies – in the style of those vast red-brick artists' studios, like Leighton House, which stand in London's Holland Park. On the left-hand side of The Avenue was a discreet gate leading to a passage by which the Prince of Wales, the future Edward VII, might gain entrance to the back door of the Jockey Club.

On the High Street itself, inns like the White Hart and the Rutland Arms (whose arched coach entrances are still intact) were a focus of activity. There was also, of course, a continual procession of racehorses, taking their daily possession of the town, stepping out elegantly from yards like Queensberry Lodge, Stockbridge House next door, Park Lodge (still in use, once owned by William Crockford), Ellesmere House and Primrose Cottage (both now demolished to make room for Fred Archer Way and the Rookery shopping centre), and Palace House. The palace itself – which had languished, unwanted and unloved, in royal ownership – was finally sold by Queen Victoria in around 1850. She was not a fan of racing, although it is recorded that she once became very agitated when she thought she had drawn the winner of the Derby in a sweep. Palace House was really far better off in the hands of the Rothschild family. After the sale, much of the original palace and stables had been demolished, which to anyone with any curiosity must be seen as a terrible shame. But Baron Meyer Rothschild, who bought the whole wrecked caboodle in 1867, brought to it his own good fortunes ('follow the Baron!' was an axiom among racegoers) and his immensity of wealth. Palace House was rebuilt as a solid and comfortable family home – a good deal nicer, no doubt, than the royal residence had ever been – and the Rothschild yard, out of which came a stream of wonderful horses carrying blue colours with yellow cap, became one of the most successful of the late nineteenth century.

This was the kind of set-up which helped to strengthen Newmarket. Somewhat unbelievably, its reputation as a training centre had suffered in the early Victorian era, and it was only Derby winners like Hermit who came galloping up to restore it. It had been said that the Heath was too hard on horses; the craze was for the South Downs instead. It is true that, unless kept in good repair, the springy Newmarket turf can be very demanding, and the means of maintaining it must be kept constantly under review. Yet from the 1820s onwards the Heath was in unprecedentedly good condition, thanks to Lord Bentinck's father, the Duke of Portland, who – as a truly conscientious landlord – had put huge amounts of money into improving the land. What had probably happened was that trainers like William Chifney, whose harsh methods had caused a lot of horses to break down, had created the impression that the culprit was not him but the Heath ground. Add to this the inevitable element of cause and effect – people would see that fewer good horses were coming out of Newmarket, so fewer would be sent there – and a 'problem' has arisen. It happens all the time in racing.

Although the problem was pretty well illusory, it had very real consequences in terms of unemployment. This was why the bells of All Saints' rang out in 1863 when the Newmarket-trained Macaroni won the Derby: it seemed like the dawn of a happy new era. A nonsense, really, as nothing about the Heath had changed from the previous year, but that was not the way in which it was seen. Two years later, Gladiateur was also trained in Newmarket to win the Triple Crown, although this was not quite so favourably viewed (Tom Jennings, who looked after the French-based horse, was regarded as a traitor in certain idiotic quarters, and had to hire bodyguards for himself and his charge). Then, two years on again, came Captain Machell and his bold yet tender nursing of Hermit.

And so, from the 1860s onwards the 'reputation' of Newmarket underwent a magical renaissance; illusory, again, but again with real effects, so much so that by the last years of the century the town had reached its apotheosis of popularity. Of course there were successful yards elsewhere – the dubious Days of Danebury, to whom Lord Hastings had given his horses; the astute John Porter at Kingsclere, who was the first trainer used by the Prince of Wales. Nevertheless Newmarket was really starting to fly. Men like Machell, Jennings and Jem Godding of Palace House (who got Macaroni raging fit on the Limekilns gallops) were entrepreneurial types, who took risks and got on with things. They helped to make the Newmarket that we know today. Jennings, for example, set up Phantom House yard in 1857 then, with handsome dark red bricks from his own kiln, built Lagrange Stables across the road and named it in honour of the owner of Gladiateur. When he moved he put his son, Tom junior, in at Phantom, and another little racing dynasty was established.

A burst of good, strong energy was now pushing out of Newmarket, into the roads that led off eastwards from the High Street. Many of the big, important yards which stand there were established around this time. Kremlin House, for example, next door to Phantom, was built in 1874 by a Russian prince, Dmitri Soltykoff, who had arrived in England when the embarrassment of the Crimea was over, and fallen in love with Newmarket. Before Kremlin was used as a yard, the prince's horses were trained at Lagrange, and – writes Thormanby – he 'could sit at his window and watch his beloved mare and foals grazing, and walk from the house into his stables in his slippers'. Heath House, which had been the home of Tregonwell Frampton, was rebuilt in the 1870s, not quite where it now stands but on the site of the Heath Court Hotel, at the foot of the Bury Road.

Bury Road itself has the aspect of a calm, broad, Victorian avenue: steeped in inviolable wealth, shaded with trees, lined with huge, unshowy houses set behind brick and stone. It could be a tasteful part of Hampstead Garden Suburb, except that these houses are mostly yards, there are two pavements – one for people and one for horses – and the road often reeks of dung. The serenely purposeful, quietly imminent atmosphere, too, is a long way from London NW11. There is something wonderfully reassuring about walking along it in the near-silent afternoon, with the Heath beyond and the old railway line running beneath, reading the lapidarian litany of names – Bedford House; Sefton Lodge; Highfield; Shalfleet; Stanley House; Freemason Lodge; Abington Place; Beechhurst; Carlburg; Clarehaven – that punctuate the road until it stretches out again into the wider landscape. Behind those names, carved in stone, the yards stand like bastions of racing's grander past. On an early morning on the Bury Road, when the stable doors open and the strings pass through those wide, proud, unchanging façades, it feels as though nothing much has changed from a century ago.

Of course, for all that they present this smooth collective front to the outsider, every one of these yards has its own complex origins. Sefton Lodge, for example, was built by a M. Lefevre, a Frenchman (for all its Englishness, Newmarket has had its fair share of foreign influence) in the 1870s, then taken over around ten years later by the Duchess of Montrose. And here we have the first – and very rare – example of a female 'character'. The duchess was a great big woman, physically not unlike a heavily maquillé Edward Heath, and known, in more robust circles, as Six Mile Bottom. Having married the Duke of Montrose at eighteen, in 1836, when he died in 1874 she took up with a successful owner named Stirling-Crawfurd, after whose Derby winner, Sefton, the Bury Road yard was presumably named.

The duchess was a good sort, but exhausting; determined, perhaps, to prove that she could be eccentric with the best of the men. Her capriciousness was feminine, as was her almost theatrical use of cosmetics and her eye for a pretty young fellow. But her forthright manner was not, nor was the Homburg hat that she wore pulled over her dyed red hair – nor, at that time, was her profound knowledge of racing. She gave her trainers a terrible time, but at least she usually knew what she was talking about, and for all her bluster it was possible to answer her back in kind. Once she went sailing like a galleon up to her first trainer, Alec Taylor of Manton in Wiltshire, and demanded to know what, if anything, could beat her horse in its race: 'Damned to hell if I know, your Grace,' he said, which she probably loved. Like most bullies, she rarely picked on people of her own size. This perhaps explains why – according to the sporting paper, the *Pink 'Un* – the jockey George Fordham, on being told by her 'to send in his cap and jacket . . . did so instantly, for fear that the Duchess might change her mind'. Later she was to conceive a mad passion for Fred Archer, which was enacted for the London *cognoscenti* in a musical comedy entitled *The Sporting Duchess*. As will be seen, her obsession with having Archer sit on her horses, at least, was to play its part in the tragedy of his life.

In 1883, Stirling-Crawfurd died – or wore out, perhaps. Although five years later the seventy-year-old duchess was to rally and marry a man of twenty-four, she was grief-stricken at first and, Queen Victoria-style, built the Bury Road Church of St Agnes as a memorial to her second husband.[7] It was from here that she dismissed the vicar after he had preached a sermon praying for a good harvest. He should, she said, have known that her St Leger horse would only go on the soft. This was bluster on the Lord Glasgow scale; the duchess was not as mad as all that, and she soon reinstated the man. Certainly she was not mad enough to request that her horses be raised in the handicap. Indeed she had the more usual disease of thinking that they were all carrying far too much weight: 'I see,' she said to the handicapper, 'that you are desirous of riding them yourself' (lucky that *you* are not desirous of riding them, he might have replied).

When the duchess died in 1894, the land on which her Sefton stud had stood was sold, and became Stanley House. This wonderful and extensive yard was, for much of the twentieth century, to be the private stable of the Earls of Derby. At the end of the 1999 season, it stands empty.

Of the other yards on the Bury Road, it is Bedford House – and its surroundings – which has the longest and liveliest

---

[7] The date of the church – 1886 – raises the possibility that the duchess also thought of it as a secret memorial to Fred Archer, who died that year.

history. In the days when Hermit was trained from there for the 1867 Derby, there was little but fields beyond, for that great rush of building was still a few years away. The yard's history is also intricate, indeed complicated to the point of boredom: its name was changed from Bedford Cottage, but then there was another Bedford Cottage which is now Rockfield House; there was also a Bedford Lodge yard next door, which was split in two in the 1930s and became the Highfield and Shalfleet yards; and then, in the middle of it all, there is the Bedford Lodge Hotel, the best in Newmarket, which was originally the house that went with Highfield.

Detail may be all important in the present tense of horse racing, but its past requires one to look more at the essentials. And in the second half of the nineteenth century, what mattered about Bedford *House* – to take its modern name – was that it was the headquarters of Captain James Machell.

He, or at least his shrewdness, was the lure to young men like Henry Chaplin, who had just enough brains to know that they should put their horses into his hands, rather in the way that they would all have used the same tailor or stockbroker. Machell was not actually a nuts and bolts trainer. At the time of Hermit's Derby, the graft was being done by two brothers by the name of Bloss, one of whom slept in the horse's box in the days leading up to the race (for which Chaplin gave him £5,000; the bed was subsequently kept on proud display at the yard). But Machell was a planner, a strategist, and he must have been fairly good at it because he won enough money to buy back his family home in Westmoreland – he was posh, in his brusque way – and a lot of Newmarket property, including what was to become known as Machell Place yard.

In a sense he was a Tregonwell Frampton for the Victorian age, someone who organised for other people while cutting a thick slice off every deal for himself. But whereas Frampton's reputation for cunning is rarely borne out by the facts, with Machell it is a different story: he really did pull off some triumphs. Twenty-six years after Hermit, for example, he overrode the trainer of the magnificent Isinglass, who said that the horse could never be prepared for the Two Thousand Guineas on the then wretchedly dry ground at Newmarket. Machell used his brains, got the horse fit by little short canters – what we would probably now call 'interval training' – which put no strain on his legs, and no doubt won fortunes when Isinglass seized the day on the Rowley Mile. Whatever his motivation may have been is not the point. Horses of that kind deserve that kind of attention. Having created the concept of greatness in the thoroughbred, racing people have a responsibility to that greatness, to make sure that it fulfils itself and – far more than the more craven souls who would have scratched both Isinglass and Hermit – it was Captain Machell who did right by those two.

In fact, everything one reads about Machell creates an image of someone slightly more sensible than everyone else – bolder, too, but then that is not so hard if one knows what one is doing. Yet, as with Frampton, his moral reputation is not particularly good. There are no terrible stories about cruelty to horses; but Machell tends to be portrayed, rather like an upmarket drug-pusher today, as having ruthlessly encouraged the idiots who came to him with hope in their callow eyes and money falling out of every pocket. He knew that 'shrewdness' was a commodity in which they were prepared to invest, and he made them pay for it. A sketch of him from the time emphasises this image. His face, despite a ridiculous walrus moustache, is stern and predatory and, seated on a horse in his bowler hat and Sherlock Holmes cape, he looks impatient to be off and doing business. It is a surprise to learn that he was born in 1838, and was thus hardly any older than the 'boys' whom he was supposedly luring like a perverted uncle into his clutches (and, at least in the case of Chaplin, helping to win them over £100,000).

Certainly there is something unattractive about the idea of those who – like Machell, apparently – get no pleasure from the sport beyond the rather miserly one of scoring points. Although obsessed by racing, they have no love for it. This is impressive to some people, who see it as the ultimate in professionalism, but if the thoroughbred horse, above all things, cannot be seen as romantic then, really, one might as well give up, play the stock market and watch the football.

Of course, we don't know that this was Machell's attitude. Yes, he wanted to run Isinglass and Hermit because he stood to win thousands on them; that does not mean that he didn't take another, more disinterested pleasure in the sight of their victories. Racing cynics are often thwarted romantics, desperately concealing what they feel to be their own vulnerability beneath a carapace of toughness. After all, the worst kind of bookmakers have been seen, faces reddened from the strain of hiding their feelings, after a late-career victory by a Brigadier Gerard or a Desert Orchid.

Nevertheless, racing – especially at that time – did present a huge opportunity for money-making of the least romantic kind. Although the sport had been cleaned up no end from the era of the four-year-old Derby winners, it was still sufficiently robust and unregulated to allow for coups of a monumental kind. These were not necessarily illegal, just sharp in the extreme, and, one might ask, what was the difference between the two? As ever this was dodgy ground. There was an attempt at a decision in the 1887 case of Sir George Chetwynd – second husband to little Lady Florence Hastings – when he was accused of dishonesty by the Earl of Durham, sued and was awarded a farthing in damages. In other words, no decision was really possible. Chetwynd, in cahoots with his jockey Charlie Wood, had turned Chetwynd House (later Machell Place) into a very hot gambling stable indeed. Wood was pulling horses for the benefit of owners and – in the main – for himself. It was the old, old story that everyone has heard a thousand times and pretends that they never want to hear again. All the same, the Earl of Durham was right to draw attention to it, as it had passed that mysterious barrier between what is acceptably spicy and what is downright scandalous. No doubt the shock of the court case pulled everyone up for a time. Wood was warned off and then let back in again, although he was probably too rich to care. In the end, there were reconciliations all round. Life went on.

Chetwynd had started out, in 1870, as one of Machell's 'boys' at Bedford House, but Machell seems not to have given Chetwynd quite what he wanted. In fact Machell has a kind of straightness about him, for all that he was mixed up in things that were by definition crooked. He once accused George Fordham of pulling a horse after losing a huge gamble in a selling race; Fordham, who guarded his reputation like a miniature bulldog, refused ever to ride for Machell again.

Machell complained, 'That damned horse was no good and I lost the best jockey in the world.' He was later to do something similar to Fred Archer, with rather more serious consequences.

So there was nothing especially lovable about Machell, who had a typical tedious gambler's belief that 'fast ones' were being pulled everywhere. He would have suspected someone of being a non-trier in a primary school three-legged race but, it has to be said, in most cases he was probably right to stay alert. How else was he to keep ahead of the game? Look what John Astley did to him, given less than half a chance. He got it wrong with Fordham and Archer – those were bad and important misjudgements – but, on the whole, he treated people according to their deserts. With Henry Chaplin, who was a gentleman, he was at his straight and sensible best. With George Alexander Baird, who was not, he behaved rather less respectfully; as will be seen, with some justification.

Baird was a nightmare. Even the greatest of racing nostalgics would find it hard to dignify him with the name of 'character', for he was nothing of the kind, just a misfit to outrank them all. Where he differed from the others – Hastings, Glasgow – was that they, *au fond*, abided by racing's code of behaviour. Baird wanted to tear this up and throw the pieces over the steps of the Jockey Club. This, of course, was impossible, because it was made of stuff that was both unbreakable and incorporeal; in the end, it was Baird himself who succumbed. An unattractive-looking person, skinny, stooped with a bland and youthful smirk, he was the sort who might well have become a modern day hero. Like the cows in *Cold Comfort Farm*, he was graceless, pointless, feckless and aimless; he was also vastly rich, a terrible show-off, talented at something purely physical and the lover of someone famous. A very sexy combination, nowadays. A century ago, society had slightly better taste.

Baird's problem was very simple: he was *nouveau riche* and he minded about it. His money came from just two generations back, when his poor and clever grandfather took shares in the railway companies whose tracks he had helped to lay. This, at the start of the nineteenth century, was like oil speculation in the 1970s – the wealth just kept on growing. It was invested in mines and Scottish ironworks until, in 1882, around £3,000,000 worth of it – plus £100,000 a year in rents – fell into the hopeless hands of the twenty-one-year-old George Baird.

The Industrial Revolution had built this edifice of prosperity, and it must have seemed as tough as iron itself. Even Baird couldn't quite destroy it, although for the next ten years he did his best; in the end, though, it was that unyielding and virile wealth which did for him. Like Lord Hastings, Baird grew up fatherless and uncontrolled. At Eton, which he took in *en passant*, he once threw a gold watch to the ground, jumped on it and crushed it – a little early sign of wildness. It was not surprising that, after Cambridge, where he did not shine, he should hurl himself into the world of racing; which he did under the name of 'Mr Abington', in order that his trustees should not know what he was up to.

It has been said that Baird was not really interested in owning horses. His passion was for race-riding, which he was taught, at a stinging price, by Fred Archer and in which he did extremely well. In 1889, for example, he rode 61 winners, 48 of them at the expense of professional jockeys, with the second-placed amateur riding just three. This was phenomenal, but then Baird was *not* a 'gentleman' rider. He treated races just as a professional of the most determined kind would have done, riding as if, instead of owning millions, he was trying to earn five guineas for a win (only three, otherwise). He dieted viciously, like all good jockeys, living on fruit and running up £2,000 a year bills from London greengrocers; although, again like many jockeys, he did not stop drinking. Talented though often out of control, in 1882 he was warned off for two years by the Jockey Club, for threatening to put the Earl of Harrington over the rails during a bumper[8] at Birmingham racetrack.

This, in Baird's peculiar mind, seems to have confirmed his own profound, unacknowledged belief that he did not belong to the world in which his money had placed him. From then on, the Jockey Club was the enemy – an attitude

---

[8] A flat race for National Hunt horses. There is a school of thought that says that Baird was set up by Harrington and innocent of this charge. As with Sam Chifney, he may have been caught for all the other accumulated crimes against the spirit of racing.

that one can understand, except that what Baird represented was so very much worse. This, all too often, is the problem with attacking seemingly indefensible entities like the Jockey Club. If it was a choice between George Bentinck or George Baird, then no question that Bentinck was the lesser of two evils.

And the sad joke was that, although Baird affected to despise the racing Establishment, it was all too obvious that he did so because he doubted his ability to hold a position in it ('Never speak disrespectfully of Society, Algernon: Only people who can't get into it do that'). This was why he behaved with such pathetic subversiveness. During his two-year exile, for example, he tried to buy the Limekilns gallops, which were then being sold out of private ownership. He did so, not because he wanted them (although they would have been very useful), but because it would annoy the Jockey Club – who, let it be noted, moved pretty smartly to get a leasehold on the land for themselves.[9]

On his return to racing – which, if he had truly loathed it, he would have abandoned altogether – Baird took a lease on Bedford Lodge and lived in what is now the hotel. This property was then owned by Captain Machell. Although, living next door as he did, Machell might have been thought the obvious man to look after Baird's racing interests, he chose not to do so, and in this he was very wise. Instead he contented himself with charging a very hefty rent indeed, and letting Baird spend fortunes on maintenance.

Nor did this stop Machell from storming in to buy Baird's horses after they had won in sellers: 'in flat defiance of the unwritten rule, but then Captain Machell was not quite a gentleman and he suspected that anything good enough for the young plutocrat was, of its sort, very good indeed'.[10] Indeed Machell *was* behaving badly but, equally, Baird should not have been running decent horses in sellers that he wanted simply to back and keep. Machell was treating Baird according to his deserts. From what he had seen of his next door neighbour, gentlemanliness would be a waste of time and – more importantly – money.

---

[9] The Heath was still being acquired piecemeal: it was not in fact until 1930 that the Jockey Club actually bought the Limekilns.

[10] From *The Squire: George Alexander Baird, Gentleman Rider* by Richard Onslow.

So Baird appointed Bob Peck, who had been running Park Lodge yard, as his racing manager. Peck stuck it out to the bitter end, although it did his health no good at all. Meanwhile his former head-lad, Martin Gurry, was appointed trainer of Baird's sixty-odd horses. This was not a success. Eventually the poor little man could stand it no longer (nor would his successor, Charlie Morton) and, forcing a pay-off, he moved up the road to establish his own yard. Rather oddly, considering his disastrous relations with his former employer, Gurry used Baird's *nom-de-course* for his Abington Place stables.

Gurry had actually won the Derby for Baird, with Merry Hampton in 1887. This was one of Baird's least impressive moments. After the race, which almost any other owner would have given a year of his life to win, he refused to lead his horse into the enclosure and just leant against the rails, affecting indifference, killing people's pleasure. 'The truth,' wrote Richard Onslow,[11] 'was that he really would rather have ridden a selling race at Wolverhampton than own a Derby winner ridden by a professional . . .' Maybe, but the suspicion is that Baird behaved in this way for his two usual reasons: to show the Jockey Club that racing's greatest prize meant nothing to him and, beneath this, to conceal the fear that he would not measure up to the task of being happy and gracious and *comme il faut*. Riding, he could be himself; racing, he felt obliged to be something else; and, because he could not be it, he knocked himself out pretending that he did not want to.

This, in fact, was the guiding principle of his short life. Like a lot of men who have money but no self-worth, he surrounded himself with those to whom he felt superior: boxers, heavies, drunks and a simpleton aristocrat called Lord Billy Savernake, with whose wife Baird slept. He later had her kidnapped (at a cost of around £50,000) after she had run away from him. That was the kind of thing that happened with Baird. On another occasion, after he had given a racing wife £100,000 to abscond with him, she returned gleefully with the money to her husband. Later Baird sent her a package: it contained a cat with its throat slit.

---

[11] From Richard Onslow's magnificently researched history of Newmarket, *Headquarters*.

In so far as he found it possible, Baird was fairly friendly with Sir George Chetwynd (no hint that he slept with little Florence) and dined with him one night at his house in Curzon Street, now the home of the Qatar National Bank. Both men got slaughtered. The next morning, Baird woke up to find one of his gruesome minions hovering, and asked where he was: 'At home, Squire.' Although Baird had no recollection of having done so, he had bought Chetwynd's house from him the night before.

A jolly jape! What was less amusing was Baird's love of cock-fighting, rat-fighting and dog-fighting – he would send his entourage out into the villages around Newmarket, looking for strays to throw against his own bull terrier. He also had a passion for boxing, and built a little ring on the side of Bedford Lodge. Fights were popular in Newmarket at the time – Lord Lonsdale had a home there, after all – and a lively, jostling crowd would congregate to see them staged in a room behind the bar of the Greyhound pub on the High Street (now demolished). Unfortunately, the fights were not always between grown men.

In the end, it was boxing that precipitated Baird's death, although boxing of course was merely the agent. By 1892 he had become obsessed with a fighter named Charlie Mitchell, who had fought John L. Sullivan and now acted as Baird's bodyguard. Mitchell, whom Baird seems really to have loved, in a pitifully dependent way, was an appalling influence on his employer – not that such a thing was really needed. By keeping Baird in London, drinking and wasting his time, Mitchell also kept Baird from doing the one thing that preserved his sanity and self-respect: race-riding. Newmarket was not good for Baird, but it was a hell of a lot better than London. Eventually things became ridiculous. The trainer Charlie Morton was told that Baird's horses could not run unless their owner had a ride at the meeting, but Baird no longer wanted to ride. The horses would regularly be taken to the track, stabled, then – poor bewildered things, subject to the whim of their even more bewildered owner – sent home again unraced.

What Baird *did* want to do, because Mitchell had told him so, was subsidise a trip for his grisly gang to New Orleans, where he would finance a heavyweight title fight for Mitchell with 'Gentleman' Jim Corbett. Yet at the same time – having, perhaps, been softened and sobered by several bouts of pneumonia – he was yearning for a different life. Charlie Morton had finally walked out, but Baird then bought the lease to the beautiful Moulton Paddocks yard, just outside Newmarket, and the better part of him was looking forward to seeing his home-bred two-year-old, Meddler, have a shot at the Derby in 1893. The trip to America was booked, however; and when Baird's new trainer, Joe Cannon, turned up at Curzon Street to persuade him not to go, a dazed and frightened Baird begged to be taken back to Moulton Paddocks. Yet when Cannon returned for him, the house was so full of Baird's hangers-on – who were damned if they were going to let their big foolish fish slip off the hook – that the trainer could not even get in through the door.

And that was it: intolerably weakened by drink, starvation and illness, Baird contracted pneumonia again in New Orleans, and died there at the age of thirty-one. Charlie Mitchell's fight with Corbett never happened. Back in Newmarket, meanwhile, at the start of the 1893 season, the bright young Meddler was burning up the gallops. According to the rule of the time, however, the death of his owner rendered his engagements forfeit,[12] and the classics were left for Isinglass. At Baird's dispersal sale, his unbeaten son of a Derby winner and an Oaks winner was – despite his abortive career – sold to America for 14,500 guineas, where he was twice the leading sire. The stud at which Baird had bred him, in the little village of Kentford, was renamed – and still is called – Meddler stud.

It was a sad, silly story, the worst of which was that Baird, in the last, truncated chapter, was showing signs of wanting it not to be. But how these not-quite-tragic Newmarket casualties piled up, and how easily they were snuffed out, in the end, too exhausted by their lives to put up a fight for them.

With Baird, one can't even say that he was done in by lack of money, quite the opposite; it was his personality that was the problem. He actually hated racing at the same time as

---

[12] In 1927, this rule was amiably challenged by the thriller writer Edgar Wallace – who, it was said, would write a book in a night to fund the next day's racing – and no longer applies.

being obsessed by it, otherwise he could never have reacted to Merry Hampton's Derby win in the way that he did. Backed by his troops of thugs, he waged war on the sport, and – despite its fighting skills – his side was bound to lose.

What would the racing Establishment make of a Baird nowadays? The equivalent would probably be – what? – a Liam Gallagher, a Prince Naseem Hamed, swaggering in with his millions and his inadequacies, threatening to rewrite the form book, giving the world a cheap thrill by refusing to have tea with the Queen after his horse had won the Derby. Of course racing today is a good deal less self-assured than it was a century ago. Its strange naïvety, combined with a panicky desire to seem 'relevant', might make it willing to welcome this kind of person: hence its encouragement of Frankie Dettori, whose former naturalness of personality has become painfully contrived but who, it is thought, reaches out from beyond the tight racing sphere to this other, modern, indifferent world.

Rather like the Conservative Party since the 1997 General Election, racing has become in many ways very craven. Yet it clings stubbornly to those traditions and mysteries – snobberies, if one sees it in that way – which are its history, its very fabric. What does it fear more: obsolescence within the wider world, or absorption by it? In the days of Baird it knew very well. He did not play according to Jockey Club rules and so – despite the fact that his money, his situation, his horsemanship all fitted him for the world of racing – he was not wanted.

Almost certainly, he saw his rejection as a question of class. In a sense, this was true. Yet the British, constantly masticating this particular obsession, are all too ready to mouth it even when it is not, quite, the right answer. Racing's snobberies – if that is what to call them – are not solely those of birth and breeding. Often, yes, they coincide with them. But really they are about a code of behaviour, which can be understood by anyone with a mind to do so: its first principle being tacit submission to the rule of the thoroughbred horse. From that, all else of importance follows. It is not a modern ethic; nor was it that of George Baird, a very modern 'character'. Completely fixated as he was upon his own role – that of the *parvenu* outsider – in the racing drama, he put the part before the horse. And it was for this reason, in the end, that he was a misfit on the racecourse as well as everywhere else.

Still, he could die knowing that he had done something that other men only dreamed of: slept with Lillie Langtry.

What she was doing with him, God only knows. He may have had a certain wild attractiveness, but above all he reeked irresistibly of money. The pair met at Newmarket in 1891, when Baird was twenty-nine and Lillie a ripe and legendary thirty-eight. He, moving in quick and hard, told her to back one of his horses, offering three times her stake if it lost: not a bad line. Later they dined together and Baird soon became a regular visitor to her elegant house in Pont Street.

But she had taken on something that must have made the Prince of Wales (of whom more later) seem like a vast stuffed toy in her bed, for Baird, ever insecure, was insanely jealous and would beat her up regularly, with or without cause. She may have got some sort of kick out of it, as she disappeared to Paris with another man, surely knowing that Baird would follow in a violent rage. And how – he ripped all her clothes, smashed up the hotel room in which she was staying, and put her in hospital for a week, but she went back to him when he gave her £50,000 and a yacht named the *Whyte Lady* (the Black Eye, the wags called it). He also backed her theatrical ventures, then stood all night drinking in the bar and making a nuisance of himself. On one occasion he staged a dog versus rat fight in the foyer of the Haymarket, but again she put up with it – presumably because he gave her a cheque for £5,000 every time in lieu of an apology. This was prostitution of a very special kind.

Yet worth it, perhaps, as he also gave her racehorses. 'My life had been consecrated to the theatre for so many years that any extraneous interest seemed superfluous,' she trilled in her autobiography, *Days I Knew*, but she accepted the horses anyway. One of these, Milford, bred at the Kentford stud, was a crack two-year-old, for whom Lillie was offered the truly astonishing sum of 20,000 guineas *before* he won the July Stakes at Newmarket. She held on to him, thinking that she was almost certain to become the first woman to own a Derby winner, but in this ambition she was thwarted by the very man who had 'given' her the horse. When Baird died, it was discovered that Milford technically still belonged to him, and all engagements were therefore forfeit. Not only that, after her lover's death, Lillie had hastened back to England from the Mediterranean only to find that his will bestowed everything upon his mother. All those bruises had been for nothing, it seemed, but she nonetheless held on to Milford, who went on to win ten more races.

Then Lillie found that she loved racing for its own sake: the thing itself. She continued to race horses, keeping a private string at Etheldreda House[13] just outside Newmarket. As mentioned earlier, she won the Cesarewitch twice, two Jockey Club Cups, the Goodwood Cup and the 1900 Ascot Gold Cup, all of them good, stalwart, staying contests. Lillie was a proper racing woman. For all her extreme beauty in youth, part of the charm that she held for men may have been an earthy, sporting streak, a readiness to *do*, which was at piquant odds with an appearance that would have allowed her just to *be*.

Since the time of Queen Anne, the ability of women to engage in this way with racing had been rather stymied. The best they could hope for was to tag along for the ride, sitting in carriages surrounded by their skirts, seeing nothing, while the men had all the fun. In the second half of the nineteenth century this started to change.

The convention was still that women did not own horses, rather as they did not write books. Thus the Duchess of Montrose raced in the name of 'Mr Manton', and Lillie Langtry in that of 'Mr Jersey'. Not until 1918 would a woman – Lady Jane Douglas – own a Derby winner in her own name. As it always had been, racing was still an essentially masculine world (and remains so, thank God: only contemplate the shrieking miasma that is Royal Ascot to think of what supposedly 'feminine' values do to the sport). But the presence of women – hitherto almost invisible – was now making itself felt, having its effect upon the image and indeed the substance of racing, turning it into the more demonstrably civilised and 'social' event that we recognise today.

---

[13] A jolly little irony is that Etheldreda took its name from the Exning-born princess, daughter of the king of the East Angles, who, despite two marriages, 'remained glorious in the perpetual integrity of virginity'. She founded a religious house at Ely which developed into the cathedral, visible on a clear day from the top of Warren Hill.

For a sport that is supposedly so unrepentantly male, it has been susceptible to a good deal of female influence – more, perhaps, than any other sport.

In the earlier part of the century, according to Vincent Orchard's history of Tattersalls, 'no respectable woman was connected with racing and breeding'. Queen Adelaide, whose husband William IV took a cursory interest in horses ('send 'em all!' he once said to a trainer asking which horse he wanted to run at Goodwood; 'one of 'em's bound to win'), would go along with him to Ascot, but took out her sewing between the races. Queen Victoria, as has been seen, had a rather shocked and shuddering attitude to the whole business. Yet an article from the *Pink 'Un* sporting paper, recollecting a picture of Newmarket in the 1860s, shows that racing men were then taking their wives to meetings in a perfectly relaxed and accepting spirit. The writer mentions 'the handsome figure of Lady Westmoreland on horseback, the beautiful seat of Lady Astley, and Madame Lefèvre, the handsomest woman we ever saw at Newmarket, with her first baby in the charge of its *bonne* . . .' He even refers to 'Mrs Rous in her yellow chariot', which is a bit of a surprise.

The article contrasts this idyll favourably with what it perceives as the nastier Newmarket of twenty years later; yet the memoirs of Lady Randolph Churchill look back upon the 1880s as a symbol of vanished paradise:

> Newmarket has become very different from what it was in the early eighties, when I first went there . . . The ladies who came were habituées, and did not muster a dozen at the outside. Among them were Caroline, Duchess of Montrose, who was a large owner of horses, the Duchess of Manchester (now Duchess of Devonshire), and Lady Cardigan,' (sister of Mrs Rous) 'who would drive up in an old-fashioned yellow tilbury, in which she sat all day . . . It was the fashion to ride, those who did not appearing in ordinary country clothes.
>
> Nowadays velvet and feathers are worn by the mob which throngs the stands, many not knowing a horse from a cow, but coming because it is the fashion. I have heard amusing tales of the ignorance displayed on these

occasions. One lady was overheard declaring that as she had not been to Newmarket for years, she had quite 'forgotten the names of the horses', and another, that someone had told her the name of 'the yearling which was going to win the Derby at the next Newmarket meeting'.

As Lady Randolph Churchill makes rather cattily clear, the implicit code of racecourse behaviour applied to women too.

Not, though, to Emile Zola's Nana, the daft, doomed young courtesan who is taken in a landau to the Grand Prix de Paris at Longchamp, a few years after its first running in 1863, and the joy of whose day is that the winner of the big race is a filly named Nana. From this, Zola creates an eroticised confusion between woman and horse. Racing's subliminal sensuality bursts out into blatancy: '. . . the sudden sunlight lent the chestnut filly the golden sheen of a redhead's hair. She shone in the light like a new louis; her breast was deep, and her head and neck rose lightly from the delicate, sinewy line of her long back . . .'

Zola, in this, the finest piece of all racing writing, shows the powerful fascination that the sport held in the second half of the nineteenth century, the broad sweep of people that it now took in. He shows, too, how the growing presence of women went hand in hand with this new popularity, for neither would have been possible without the other. And Nana, boldly dressed in the blue and white of 'her' filly's colours, can be seen as a symbol of this changed ethos of racegoing. She is an assault from the outside. Her fresh, vulgar, self-centred candour pierces the mysterious world of racing like a child popping a balloon. The weighing room – that holy inner sanctum – is a disappointment to her:

for she had been picturing to herself something on a vast scale, a machine for weighing horses. Discovering that they weighed only the jockeys, she declared that it wasn't worthwhile making such a fuss about their weighing. On the scales a jockey with an idiotic expression was waiting with his harness on his knees for a stout man in a frock-coat to check his weight; while outside the door a stable-boy was holding his horse,

Cosimus, round which a silent, fascinated crowd was clustering.

The course was about to be cleared, and Labordette urged Nana to hurry up. But he turned back to show her a little man talking to Vandeuvres some distance away.

'Look, that's Price,' he said.

'Oh, yes, the man who's riding me,' she murmured, with a laugh.

She found him terribly ugly. All the jockeys struck her as looking imbecilic – probably, she said, because they were prevented from growing bigger. This particular jockey was a man of forty, and with his long, thin face, hard, expressionless, and deeply furrowed, he looked like an old dried-up child. His body was so small and gnarled that his blue jacket with the white sleeves looked as if it had been thrown over a piece of wood.

'No', she went on as she walked away, 'I don't think he could make me happy'.[14]

Ma chère, you should have been in England – where racing had acquired its first romantic icon for over two hundred years, since the days when Charles II set the women alight with his flying lovelocks and flourishing whip. Skinny, stooping, shivering in his greatcoat, this new hero was an unlikely sex symbol, although the many females who pursued him may have been intrigued by the paradox that he presented, of a lost melancholic boy who could ride a finish stronger than anyone. He was, undoubtedly, a product of the sport's new popularity, and the time was ripe for a recognisable star. But still he was for real, not a media construct, and the diverse passions that he inspired were also real. He was the most famous jockey of his age, the most celebrated of any age, and the greatest casualty that racing would ever claim: Fred Archer.

---

[14] All from the Penguin Classics edition, translated by George Holden.

7 Archer's up

"'Tis the Pace that Kills' – 1874–1887

THE GHOST OF FRED ARCHER is said to haunt Newmarket and, on a dark night on the Heath, there is nothing that one would rather see. People claim regularly to have done so: the familiar concave figure, out on the gallops, mounted on a pale grey horse. The story is told of an amateur rider who heard a steady clip-clop behind him as he cycled home to his lodgings. 'Oh, that'd be Fred,' said his landlord, an ex-jockey who had raced against Archer. 'He goes for a ride occasionally.'

After his death in 1886, the presence of Fred Archer was still more real to Newmarket than that of anyone who was then alive in the town. Now, although he would not be widely known in the world outside racing, within it his myth is still similarly vital. In Cheltenham, where he was born in 1857, and which is of course a racing town in its own right, people still boast with quiet pride of being related to him. Yet he was just a jockey, albeit a phenomenally successful one, a semi-literate horseman, pallid and buck-toothed, with a reputation that was not all one would wish. Yes, the age into which he emerged was ready for a racing hero. But how did it happen, all the same?

Archer had romance, a rare commodity. If one were to say that he had it because he was tall, how ridiculous that would sound; yet the fact is that Archer's life would have been completely different if he had been four inches shorter. It was his peculiar luck – good or ill, however one likes to see it – to be 5 feet 8 ½ at a time when the minimum weight in a big handicap was 5 stone 7. In 1871, when Archer had not yet grown to his full height, he won the Cesarewitch on Salvanos, to whom Rous – mistakenly, his eyes were going – had given bottom weight: '. . . little F. Archer rode him wonderfully well,' wrote Sir John Astley. 'The gigantic horse tried to run out of the course, but the tiny mannikin kept him straight.' Four years later, however, Archer was riding at a stone and a half heavier, and by the end of his life, he found it impossible to ride at 8 stone 6. The struggle between the extraordinary talent that he had for jockeyship, and the body that resisted his burning desire to express it, was what marked his life. The crowds who watched him did not, of course, know of the agonies that he suffered, but they intuited the presence of the sad and raging demon in Archer. They saw the supernal strength with which he rode, and gaped at the sight of it coming out of that crooked string bean of a man. They were compelled by this wild, whirling force who, when the race was won, would uncurl himself to his stooped height, put on his sober bank clerk's collar and tie and become quiet, remote, rather refined, unlike any jockey they had ever seen before. This was no strutting little monkey like a Chifney or a Robinson. Archer was more like a changeling, a displaced aristocrat. It was said that his real father was not, in fact, an uneducated Cheltenham jump jockey, but Lord Wilton, with whom he would often stay in the winter for the hunting season and, although there is no real evidence for this, it is not impossible. Archer's mother was an attractive woman (tall, incidentally), far too good for her rough little husband. It was unusual, to say the least, for Wilton to invite a professional jockey to stay at his home. And an early biography of Archer, owned by Lord Rosebery and sold after his death, was found to have been annotated beside the name of Lord Wilton: 'who was said to be his father'.

But the mere fact of this rumour proves Archer's fascination. It is hard to imagine it arising over any other jockey (Charlie Wood, for example, looked more like the illegitimate son of a tree-shrew). Even now, when many riders are obviously superior, intelligent men, Archer would arouse an interest that would, in all probability, transcend his sport. The romance of him would still weave its strange spell.

After death, of course, the myth bloomed. For a time, at least, he became an Adonais, and indeed poems, rather less good than Shelley's, were written for him ('The rider pale, upon his great white horse/Has beaten thee!'). Upon the dead figure of Archer – who, even in life, had looked as insubstantial as a spectre – converged all the romance of racing itself. What power did it have, what urges did it inspire, to cause people to engage in such doomed and feverish battle with it; or, in the case of Fred Archer, quite literally to give his life?

Racing was probably never so widely popular, so colourful a part of the fabric of daily life, as in the years after Archer's death. If, in life, he had made the sport important, in death he made it even more more so. Immediately after he died, people may well have gone to a meeting in the excitable, pleasurably sorrowing way that they went to Kensington Palace in the last months of 1997 (it is not much of an exaggeration to compare the impact of the deaths of Princess Diana and Fred Archer; on the day of the tragedy in November 1886, buses were stopping every few yards on the London streets so that people could pick up an evening paper, and get all the gory details. *The Times* gave up two densely detailed full-length columns to the event, which was probably the Victorian equivalent of a big splash). And, for the next twenty years or so, racing continued to play a role of amazing liveliness on the national stage.

But – to state the obvious – the impact of Archer's death depended on the impact of his life, the style and success of what he did. And this, in its turn, depended upon the health of racing at the time, which was very good. He had emerged into racing at a time when the sport was turning golden, when horses, owners and trainers were beginning to shine with an unusual lustre. Of course this gleams more brightly with hindsight than it probably did at the time. Of course, too, the nostalgics looked back to the age of Rous and wished the outside world away. But these *were* glorious, perhaps unparalleled, years for racing, and glorious too for Newmarket – sitting poised and firm at the sport's centre, surrounded by its handsome new yards, buoyed up by a sea of money. If one could relive any era in the life of the sport and the town, it would probably be the years between 1880 and 1900: when horses of undisputed greatness – about whom no argument is possible – were bounding across the Heath; when Fred Archer rode Ormonde to win a Derby and St Leger for the Duke of Westminster; when Mat Dawson trained St Simon to win a Gold Cup by twenty lengths; when the Prince of Wales' Persimmon raced against Leopold de Rothschild's St Frusquin; when confidence was so high that it seemed it might never be lost again. This was a time when racing believed, unquestioningly, in its power, and the public, happily dazzled by the riches with which it was presented, began to believe in it too.

This is what Fred Archer was a part of, and what he helped to create. It all began in 1868 when, having been taken there by his father, he was apprenticed to Mat Dawson at Heath House ('the said apprentice his Master faithfully shall serve his secrets keep his lawful commands everywhere gladly obey . . . he shall not commit fornication . . .'). He arrived at the age of eleven – surely even jockeys do not fornicate so young? – when he weighed 4 stone 11. 'I have a wonderful boy here,' said Dawson, 'who will do wonderful things.' Archer's pay was seven guineas a year, rising to thirteen guineas by the fifth year; five years after that, he would be earning upwards of £10,000 and running from the food that he used to steal from Mrs Dawson's kitchen.

Heath House was the place to be in the second half of the nineteenth century, whether one was a jockey or an owner. It emanated success. It resounded with it. Not since Robert Robson had a stable dominated in such a way, and in Robson's day the competition was far less intense. Of course success breeds success in racing – train a classic winner and you will have classic winners to train. But the job still has to be done, and Dawson did it in such a way that he is recognised as the first great trainer of the 'modern' era. Like a Cecil or a Stoute, he had huge numbers of horses – over 100 at a time (Cecil would have more like 200, but then facilities and so forth are now vastly improved) – which means that he must have had very good staff. Indeed, he employed several men who were to become trainers. Felix Leach, for example, took over Trillium Place yard on Birdcage Walk, George Blackwell went to Lagrange Stables and Richard Waugh (member of a huge Newmarket dynasty) ended up in Germany, training for the Kaiser. And, again like a Cecil or a Stoute, Mat Dawson concentrated his energies upon bringing out the best in the best horses. No handicap coups for him – leave those to the poor souls who could aim no higher, who had to content themselves with cleverness because they could not achieve greatness. Dawson kept his eye on more glittering prizes.

What *was* different from nowadays is the brusqueness with which he often treated owners, men of the greatest wealth and position who nonetheless – as he well knew – were yearning to get their horses into his clutches. Today, although some trainers can be off-handed buggers when they want to be, or might nick a few quid out of owners on the side, this is not a good idea – they operate in dodgy times. Owners are effectively subsiding the sport of racing – to be blunt, 99.9 per cent of them are throwing away money in exchange for kudos, pleasure, kicks, whatever. It therefore makes sense to keep them as happy as possible, feeling good about their own generosity. The more intelligent trainers do this. A man like Cecil is in a position of strength, of course, in that he has the pick of owners, but in a sense this just changes the nature of the pressure. People who pay more are always likely to demand more, and even more likely to walk away when they don't get it. Cecil lost the patronage of the Maktoum family in 1995 and, whatever the facts behind that peculiar affair,[1] the one certainty is that the Maktoums had the right to do what they did. The trainer, in his apparent omniscience, may be like God to the owner, but in the end the owner has the power to move to another church.

And really he had that power when Mat Dawson was training for him – after all, where would Dawson have been if everyone had taken their horses away? But the racing world

[1] The story was that the Maktoums had objected to interference from Cecil's young wife, Natalie. The rumours to this effect were strong and convincing, although it must be said that Natalie Cecil was often used as a convenient scapegoat by Newmarket society. Perhaps just as important was the allegation that Cecil had failed to inform the Maktoums of an injury to a crack two-year-old, Mark of Esteem. He and the other forty or so horses were removed from the yard. Mark of Esteem went on to win the 1996 Two Thousand Guineas.

was so different then: trainers were not fighting to stay afloat, owners were not getting a laughable return on what they spent, above all there were no Bookmakers PLC bleeding the sport dry. There was not the *fear* that there is now, a fear which gives too much power to anyone who has money to bestow – or withhold. And so a man like Dawson could comfortably tell owners that he was in charge, that he was going to make all the decisions, that this was the way in which his job could best be done, and if they didn't like it – tough. He could tell Lord Falmouth, one of the most important owners of the time, to take his horses away after he had contradicted Dawson's orders to a jockey (the animals all came trailing back, but only after Falmouth had made the first move). He could break with another owner – for good, this time – who had come round to the yard on a Sunday demanding to see his horses, during what everyone knew to be Dawson's sleeping time (very precious to anyone who works in racing). It wasn't exactly that Dawson had power over the owners. It was simply that he saw no need to be frightened. If this sport was becoming a business – and the size and success of Heath House says that it was – it was still being conducted in a highly idiosyncratic, personalised, unaccountable way, which suited it very well indeed.

Dawson's first Newmarket jockey was Tom French who, just as Fred Archer was to do, died at the age of twenty-nine. The cause of death was consumption brought on by wasting; again like Archer, he was really too tall for the job. That year, 1874, Archer became champion jockey for the first time – as he would continue to be until his death – and shot up to his full adult height. His magnificent career was launched; so too was the anguish of starvation, sweating and purgation.

During his thirteen seasons as champion jockey, Archer probably ate less than a normal man would eat in thirteen weeks. In winter he would have more, obviously, and his weight would go up to about eleven stone. Then the season would come around again – alluring, terrifying – and with it the knowledge that forty or so pounds would have to come off and stay off. As he grew older so this became harder. At first, starvation and saunas did the trick: for breakfast, a spoonful of hot castor oil and half an orange, for lunch a sardine and a glass of champagne, hours in the Turkish bath that Dawson had installed to sweat the horses and dinner a dirty word (he would gain three or four pounds if he ate at night; it was said that he had once run out of a dining-room when a steak and kidney pie was served). Later, even this appalling regime was not enough to keep the weight off, and he resorted to what became known as 'Archer's Mixture': a vicious aperient, which he got from a doctor living at Rous Villa on Old Station Road. It was so unspeakably strong that a friend to whom Archer once gave a spoonful was unable to go racing the next day. Archer, meanwhile, was drinking it out of sherry glasses, and there was nothing inside him for it to get rid of.

While he was doing that – living on less that Lester Piggott's 'puff of cigar smoke' or Australian jockey Brownie Carslake's 'cup of tea and hope' – he was also doing this: winning 2,748 races, including 246 in 1885 – a record which stood until Gordon Richards broke it in 1933 – and five Derbys, four Oaks, six St Legers, four Two Thousand Guineas and two One Thousand Guineas. Only six other jockeys have ridden 200-plus winners in a season, four of them in the past ten years, and it is still regarded as a great feat. When Kieren Fallon achieved it in 1999, he had the help of cars, helicopters, telephones, faxes, evening racing, an agent. Fred Archer did it with none of those things, nothing but the horse and the train and the telegram, and his own shaky ability to write down what he had to remember. And – even by a jockey's standards – no food.

Those who write about Archer's record are properly amazed by it, but still one gets the sense that they have never really dieted, and so have no real grasp of what it is like to feel sick with hunger, in pain with it, light-headed with it, ready to kill for food and then, most sinisterly of all, to have the sense that hunger has disappeared, leaving in its place an empty, dreamlike state: a high with no substance to it. Most women with any vanity have gone through this hell. But to go through it without the knowledge that somewhere, at the end, a good dinner awaits, to know that this is what it will be like for the next five or ten years, and that, rather than lying on a sofa hallucinating about a baguette and a ripe Brie, one has to be up at dawn on the Heath and on the racecourse all afternoon, grappling at forty miles an hour with a succession of recalcitrant thoroughbreds, fighting for space and victory amid a throng of other starving maniacs – that was the life of Fred Archer and, to endure it, the triumphs would need to have been very sweet.

Of course, although he is as extreme an example as one will find, Archer is far from being the only one who lived like this. Indeed, reading about jockeys, it seems as though they are divided into the ones who had to starve and the ones who did not. Neat, cocky little Sam Chifney senior had, throughout his life, no trouble riding at 7 stone 12. Frank Buckle had his first ride at 3 stone 13 and, although he always pigged out on a goose at the end of the season (how he must have dreamed of that roasting smell), again had no real weight problems. Yet Sam Chifney junior and Jem Robinson both ballooned, relatively speaking, when they were not riding.

And so it has gone on, up to recent times, with Walter Swinburn forced into possible retirement because he cannot maintain a low weight, Steve Cauthen having resorted to bulimia and other jockeys, we are told, having used diuretics and laxatives. Piggott famously never ate; Willie Carson, on the other hand, did; like the 4 feet 11 ½ Gordon Richards, he was saved by shortness. But even jockeys who were far smaller than Archer or Piggott had problems. Jack Watts, who rode Persimmon to Derby victory for the Prince of Wales, had been unable to make the weight for the race just two days beforehand. Danny Maher, the American who rode three Derby winners in the first decade of the twentieth century, was consumptive but smoked like a fiend to keep thin. He died a week after the 1916 Cambridgeshire, which he watched, lungs collapsed in two heaps, propped up in a car that had been parked, by special permission of the Jockey Club, beside the Rowley Mile. His great rival Frank Wootton was forced to go jump racing because of his weight. Brownie Carslake, who won seven classics between the wars, was said always to look as if he were about to die. And the correlation between premature death and a lifetime of wasting, though not absolute, is still pretty hard to miss. Gordon Richards died at eighty-two; but Carslake died at fifty-five, Wootton at forty-seven, Watts at forty-one, Maher at thirty-five and Archer, of course, at twenty-nine.

George Fordham never needed to waste, which may have made his rivalry with Archer harder to bear for the starving, fiercely ambitious, younger man. Although nowadays Archer's name is legendary and Fordham's nearly forgotten, opinion was divided at the time as to which of them was the better jockey. One gets the sense that people were trying very hard not to be bowled over by Archer's superior glamour. Richard Marsh, for example, who trained in New-market for the Prince of Wales, wrote that Archer 'had some uncanny means, I thought, of imparting extra vitality to his horses . . . yet, on the whole, I am inclined to name George Fordham as the greatest all-round jockey I have ever known'. Even Mat Dawson said that Fordham was better, but he may have been trying to get a rise out of Archer. Fordham, it was generally agreed, had better hands and racemanship; Archer more fire, more style, more insane courage. After his death, these qualities won the day in people's minds; during his life, more sober judgement prevailed.

In the 1880s, whether one preferred Fordham or Archer was probably a question of one's own temperament, a question of Gielgud or Olivier, Charlton or Best, claret or champagne. The two men could hardly have been less similar. Fordham did not have Archer's almost frightening self-discipline, and he liked a drink. A trainer who wanted to give a drop of port to a horse was told by Fordham that it should, first, be tested by him, then that as only the dregs were left it was hardly worth giving them to the animal.

He was the elder of the two riders by twenty years, and had been champion jockey for the first of fourteen times back in 1855. He had also played his part in distant dramas like that of Lord Hastings, having ridden Lady Elizabeth in her wonderful two-year-old career. Perhaps because of Archer's arrival, he retired in 1876, but having nothing to do but drink he came back almost immediately. 'Fancy,' wrote 'The Druid', 'Fordham, with all his knowledge and experience and able to ride at 7 stone 5; it seems like a gift from heaven.' Or, to Archer, a twist of the knife in his non-existent guts.

The differences between Fordham and Archer exacerbated, if anything, the intensity of competition between the two; they did not like each other much and it was probably Archer who started the animosity. 'You have taken a liberty with me, Mr A,' Fordham once said after a race. 'You must not take a liberty with George.'

There was something implacable, something relentless about Fordham, with his plain and smiling face, that seems to have driven Archer mad. He was vastly irritated – and one can understand it – by Fordham's famous ability to 'kid' during a race. Whenever he thought he knew where Fordham was, he was somewhere else, doing something else; he also had a habit of 'clucking' at his horse as if it were in trouble, so that the other jockeys would make their move too soon and let him pounce at the death. 'Fordham was cluck-clucking at his mount for the whole of the race,' he once said. 'I thought I had him beaten two or three times in the two miles. But with his infernal cluck-clucking he was always coming again.' Small wonder, perhaps, that Archer had Fordham's photograph beside his fireplace; if he couldn't get rid of the damn man, he was going to face him down.

It is significant that, when the two jockeys met in Newmarket match races, set up by the aristocratic men for whom they both rode, Fordham – what with his 'kidding' and 'clucking' – would almost always win. In big races like the Derby, Archer was supreme. Fordham did not have that sort of nerve. Epsom, especially in those days, was a terrifying track, on which Archer had perhaps his finest hour. Yet the circumstances of that hour would never have arisen with Fordham.

It happened in 1880, the year of Bend Or's Derby. Bend Or – a chestnut horse of unusual beauty – belonged to the first Duke of Westminster, with whom Archer had a £1,000 retainer. Although Lord Falmouth had first claim on the jockey, in his usual gentlemanly fashion he released him to take the Derby ride on the fancied colt. It nearly didn't happen, however. Less than a month before the race, Archer was out on the gallops with a horse called Muley Edris; in a brief, inattentive second, he had been seized and savaged, the muscles of his arm quite bitten through. Despite a visit to Falmouth's London surgeon ('shall I be fit to ride the Derby?';

Above 'The Cockpit' by Hogarth (1700–1799)

Right Lord George Bentinck (1802–48), second Dictator of the Turf, in his beautiful buckskin breeches. From a sketch by the Count D'Orsay.

The jockey as national icon. Fred Archer (1857–86)

Right Selection of memorabilia relating to Fred Archer, including the revolver with which he took his own life

Below Fred Archer on Ormonde, a painting by A. Wheeler (1815–1932)

Opposite top The second leg of the Autumn Double. Masked Marvel (carrying seven stone nine) wins the 1925 Cambridgeshire for his owner, Mr Macomber, whose horse, Forseti, had won the Cesarewitch earlier that year

Opposite bottom HH Aga Khan III leads in his Triple Crown winner, the immaculate Bahram, after victory in the 1935 Epsom Derby

Above Lillie Langtry (1853–1929), winner of the Cesarewitch in 1897 and 1908, lover of Edward, Prince of Wales and George Alexander Baird

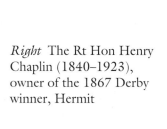

Right The Rt Hon Henry Chaplin (1840–1923), owner of the 1867 Derby winner, Hermit

The start of the 1941 Derby, run at Newmarket, and won by Owen Tudor, a son of Hyperion

The morning of the Two Thousand Guineas. Racegoers in the courtyard of the Rutland Arms Hotel on Newmarket High Street

Winston Churchill, staunch defender of wartime racing, gets his reward. Colonist II carries his owner's initials on his rug after winning the 1950 White Rose Stakes at Hurst Park

Queen Elizabeth II watches the finish of the 1956 Two Thousand Guineas on the Rowley Mile, won by the 50/1 shot, Gilles de Retz

Stable lads at work in Harry Wragg's Abington Place yard, on Newmarket's Bury Road, 1956

'better drive, better drive'), he was still unable to work nearly three weeks later, and was a stone over racing weight.

Now this seemed like the worse kind of luck, but in fact it was vengeance on the part of Muley Edris, who in the past had been whipped so viciously by Archer that, when the chance came, he had gone berserk at the jockey. And this is where George Fordham – plain, unglamorous, ageing – becomes the more heroic of the two men. 'Don't you think that you had better leave that pretty whip behind?' he once said to an apprentice, who was flashing it around before riding the Cesarewitch. This, after all, would be nothing like a whip today, which can itself be bad enough; a whip then was a long, evil thing that could slice into a horse. Spurs, too, which are no longer used, would leave a horse with flanks gnawed and bleeding by the little spiked rowels. Fordham often rode with neither whip nor spurs. He had much of his success with fillies – winning a record seven One Thousand Guineas – and this was probably due to his sensitivity. He was, above all, a kindly jockey, and a kindly man: 'When I get down to the post on these two-year-olds and I feel their little hearts beating under my legs I think, why not let them have an easy race, win if they can but don't frighten them.' This was not the philosophy of the time, which makes it both remarkable and touching.

Nor was it Archer's style. In 1884, he was to say: 'It's a great mistake to knock a horse about and I know that a few years back I was a severe rider, but I've learned better by experience.' In 1880, however, he had no such self-restraint. Brigg Boy, the horse that he rode for John Astley in the match against Captain Machell, was never any good afterwards; Archer had driven him too hard, in his compulsion to get up by a short neck.

He was not unusual in his ferocity. After his death, the jockey Tom Cannon took the rides on Archer's last Derby winner, Ormonde. Another jockey, aggrieved at having missed out, took his revenge (on the horse? – a strange logic) by barging into Cannon during the 1887 Hardwicke Stakes at Ascot, and tearing four-inch flaps away from Ormonde's near hind. Not that this was Archer's style, either. It was crass, nasty and above all pointless – if Archer had done it, he would have made damn sure that Ormonde did not still go on to win the race. But it was a different world, and George Fordham was the representative, within it, of a more enlightened future: the one in which the all-conquering Steve Donoghue would say of his 1921 Derby winner, Humorist, 'I would rather have cut off my right arm than show him the whip . . . I loved him like a child.'

Yet for every Donoghue there was, and still is, a great jockey with the devil in him. Piggott, for all his class, was a terrible barger and hitter; Kieren Fallon rides like a man with a hellhound on his trail. But it is not cruelty so much as *urgency* that characterises these jockeys. They all want to win, obviously, but with Fallon one can *see* the desire; with Archer too, presumably, which was part of what made him exciting. Perhaps no jockey before or since ever showed the desire so clearly. 'I am so thoroughly wrapped up in racing, my mind is so entirely upon it, that I really never think of anything else, not even of where I am.' It was a kind of madness, enabling him to override the starvation which, at the same time, was fuelling the madness. And so, during a race, his head was not in the right place to be able to think, as Fordham did, of the horse as a *horse*.

This is not to excuse Archer for his biting whip and digging spurs, but to attempt to explain him. All he knew was the contest. A story was told that he was found in tears after finishing first in a dead-heat, because he had not ridden both the winners. He would shamelessly approach owners and trainers to get rides on horses he liked the look of (Piggott, too, went in for this). Before the 1881 Derby he told Bob Peck to give £1,000 to the jockey of Peregrine, who had won the Two Thousand Guineas, and give him the ride instead. Peck refused and Archer won the Derby anyway on Iroquois, who beat Peregrine by a neck. That was what Archer could do; in the 1880s, it was nearly useless to resist. That was why the town-crier of Thirsk, heralding his arrival at the racecourse in 1884, proclaimed that 'Fred Archer, the celebrated horseman . . . will ride the winner of the Foal Stakes. Gentlemen! Come and see the wonder of the world.' And Archer did win.

Muley Edris, who had done his best to put an end to this whirling phenomenon, lost. In the week before the 1880

Derby, Archer lost a stone in weight and started riding again like a lunatic. By the day of the race itself, he was quite bonkers, shaking and hissing, with a piece of iron stuck up his near-useless arm. Fortunately for him, Bend Or was a horse of wonderfully calm temperament, else he could very well have killed himself as he hurled his mount round Tattenham Corner, swearing and screaming at the other jockeys to get out of the way of the rail (Archer always had a mania for sticking to the inside of a racecourse; it was said that he rode the Derby with one leg over the rail, hardly likely, but he did once rip his boot open on it).

One hundred yards from the winning post, Archer forgot that he had an iron bar instead of an arm, went for his whip on Bend Or and dropped it. All he had was the other arm, the long legs that gripped 'like a pair of tongs', and a desire that burned like the fires of hell. Seeming almost to lift his horse past Robert the Devil, whose lead in the straight had looked unassailable, he got Bend Or home by a head.

Archer rode better races both before and after this, but never one that was so dramatic.[2] In reality he had terrorised Robert the Devil's jockey, Rossiter, into submission. 'It was not wise, perhaps, to turn round,' Archer said of him afterwards, when the fever of victory had abated and he had reverted to his quiet, judicious, other self; but it was fear of the approaching Archer that had made poor Rossiter look behind in the straight and allow Bend Or to overcome him. 'Fred Archer was a powerful personality as well as a brilliantly successful jockey,' wrote the trainer John Porter. 'Very masterful, he generally had pretty much his own way . . .'

And so the trail of success continued to blaze. Retainers piled up. The 6th Duke of Portland and the new, more sensible

---

[2] The race also had a dramatic aftermath. The owner of Robert the Devil claimed that Bend Or was in fact a horse named Tadcaster, and that the two had been mixed up in the Eaton Stud book. Corroboration came from a groom, but his word was of dubious value as he had been sacked from the stud. However, he repeated the story on his death bed, and it was not wholly dismissed; but, frankly, by then, scandal had become more boring than rectitude and the general feeling was one of wanting to believe in Bend Or. Incidentally, Robert the Devil's preserved body can be seen in Gibsons Saddlers, off The Avenue, where he is a handsome model for riding tack.

Lord Hastings paid £2,000 jointly for Archer's services, Lord Alington £500 and, although Lord Falmouth gave only a nominal £100, he was so important an owner that this was then the best job of the lot – the Earl of Rosebery had a special form printed on which to send him congratulations after a win. This triumvirate of Falmouth/Dawson/Archer was a glorious thing. Between 1872 and 1883 Lord Falmouth won – in prize money alone – at least £10,000 every year from his racing, and about £220,000 in all. His victories with Archer up included three Two Thousand Guineas, two One Thousand Guineas, a Derby, three Oaks and three St Legers; all within a relatively short space of time, during which competition was at top pitch. Falmouth was hugely popular for the honesty with which he ran his horses. As Thormanby put it, 'he let the public know as much about them as himself,' which he was entirely happy to do, because he had absolutely no interest in gambling. A new breed, indeed! the owner who loved the thoroughbred so much that the horse, itself, in all its classic winning grandeur, was enough for him. No doubt that £220,000 could have been multiplied by ten – and would have been, in almost any other hands. But Falmouth was frankly too rich to worry and, unlike those other aristocrats who had gambled, not for money, but for a matchless thrill, he 'wanted no such stimulus' (Thormanby again).

Indeed, the towering tide of gambling seems now to have receded, at least in the lives of these powerful and assured owners. The passion had burned itself out; the fashion for self-destruction was over. The Duke of Westminster was described as a man 'who races for the love of the sport and not for the sake of making money' (when approached to sell his 1880 Derby winner as a stallion to the USA, he said 'there is not enough money in the great American republic to buy Bend Or'). In thirty years of racing, he won prize money of around £300,000, the sort of sum that a Lord Hastings might have conjured in thirty hours, but at least Westminster held on to it – not that he needed to.

The Prince of Wales, meanwhile, gambled in dear little sums that George Bentinck would have laughed to scorn ('I quite see how the mistake occurred in the entry in my book,

so shall claim only £120 instead of £140 on Friar's Balsam,'
reads one of his letters. Timid as an old lady at a Tote
window, he continues: 'I backed St Mirin last week and shall
hope to be able to "hedge", as I fancy Machell's stable must
be dangerous . . .').

It was as though these men, living as they were in the
plush, secure, respectable world of England at its imperial
height, quite simply had no need to prove anything about
themselves; which was, after all, what someone like Lord
Hastings had been doing. The Earl of Rosebery, for example,
was a typical unlucky gambler, but not a frenzied one: where
was the need? He was married to one of the richest women
in the country, Baron Meyer de Rothschild's daughter. He had
horses with Mat Dawson; then, when Dawson went into
semi-retirement in 1895, raced them from his own private
stable, Primrose Cottage, behind his pretty yellow house
(now a pair of shops) at 38, Newmarket High Street. He won
ten classics. He even pulled off the double of winning the
Derby and being prime minister, when Ladas won the race in
1894. Why on earth should he want to wage war on such a
life?

Of course, one might have said exactly the same thing
about those many casualties who littered the Heath. Their
lives had hardly been deprived, yet they had wrecked them,
nonetheless. The compulsion to do so was their own, but at
the same time one has the sense of a strange and irresistible
pressure within the world of racing – rather like the push of
events within a Shakespearean tragedy – which was making
them behave in the hysterical way that they did. Now, at the
end of the nineteenth century, in that *belle époque* before war
and taxation came to do their worst, racing seemed to have
attained a sense of stability, of rich and blissful contentment
with itself. The spinning world had, for a while at least, come
to rest upon its axis. And there is no more perfect image of
that axis than the dining room inside the Jockey Club in
Newmarket. The aura of solidity, of wealth, of pleasure
indulged in a fine, full and gentlemanly manner, is, even
now, as thick and patrician as the *General Stud Book*. The
dining table was presented to the Club by Edward VII, and it
requires little imaginative effort to see him and his set sitting

around it, plump as partridges in their *tenue de soirée*, lighting cigars and chatting about their magnificent horses. Above their heads, exquisite Czech chandeliers were perilously suspended. At one end of the room stood a vast champagne cooler, attributed to Robert Adam, that would hold forty magnums.[3] And all around, on the walls, were the icons, the painted totems: Ormonde, Archer up; Isinglass, Triple Crown winner of 1893; Flying Fox, Triple Crown winner of 1899 . . .

The sense of stasis, of a timeless idyll for an enchanted circle – whose years were in fact numbered – is conveyed in memoirs of the late nineteenth century. This is Daisy Warwick, one of the Prince of Wales' mistresses (who later stood as a Labour parliamentary candidate, and would charmingly point out to visiting comrades the bed in which she had slept with the future king):

At Newmarket there was a set with which one was on the best of terms. All our intimate friends appeared to be either patrons or real lovers of the turf. The group included Henry Chaplin and Lord and Lady Bradford . . . Others always in evidence were the Duke of Devonshire, then Lord Hartington, Lord and Lady Cadogan, whose entertainments at Chelsea House were part of the pleasures of the London Season; Lord Derby, always a sportsman . . . and Lord Falmouth. The Prince of Wales never missed Newmarket, and would frequently ride out with the rest of us in the mornings to see the horses exercised . . .

The Duke of Portland wrote, in similar style:

We were called at seven o'clock in the morning. At eight, our hacks were waiting at the door . . . After breakfast the newspapers arrived, and much discussion, most of it foolish, took place on the prospects of the ensuing day's sport. For an hour or more before the races, a constant procession of acquaintances and

---

[3] This was later converted into an enormous washing-up 'machine', in which the gold cutlery could be cleaned without fear of theft.

friends passed our house, which was in the High Street, and we greeted them through the open windows. Our hacks were again brought to the door, and we then rode to the races. At luncheon, during the Spring Meeting, there were plovers' eggs and prawns . . .

And what of the people who did not inhabit this golden galaxy? No revolutionaries they. They would congregate outside Palace House, then the home of Leopold de Roth-schild, hoping for a glimpse of visiting royalty – diversionary tactics on the part of policemen became necessary to disperse the crowds. They would line the High Street by The Terrace and cheer the aristocratic carriages as they left for the racecourse. This, of course, was an era which did not question the prevailing hierarchy: Lord Rosebery was cheered with apparent sincerity when Ladas won his Derby and Guineas; the royal victories were greeted with wild delight. The man who shouted to Edward VII, after Minoru's Derby victory in 1909, 'Now, King, you've won – go home and dissolve this bloody Parliament,' was very much the exception.

But racing has always had a very particular relationship with wealth and privilege (even today, a racecourse is the one place where a nob can be assured of deference, even if it does now take a rather theatrical form); and this is true, too, of Newmarket. In the late nineteenth century it was, beneath its gleaming top stratum, a town with a workhouse, with tiny terraced houses behind the High Street, with pitifully under-paid stable workers (that, at least, does not really change). Yet it rubbed shoulders with the *richissime* in a way that no other town could. Certainly not London, where invisible walls of impenetrable density stood between, say, Mayfair and Soho. Newmarket had a unique intimacy with rich people, who for all their superior position were – just as they are now – in eager thrall to the place, to its clever little horsemen, its impassive trainers, its accretions of knowledge and tradition, its thoroughbreds, its Heath. Although, as racing became ever more Newmarket's *raison d'être*, so the town became ever more dependent upon the patronage of racehorse owners, it had a kind of ease with its patrons: after all, it had something that they wanted.

And so, even if there was resentment of all that plenitude – which there surely must have been – there was not quite the same class structure as existed elsewhere. Racing has been called egalitarian, in that all classes can meet on the track; it has been called élitist, in that these classes are kept separate; neither of these two is quite accurate. Racing has its own, subtly different hierarchy. The crowds may have gathered for a glimpse of the Prince of Wales, but they would have waited all day and night for Fred Archer.

What is extraordinary is how Archer's fame transcended Newmarket, racing, even sport. When he arrived at a London theatre, it was said that 'no king could have had a greater reception' (and they can't *all* have won money on him). The special first-class train was once held up for him at Ascot. His name entered the language: people would say 'Archer's Up' as they would now raise a thumb, to show that all was well.

Women pursued him relentlessly, rather as they might now a footballer or soap opera star. It is a little hard to credit, looking at his photographs; but if a man has romance, he has it. And then there was the jockey thing, which for some women exerts a real fascination. Of course, communal crushes of this kind can never be taken too seriously. If one person said that she found him attractive, others would have said the same. Nevertheless, Lady Hastings wrote that 'the way in which some women ran after Archer was amazing'. Upper-class women in particular, apparently; to whom he would have been a novelty but a well-mannered one, whose table manners they need never know about. His sister once found a letter in which one such well-bred wife was 'asking why he was so cold to her and all that . . .' And the Duchess of Montrose, nearly forty years his senior, does seem to have been truly infatuated. After the death of Stirling-Crawfurd she considered marrying him. 'I don't think I had better do it,' Archer said to Captain Machell. The etiolated, remote, polite jockey must have seemed like a creature from another world to the duchess, with her monumental bustles and her unstoppable mouth, and she was obsessed in the way that a child would be by a perfect doll. She sent Archer constant invitations to parties at Sefton Lodge; wanting him to ride her horses was only the half of it.

But he was polite with all these silken women and married the niece of Mathew Dawson, Nellie Rose, a girl about whom little is said except that she was quiet and sweet and, presumably, a refuge to whom things did not have to be explained. He seems really to have loved her. The wedding took place at All Saints' Church in 1883 – almost every staging post in Archer's life has its Newmarket landmark – and the town came out to watch, lining the route all the way to the railway station, where a special carriage took the couple on the train to London. A ball was held for guests at the Rutland Arms and there was a whoop-up on the Severals, where an ox supplied by Lord Hastings was roasted. Archer then moved out of Heath House, and set up home in a large, grand, rather isolated establishment – with a conservatory and, *entendu*, a Turkish bath – which he had built amid some paddocks off the Fordham Road. He named it Falmouth House[4] after his chief patron.

Did he do this, perhaps, because the relationship with Lord Falmouth, hitherto so pleasant and secure, had recently been somewhat shaken? A strange little story had surrounded the previous year's St Leger, which must have left Archer feeling unsettled and uneasy. Falmouth's filly, Dutch Oven (possibly the least meaningful name ever given to a classic winner) had won the race at 40/1, having run very badly in her previous outing and in the Derby. The result was referred to the stewards by none other than Sir John Astley, who had gone bustling off with his suspicions in a very high-handed manner. This was a bit rich, coming from a man who so dearly loved his little coups. No doubt he would have said that he was voicing the general concern. What almost certainly *had* happened was that he had backed the 8/13 favourite and lost his money; there is nothing more irritating than the gambler whose private losses cause him suddenly to acquire a public conscience.

The stewards dismissed his objection, which really had very little substance, especially as Archer had done everything he could before the race to get out of riding Falmouth's filly. But he had been tainted all the same; and worse was to come.

---

[4] The house was demolished in 1970.

In 1884, Lord Falmouth suddenly sold almost all his horses, offering as a reason his advanced age – he was sixty-five – and worsening health. The real reason, people said, was that he believed Fred Archer to have stopped his colt, Gaillard, in the 1883 Derby.

Could this possibly have been true? Gaillard had won the Two Thousand Guineas that year. The day of the race had its own excitements, as the owner of the horse's sire, a charming Hungarian nobleman named Prince Batthyany, had dropped down dead – overcome, perhaps, at the prospect of the race, and how one understands that – half an hour beforehand in the Jockey Club stand. On Derby day, Gaillard unsurprisingly started favourite. But he was a bit of a jinx, no question. Archer got a less than perfect run round Epsom, having lost his beloved rail to Charlie Wood on St Blaise; Gaillard finished third, with St Blaise the winner. A neck behind, in second, was Highland Chief – the horse trained by Archer's brother, Charles, and backed by him very heavily. So it was inevitably and immediately said that Fred as well as Charles Archer had gambled on the horse, and that Fred had tried – and failed, just – to let Highland Chief win.

It is very, very hard to believe that Fred Archer would ever have given anything less than his utmost in a Derby. Quite simply, that was not his nature. However much he loved money – and the stories of his miserliness are not terribly well-founded; he left £60,000 when he died and far more than that had gone through his hands – he loved winning races infinitely more. The torture that he put himself through was too hellishly pure to be satisfied by finishing third and making a few grubby hundred pounds.

But did Lord Falmouth think otherwise? Again, the truth will never be known. He had spoken of retirement before the l'affaire Gaillard; even so, he did it a bit too smartly afterwards for the good of Archer's reputation. The blow was softened – perhaps – by the fact that he left a few horses in training. As always, he conducted his affairs like a gentleman. After all, if he *had* heeded the rumours – which were being whispered very stagily, and would have been difficult to ignore – then he was entitled to feel hurt and disillusioned. It would have seemed as if the notion of integrity, upon which he had based his whole racing career, had been shown up for a sham.

Not that the average racegoer had ever really doubted this. Integrity was the ideal and ideals were necessary but the world was the world. Fred Archer remained the popular hero *ne plus ultra*, whether or not he was also a bit of a cheat. To him, though, the slurs must have been agonising. Jockeys have always had to put up with this stuff – a certain type of racegoer wears his suspiciousness like a badge of honour, seeing tricks and mischief in every race – but some riders are more robust about it than others. Fordham had the strength of mind simply to walk away from anyone, like Captain Machell, who impugned him. Charlie Wood, who was guilty of pretty well anything that was said about him, and who died aged nearly ninety with a large fortune, couldn't have cared less. But Archer was a dangerously sensitive soul. And his career had been such a shining thing, with its top-of-the-range retainers and its peerless results: surely it was not meant to have mud thrown at it?

And the mud was sticking, in bigger and dirtier clumps. There was now a rumour that Archer was part of a jockeys' ring run by Wood, which was frankly unbelievable. He did, on certain occasions, offer advice to a betting syndicate and, like most riders, he did gamble, but the losses that he sustained hardly suggested membership of some cunning inner circle. Then he lost his retainer with the Duke of Portland. This was probably because yet more rumours had linked Archer with the dreaded name of George Alexander Baird, who – when he returned to racing after his two years in exile – had wanted to set up a stable in partnership with the jockey. Again, it is barely credible that Archer would ever have been tempted by this. His situation with Mat Dawson was far more attractive than anything that Baird could offer. Portland, however, seems to have thought otherwise: he gave Archer some sort of ultimatum – me or him – and Archer, rightly disgusted by the whole business, walked away from both.

Of course he was still the most sought-after jockey in the country, and his stream of successes did not stop. 1885 was probably his finest season, the one in which he rode his 246 winners. He won the Derby on Melton for Lord Hastings, Portland's former partner, who sensibly kept up his retainer with Archer ('Had rather exciting moment,' he telegraphed to his wife from the Epsom grandstand). Earlier that year Archer had won the Two Thousand Guineas on Paradox. When the horse was beaten by a head in the Derby, Oscar Wilde sent a telegram to his friends, the Hastings: 'I understand that Milton's *Paradise Lost* is being revived and will appear in Derby Week and will be published under the title *Paradox Lost* by Melton.' Archer also won the St Leger, again on Melton, and the Oaks on Lonely, a daughter of Hermit. It was a year of achievement which, all in all, no jockey has ever equalled. 1886, too, had its moments of magnificence, with the Duke of Westminster's Ormonde winning the Derby and St Leger (at odds of 1/7), Archer up. But the wolves were circling, nonetheless; and the story was nearly over.

There is a sense – no more than that – that Archer, having been created as a sporting hero of transcendent power, was afterwards helped to destroy himself. So as well as being tragic the story is a modern one, and a very English one, in this sense.

The rifts with Lord Falmouth and the Duke of Portland were ridiculous, really, and need never have happened – or at least, not in the way that they did – had there not been a climate of semi-hysteria surrounding Fred Archer at the time. Anyone with a clear head would have seen as much. George Lambton (later to train at Stanley House) dismissed the rumours about Archer as so much implausible nonsense. True, the two men were good friends, but Lambton, a hugely respected figure within racing, was writing some time after the event and his judgements convince.

Rather like Sam Chifney senior, Archer found himself in an unprecedented position: a hired servant with huge power, and popularity of which others could only dream. He worried people, this lanky genius with the gentleman's air and the fatal attractiveness, whose drive and courage put most of them to shame. Later, the untouchable supremacy of Lester Piggott would have a similar effect. After he was sent to jail in 1983 and the expressions of sadness had been conventionally made, some of those who knew him could hardly wait to start putting the boot in. And if Piggott was something out of the ordinary, how much more so was the glamorous Archer, whose fame had spread by God-knows-what means to cover the country! No wonder the desire began to emerge to bring him down to earth, to accuse him of pulling a horse, for heaven's sake, as if he were any greedy little glorified work rider off the Newmarket streets.

It would surely have been the injustice, above all else, that struck Archer about the loss of his patrons – but then, as now, jockeys were liable to suffer that kind of thing.[5] And there was still plenty to look forward to. Mat Dawson remained as firm as a rock. Nellie was pregnant for the second time, the first child having died at birth. At the end of the 1884 season Archer went up to Liverpool to ride a winner for the Duchess of Montrose; afterwards he was given a telegram saying that his baby had been born, all was well, looking forward to your return. His exhausted body must have felt free and uplifted on the train back to Newmarket. In this rare, relaxed state, his mind turned to planning a funny little surprise for his wife, a variation on an intimate theme: before going in to see her and the baby girl, he would change into the hunting outfit that she so loved him to wear. Had he not done so, he might have seen her briefly before she died. As it was, he arrived to the sound of screams from his sister, saying that Nellie was having convulsions. She recognised neither her husband nor his clothes in her last few minutes of life.

And so Archer rode more fiercely than ever through the 1885 season, as his results showed. But by 1886 he was nearly at the end of the line. The wonderful Ormonde gave him his final triumphs, as good as any he had achieved; yet he had chosen not to ride the horse in the Two Thousand Guineas, a rare misjudgement. He also saw signs of what he must most have feared, that his riding was not what it had been. Anyone, he said, could have won on Ormonde, and this was probably true; some thought him the greatest horse of the century.

---

[5] In 1999, for example, Kieren Fallon was sacked from his position as stable jockey to Henry Cecil; the strong implication of a newspaper story was that he had slept with Cecil's wife, but Fallon always denied this and there was indeed no proof – only rumour.

However it wasn't Archer's riding that was failing, it was his health, which was shot to pieces. It was dealt what was probably the final blow by none other than the Duchess of Montrose, who had never missed a meal in her life, and who blithely expected Archer to ride at 8 stone 6 in the Cambridgeshire. Her horse, St Mirin – 'I *count* on you to ride it' – had run third in the Derby, so this was a pretty kindly weight for him; though not, of course, for his would-be jockey, who was now twenty-nine and finding it near impossible to get below nine stone.

Before the October Meeting Archer went to ride at the Curragh, where he had been asked to ride at 8 stone 7 just one day after he had purged his way down to a weight of 9 stone 4. Really quite mad by now, he spent the intervening hours in a Turkish bath, drinking his terrible mixture, only to find that at the end of it all he still weighed 8 stone 12. The horse won anyway, but the Cambridgeshire loomed. 'I never saw you look half so bad as you do now,' he was told by a friend. Archer laughed. 'If I look bad now, how shall I look next Wednesday?'

For the three days before the race, Archer again ate nothing and sat sweating and purging. He now weighed 8 stone 7 and looked like a walking bone, loosely wrapped in livid skin. A year earlier he would almost certainly have found the strength, somewhere inside himself, to lift his horse over the line, as he once had done with Bend Or, but now there was not much more that his poor wrecked body could do for him, and he lost the Cambridgeshire on St Mirin, by a head, to a horse carrying a stone less in weight. It was as fine a performance as Archer ever gave, in fact.

Not long after this, the rumours began again. It was as though the world of racing had scented Archer's appalling vulnerability and was moving in for the kill; not consciously, of course, but irresistibly all the same. It was said that he had paid the jockey of the Cambridgeshire favourite to lose the race. There was no evidence for this at all, but the rumour had its nasty little day of glory. Then, on the last day of the meeting, the day that Fred Archer rode his last ever winner – at Newmarket, on one of Lord Falmouth's few remaining horses – he was cruelly cut by his old friend Captain Machell.

Archer had advised Machell to back one of his rides, a filly who finished second by a head. Afterwards Machell met a female acquaintance who said oh, how *funny*, that Archer had told her *not* to back the horse! He had known the jockey for many years, but Machell had had a bad meeting, he was in a bad mood and he decided, suddenly, to believe this trouble-making fool of a woman. When Archer entered the paddock after the race, Machell publicly turned his back on him. 'Save me from my friends,' he said.

The thought of Archer's life after this, of the return to the lonely, secluded house which, for all its grandeur, was too large for that insubstantial ghost of a man to fill – the baby girl whose birth had killed Nellie Rose now lived with her mother's parents[6] – is almost unbearable. He rode again, at Lewes, where he lost on the favourite, then went back home. The end came quickly after this. On 6 November 1886, a medical bulletin was issued from Falmouth House saying that 'Mr F. Archer has returned home suffering from the effects of a severe chill, followed by a high fever.' The Lords Falmouth and Hastings sent telegrams; nurses were employed; the doctor was in frequent attendance. The next day was the second anniversary of Nellie Rose Archer's death. On Monday, 8 November, another bulletin spoke of an improvement in Archer's symptoms. Although suffering from typhus, his temperature was down; but he was still rambling in his speech, talking about the defeat of St Mirin, the death of his wife, his own imminent death.

Later on the Monday he asked to be left alone in the room with his sister. She had her back to him, looking out of the window on to the Fordham Road. 'Are they coming?' she heard him ask. She turned to see what he meant, and saw that he had taken from a drawer the revolver that he had put there, three years earlier, at a time when there were burglaries in Newmarket. She struggled with him and said afterwards that he was still very strong. He had his arm around his sister as he put the gun into his mouth and pulled the trigger.

---

[6] The John Dawsons of Warren House, the establishment built at the foot of the Heath by William Chifney. Mrs Nellie Tosetti, née Archer, died in Sussex in 1930, aged forty-six.

Grief, it was said, or derangement from the fever: 'suicide while in a state of unsound mind' was the inevitable inquest verdict. Whatever the reasons – and surely it was an accumulation of them – it is hard to think that Fred Archer would ever have killed himself if he had not starved, with the masochistic frenzy of an anorexic, for the whole of his adult life. But then he would never have starved himself in that way if it had not been for the strength of his desire to win races. He would have lived a sensible life instead, and not become racing's most famous ever casualty – nor its greatest ever human hero.

In the comfortable solidity of Victorian Newmarket, Archer had burned with the heat of a Smithfield martyr, with the passion of a lover; and after all, without passion, sport is a dead thing. That bent scrag-end of a man showed the wider world what racing itself had always known: that it was born of passion, that the thoroughbred horse had been created by passion, that passion was the flame that lit the Heath. Racing was never quite so intensely alive again, after the death of Fred Archer.

The funeral was, for Newmarket, on the Churchillian scale: the town simply stopped. Perhaps it was enjoyable in some wretchedly exciting way. The Prince of Wales sent a wreath, the Duke of Westminster wrote a sincere tribute ('Racing will be a different thing for me now – so much *heart* cut out of it'), as did Lord Falmouth, and the Hastings requested that a small cross from them be placed on the coffin. Of course, this should have been buried in unconsecrated ground; but it was put in the grave with Archer's wife, and their first dead baby, William. A large pale marble cross marks the place in Newmarket cemetery. The combined age of the three people in the tomb was fifty-two years.

Souvenirs of Archer – ashtrays, jugs, matchboxes, plates – were being bought almost faster than they could be got into shops, and were still being produced in 1897. There was also a waxwork put in Madame Tussauds, in which the jockey wore Lord Falmouth's colours: 'magpie' jacket – black with white sleeves – red cap. The almost fetishistic interest in Archer continues to be indulged. At the National Horseracing

Museum, the gun with which he shot himself (sending the bullet out the back of his neck, as *The Times* was good enough to inform its readers) sits in a glass case; although there is a story that the revolver which Archer really used was buried soon afterwards on the Heath.

Afterwards, Captain Machell spoke of the events on the last day of the Houghton meeting. 'Could you believe it possible that, after seeing a horse beaten by a head in a desperate finish, I should think Archer was not trying ... I am haunted by the look on his face when I refused to speak to him after the race.' In 1893, Machell was found crouching on the narrow balcony outside the fourth-floor window of his hotel room in Liverpool; he was persuaded back inside and taken home to Newmarket. There he said that he was visited by the ghost of Fred Archer, who came and stood beside his bed, then touched his hand.

Just a year after Archer's death, his rival George Fordham died at the age of fifty. On his tombstone were the words: ''Tis the pace that kills'.

8 A Golden Age

'No Doubt they are both Great Horses' – 1884–1909

A ND NOW LET THE PURISTS have their say: the real star of this golden era was not Fred Archer. It was simply that his stellar qualities allowed those of the real stars to be appreciated, widely and gloriously and as never before.

The question of greatness in the thoroughbred is one that is debated constantly nowadays. How far is it an absolute, how far is it in the eye of the beholder? Does it lie in what a horse does, or in the impression that he makes while he is doing it? No doubt the horses who ran at the turn of the last century created debates of their own at the time. Was this one truly a great Derby winner, or was he beating an inferior field? Was Bend Or greater than Robert the Devil, or was he lucky enough to have Archer at his manic best on his back?

With the thoroughbred, although the right to be placed in the pantheon is earned in a series of moments – transcendent, ephemeral, utterly of the present – it is the steady passage of time which allows the judgement to be made. And so, a hundred or so years after the event, the names stand elevated and unassailable: Bend Or; St Simon; Ormonde; La Flèche; Isinglass; Persimmon; St Frusquin; Flying Fox; Diamond Jubilee; Sceptre; Rock Sand; Pretty Polly; Minoru. They themselves stand in portraits, eternally poised between reality and myth: a gleaming St Simon, with his head moving towards his manger; elegant Isinglass; immaculate Diamond Jubilee; big, calm Pretty Polly in her box. Between them they won 31 classics. Sceptre on her own won four; seven of the others won Triple Crowns; the Triple Crown was won ten times between 1880 and 1910. By today's standards this is astonishing and inconceivable. Nijinsky, in 1970, was the last horse to win the Triple Crown and the first for 35 years.

These extraordinary horses, who bestrode the turn of the century like colossi, were not 'better' than horses today – how can they be? But they were products of a different era, in which the thoroughbred was raced rather than protected, and in which it had less to be protected against. Nowadays, dominance is harder to achieve. Fear has its hold upon racing, dressed in its familiar businessman's disguise. It takes someone as rich as Sheikh Mohammed al Maktoum, who does not have that urgent need to protect a horse's reputation for the breeding market, to run a horse over and over, at four and five and even six. And the horses themselves have changed. Then, along with their greater freedom, they also had greater scope. They would run a Guineas, a Leger, a Gold Cup, a Cambridgeshire: the circumscription of specialist breeding had not yet narrowed their horizons. Speed and stamina had not yet begun their sad process of separation within the thoroughbred, which has brought 'improvements' that sometimes seem like nothing of the kind. If, a hundred years ago, their careers were harder, they were perhaps better equipped to deal with them.

Impossible to say that they represented an apotheosis. Yet the way in which they arrived, in steady sparkling succession, at a time when racing was at its popular height, seemingly unassailed by the troublesome past and future, gives an impression of serene grandeur that was never quite rediscovered. There would be more great horses and the twentieth century would be punctuated by their blessed appearances. In 1999 one of the greatest of them all, the grey Daylami, was bought from France and trained until the age of five on Newmarket Heath. But the whole country knew Bend Or and Persimmon, and (*pace* his jockey, one L. Dettori) just a few mesmerised thousands had the joy of knowing Daylami. The horses stayed the same, but the times changed around them. At the turn of the century, horse and time were in brief, exquisite harmony.

Perhaps the greatest of them all – and yes, a meaningless, because unprovable, statement – was St Simon. Who knows?

Ormonde was a great horse, who won his 1886 Triple Crown with an ease that seemed to grow with every furlong that he ran. His trainer, John Porter of Kingsclere, thought him the best horse of the century. At the end of his career he developed breathing problems and, sent to stud abroad, he was not a prodigious sire. Before he left England he sired Orme, a classic contender who was nobbled in 1892: an occurrence which had, by that time, became somewhat shocking. Five years earlier, during the celebrations for Queen Victoria's jubilee (when the trainer Charlie Blanton presented to Newmarket the famous Clock Tower, which stands at the end of the High Street), Ormonde was guest of honour at a party thrown by his owner, the Duke of Westminster, at his London home. The horse paraded in the garden of Grosvenor House, where the hotel now stands, and ate the flowers presented to him by the Queen of Belgium.

His racing career was perfection, as near as damnit. But St Simon – there was something about St Simon that recalled the days of Flying Childers and Eclipse, when a horse could make one of those inexplicable, miraculous leaps that took the breed forward. And although there are many races that one would give a lot to have seen, for St Simon's Gold Cup win in 1884 one would perhaps give the most. Not that it was a race, in the usual sense of the word. Charlie Wood, sitting cosily for the first two and a quarter miles, just let the horse lollop along behind the previous year's winner. He had been told by Mat Dawson that there was no need to win by more than two lengths. Usually Dawson barely bothered to train St Simon, who had, for example, won a two-year-old race at Doncaster by eight lengths, having given more than three stone to the lowest weight. Before Ascot, however, he had worked a little harder with the horse.

With two furlongs left, Wood let him go and, instantly, he moved into that other sphere which great horses inhabit. He won the race by twenty lengths, after which he was just getting into his stride. Awesomely helpless on his back, Wood went along for the ride as St Simon made another joyful circuit of Ascot racecourse.

He had been owned by Prince Batthyany, the man who dropped down dead before the 1883 Two Thousand Guineas.

This meant that his engagements were forfeit; and he did not, as Ormonde was to do, contest any of the classics. In fact he had only been entered for the Guineas, though it is hard to think that he would not have produced an incontestable result to the Derby, which finished in a dead-heat between St Gatien and Harvester (whom he had ridiculed in a two-year-old trial), or would not have savaged The Lambkin for breakfast in the St Leger. But it was this off-the-wall career of his that enabled him to dominate as he did, at Ascot and on eight other occasions. Even he, surely, could not have won a classic in quite so cavalier a manner.

And so comparisons between St Simon and Ormonde are impossible. They were like Shakespeare and Sophocles: the magnificent anarchist and the pure classicist. All that can be said is that, between them, they had the whole business covered.

St Simon had not been the intended purchase of the Duke of Portland when he attended Prince Batthyany's dispersal sale in Newmarket, but the other horse went for too much money (and yes, this was the man who owned whole chunks of London W1; sometimes the rich can be very careful indeed). So he paid 1,600 guineas for the unraced two year old instead, who had been in the Warren House yard of Mat Dawson's brother. John Dawson had a fair idea of what the horse might be capable of and to this end he painted his leg with what was supposed to look like a blister, hoping that this would put off buyers. Mat, smelling paint and mischief, advised his Grace that St Simon should be snapped up, pronto.

The horse should have been Fred Archer's ride, but around this time came the falling-out with Portland and he could not have made the Gold Cup weight anyway. He work rode St Simon at the start of his three-year-old career, when Mat Dawson had said that he needed 'waking up' a bit; Archer touched him lightly with a spur, whereupon he took off as he was to do at Ascot, flashed through two strings of horses and ended up nearly in the High Street. He was not an easy animal. Previous to this he had been exercised on a straw floor, the weather being too bad to go on the Heath but, like a recalcitrant child, had wandered off it seventeen times

(George Fordham counted them) and fallen over on the ice. He had to be muzzled before grooming, sweated like a pig and took hours to get on a train to go racing, for he would only enter the box backwards. Later it was discovered that he could be made tractable by the sight of an umbrella. Lads learned to improvise with walking sticks topped by a bowler hat.

He was fiery as the devil, in fact, but magnificent as perhaps no other horse has ever quite been; 'the only smashing good horse I have ever trained', said Mat Dawson, whose Heath House had been stuffed with an embarrassment of classic winners[1] and whose vote went, nevertheless, to an animal who never even needed to contest one. And it is again meaningless, because unprovable, to say that he is the best horse ever to have been trained at Newmarket. But sometimes it is extremely pleasurable to make statements of that kind.

St Simon was also, unlike Ormonde, a truly influential sire. Portland said that his progeny were 'more nearly robots' than any he had ever known, perhaps a strange way of putting it but he meant, presumably, that there was a kind of certainty about them. What Mat Dawson called the 'electricity', which showed itself even as St Simon walked around his box, seems to have been transmitted through his blood, right through to supercharged twentieth century sires like Hyperion and Nearco. He was also completely sound, which many sires are not; indeed seemingly indestructible until the day in 1908 when he collapsed, swiftly and suddenly as he did everything else, on his return from exercise.

He had been champion sire nine times (more often than any stallion since 1787), with ten of his immediate progeny winning seventeen classics. Among these were La Flèche, St Frusquin and the Prince of Wales' Persimmon: double classic winner of 1896, whose elegant, greenish-blue statue stands outside the Royal Stud at Sandringham and whose stuffed head – a surprisingly attractive, alert-looking object – is in the National Horseracing Museum. Persimmon was not the first horse owned by the Prince, who had been struggling for success since the 1870s. But his Derby and Leger wins

---

[1] He won 28 classics in the years 1853–95.

symbolised the full-bodied return of royal patronage to racing, and to Newmarket.

This set its triumphant seal upon the golden age. Almost a hundred years after Prinny had flounced off the stage, a Prince of Wales – God bless him – was back in town. The future Edward VII, a man whose Jockey Club breakfasts 'were almost appalling in their length and solidity', could hardly have cut a more different figure from Fred Archer, yet the presence of both men was similarly important. Both played an essential part in this suddenly brightly lit theatre. Newmarket had been created by royal patronage, after all, and although in a way its self-assurance was absolute, needing no outward confirmation, there was still a sense that this was as things should be: a prince submitting once more to the benign and rigorous rule of Newmarket. There he is in a photograph, in one of his terrible country suits, a bowler on his head, racing glasses slung across his chest; standing to one side with the eternal, proud humility of the thoroughbred owner while beautiful Persimmon fills the frame and the eye.

Mummy disapproved no end, of course. 'What will become of the poor country when I die?' But Victoria had it wrong: few monarchs ever reached the apotheosis of popularity attained by Edward VII when, in 1909, his horse Minoru won the Derby.

As the Prince Regent had been before him, Edward was a *bon vivant*, but on the whole he got away with it. Indeed, as with Charles II, it may have worked in his favour, especially when his mother was doing her Widow of Windsor act for all it was worth. The normality of Edward, the openness with which he and his 'Marlborough House set' went out and about in hansom cabs to London music-halls and gambling clubs, to Epsom, Ascot and Newmarket, must have had a certain attractiveness. For Victoria, it destroyed the mystique of monarchy – an argument that continues to rage, this – but people seem to have been happy to have a stately, Saxe-Coburgian Prince Hal in their midst, living the life that surely most men would like to have lived, taking his pleasure without shame but not shamelessly.

As a young man – he was born in 1841 – Edward's rakishness had a wilder aspect. Some of his friends, like

Henry Chaplin, were implicated in scandals – this, after all, was the time of Lord Hastings' elopement with little Lady Florence. Lord Euston of the Grafton family was discovered to have married a bigamous woman (worse yet, she was considered very common); Lord d'Eresby stole his mistress' money and eloped with her maid; and in 1871 the Prince himself was in a divorce court, denying adultery with Lady Mordaunt, his letters to her printed in *The Times*. This went down very badly, although the furore was nothing compared to what it would be nowadays. There was also a lot of excitable talk about what Edward got up to in Parisian nightclubs (orgies at the Café Anglais, no less) and about gambling debts (cards rather than horses).

Yet as the Prince grew older and fatter and more of an immovable object, so his capacity to shock seems to have waned. His 'debauchery' became comfortable, jolly; frankly it was impossible to imagine him with his spats off. If he had looked like Fred Archer it might have been different, but he was such a waddling Lothario, so very fond of sedentary pleasures like cigars and food. He once ploughed his way through six courses, having said at the start of the meal that he was not very hungry, then looked up from his plate plaintively: 'Is there no cheese?' At the dinner in Paris when a serving tray was lifted to reveal the renowned courtesan Cora Pearl, wearing only a sprig of parsley, one cannot help but wonder if the prince would have preferred a plate of *boeuf Bourgignon* instead.

So too, with his racing, the impression is given of a passion indulged within secure, gentlemanly boundaries. There was none of that maniacal fervour which characterised an earlier age, a younger man. Racing *was* a passion, of that there is no doubt, but it was an affair conducted with an eye to the conventions; and, most importantly for public relations, without spending insane amounts of money. The letters that Edward wrote on the subject have, as has been mentioned, a rather careful and old-womanish quality to them:

'I am sorry your horse did not win. But I do not in the least mind losing a "tenner",' he wrote to his friend, Colonel Paget, who did most of his betting for him and had given him this ruinous tip. On another occasion: 'As I always like paying my debts at the appointed time, I enclose £100 which you kindly put on l'Abbesse de Jouarre for me.' £100! George Bentinck would have burned that to heat his curling iron. In 1886: 'I am very flourishing, thanks, but had not a penny on Ormonde for the Derby – alas! Try and get Sir Hugh for me as cheap as you can.'

In fact he had no luck at all for nearly twenty years, which might have led most people to jack the whole thing in. He had made a tentative *entrée* into ownership, registering his colours two years before he actually raced his first horse, an Arab who was beaten thirty lengths at the 1877 July meeting (and this, now, was the difference between the average thoroughbred and his outdistanced forebear).

An oleaginous book entitled *King Edward VII as a Sportsman* (which portrays its hero as a dashing big game-hunter and the finest shot since William Tell, rather than a bearded balloon precariously buttoned into a Norfolk jacket) hints at what might have been going on in those missing two years. 'In the early seventies,' the book intones, 'HRH was understood to be interested in some animals trained under the superintendence of the late Captain Machell, but whatever this interest may have been, it was a private matter, and it would be improper to discuss the subject in detail!' What could have happened? If only this silly book had fewer scruples. All one can assume is that Edward considered becoming a part of the oh-so successful Machell set-up, then realised that this dubious temptation would have to be resisted, if only to stop Victoria from telling him what Albert would have made of it all.

So he went to John Porter instead and, through no fault of the trainer, had a disastrous time of it. He bought a daughter of Hermit as a possible foundation mare, but the poor girl had a huge, diseased heart and died as she approached the winning post in her second race. A fortnight later, the Prince was back at the Newmarket sales, spending 3,100 guineas on a brother to Paradox (second to Melton in the Derby) who never even raced. His horses, he said, were 'awful'. In the eight years up to 1893, he won £5,904 in stakes and eighteen races, which was really pitiful; and this at a time when Porter was tactlessly training animals like Ormonde.

But it was Porter who handed Edward the unlikely key to good fortune, all the same. Six years earlier, he had gone to have a chat with the Prince – who was sitting in a dressing-gown, writing his letters – in which he advised him to buy a mare named Perdita II. She cost £900. 'You will ruin the Prince if you go on buying these thoroughbreds,' scolded the comptroller of Edward's household. In fact she was to become one of the greatest bargains in racing history, quite possibly the greatest brood mare, and to become known as The Gold Mine. The repeated success of her matings to St Simon – three couplings, three champions – was almost freakish; Perdita was only an ordinary sort of horse, but something in her blood certainly roused the mettlesome stallion.

John Porter, however, did not reap the benefits of his prescience. On the first day of 1893, Edward moved his horses to Newmarket, to Egerton House on the Cambridge road, which had been rebuilt over the past two and a half years as a state-of-the-art training establishment (the money to do this had been earned by one stallion, Hampton, who had stood at Egerton stud for so long, and so prodigiously, that he had made £50,000 for his owner Lord Ellesmere's estate – and that is what one *calls* a gigolo). Egerton was a wonderful set-up, but these awe-inspiring yards can bring their own problems. It was estimated that a trainer would need to bring in £13,000 a year just to cover costs – which sounds very familiar to an age in which upmarket stables are in constant quest for horses, just to keep the numbers up, the books balanced and the equine swimming-pool heated.

Installed at Egerton was Richard Marsh, a former jump jockey, which perhaps gave him the nerve to cope. Indeed when he was offered the job of royal trainer, his first reaction was to say that he would have to consult with his principal owner, the Duke of Hamilton; a piece of *lèse majesté*[2] that Edward in fact appreciated. It is unclear, though, why the Prince made the move from John Porter. Yes, Egerton was as smart as a pin and convenient for Sandringham (where Edward brought in 'Sandringham time', in which the clocks

---

[2] It was politer, at least, than Steve Donoghue was to be when offered the position of royal jockey to George V: 'I would love to,' he said, 'but His Majesty has very few good horses.'

were put back an hour to allow more shooting time; Edward VIII brought them forward again). And, of course, Newmarket was Newmarket. Nevertheless there is a suggestion that the change was prompted, Warwick Lake-style, by the Prince's racing manager, Lord Marcus Beresford, who may have had his own little private power struggle with Porter. To all intents and purposes, however, the break was amicable. The trainer subsequently had made for Edward a shield, surrounded by little medallions containing hair from his horses' tails, now in the National Horseracing Museum:[3] 'this', the oleaginous book assures us, 'Porter was always gratified to believe that the Prince particularly valued'.

Whatever the reason for the split, there is no doubt that Newmarket brought forth the fruits that had been planted at Kingsclere and the association between Edward and Egerton was a hugely happy one. First of all came Florizel, the least successful product of St Simon and Perdita, but a veritable world-beater when compared with what the Prince had been racing before. In 1895, at the age of four, he won all sorts of staying races including the Jockey Club Cup at Newmarket, and nearly as much money as had been cobbled together in the past ten seasons. No doubt about it, things were looking better. And Florizel's two-year-old brother was looking better still.

Yet the gallop that Persimmon did at the 1896 Craven meeting, at the start of his three-year-old career, had a very depressing effect upon those who watched it. 'Call that a Derby horse?' said Marcus Beresford, rather nastily, to Richard Marsh, who must have been feeling very uncomfortable as his stable star finished three lengths behind the horse that he was supposed to flatten. 'I don't think that I have ever had a horse come to hand so sluggishly and slowly as did

---

[3] There was a great fashion for fetishistic artefacts of this kind. Hooves were cut from Eclipse, St Simon and Persimmon (now in the Jockey Club), and from Hermit; Gladiateur lost his tail and Persimmon his head; St Simon's skeleton stood in the Natural History Museum, Eclipse's and Hyperion's in the National Horseracing Museum; and Ambush, who won the Grand National for Edward in 1900, was buried on the Heath then dug up again when the Prince decided that his skeleton, too, should be exhibited. There is nothing macabre about this impulse towards preservation. These bits and pieces of horse are simply repositories of magic, totems in the most primitive sense. And they are, perhaps, a way of finally holding on to what, in life, was so unknowable and elusive.

Persimmon,' he was afterwards to say. As the season began the horse still wore a coat like a woolly mammoth. The talent was there, but the question was whether it could be drawn out of the hat in time. Meanwhile Leopold de Rothschild's St Frusquin, trained in town at Palace House, won a scintillating, shiny-coated Guineas at a price of 12/100, and looked all set for Derby victory (he started 8/13 favourite on the day of the race).

Persimmon was found to have had a raging abscess at the time of the terrible gallop; all the same, the day of his final spin before the Derby was surely very nerve-racking for Marsh. It took place on the private gallops at Egerton – the moss litter surface had been copied from Chantilly – and Edward came down to see it with (for a wonder) his wife Alexandra, the future George V and other members of the Royal Family. One can imagine them all sitting there like Teutonic dummies, waiting to be entertained. The show was on; would the star shine?

He gave 21 pounds to a decent horse and cantered up. 'We have only one to beat, Your Royal Highness,' said Marsh to Alexandra. And, to the Prince: 'I think we will win the Derby.'

The sons of St Simon – Persimmon and St Frusquin – were all set for the Epsom showdown. And it was, indeed, the presence of St Frusquin that gave such moment and substance to Persimmon's victory. The nightmare had continued right to the end for Richard Marsh: very much his father's son, Persimmon had refused to get on the train to Epsom – with only minutes to spare before departure, twelve men manoeuvred him into his box – and the sweat was cascading off both him and his trainer by the time of the Derby. So precoccupied had he been with keeping his charge calm at the start, Marsh never even saw the finish. But his tricky, courageous horse had fought it out with St Frusquin down every inch of the Epsom straight. It was a real race, an absolute race, and Persimmon won it by no more than a neck. 'No doubt,' said the Prince of Wales, to his friend Leopold de Rothschild, 'they are both great horses.'

A film was made of this 1896 Derby, which one would give a great deal to be able to see. According to *Strand Magazine*, a camera was set up twenty yards past the winning post and, as the runners approached, 'the inventor paid little heed to the appalling uproar that marked the finish of the race; he only turned his wheel for dear life and for the benefit of the public who weren't there.' The following evening, this piece of newsreel was shown in the Alhambra Theatre, Leicester Square, to a soundtrack of 'God Bless the Prince of Wales'. A drawing of the Prince leading in Persimmon after the race was published in the *Illustrated London News*; the artist, Samuel Begg, was criticised for having underplayed the enthusiasm of the crowd. 'Owner, horse and jockey came in for a perfect ovation, and the Prince was kept bowing like a Chinese manadarin for several minutes,' the racing writer W.A. Blew later recollected, 'the cheers being renewed when he went forth to lead his horse to the weighing room. Many hats which were thrown into the air on that occasion must never again have reached their owners.'

And this fond excitement seems to have been quite genuine. Persimmon's victory showed, of course, that the Prince of Wales was at one with so many of his subjects; unlike them, he had everything but, like them, he wanted above all else to win the Derby. This was the sense in which racing could be, up to a very certain point, a leveller. The means to achieve it were different, but the desire was the same. Of course this is no longer true. Nowadays, the desire to win the Derby is, as it was two hundred years ago, confined to those who inhabit the racing world. And so even if Sir Alex Ferguson, racehorse owner and the closest thing that we now have to popular royalty, were to pull it off, the sense of communion with his achievement would not be there. In fact, in a strange way it might be stronger if the Queen were to win the race. Although less 'popular', in the silly sense of the word, than a Ferguson, it is clear that her presence at race meetings still means something. It is as though she and racing have a communal significance, both of them representing something that often seems to be moving gracefully towards obsolescence, without anyone caring very much, but that people do not, in fact, want to lose. And so her Derby victory might still be the most popular of them all.

Not, though, to the orgiastic extent displayed in 1896: that was as if the Prince of Wales had scored the winning goal in the World Cup. For him, of course, it must have been amazingly satisfying. Better than sex with Lillie Langtry, better even than a twelve-course dinner cooked by Mrs Bridges; this was his boy, his home-bred, his most beautiful and mysterious possession. Persimmon went on to win the St Leger and, at four, the Gold Cup and Eclipse Stakes (carrying 10 stone 2). Then he was retired to Sandringham where, in his first crop, he threw Sceptre: the St Simon blood continued to pulsate with alarming life.

The Prince had been keen to set up a stud of his own, even though Hampton Court had been revived (not for the first time) in 1850. Victoria, ever the caricature, set the condition that the stud could be re-established as long as all the produce were sold as yearlings at public auction – in other words, as long as the Royal Stud was not contaminated by the presence of racehorses for longer than was absolutely necessary. It was the most respectable of set-ups, and it was also very success-ful. Orlando, the 'winner' of the Running Rein Derby, stood there; The Earl, who should have won the 1868 Derby for Lord Hastings, was bought there. So, too, was La Flèche, the filly who won the 1892 Triple Crown for Edward's friend, Baron de Hirsch.

'She was a pronounced specimen of the varminty, grey-hound and wiry type,' said Richard Marsh. 'When she was ragged and thin she could be relied upon to give of her very best form.' She was also the most expensive yearling sold to date. Bidding against the ever-cautious Duke of Portland, Hirsch blew him out with an offer of 5,500 guineas, which she was more than worth (small change to Hirsch, however, who left £8 million when he died). Yet her ending was not good. After the death of her owner in 1896, she was sold at the Newmarket July Sales for 12,600 guineas. This was more than the buyer, Sir Tatton Sykes, had authorised Marcus Beresford to pay; perhaps that was why he refused to take her home after she had arrived at his local railway station. He was sulking with her. And so the great La Flèche was left starving in her box, fed by a station master with food from his smallholding, until Sykes finally consented to receive her two weeks later.

Baron Hirsch would have been appalled. He was not really a racing man, and although La Flèche was very distinctive, with her varminty look, he had once failed to recognise her when Richard Marsh took the name down from her box. But he was kind in the extreme. He had come into the sport after the death of his son: it had been the son's passion, and so he took it over. Anything that he won he gave away to London hospitals – £35,000 in La Flèche's year. 'Matrons and nurses,' wrote Thormanby, 'might be seen scanning eagerly the sporting column of the daily papers . . .'

Hirsch was, in fact, a marvellous man who put to shame those who sneered at the Prince of Wales' friendships with Jews; which they continued to do, all the same. A mad story started up that he actually had Jewish blood (Albert's father being his wife's Jewish footman, no less). Anti-Semitism, as was made distressingly clear in the 1930s, was instinctive in a certain type of English person who, at the same time, was extremely willing to mix with Jews when it was to their advantage. The Rothschilds were well enough liked – Baron Meyer had become the first Jewish member of the Jockey Club in 1876 – but it was said, nevertheless, that the Prince was so attached to them because they bailed him out of his debts, for which there is no evidence whatsoever. Edward was a cosmopolitan, not narrow-minded at all, and he probably found these clever men rather more interesting and worldly than the average English sporting gentleman who, for all his charm, could be wearingly one-dimensional. The ESG was a child, in fact, whereas Leopold de Rothschild was a grown-up.

Edward would also have enjoyed the atmosphere of sybaritic luxury that hung around these fabulously rich people, and very sensible too. Palace House was no doubt a good deal more comfortable than the average English house. Moulton Paddocks, once leased by George Alexander Baird, and by now the home of Sir Ernest Cassel, was sumptuous in the extreme. Cassel, the son of a German money-lender, had arrived in England aged sixteen with his violin and, by the age of forty in 1892, become a multi-millionaire – an impressive character. After Baron de Hirsch's death, he took over as Edward's financial adviser, which does not mean that he was not, also, his greatest friend. It was Cassel who built the Edward VII Memorial Hall and Gardens in Newmarket High Street, on the site of Lowther House, where his horses were formerly trained (there are a few tethering rings on the brick wall of the garden, which once formed the inside wall of some of the Lowther House boxes). Cassel's horses were not, incidentally, up to much. He won the 1901 Two Thousand Guineas with a £300 horse, named – appropriately – Handicapper: 'by what miracle it is impossible to guess', spat the writer of *King Edward VII as a Sportsman*, whose sycophancy was very much confined to the regal sphere.

Two years after this victory, Cassel moved himself and his horses to Moulton Paddocks, where he had a wing built especially for Edward's use. When the property was sold, after Cassel's death in 1920, it was described as 'the famous sporting estate' and as having twenty bedrooms and 1,300 acres of ground. Now the site of the Godolphin racing operation, it was then bought and briefly inhabited by the millionaire financier Jimmy White, who six years later was to drink prussic acid, having lost everything by the return to the Gold Standard. His widow, living in one room in Victoria, refused to sell his racing trophies.

After Persimmon, Diamond Jubilee: the wickedest of them all, and the most physically immaculate. Henry Chaplin once bet Richard Marsh £5 that he would be able to find a fault with the horse but, after long minutes of study, had to concede that here, as far as was possible, was perfection.

He really was a terror, though. As a foal he would walk straight at grooms and, if they did not get out of way, right over them. He bit off a stable lad's thumb. Before the July Stakes in 1899, he threw Jack Watts (who had ridden Persimmon to Derby victory then entered the enclosure 'looking as solemn as a judge who had just passed the death sentence'[4]); ran riderless down the course, refused to start with the rest and finished last.

So Marsh tried him with Mornington Cannon, a kindly jockey but one who did nothing for Diamond Jubilee: 'The colt had a way of turning his head around and looking at his rider in a manner which was far from encouraging.'[5] Event-

---

[4] From George Lambton's *Men I Have Known*.
[5] From *King Edward VII as a Sportsman*.

ually he had a go at Cannon, swinging him around with his teeth like a tiger playing with a bone, and the only thing left to try was to put the stable lad Herbert Jones on his back. Jones was just a boy, with two wins from 43 rides, but the horse seemed to like him.

It was said, and plausibly, that Diamond Jubilee was wayward to this extent because as younger brother to Persimmon he had been spoiled. What is done to a horse is done, though; if he had been indulged as a baby then, at three, everyone was going to have to cope with the consequence. And it was more than that. Diamond Jubilee was teetering upon the summit of thoroughbred perfection, high and proud and dangerous; Richard Marsh knew this, and his respect for what the horse was, what he had been made, was complete and magnificent. 'You must never hide' (i.e. hit) 'the high-class horse of great courage. It is courage which makes him high-class. Break that and you destroy the whole fabric of the splendid racehorse.'

And with this degree of understanding to help him, Diamond Jubilee won the first Triple Crown of the new century. Yet he *was* standing on the precipice that topples into over-breeding; the lively blood that had produced Persimmon had, with him, come close to boiling over. In fact his talent was greater than his ability to use it, and Marcus Beresford said that the only time it was truly seen was in the Two Thousand Guineas, which he had won from the first furlong. A letter written afterwards by the Prince read: 'Thanks for your congratulations on Diamond Jubilee. He won the Leger easily, but was, alas! beaten for the Jockey Club Stakes as he was both leg-weary and sulky.' And that, thereafter, was to be the story. The horse raced at four but his heart did not seem to be in it; he never won again, and was eventually sold for £30,000 to stand at stud in Argentina, where he was a success.

The year 1900 was to be the Prince of Wales' greatest as an owner. He won not just the Triple Crown but the Grand National; even the Maktoums have never pulled that one off. His Derby win was considered sufficiently important to warrant a telegram from Lord Roberts, at that time commanding the British army in the Boer War: 'News of Diamond

Jubilee's victory was conveyed to me by Stanley during attack on Blandfort yesterday. Army in S. Africa beg to offer respectful congratulations.' War would come and war would go, but the Derby was still the Derby; a truth that would hold, well into the next century.

For Edward, however – as was almost inevitable – things now went very quiet. The standard of his horses dropped at times to the desperate pre-Perdita levels. Florizel and Persimmon were wonderful stallions to be standing at Sandringham but, while other owners were winning all over the place with their progeny, the King seemed to have kept the rubbish for himself. He actually began to apologise to his trainer about it: 'We have some very bad horses, Marsh.' In 1907, he won the July Stakes with Pearl of the Loch, which even *King Edward VII as a Sportsman* was obliged to admit was among 'the worst animals that ever took this'. In 1908, his Derby horse, Perrier, ran appallingly. Marcus Beresford subsequently used his upmarket salesman's patter to try and sell the colt to a Frenchman: 'He was going well, when at a critical point of the race six or seven others came past him, and he lost.' '*Quel malheur,*' said the Frenchman, reaching for his cheque-book.

But the real unhappiness of 1908 was the death of Persimmon, aged sixteen. He was found one day in his box with his pelvis broken; there are few more terrible sights than a stricken thoroughbred, and this had been such a very fine example. Everything was done for him, he was suspended in a sling in the desperate hope that he would mend, but in the end he had to be destroyed. Edward had really loved him. 'Isn't he beautiful, isn't he beautiful,' he would murmur, gazing as the horse was led out to him in the grounds at Sandringham. The Jockey Club has in its possession a Christmas card, designed to hang on a bridle, inscribed 'Persimmon from Edward R'; perhaps the King sent these to all his horses. After his favourite's death, an exquisite little statue of him was made in silver by Fabergé, and Mrs Leopold de Rothschild commissioned a similar item for her husband: a model of St Frusquin, the horse whose greatness allowed that of Persimmon to shine all the brighter.

The glory days were not quite over, though. In the year of Persimmon's death, the King – despairing of his home-breds

– gave it one last shot by leasing six horses from a man named Colonel Hall-Walker, who believed himself to be the reincarnation of Charles II. It was Hall-Walker, later Lord Wavertree, who laid the foundations for the National Stud which is now in Newmarket. In 1916 he had offered his bloodstock, including 43 beautifully bred mares, to the nation, on condition that the government bought his breeding establishment in Ireland. The original purpose was the production of good quality Army horses. However, after the First World War the admirable concept was established of a thoroughbred stud which would attempt to preserve blood-stock for the 'nation', and, very soon, it had produced Blandford, a champion sire of the 1920s and 1930s. The National Stud moved from Ireland in 1943, and to Newmarket in 1963.

The horses leased by the King, however, were not all that he might have wished. The only one that Richard Marsh thought anything of – although not much – was a light-framed colt called Minoru, who had won at two then, when crossing the Cambridge Road to gallop Racecourse Side, had slipped and, according to Marcus Beresford, 'nearly split himself in half'.

It was all fairly inauspicious but then, at the start of the 1909 season, it was as if a light had been switched on above the horse, and in a sustained burst of success, which had Marsh gasping with disbelief, he won the Greenham Stakes (£879), the Two Thousand Guineas (£5,000), the Derby (£6,450), the St James' Palace Stakes at Royal Ascot, the Sussex Stakes at Goodwood and the Free Handicap at Newmarket (now staged in April, then run at the Houghton meeting). The King had only a year to live, but Minoru was taking him out in style.

He was not quite a Persimmon or a Diamond Jubilee, but he was brave: Hotspur in the *Daily Telegraph* described how, in the Free Handicap, the horse gave chunks of weight to his three opponents, 'of whom Cattaro was in receipt of no less than 16lb. In the Abingdon Mile Bottom, Minoru appeared to be beaten. Then it was that Maher' (Herbert Jones, now the royal jockey, was injured) 'displayed his superb horse-manship. The jockey rode the race of his life. Spectators were absolutely thrilled as Minoru, distressed as he was, responded with courage to the calls of his rider . . .

'Minoru's victory not only furnished the opportunity for a loyal demonstration of enthusiasm such as is rarely witnessed on a racecourse, but it also provided the setting for a pretty incident. His Majesty came from the Jockey Club enclosure to congratulate Maher upon riding a wonderful race. It was probably the proudest and most memorable moment of the jockey's life.' Oh, *autres temps*! Except that, again, the world of racing has changed less in this respect than most other worlds. Jockeys are still asked, today, about the thrill of riding a winner in the royal colours; they still agree that it is special; and it makes little difference, really, if they are doing this from courtesy or from honesty.

Again, though, it would be hard to re-create the kind of scenes that greeted Minoru's Derby victory – and not just because the poor Queen no longer has anything remotely capable of winning the race.[6] This day, 26 May, 1909, was a high point in the fortunes of both the monarchy and of racing. They had, both of them, attained a popularity that had not yet strayed over into the wild hinterland of populism: that had been achieved because of, not despite, their mystique.

The forces of idiocy were present, of course, as they had been for the past ninety years and would be for the next ninety. As Minoru walked into the winners' enclosure people were trying to pick hairs out of his tail – 'Please don't touch him, or he will kick,' said the King; and racing's code of behaviour prevailed, as it rarely now does on Derby day.

This was the first – and the last, probably – Derby win for a reigning monarch. There was a lot of singing of 'God Save the King', and cheering, and trying to shake the King's hand, all of which appeared to leave Edward very moved for inside that bulbous chest was a susceptible heart. Sir Edward Grey, the Liberal foreign secretary, wrote that 'the humblest devotees of horse racing in a Derby Day crowd knew that King Edward was there to enjoy the national festival in precisely the same spirit as themselves . . . There was, in fact, a real

---

[6] Wrongly advised, perhaps, by those who fear the envious forces of republicanism? At any rate, it is hard not to see significance in the fact that her last decent horse, the dual classic winner Dunfermline, ran in the Jubilee year of 1977.

sympathy and community of feeling between himself and his people.' This may sound like idealism after the event, but it probably *did* feel like that. It is one of racing's central paradoxes that something so rarefied, so dedicated to the principle of élitism, can cause a crowd to bathe in a shared and blissful warmth; it is another, similar paradox that a King can be brought close to his subjects by that most elusive thing of all, a thoroughbred classic winner.

As for the man who shouted 'Now, King, you've won the Derby; go home and dissolve this bloody Parliament,' he was a voice from another world altogether, who refused to collude in *la grande illusion* that is racing. For that is what it is, no doubt about it: a romantic construct based upon hope, continually pulled down, continually rebuilt. And the Edwardian age, which was a great illusion in its own way, was perfectly at home in it. One hundred years or so ago, all the theatre that is now re-created on a racecourse was for real. Perhaps it gave its finest performance on the day of Minoru's Derby win.

Just a few weeks afterwards, the King told Marcus Beresford that he intended leaving Egerton House and moving to a public yard in Newmarket. He refused to discuss the matter: perhaps he had become capricious in his old age; perhaps pressure had been put on him to reduce his expenditure. But it was a bizarre and ungrateful action, seemingly very much out of character (of course it does beg the question of what had caused him to leave John Porter's yard in 1893).

The day was saved for Richard Marsh by none other than Lillie Langtry who, in her new guise as good sportswoman, chatted obliquely to her ex-lover in the Jockey Club enclosure at the July meeting. To her, he admitted that Egerton had become too expensive to run (although this is hard to credit, as he had earned £270,000 in stallion fees during his racing career, was to win over £20,000 in 1909 and was never in arrears with his Weatherbys account). Whatever his reason, or whim, it cannot have been very substantial. Lillie reminded him that he would lose all the privacy that went with his present set-up; he agreed almost immediately, and Marsh and Egerton kept the King's horses. 'You're a brick,' said

Marcus Beresford to the face that once launched a thousand aristocratic heart murmurs. The strange little episode was over.

And then, not much more than a year later, the King suffered a severe bronchial attack. News of his last winner, Witch of the Air at Kempton Park, was telegraphed to Buckingham Palace. 'I am very glad,' he said; and died six hours later. Minoru, the most successful royal owner's last champion, was sold as a stallion to Russia. There is a story that he was one of the horses used to draw the Romanoff carriage through the streets, in an act of defiance before the start of the Russian Revolution.

Weird and wonderful things had meanwhile been going on during the reign of Edward VII, not yet disturbing the serene façade presented by the King and his friends, but portents of a less certain future. There had, for example, been an invasion.

The Americans had come to Newmarket and, as always, they brought change and irresistible influence, little of it for the better. They also seemed to have a rather insulting notion that they could behave far worse in England than at home. John Huggins, who trained at Heath House at the turn of the century, was asked if there were many crooks in racing in his native USA. 'No, they have all come over here.' The charming belief that this country exerts a pressure upon Americans to say 'please' and let the other guy win was, in early twentieth century Newmarket, turned on its head.

Not always, of course. Men like Pierre Lorillard, a tobacco millionaire who owned Iroquois (ridden to 1881 Derby success by Fred Archer), or James Keene, whose Foxhall won the Autumn double in the same year, were completely reputable. So too was Huggins and Lorillard's trainer, Jacob Pincus, who got Iroquois fit by the then unknown means of galloping him against the clock. But the Americans who came a little later were doing so to make a quick and very dirty buck; as was to be revealed, in circumstances of high drama, in 1903.

It was a concerted coup on the part of two men, William Gates and James Drake. Gates was a barbed-wire millionaire (selling the stuff was how he made his fortune), Drake was a professional gambler and the chief ingredient in their nasty plan was dope: still a very dubious word in connection with American racing. Every year since 1984, as the European horses have made their annual assault upon the US Breeders' Cup races, the question has been: to drug or not to drug? Of course Lasix – administered to horses to counter the debilitating effects of broken blood vessels – is not a malign substance, but it is banned in Europe, and the freedom with which Americans dole it out to their animals (like Prozac) has, perhaps illogically, perhaps not, a slightly sinister aspect. All the same, if 'They' are using it and 'We' are not, the playing field is not very level. And so the European Breeders' Cup horses often do run on Lasix. The Americans, as usual, are laying down the *de facto* rules of engagement.

At the start of the century, however, the last thing they wanted to do was tell anyone what rules they were playing by. Gates and Drake had set up in Newmarket at a stable called Red House, now demolished, which had stood by St Mary's Square; with them was their own personal Dr Crippen, a trainer named Enoch Wishard who was feeding his horses on little cocktails of cocaine and arsenic. In a sense, cocaine was not so different from Lasix, in that it achieved the same purpose: of allowing a horse to run better, or harder, than it might naturally have done, allowing it, in effect, to become a different horse, just as drugs can turn one into a different person. It was and is a horrible idea, frankly antithetical to the spirit of racing, but then, of course, so many things within the sport are.

At the turn of the century, the American crooks were having a field day. Their version of pulling a horse, and then letting it run to its capacity, could hardly fail; all they had to do was race an animal without drugs and then with them; it was almost impossible that it should not improve sufficiently to win. It might kill itself, as a drug-crazed horse did in 1903, when the jockey was unable to pull it up and it ran into a wall. But that was unfortunate – a hazard of the game. The plus side was too great to let oneself get sad and sentimental over the odd dead horse. It was estimated that the dopers won around £2 million in the years between 1897 and 1901, a sum which makes something of a mockery of the sport and the air that it then had of impregnable solidity. Of course, if one chooses to look at it differently, it is the dopers who were the real joke.

Their antics were brought to an end in 1903 by George Lambton, by then training for Lord Derby at Stanley House, whose suspicions were so strong that they had become knowledge, as near as damnit. He proved in the simplest and most effective way possible exactly what was going on: by doping five useless horses of his own, then telling the Jockey Club to watch in amazement. Four winners and one second later, the point was made. A rule was passed stating that 'If any person shall administer, or cause to be administered, for the purpose of affecting the speed of a horse, drugs or stimulants internally, by hypodermic or any other method, every person so offending shall be warned off Newmarket Heath and other places where these rules are enforced.'

So the crooks went to France, there to practise a spot of *le doping*; and a shadow was lifted, if not completely removed, from Newmarket.

With the Americans had come a handful of jockeys, whose influence was to be rather more ambivalent. Tod Sloan, for example, had an effect upon race riding that was to be as revolutionary as that of Sam Chifney senior had been, over one hundred years earlier. Up went his stirrups, in came his rein, and hey presto, he was the 'monkey on a stick' that is now so familiar an image one can scarcely picture the lengthened, elegant style in which jockeys rode beforehand. 'He used to crouch right up on a horse's neck,' said a transfixed Steve Donoghue, 'balanced like a bird . . .'

It is said that the short rein and stirrups may have been invented by default, as it were, when black jockeys at out-of-town American meetings were thrown on to horses – no saddle, no leathers, nothing – and all they could do was cling on to the mane and neck with their knees pulled up. It seemed ridiculous, except that the horses they were riding often won. One of these black boys, Willie Sims, actually rode and won at Newmarket; but it was Tod Sloan – a very good horseman anyway – who gave the style legitimacy. Whether or not he had learned from the black jockeys, he had little choice in the matter when it came to riding with short stirrups: his legs were only the length of a garden gnome's. The name Tod came, in fact, from 'toad', in reference to the fact that his legs were more like hunkers than limbs.

Born in Indiana in 1874, Sloan came to England in 1897 and made an instant impression, riding twenty winners in a very short time. In 1898 he won 43 races out of 78; in 1899, there were 108 winners from 345 rides. It was very, very startling – what would have happened if he had ridden against Fred Archer, is the fascinating question? – and, had it not been for the fact that Sloan was also bumptious, brash and crooked as an S-bend, it would have been welcome. Of course change such as he represented was disturbing, but racing is less resistant to innovation than is generally supposed. If sitting on a horse's neck was better than sitting on its back, that is what jockeys would do – no question. And, indeed, it is what they did. 'You cannot like it,' said George Lambton, 'but it has come to stay and we must make the best of it': which might reasonably be called the reluctant, guiding principle of racing.

Sloan was also at an advantage in that the starting gate, which had been brought into use in 1897, was already familiar in the USA. And he had the supreme advantage, that of being new. Just as the England football team could win the World Cup because no one had ever played quite that way before, so Sloan could win races because he judged pace differently from English jockeys. He, of course, saw it as simple superiority: 'Without brag or bounce I must say that there was such a hopeless ignorance of pace among the majority of those riding in the race that I suppose I managed to kid them,' he said, after winning the 1898 Middle Park Stakes. Yes and no. Richard Marsh was unconvinced that Sloan was any better than, for example, Herbert Jones, and his record in the classics was not outstanding: his style was not sophisticated enough for Epsom. Yet Fred Rickaby, who rode for Lambton, said that 'If I were an owner, I should not run a horse unless Sloan rode it.'

But he was such a little *bugger* – he rode for John Huggins, for example, and the trainer's chief owner Lord William Beresford had to bail him out, in 1899, after he had given a waiter a cut lip with a champagne bottle. He also rode for Lillie Langtry and, in 1900, even for the Prince of Wales, winning a race by a short head, after which his 'foul riding' of the finish drew severe censure from the stewards. Nevertheless he was in line to get a retainer from Edward in 1901, had he not been booted out beforehand.

It was his corruption that brought his lively stay in England to an abrupt end. He was implicated in the doping scandals, although he had left the country by the time these came to a head; it was the society pet American brothers, Lester and Johnny Reiff, who rode most of the drugged-up Wishard horses. But Sloan was a simply terrible gambler and, if such a thing were possible, an even worse loser. In the 1900 Cambridgeshire, he defied the new rule that banned jockeys from betting and, with the rest of his merry gang, plunged madly on his own mount, Codoman. Accounts differ as to how much he would have won, but it was not less than £66,000 and perhaps as much as £300,000. Not so surprising, then, that his rage in the weighing room after the horse was beaten was something to behold: 'You Irish devil,' he said to the winning jockey (whom he had tried and failed to bribe), 'if I'd won that race the stewards could have had that hat and this shirt for breakfast.' The stewards, who by now had had more than enough of tiny Tod, were most interested to hear this. Sloan was informed that any request to renew his jockey's licence in 1901 would be refused.

Apparently stunned, he reapplied fifteen times for his licence; how could our poor old racing get by without him? He was then warned off in France, and finally deported from England in 1915, for running a London gaming-house. He was a lost soul, in fact, discovered after the war, by Damon Runyon, working as a gateman at a racecourse on the Mexican border. He died in 1933, in the charity ward of a hospital.

Then it was back to the Edwardian era, but again with a twist. In 1899 the Duke of Westminster died, leaving an heir – always known as Bend Or, after the horse who had won the Derby when he was a baby – who was not yet of age. The late duke's bloodstock was therefore sold through Tattersalls.

Among the lots was a yearling daughter of Persimmon, out of a full sister to Ormonde. This was Sceptre, who was to set a record of four classic wins[7] that will never, now, be broken.

Tattersalls, which had originally conducted its sales at Hyde Park Corner, was now established in Newmarket, although until the 1940s it continued to stage London sales at Knightsbridge Green. In 1884, however, the family business had bought a piece of land behind Queensberry House and built on it. The July Sales had been held on this site since 1870, out in the open air, which must have been a delight; but as the Newmarket sales took over from those of the Middle Park and Hampton Court studs, so proper premises were needed. By the 1880s, the July Sales had become a slightly recherché part of the Season. Women would turn up in full summer fig; it was reminiscent of the days when Hyde Park Corner held an essential place on the social circuit, and the eighteenth-century playwright, Farquhar, could write: 'Oh yes! I stopped at Tattersalls as I came by, and there I found Lord James Jessamy, Sir William Wilding and Mr ————...'

Before the sale of the Westminster stock, a man called Robert Sievier – actor, journalist, gambler, adventurer, you name it – had won £30,000 on Diamond Jubilee's Derby. During the week at Epsom, he had cleared in all about £53,000. This would still buy a decent yearling nowadays – with luck, it would buy a champion, like the 1996 King George winner, Pentire, later sold to Japan for six million dollars. In 1900, it would certainly buy the thing that Sievier had his eye on: Sceptre. And he was willing to spend more of it than anyone had ever spent before on a yearling.

The night before she was due to be sold, he strolled into the Rutland Arms and handed £20,000 to Somerville Tattersall. He had no account at Tattersalls and therefore thought it best to put down a deposit on the filly. Highly surprised, and somewhat discomfited by finding himself in sudden possession of the sort of sum for which murders are committed, Tattersall stashed the money in the wardrobe of his hotel

---

[7] Sceptre broke a record set in 1868 when Formosa won the fillies' Triple Crown and dead-heated first for the Two Thousand Guineas.

room. The next day, confident but no doubt very geed-up, Sievier arrived at the auction to claim his prize. And he got her cheap, in a way; the bidding stopped at £10,000. But Sceptre was still the most expensive yearling ever bought at auction, almost twice as expensive as La Flèche had been, ten years earlier, when three cheers had been given at Hampton Court for the boldness of Baron de Hirsch.

Sceptre was worth it, of course she was; she may well be the best filly ever to have raced, although just two years later Pretty Polly would come along with her triumphant challenge. They were both, as Edward would have said, great horses. Where Pretty Polly was more blessed was that she had not been bought by a man like Sievier, who was an uneasy mixture of old-style Cavalier and new-breed entrepreneur. He had something of Dennis O'Kelly about him, that bold colonial cleverness which could leave the Old World gasping for breath (Sievier was Australian); but there was also something coldly modern, which let him know Sceptre's price but not her value. He did, in fact, the unforgivable thing: prized her not for herself but as a commodity. She was a means to an end, and she deserved to be much more than that; which is why the £10,000 purchase was not just a thrilling kickstart to the century, it was a warning. Bob Sievier was not, of course, the first to buy a great thoroughbred in the hope of what he could get out of it. Yet he was a sign, all the same, of what was to come in the next hundred years, when racing would try – and fail, ultimately – to turn itself into a business.

Sceptre won four classics and, without Sievier, who had set himself up as her 'trainer', might have won all five (Pretty Polly, too, was surely capable of this, but she only contested the fillies' Triple Crown). However, just as Lord Hastings had with Lady Elizabeth, Sievier treated Sceptre as if she were no more precious than a tough old handicapper; and he did not, as Hastings had done, have the excuse of being out of mind with fear at the time. He was merely greedy.

For here was a classic horse, if ever there was one. Quality was finely sketched all over her frame. Her blood sang aloud with vitality. Yet Sievier began her three-year-old career by running her in the Lincolnshire Handicap: which was, and is, the first big gambling race of the season. This was obviously the attraction, but the idea that a horse would run in it before contesting the classics is, and would always have been, beyond belief. Sceptre, unprepared, ran second. Then, soaring gracefully above the idiotic shenanigans of her guardian, she showed what she was really made of.

After the two Guineas races, which she gathered up with cool relish, she finished fourth in the Derby before winning the Oaks in a canter. It was a very popular triumph. Hotspur had described the disappointment that greeted the victory of Ard Patrick in the Derby – which is always so ridiculous, as a result is a result, but racegoers cannot help their longing for fairytales – and now wrote: 'I was inclined to wonder if things would have been different had Sceptre followed in the footsteps of Derby–Oaks winners Eleanor and Blink Bonny. The answer must now be given in the affirmative, as neither the rain nor an attendance apparently much below the average could check the display of public acclamation. The filly was the one that commanded the people's sympathies . . .'

Interestingly, although there is no doubt that a Mill Reef, say, or a Brigadier Gerard, were among the most popular horses of the century, the response aroused by a truly great filly can be even warmer. In recent years, the exquisitely beautiful Bosra Sham – winner of the 1996 One Thousand Guineas and Champion Stakes – caused swooning around paddocks. 'I'd leave my wife for her,' a man was once heard to say, and indeed it may be the heavy masculine presence at racecourses which is the factor here. Men really do fall half in love with these fillies. They are, indeed, a good deal prettier than any woman, but there is also something fascinating about the mixture of two ideals: that of the thoroughbred and that of femaleness. Filtered through femininity, the thoroughbred's remoteness becomes coquetry, his beauty becomes alluring, his speed becomes miraculous, his bravery becomes feisty, unexpected, touching beyond belief.

And so, Sceptre's treatment after the Oaks makes any real racing man want to ask Bob Sievier to meet him on Wormwood Scrubs, where George Osbaldeston is waiting. She had run four classics. She had surely won her owner a fortune. 'The mare', as she was now lovingly called, deserved a metaphorical fortnight in the Seychelles. Instead, what was she asked to do? Run at Longchamp in the Grand Prix de Paris, where she was beaten by her own jockey's race tactics; go to Royal Ascot, lose the Coronation Stakes then – in the same week – win the St James' Palace Stakes; go to Goodwood, lose the Sussex Stakes then win the Nassau Stakes; and finally, most grievous of all, after her wonderfully luxurious victory in the St Leger, run in the Park Hill Stakes two days later, in which she was defeated by exhaustion. The following season, it was all set to start up again when Sceptre once more contested the Lincoln. And one must be glad that she finished fifth – such an insult to her, though! – otherwise Sievier would no doubt have won thousands, and would not have been obliged to sell his filly for £25,000. A year earlier he had turned down £35,000. 'Treat her like a selling plater,' he said to Alec Taylor, the Manton trainer who now handled her career.

Taylor had more sense and grace and, in his reassuring hands, the gleaming Sceptre found its lustre again. She won five times as a four-year-old, including the Champion Stakes at Newmarket, but the damage had, perhaps, been done to her. At five, she was finished; at stud, she was unexceptional; and indeed she was barren for a long time before her death. These things can happen to any filly, but it is hard not to compare Sceptre's disjointed, hysterical three-year-old career with the life of Pretty Polly who, safely stowed at Clarehaven on the Bury Road, was treated like the princess that she was. She attended race meetings with a cob horse, Little Missus, whom she loved and who always accompanied her round the paddock.[8] She ran through to the age of five, winning – as well as her three classics – the Coronation Stakes, the Nassau Stakes, the Park Hill Stakes, the Free Handicap and two Coronation Cups; a lot of racing, but arranged in a seemly manner that allowed her greatness to flow without strain. The records of Sceptre and Pretty Polly are similar; the way in which they were achieved was very different.

Bob Sievier was not a villain. Indeed, he has had a good press throughout the century for his vigour and his daring,

---

[8] Her shock defeat in the 1906 Gold Cup has been explained, by some, by the fact that Little Missus was not with her that day.

and for stylish swaggering little gestures like the wreath that he sent to Danny Maher's funeral: 'Weighed in, old boy, farewell'. But it would have been better, all the same, if the Duke of Westminster had died a few years later than he did, and Sceptre had stayed in his hands. This is not snobbery; it is fact. Sceptres do not come around often enough for them to be run into the ground by someone chasing riches. Nowadays, a Sievier would probably do the opposite thing: race his filly a few times then make as much as possible out of her as a brood mare. Both courses of action are governed by the same principle: that the money a horse is worth has more value than the horse itself.

That is not, cannot be, what racing is about. The thoroughbred was not brought to a pitch of perfection in order that, as a final flourish, a price tag could be tied around its elegant neck. Throughout the evolution of flat racing – a process which, by the start of the twentieth century, had effectively come to an end – the unspoken paradox has always been this: that money is of the essence, but that this money is subsumed into the fabric of the sport. Ridiculous, yes. Nonsense, of course. Except that, as soon as this paradox is questioned, so too is racing itself. And this was to be the story of the twentieth century; but not, thank God, the whole story.

9 War

'An Insane and Unseemly Spectacle' – 1914–1945

ACING AND THE TWENTIETH CENTURY did not suit each other very well, although it was some years before this became clear. Meanwhile Newmarket moved with the times, without ever really changing – the one constant in the world of the sport.

War came and went, came and went, and other racecourses succumbed, but Newmarket remained. The RAF came to the Heath, but the gallops stayed in use; a tank was driven down the High Street, and the soldier in charge of it was reported for frightening the horses. Newmarket staged every one of the wartime classics, except for the St Legers of 1940 (Thirsk) and 1941 (Manchester).[1] These races attracted crowds for which meetings nowadays would – in a manner of speaking – be prepared to die.

Understandably, when war first announced itself to the century, there had been a great deal of confab as to whether it was correct even to keep Newmarket open. What is perhaps surprising is that men like the Duke of Portland (now fifty-eight, he would live to see the next war as well) were very much against the continuation of the sport. He wrote to *The Times* saying so, citing a sorry story about how wounded servicemen had been evicted from Epsom grandstand – then

---

[1] There was no St Leger in 1939, the only time that a classic race has been cancelled. The Legers of 1915–8 were technically not St Legers but substitute races (with classic status) called the September Stakes – Doncaster thought that no other racecourse should stage the real thing.

a temporary hospital – so that the Derby could be run (there are doubts as to the truth of this; did these men really have to be removed a month before the race?)

Other members of the Jockey Club, however, regarded the Portland attitude as a betrayal of fundamental principles. And from the fellow whose ancestor had owned great swatches of the sacred Heath! This is when racing people could, and still can, be very irritating. It is one thing to live in a world of one's own, another to pretend that the world outside does not exist and that, if it does, its laws do not apply. There was a very nasty Jockey Club meeting in which the Earl of Durham (brother to George Lambton), backed by Lord Rosebery (ex-prime minister), accused Portland and his gang of caving in to puritanical, alarmist public pressure. This was in May 1915: Gallipoli had just been fought, the *Lusitania* had been sunk, but the Derby still had to be run, damnit.

And, in a way, it did. This would be Churchill's position in the Second World War: people wanted something festive and normal to do. Racing was like drawing stocking seams up the back of one's legs with a bit of charcoal, like going to the pictures and dreaming of Robert Taylor or Veronica Lake: frivolous but necessary. If everyone were to live like Herbert Morrison, going round like a witchfinder, hunting out poor souls who were taking a bit of pleasure at the races – horses or dogs – before a bomb came crashing on their heads, then the war would be lost out of sheer depression. 'Is the Home Secretary aware,' Morrison had thundered, 'that women working in munition factories for twelve hours were having to walk two or three miles to their homes because conveyances were filled with people going *greyhound racing*?' A certain kind of socialist has never been very keen on pleasures that he himself does not enjoy, and Churchill won the day on this one. 'Will you kindly let me know beforehand what you think of saying?' he wrote to Morrison, lethally, when the vexed subject of racecourse closure began to loom in 1941. 'If anything were done which threatened to terminate horseracing in time of war, or ruin the bloodstock, it would be necessary that the whole matter should be thrashed out in Cabinet first.' Not very subtle, but it did the job. Of course Churchill himself – who, though a consummate politician, was also a human being – later owned a horse or two: Vienna ran in the 1960 Derby, and a lovely crowd-pleaser of a grey, Colonist II, won the 1950 Jockey Club Cup.

Probably because of Churchill's robust influence, there was more racing in the Second than the First World War. In 1915, the House of Commons was violently opposed to continuation of the sport, although a speech by the President of the Board of Trade acknowledged – rather as it would today, if football were to be suspended – the terrible sacrifice that this would entail for the 'people at home'. But on 19 May he wrote a letter to the Jockey Club senior steward, Captain Sir Henry Greer, which no doubt caused a lot of spluttering:

> I have to inform you that owing to the circumstances of the war, and in particular the necessity of keeping the whole of our British railway system free from conges-tion at any time . . . we think it necessary to ask the stewards of the Jockey Club to suspend all race meet-ings in Great Britain after this week for the duration of the war.
>
> The only exception to this general suspension should be at Newmarket . . .

Headlines boomed excitably, as if the end of the world had come (which it had, in a way): 'Racing Ends This Week . . . Only Newmarket Meetings to Go On . . . No Derby and Ascot . . .' This was not entirely accurate, as Newbury limped along for the duration (presumably because it was also a training centre), there was some racing at Lingfield and Windsor (so convenient for London), while the Grand Nation-al was run at Gatwick (which did not make it through the next war, closing for good in 1940). Bizarrely, the other tracks were obliged not just to maintain themselves but to contrib-ute to the prize money at Newmarket – this has the ring of a Jockey Club decree, coming down from the heavens – and poor old Epsom sold off the contents of its wine cellar in order to find the necessary.

And, for the first time in 135 years, its classics were staged elsewhere. On what should have been the first day of Royal Ascot, the Derby was run at Newmarket. A confused world, indeed. The race was won by Solly Joel's Pommern, Donoghue up, a partnership that would take the first wartime Triple Crown. Joel was a popular figure, a self-made man of some style (his black colours and red cap the nicest in racing) who would later move to Moulton Paddocks, and later yet stage *Desert Song* on Drury Lane. His victories with Pommern were terrifically well received at Newmarket. The year before, the *Daily Express* had despaired as the Derby was won by a featureless French horse at 20/1, with the English lolloping feebly behind. 'It is mostly tragedy so far and I wish I could anticipate a happy ending,' was how the newspaper summed up the situation in the summer of 1914, irony bristling on the statement like quills. But in 1915, as the known world began to fall, taking more than ten million men with it, the Derby gave cause for jubilation.

Of course Newmarket only kept going on a makeshift basis. Whereas before there had been bustle, a constant movement of horses in their rugs and tiny, purposeful men in caps and boots, now the criss-crossing lines of activity had become thin, spare, much as they would have been in the fallow period of the 1850s. Although the huge size of some wartime fields shows that a good many horses were still in training, inevitably there was culling in both stables and studs. Breeding operations were checked in their stride. At the 1915 Tattersalls yearling sales, the average price was 196 guineas, and in a way it is hard to imagine anyone even paying that. In 1917, things got really bad. When Lloyd George came blundering in, trying to get a complete ban on the sport ('it was against public opinion that racing should be continued' – a downright lie), the breeders decided that something had to be done. The Thoroughbred Breeders' Association, whose headquarters are now on The Avenue in Newmarket, was formed in order to put a case for the 'industry' to the government. Despite the fact that the TBA had the dubious backing of racehorse-owning fraudster, Horatio Bottomley, the concession of forty days' racing a year was won.

Meanwhile, it was hardly the time to moan, but Newmarket was finding its role as entertainments officer to the nation's racegoers rather tricky to fulfil. Jockeys and stable staff were called up; and, heaven preserve us, a couple of women actually made their appearance within the ranks. Cicely Lambton, wife of trainer George, recalled the arrival in Newmarket of 'Sir Robert Wilmot with a small string of horses and, with him, his two daughters. They were, I think, almost the first girls to ride and "do" their own horses, certainly the first I had ever seen, and I well remember the small sensation they created when they first rode out on Newmarket Heath in very neat breeches and tweed coats like a couple of boys . . .' It reminds one a little of the legendary Miss Pond – daughter of the publisher of the *Sporting Kalendar* – who in 1758 rode a thousand miles in a thousand hours (not all at once, let it be noted) for a 200 guinea bet, and who was much admired by an intrigued Dr Johnson.

Not much seemed to have changed in nearly two hundred years. Mrs Lambton was an enlightened woman, whose mother Lady Horner had belonged to The Souls, but her attitude towards the Wilmot girls was not very encouraging. One of them, Norah, later took over her father's stable and longed very much for official recognition in the form of a trainer's licence. 'The Jockey Club have always been ada-mant over this question,' Cicely Lambton wrote in 1950, 'and I must say I think rightly so: once the door was open and women allowed into the sacred precincts of the weighing room on the official footing as trainers, what is to stop them from becoming jockeys too? . . . I think it will be a very long time before feminism asserts itself to this extent; in fact, the Turf will remain the last ditch!'

This was true, but it is one thing for racing to be a masculine world and quite another for it to be ridiculously discriminatory, as the quality of female trainers today (and indeed, of a jockey like Alex Greaves – who in 1996 became the first woman to ride in the Derby, albeit on a 500/1 shot filly) makes it only too clear. Yet Norah Wilmot did not receive a licence until 1966, having waited for 35 years while, beneath her name in the *Horses in Training* publication, had been printed the words: 'Licence may be held by R H Swash'. The change finally came when Florence Nagle, who had also been training horses since the 1930s, decided that enough was enough and brought a case against the Jockey Club. It required a verdict from the Court of Appeal to win the day. And it was the 1975 Sex Discrimination Act that enabled women to ride under Jockey Club Rules; sometimes the laws of the world outside have, necessarily, made themselves felt.

The war did bring the first female owner of a Derby winner – Lady Jane Douglas, whose Gainsborough pulled off the 1918 Triple Crown – and, to date, the last female winner of the race itself.[2] Fifinella, who was better than her silly name suggests, won the Derby and Oaks in 1916. Hotspur in the *Daily Telegraph* described the large crowds that gathered at Newmarket, as the Battle of Jutland raged, to watch her become only the fourth filly ever to bring off this double: 'The general public were present in large numbers, and conspicuous were officers of all ranks, while many of the rank and file stationed locally, and a large company of convalescent wounded, made a khaki and blue border to the rails on either side of the course . . .'

Hard to believe that, just seven years earlier, Newmarket had floated on a calm, glittering sea of assurance and prosperity: that it had been an impregnable idyll, where women drifted in trailing voile and men strode behind confidently placed shooting sticks, where complacence had not extinguished vitality and memories of Triple Crown winners still vibrated in the lustrous air. Seven years earlier, the King had marched cheerily into the winners' enclosure to greet his Guineas winner, Minoru, had shaken brisk hands all around and had acknowledged the Newmarket crowd, whose congratulations had just that ineffable added savour: of expertise, of coming from the horse's mouth, of assumed and accepted equality. Now Newmarket had the Derby, and with it had come informality, drabness, a different kind of good humour, young boys limping determinedly between paddock and stand, other young boys losing themselves in contemplation of the next race, rather than their own future – the blessed importance of triviality . . . Perhaps Newmarket had

---

[2] In 1998, Cape Verdi's gorgeous, silky victory in the One Thousand Guineas led romantics – which is everyone, although the carapace of cynicism varies in thickness – to believe that she would break the jinx, and she was sent off favourite on Derby Day. The poor girl finished ninth and was never afterwards the horse she had been at Newmarket.

never had greater importance in the life of the nation. But the golden age, as everyone surely knew, was well and truly over.

In Newmarket as elsewhere, the effects of the First World War were both obvious and insidious. George Lambton, for example, felt them directly. His Stanley House yard had stayed open, as Lambton was popular and persuasive enough to gather around him some unlikely but willing volunteers: 'A very fine, keen-looking lot of elderly gentlemen', as his brother Billy described them when home on leave. Lambton himself was born in 1860, was far too old to fight, and was therefore best employed in adding to the gaiety of the returning soldier. To this end he won the One Thousand Guineas between 1916 and 1918; somebody had to do it, but one speculates as to how much pleasure these victories gave him. One of his brothers, Francis, who had trained at Park Lodge in the early years of the century, had joined up at the age of forty-three, and in 1915 was killed at the Front: a shell having burst on the parapet of his trench, he got himself out from under the shower of sodden earth but, as he stood up, was shot in the head by a German rifleman. Cicely Lambton's brother, Edward Horner, one of those beautiful and lovable young men that war always seems to claim, also died. Then, in 1918, the Stanley House stable jockey Fred Rickaby was killed in action, aged twenty-four, leaving a wife and two children. The war was nearly over when this happened, but he had refused the opportunity to return home without seeing the thing through to the end. 'Poor little Rick,' wrote his employer Lord Derby to Lambton. 'It was very sad indeed his death. I had no idea that he was even in France and if I had known he had been wounded I would have tried to have got up to see him . . .' (Derby was at that time the British Ambassador in Paris). But life – the remorseless renewal of the racing season – went on. With the war having only a week to run, he wrote again: 'Do you think any arrangements could be made to secure Carslake now that poor little Rickaby has been killed . . .?'

Insidious, though, was what happened, as a result of the war, to the class of people whose patronage had underpinned racing from the first. As their wealth became eroded by taxation, so their support inevitably became weaker. Patronage, to be truly effective, requires what is tantamount to infinite wealth: that is what the Maktoum family of Dubai has and that is why, today, it can very nearly support Newmarket on its own, with the four brothers holding up each corner of the town. Rich is not enough. *Richissime* is what is needed. And *en masse*, or even singly, the owners of the golden age had it. Falmouth and Westminster and Portland and Edward VII and even ghastly George Baird – they had money to burn, to waste, to throw at the sport. If they won, hurray; if they lost, Belgravia and Marylebone were still standing.

Of course these people did not become poor, but their wealth no longer seemed illimitable since for the aristocracy, the sense of what one might call *unaccountability* had gone for ever. And, however right and proper that passing may have been, it pulled the rug out from under English racing. This was not immediately apparent. Before the war, ownership had not been confined to these people; afterwards, they continued to own horses; certainly they continued to dominate the Jockey Club (and still do). But the point – whether one likes it or not – is that people of this kind were good for racing, because they and racing *understood* one another. It was like a marriage, there were tiffs and upsets and fallings-out but there was a fundamental mutual need; one party was bedazzled by the other's glamour, one was in thrall to the other's bounty. It worked, in fact, as well as any marriage that combines realism with romanticism – which is to say very well indeed.

It always comes down to the same thing. Racing gets along best when people are not questioning the point of it. There *is* no point, if someone has to ask what it is. Applying the principles of business, which always require goals and rationales, to something so essentially airy-fairy is bound to be fraught with problems. It is like trying to explain cricket to a Frenchman. It can be done, for so long and so far, and then it can't be done any more. The elusiveness of the thing defeats the attempt to pin it down. In the 1970s, Robert Sangster made millions by turning racing into a business. He bought and sold at the right time, he syndicated, he made stallions into commodities in which people invested as if the horses had been floated on the stock market. It was brilliant, and it seemed as though it could go on for ever, with bloodstock perpetually propagating its own increasing value. But then Golden Fleece, the 1982 Derby winner, died of cancer, and El Gran Senor was beaten by a short head in the 1984 Derby, and the Maktoums arrived carrying so much money that they did not *have* to treat racing as a commercial enterprise. These are the kinds of things that can happen in any business. But a business with the thoroughbred horse at the centre of it . . . Very, very tricky. This animal has no head for business at all.

That is not, of course, to say that people should not be treating racing with good sense, and trying to make it pay, and all the rest of it. Captain Machell did so. John Magnier, the Sangster associate who helped him decide which horses to buy in the first place, has his instinctive understanding of the thoroughbred to sustain his commercial sense, and it has made him very rich indeed. A man like Prince Khalid Abdullah, who owned Dancing Brave, does not chuck money around. His Banstead Manor stud at Cheveley, which now stands the most successful sire in England – Rainbow Quest – is an immaculate example of how to build upon one's own good fortune, and breed champions from champions. The Maktoum style, which verges upon profligacy, is not the only way of doing things. Yet the feeling persists that this is a sport which needs, above all else, a steady flow of money washing over it, sent by people who really don't care whether they get it back or not. Prince Khalid may take pride in the success of his operation, as too, no doubt, do the Princes Fahd and Ahmed Salman; but the hard fact of it is that, if the Salman brothers had not won, as they did, the Derby and Oaks of 1999, they would still have been able to eat at Le Gavroche every night for the rest of their lives, and buy a few more potential classic winners with what they had left.

Every owner does not need to be like this, but racing needs a handful of them to be like it. Sporting instincts are frankly more buoyant with a cushion of money beneath them. Of course one might say that horses should not be as expensive as they are, although – as with footballers' wages – it is hard to know what can be done about it. As Guy de Rothschild said: Horses are expensive because they are expensive. Bob Sievier proved it when he gave £10,000 for Sceptre. She became worth that much because that was what he had paid for her. Indeed, and this is the paradox, it is the 'democratising' forces of commerce which have inflated price – at the top end of the market – so far beyond value. It was the activities of Robert Sangster that caused a yearling to be sold for $10.2 million at Keeneland in 1983, not, as is commonly thought, the arrival of the Maktoums. They paid it, certainly, and for a horse who never raced. But by being prepared to pay that much – more than anyone else would or could – they eventually brought prices down again, because it became clear that the business ethic had met its match.[3]

So what does this mean? What it has always meant: that racing, like art, prefers patrons to dealers. At least that way one is assured of quality. And it is fortunate – to say the least – that certain members of Arab royalty are sufficiently entranced by English racing, and especially by Newmarket, to want to act as its patrons. Racing would never forgive itself if, in quest of the egalitarianism than it can never, truthfully, find, it were to change so much that it lost its attraction for these philanthropic gentlemen, who understand the sport every bit as well as the English aristocracy did at the start of the century. It started with their horses, after all.

But back in the years after the First World War, the aristocracy had been landed with one God almighty communal tax bill, and was selling up. London mansions crumbled, only to rise again with chrome fittings and Art Deco doors, as the hotels that would later be bought by oil money began to go up on Park Lane. In 1924, Devonshire House was demolished, the land on which it stood having been sold for £1 million. In 1928 Dorchester House went for £500,000. The Sassoon family – one of whom, Sir Victor, would later own the 1957 Guineas–Derby winner, Crepello – clung on, and by 1929 owned one of the last great mansions on the road. The

---

[3] Sangster did in fact pay $13.1 million for a yearling at Keeneland in 1985, but that was his last shot at staying top of the premier league.

Grosvenor estate began to be sold off, the houses turned into flats, the mews turned into chi-chi little *pieds-à-terre*: 'such an enormous and rapid transfer of land had not been seen since the confiscations and sequestrations of the Civil War,' as a biography of the 2nd Duke of Westminster ('Bend Or') put it, 'such a permanent transfer not since the dissolution of the monasteries in the 16th century.' An exaggeration? No doubt it did not feel like it. The symbols of the golden age were being dismantled, quite literally. It is only necessary to have a feel for the past to mind about it, just a little.

Yet the period between the wars, when all this upheaval was taking effect, has also been called a golden age for racing, and it is easy to see why. The effects of change had not yet made themselves fully felt, and men like the 17th Earl of Derby would still symbolise racing success: not just in the 1920s and 1930s, but for as long as the sport lasts. His association with George Lambton at Stanley House was comparable to that between Lord Falmouth and Mathew Dawson. Lord Derby was leading owner in 1911, 1923, 1927, 1928, 1933, 1938 and 1945, which is the sort of record that only HH Aga Khan III and Sheikh Mohammed al Maktoum can compete with. And he was breeding his own horses, one of the last English aristocrats to do so on the grand scale. In 1918 he wrote a letter to George Lambton, resonant with ill-suppressed hysteria: 'It is quite evident that in one way or another the Government mean to crush the industry of horse-breeding . . . apparently there is to be a luxury tax on racehorses and on their value, though how that is going to be discovered until they have raced I do not know . . . Under these circumstances there is no possibility of going on racing – at all events in England. In India however they are apparently very keen about racing . . .' It all sounds very familiar; yet he resisted the lure of the Viceroy's Cup and returned home to win twenty classics.

The Derby–Lambton partnership was a first, in that the trainer came from the same sort of background as the owner. This must have made life simpler in some ways, although it was to create embarrassments in others. George Lambton was a hugely attractive man, whose languid look – straight out of *The Yellow Book*, very much in contrast to squat, bluff Lord Derby – belied his vigour. The fifth son of an earl, it was highly unusual, at that time, that he should become a racehorse trainer. He started out in the familiar way of a well-born boy attracted to the turf, gambling more than was sensible and race-riding against none other than George Baird, but he then seems to have been attracted by the idea of actually working at what he loved. There was, in his nature, the get-up-and-get-on-with-it quality that characterises most successful trainers. He also had charm, which is a quality that some of them deploy to devastating effect: and was, in fact, the prototype for what would become a highly recognisable species. Gossip columnists – intrigued by this new breed of person that had sprung up in Newmarket – reported sightings of him striding across the Severals in a Savile Row suit, a pekinese dog at his heels. In the elegance of his figure, leaning on his stick outside Stanley House, an infinitely gentlemanly dandy in his trilby, his watch chain, his bowtie and button hole, is the genesis of Henry Cecil's suede loafers and coloured socks, and of the image that he presents to a fascinated world.

Lambton began training for Lord Derby at Bedford Lodge, where the walls must have been nearly falling down with the weight of history upon them. Then, in 1903, he went to Stanley House stables (living, after his marriage, in a house across the road named Mesnil Warren), which with its private gallops and spacious layout was probably, by that time, the best yard in Newmarket. Soon, the glory years would begin.

The successes of the Stanley House partnership really represent the last fine flourish of the old order. Canyon (Fred Rickaby's last classic win in 1916) and Ferry (1918) won the wartime One Thousand Guineas, and Tranquil took the race in 1923 (her name belied her; she had to be tamed, St Simon-style, with an umbrella, which Lambton would open in order to make her gallop). The 1924 Derby, run in trenchlike mud, was won by Sansovino, and the *Daily Graphic* ran a ' "Lord Derby" Day Number: At Last!' cried the headline. 'After trying to win the Derby for 137 years, victory in the historic race at Epsom was obtained yesterday by the House of Stanley ... Never before had such a great crowd crammed the Downs' (and how, exactly, did they know that?) 'and veteran racegoers cannot recall experiencing such wretched weather. It rained most of the day, but nothing could damp the high spirits of the spectators.

'Remarkable scenes were witnessed when the great procession of traffic attempted to re-form for the return home. The wheels of many motor-coaches and 'buses had sunk into the sodden turf . . . Hundreds of motor-cars and coaches, rescued from the mud, were passing through Epsom shortly before midnight.' *Ah, les beaux jours!* In 1999, if one left the course pretty smartly, it took half an hour to get back to London after the Derby.

Sansovino had been ridden by Tommy Weston, then twenty-one, who had recently been appointed stable jockey at Stanley House. After the race, his white stock was found to have got caught around the top button of his black silks; Lord Derby thereafter stipulated that his racing colours should be 'black jacket with one white button'. Weston was the son of a wagon-driver on the Lancashire and Yorkshire railway and, as such, the focus of a certain resentment among native Newmarket jockeys, for having swooped down from the north to take one of the best jobs going. 'He was a very common lad in his way,' a bookmaker who had known him from his early years was later, rather cattily, to recall. 'He used to say, when he started out, I'm a "separator": I separate the shit from the straw. And he finished up owning his own house and riding for Lord Derby.' Of course Lord Derby himself was, in a manner of speaking, from up north; indeed it was his little trick sometimes to affect a faint Lancashire accent. He may sometimes have been happer dealing with Weston than with Lambton.

He had originally tried for Brownie Carslake as stable jockey, and in 1921 – as advised by his trainer – had offered a £4,000 retainer to Steve Donoghue, then very much the pick of the bunch. This the jockey treated in typical cavalier fashion. That very year he waived it to ride Humorist – the horse he loved 'like a child' – to Derby victory; for this Donoghue must be forgiven. Two weeks later the horse was found dead in his box, surrounded by his own blood. His bad Guineas run, for which he was criticised, had been due to the fact that he had tuberculosis. 'It was his love for me which caused him to make that great effort and win the greatest race in the world with only one lung to feed his dauntless heart.'

Here was a jockey who cared less about owners than he did about their horses – 'I think of them as my friends, my greatest friends' – and this was, or should have been, enough to make any owner want to use him. His hands were once X-rayed in the hope that they would yield up their secrets, but really that was not where the magic lay. It was Donoghue's instinct, his understanding, his *heart* which was the key to the two Triple Crowns, the ten consecutive championships and the six Derbys. 'Stephen can find out more about what's left in a horse with his little finger than most jockeys can with their legs and their whip,' said Brownie Carslake, himself no slouch.

There was something terribly attractive, almost childlike, in the directness with which Donoghue went at racing. Yes, he 'schemed' in a not very clever way[4] to get rides, and yes, he tried to extricate himself from his retainers (in 1923 he was at it again, dodging Lord Woolavington in order to ride Papyrus to a third consecutive Derby win). But somehow this was forgivable, because his motives were not base; because he sincerely believed that he would do better than anyone else by a horse; because he could pull a twitching ear before a Derby and soothe it in an instant; because he said that his sixth Queen Alexandra Stakes win in 1934 on Brown Jack – an unglamorous, heart-breaking, ten-year-old stayer – was worth more to him than any Derby.

Donoghue retired in 1937, at the age of fifty-three. A dinner was given for him at which Brown Jack's owner, Sir Harold Wernher, arranged for a radio receiver to be placed in the horse's box so that his jockey could send him a message. It is reported that Brown Jack's ears stood like stalks when Donoghue said goodnight to him. Let no one despise the sentimentalists in racing – they hold the heart of the sport in kindly hands.

Meanwhile Lord Derby was giving the world his own little heart-breaker. Hyperion, who won the Derby and St Leger in 1933, was one of the most popular racehorses of the century. In constrast to Fred Archer, he was made special by the fact

---

[4] In fact Donoghue could be quite dopey in the ordinary sense. He once booked four sleepers to Scotland, leaving from King's Cross, then travelled up in the guard's van from St Pancras.

of being so small. 'Smallest Winner for a Century', thundered the *Daily Sketch* after the St Leger. He stood just over fifteen hands – absolutely tiny – and, as needs to be done every now and again, he broke every rule in the book by becoming not just a champion racer, but six times champion sire. Among his progeny was Aureole, Derby second in 1953 and probably the best horse ever owned by the present Queen.

By 1933, there were of course cameras at these races recording them for newsreels, and so – despite the jerky, speedy picture – it is possible to see how Hyperion looked as he won his Derby: like a little rocking-horse skittering along, four joyful lengths clear of his lumbering pursuers. It is possible, also, to get a sense of the ovation he received as he strolled up to the Epsom winners' enclosure, a child prodigy amongst the grown-ups, cheers breaking like benign thunder-claps above his nodding head. 'The sweetest little horse I ever saw,' Lady Sarah Bunbury said of Gimcrack in the 1760s, and Hyperion too was the nearest that a dual classic winner – proud, mysterious, separate – can come to being a poppet.

'I am too excited to say much,' breathed Lord Derby after the Epsom victory; he had not expected Hyperion to win. By now the earl, who had achieved his peak weight of 22 stone, was sixty-eight years of age. Lambton could not compete on the tonnage front, but he was five years older. For the Stanley House team, its finest hour seemed therefore likely to be one of its last; which makes Lord Derby's subsequent behaviour towards his trainer all the more peculiar.

Aged 73 years or not, Lambton had done a bloody good job with Hyperion who, for all his adorable qualities, was a lazy little beggar. 'Nobody but you could have brought him to the post in the state he was in – perfectly trained,' Lord Derby wrote after Epsom. 'He would not have blown a candle out and there is no doubt he is a smashing good horse.' Before the St Leger, Hyperion had an attack of laminitis, which caused more problems, but again Lambton had him fit as a flea for the race, which he controlled almost from the starting gate: 'making,' as 'Hotspur' wrote in his inimitable way, 'the others look so *common* by comparison'.

Life should have been merry as a marriage bell at Stanley House towards the end of 1933, as Lord Derby prepared to have his Christmas cards printed with their picture of him leading in Hyperion (even in his top hat, not as tall as the little horse). Instead, divorce loomed.

There have been many inexplicable ruptures within the history of racing, but the one in which Lord Derby decided – without warning, after forty years – to terminate his association with George Lambton is perhaps the most bizarre. When the Earl of Glasgow took his horses away from trainers, he could at least plead the M'Naghten Rules in self-defence. When the Maktoums broke away from Henry Cecil, there were at least some plausible rumours wafting about. But this . . . of course Lambton was knocking on in years, and so those commentators who have decided to plead for Lord Derby say that he was merely trying to protect his trainer, to save him the misery of so tiring a job when, dear old fellow, he should be sitting comfortably in his house (but not Stanley House). Due to illness, Lambton had not actually attended the Derby, and this seems to have given his employer the licence to say that he was failing in health. He may even have convinced himself that this was the truth, as those who want to believe something tend to do so, although the fact that Lambton actually trained Hyperion to win the race rather gives this the lie.

Also, his state of health was surely for Lambton himself to decide? It was sheer presumption for Derby to write him a letter saying that 'to continue at that pressure' (as exerted by Hyperion) 'would be too great a sacrifice to yourself . . . I hope you will recognise the motives which make me end it now and that this friendship of ours, unbroken for forty years, will continue to the end.

'One does not like at a moment such as this bringing in the financial question . . .'

It was the sort of letter that a certain type of aristocrat would send in order to dismiss a loyal but useless servant: brimful of condescension, poisonous beneath the honey (and the offer of an extra six months' wages, plus a pension). The problem, of course, was that George Lambton both was and was not a servant. He was employed by Lord Derby but he was, in class terms, his equal, a Hon. who had simply chosen to spend his life as a trainer of racehorses (and whose brother, let it not be forgotten, had in the 1920s been elected senior steward of the Jockey Club[5]). It is only a theory, but the suspicion arises that Lord Derby had found it a bit of a strain dealing with Lambton, always wanting to tell him what to do and always having to be careful about how he did so. It would have been like spending one's life with a butler with whom one had previously shared the opening bat in the Eton–Harrow cricket match: terribly exhausting, frequently embarrassing and finally leading to a kind of hatred.

For example, it was Lord Derby's belief that, as George grew older, Cicely Lambton had been doing a lot of the work at Stanley House (rather ironic, in view of what she later wrote about women trainers). He intensely disliked the idea of this. He had also convinced himself of what, when one looks at photographs of that lanky, ladylike counterpart to her husband, seems quite unbelievable: that Cicely was plotting stable coups. But had Lord Derby employed a trainer to whom – let us be blunt – he felt socially superior, he would no doubt have come straight out and said what he thought. As it was, he had to bob and weave and, in so doing, he was far nastier than he would otherwise have been. And this had been the case for years, as is shown in a snipy little letter, sent in 1921, after Lambton had recommended offering a retainer to Steve Donoghue: '. . . there was a time when you did not much like Donoghue and did not think he was very straight but apparently there is now no objection to him . . .' In fact it was Lord Derby himself who had hummed and hawed over Donoghue; and who, having said that the jockey could take the ride on Humorist, then turned nasty about the fact that he had wanted it.

In 1922, Derby asked Lambton if he would invite an American owner to stay at his home, so that the man could study his training methods. Here, Lambton got a bit of his own back: 'What an extraordinary proposal . . . I am always delighted to show strangers the horses, either in the stables or at work and do anything I can for them, but to have a total stranger coming out continually in the morning and following me about "FOR SEVERAL WEEKS" is really quite out of the

---

[5] One of Lord Durham's edicts was to ban smoking in the weighing room. This went down badly with certain jockeys, as anyone who has ever puffed on a fag to calm their nerves/suppress their hunger will understand.

question as far as I am concerned ... No one but an American would have the assurance and cheek to do it' – and you, he might just as well have added, should never have encouraged the dreadful vulgarian (Lambton was probably rather anti-USA, after his dealings with the great doping scandal of 1903).

So it had been fraught between these two from time to time, over the years. There was also the conundrum of Lord Derby's character which, though affable, had been likened to that of a 'Genial Judas'. He changed his mind constantly about things: what jockey to appoint, what his opinion was of these jockeys, whether or not he wanted other owners in the yard. And the way in which he dealt with Lambton – never discussing with him all the compassionate misgivings that he had over his trainer's alleged bad health, never facing him in person, simply dropping the bomb through the letter box without a hint of a warning – shows a kind of feeble treachery. 'A very weak-minded fellow, I am afraid, and, like the feather-pillow, bears the marks of the last person who sat on him,' was the judgement of Earl Haig, with whom he had worked when Secretary of State at the War Office. That is not necessarily the last word – Haig might be said to have had the opposite problem – but for someone apparently so strong and colourful, Derby's is a strangely elusive personality. It was said that he was a figurehead appointment at the War Office, and one might just as easily say that he was a figurehead within the world of racing: the great sporting aristocrat, the larger-than-life owner-breeder. Beyond that, it is hard to know what to make of him. One can only say that, when he finally did make up his mind to do something, it revealed a side to his nature that would have been better hidden.

Yet whatever the truth behind this unfathomable affair, the ending of the relationship seems to have lanced whatever bitterness it had collected and, four years later, the men became friends again. On Lambton's part this was saintly indeed, but he may have been too old to want a feud to sour the magnificent memories of Stanley House. 'It has nearly broken my heart to break away,' he wrote, but a month after being forced to leave the yard he had, at nearly seventy-four, set up as a public trainer at Kremlin House on the Fordham Road. One can only gasp in amazement at such a man. Did he want to prove the rumours of his 'illness' to be so much hypocritical bunkum? Did he want to set up the yard for his son, Teddy, to take over, as indeed would be the case? At any rate, he continued to send out winners and would not, almost certainly, have taken pleasure in the fact that the four-year-old Hyperion – now trained at Stanley House by Colledge Leader – never won again.

Stanley House was not finished, though: far from it. If Lord Derby had hoped to get more success by booting out Lambton then, regrettably, he got his way, along with seven more classics. There was a wartime Derby with Watling Street in 1942, and a One Thousand Guineas–Oaks double in 1945 from Sun Stream who, as a daughter of Hyperion, must have been very precious.

Both men lost sons towards the end of their lives, and died within three years of each other: George Lambton in 1945, Lord Derby in 1948. Lambton, who had lived to see Sun Stream's pair of victories, was mourned as – according to the *Sporting Life* – 'the greatest trainer of our time'. His death came four months after that of Steve Donoghue, who at the age of sixty had suffered a sudden heart attack, his life having become rather aimless – despite a shot at training – since his retirement ('The monotony is dreadful, having nothing to do except read the paper and dream of great times in the past,' as Brownie Carslake was to put it; he lasted a year after retiring in 1940 and his ashes were scattered over the Rowley Mile).

Lord Derby's reputation suffered not one whit from the Stanley House fiasco; although it had caused a sensation at the time, almost immediately afterwards it was as though it had never happened. Perhaps people did not want to think badly of such a popular figure. In 1935, a seventieth birthday party was held in Preston for the 'Uncrowned King of Lancashire' – a title he surely owed in part to his racing activities – and a present given to which 80,000 people had contributed a shilling. When he died, he was described in the *Daily Telegraph* as 'a great Englishman. In many respects he epitomised all that is best in the national character'. Certainly this could be said of the image that he presented; whether it is true of the reality behind it, however, is a question rather more difficult to answer. After Lambton's death, Cicely wrote to Lord Derby to say that she had been left her husband's bloodstock and hoped, as had previously been the case, that she would be able to mate her mares with Hyperion and Fairway (1928 St Leger winner). 'Of course I do not expect the same generous terms you gave to George but I would be awfully grateful if I can have the nominations as he did but at the ordinary fees.'

This seems like just a courtesy confirmation of an arrangement; but the reply, polite though it was, said otherwise. 'I have to reduce a few owing to stallions getting so much older and that is why I cannot make you a definite promise now to give you a nomination.' The hatchet may have been buried; somewhere, though, it still gave off a chill gleam.

And yes, Hyperion was now eighteen, but he would be twenty when Aureole was born, and he would outlive his owner by twelve years. He died, finally, in 1960, at Woodlands stud on the Snailwell Road, opposite where he was born in 1930 on the Stanley House estate; his box at Woodlands, where he was stabled next to Fairway, still stands. A visitor who saw the sweet, stellar little horse at the stud, two years before his death, described how 'although his back was swayed and massive dark circles were under his eyes because of damaged tear ducts, the personality was there. It was an intangible thing, but it was real.'

And a 1944 edition of an American[6] magazine called the *Blood-Horse* contained this, from an English writer: 'He seems to be an institution, rather than a blood horse. Maybe you criticise your President or your Prime Minister, or General Motors, or Ford ... But neither you nor we can criticise Hyperion.' With him, and through him, the same came to be true of Lord Derby.

Hyperion stands outside the Jockey Club in Newmarket High Street, neat and graceful as always, his eye gazing serenely at nothing and everything. As a symbol of twentieth-

---

[6] There was a story that Louis B. Mayer, who loved racing, offered Lord Derby a blank cheque for Hyperion. 'Even though England be reduced to ashes, Hyperion shall never leave these shores' was his owner's ringing response.

century racing, he is peerless, in that he speaks only of what is good and timeless: not the whole truth, but the truth all the same.

Two years after Hyperion's dual classic triumph, the Aga Khan's Bahram went one third better while arousing one third of the popular emotion. This was partly, it must be said, because he was owned by the Aga Khan, and the leader of the Ismaili Islamic sect was never going to strike the same jolly chord as the uncrowned King of Lancashire, however much he was just as round and jovial. But – and this is one of the great mysteries about racing's relationship with its public – there was something about Bahram himself that annihilated identification, where Hyperion had invited it. Like Tennyson's Maud, Bahram was 'dead perfection'. When he won the St Leger by five lengths there was, wrote 'Hotspur', 'never a thrill, never a moment of suspense. Everything worked like a piece of machinery'. 'Bouverie' in the *Daily Mirror* was left similarly high and dry: 'Well, Bahram is the first triple-crowned hero since Rock Sand' (and would be the last until Nijinsky in 1970). 'The Aga Khan's colt retires from racing to join the few great horses that went through their racing careers unbeaten. All that and yet it was one of the tamest St Leger days I can remember . . . Never have I seen Tattersalls so sedate before a big race, and the preliminaries in the paddock and the parade left the feeling that it was all merely a preliminary to a Bahram canter. And that is exactly what it all proved to be.'

It is a strange paradox. The creation, and constant re-creation, of the thoroughbred is about a quest for perfection, and yet, when it comes, it does not satisfy. It is as though the life has gone from the thing. There was a Bahram for the 1990s in Lammtarra, the Maktoum-owned horse who ran, unbeaten, four times in his life and who, in three outings in 1995 as a three-year-old, won what might reasonably be called a modern Triple Crown, the Derby, the King George VI and Queen Elizabeth Diamond Stakes and the Prix de l'Arc de Triomphe: a feat so astonishing, so breathtaking in its cool, ruthless, fleeting efficiency that the reaction was one of incomprehension, then criticism. Is that it? was the feeling. No – something must be wrong somewhere. Was Bahram ever really extended? Did Lammtarra ever win by a convincing distance? To which the only possible answer is: no, and so what? They did what the thoroughbred was conceived to do. They answered the questions that racing itself has elected to pose to them.

And they were both whisked off, pronto, to propagate perfection – which Bahram did not do and Lammtarra, to date, has not done, although if he does it is the Japanese who will bear the fruits of it. He was sold for $30 million in 1996, having left a sole tantalising crop of yearlings from his season at Dalham Hall stud (one of whom ran – badly – on Newmarket's last day of racing of the century). The days of Hyperion returning to die over the road from his birthplace are not quite over: Daylami, the great grey, was retired in 1999 to the present Aga Khan's Gilltown stud in Ireland, where he was foaled in 1994. But Lammtarra, born in America, trained in Dubai and Newmarket, retired to stud in Japan, is more typical. Welcome to the international world of racing, the one that Aga Khan III did as much as anyone to open up, back in 1940, when Bahram and Mahmoud (the 1936 Derby winner) were sold to America. There they would join Blenheim, who had won the Derby in 1930, and who sired Mahmoud before going to stud in Kentucky.

This, as may be imagined, went down badly. Lord Derby may have been a snake in one way, but the 1940 *Bloodstock Breeders' Review* didn't care if he was as wicked as Neville Heath, not while he had 'his inflexible resolution in retaining, in spite of world-wide offers, our most outstanding young stallion since St Simon . . . So long as we have men and horses of such a type, we may surely afford to look forward patiently to better days'. Well, no, actually. The loss of the three 1930s Derby winners would find its disastrous parallel in the 1990s, when the winner of the race in 1991–5 and 1999 was sold to Japan, and the 1997 winner went to stud in America.

But this is now accepted as a fact of globalised life. Then, the Aga Khan was seen as traitorous in the extreme, a Lord Haw-Haw of the Turf, even though English racing was something for which he may reasonably have felt respect rather than loyalty. It was an interesting question. By winning 'our' races, did these horses thereby have an obligation to give something in return for what they had received in kudos? Was it fair to snaffle England's greatest prize then go and parade its significance in America? And the Aga Khan had *said* that Bahram would not be sold; not, that is, unless a syndicate headed by a Vanderbilt and a Chrysler offered £40,000 for him. And so Bahram – suddenly perceived in all his shimmering greatness, rather as Lammtarra is now – and Mahmoud quit their positions at Egerton stud, which had been leased by the Aga Khan, and went to join Blenheim in the land of milk and honey.[7]

Of course this was wartime, even though the Aga Khan may not have known too much about that, from his hidey-hole in the Palace Hotel at St Moritz. Newmarket was not the best place in the world for valuable racehorses; one can never be sure that Bahram and Mahmoud would not have stayed in normal circumstances. Indeed, Lord Derby did lose two broodmares when a bomb fell in June 1940, so it wasn't quite so mean and cowardly as it seemed when, in December that year, the Aga Khan sold nineteen yearlings and forty horses in training. They made just over 42,000 guineas, around half of what they would normally have fetched; on the first day bids of less than ten guineas were accepted. It was all perfectly understandable; although for the Aga's trainer, sixty-year-old Frank Butters at Fitzroy House, off the High Street, it was a nightmare. Five years earlier he had had Bahram and Mahmoud in his well-stocked yard. Now he had eleven horses.

Another major trainer, 53-year-old Captain Cecil Boyd-Rochfort, who then ran Freemason Lodge (and would later train for the Queen), was in a similar situation to Butters, left with a string of twelve after his American owners had mostly pulled out their horses and, in some cases, sent them back to the US. There was even a rumour in New York that English racing had stopped. William Woodward, for whom Boyd-Rochfort had trained the 1933 One Thousand Guineas win-

---

[7] Blenheim and Mahmoud were both powerful sires; Bahram, who had already attained 'dead perfection', was less so and eventually went to South America. But the real loss was Nasrullah, whom the Aga Khan sold to America in 1950 without causing nearly such a fuss, and whose influence upon US breeding, in imparting speed to his offspring, was perhaps stronger than that of any other horse this century.

ner, Brown Betty, wrote to his trainer in May 1940: 'I do not know if it is correct that racing in England has been stopped, but assume that it is, and I would think that it should be. In fact I have been very loath to go on . . .'

This was all very fine, but what the First World War had proved was that racing, on balance, had been a good thing. Of course a lot of people felt almost honour-bound to deny this. Harold Nicolson, then an MP in the National Liberal party, wrote in his diary in May 1940 of making a speech at a dinner of the 1936 Club: 'I gave them a test question to vote on namely, "Should the Derby be put off?" They voted some 88 per cent in favour of postponement.' This, however, was just three days after the fall of Amiens and Arras, ten days before Dunkirk. Only a very bold soul would have piped up and said well actually, Harold, I can get you a bit of ten to one on Pont l'Eveque (who on 13 June did in fact win the race; being named after a French cheese may not have helped his popularity).

George Lambton *was* a bold soul, and it was at exactly this alarming time that he wrote, with his usual gentlemanly directness, to *The Times* in 1940: 'One of the arguments used by those who thought that racing should stop was that the men who were fighting in France were strongly opposed to it. I believe this to have been an absolute fallacy . . . on one occasion I went to France to see my brother, General Sir William Lambton, who had been terribly injured and whose life was in great danger . . . Before I had been in the camp a couple of days I found officers, Tommies, doctors, and nurses all talking and asking me about racing . . .'

Exchange for 'racing' the dread word 'football' – Who's top of the league? instead of What's won the Derby? – and this all rings very true.

Churchill knew as much, and Stafford Cripps, according to a letter from Lord Derby to Lambton, was 'not so violently opposed to racing as might be thought'. Nor was Herbert Morrison anything like as bad as Emmanuel Shinwell who, high as a kite on class hatred, put a question in the House about oats given to racehorses. Might they not, inquired the future peer, be given instead to poultry, in order that the nation's egg supply be increased? (What about that lovely powdered stuff, someone should have answered.) But the real reply made Shinwell look far sillier; apparently all those sackfuls of oats, poured down the patrician thoroughbred throat, would increase the supply of eggs by one per head every four years.

It was a wonder that there was no suggestion of shooting all the bloodstock to feed the public on horsemeat (stranger things were eaten during the war). And there was, indeed, an inevitable, sad culling of racehorses and bloodstock. But how interesting that those Labour party members who inveighed against the sport, as 'an insane and unseemly spectacle', had no thought for the 10,000 (peacetime) population of Newmarket, most of which was not made up of nobs and n'er-do-wells, but of people whose livelihood depended upon the continuation of racing and breeding. Were these poor souls the enemy, because they colluded in their own patronage? It was an attitude that was beginning to take a hold: the idea that racing was a symbol of all the old structures that needed to be dismantled.

'For the last few years,' wrote George Lambton in a 1941 issue of *Country Life*, 'our politicians . . . have had no interest in horse-racing or in the breeding of bloodstock . . . The present moment is a dangerous one for those interested in the bloodstock industry. We may be sure that the faddists and those people to whom the sport is antipathetic will not lose their opportunities, and they will have to be fought, and fought continuously.'

This was indeed prophetic, for the Second World War was both bringing to light and confusing the problems that racing would face afterwards. With regard to the immediate situation, Lambton unarguably wrote: 'If racing were to be stopped altogether, would it increase our output of munitions, or would there be one tragedy less? I say most emphatically "No" but it would throw many people out of work and completely ruin a large number who have all their capital invested in the racing and horse-breeding industry.' And this, put concisely, was the problem for the class warriors: they could not achieve the latter without also bringing about the former. As this unfortunate truth went against all their ideas, it was naturally not something that they chose to contemplate.

Yet there does seem to have been a stubborn, flinty resistance to the idea of racing at this time. Of course it is hard to gauge whether or not antipathy was stronger than it had been in the First World War. But the impression is that it was, that as a section of the public became more class aware, less willing to be won over by the pageant-like aspect of horse racing, less able to be lost in something outside itself, so its objections to the whole idea of the sport became more confident. And then there was the disapproval of gambling, ready as always to pop up its prim little head.

The puritans seemed to have the moral high ground. But disapproving of another person's pleasure, really for no better reason than that it brings them pleasure, is a dodgy game. And there was another section of the public (the normal, cheerful, red-blooded one) whose opinion was very different, and just as important. Resolutely refusing to dig for finer feelings, this gang held out for its good, strong, harmless indulgences. If Britain had to stand alone, then it was bloody well going to stand with more than just *Band Waggon* and *ITMA* to keep it amused.

And so, to please these hopeless – but inconveniently numerous – people, a compromise was reached. As before, racing went on at a handful of tracks including Windsor, Pontefract, Manchester, Ascot and, of course, Newmarket. Lingfield, often used in the first war, this time around became a POW camp. Windsor was very popular. Betty Kenward, the magnificent Jennifer of *Harpers and Queen*, described the extraordinary lengths to which people would go to reach the racecourse situated by the Thames, using bikes then trains then punts. She also recalled a meeting at Ascot in 1944 'where we were still dodging V-1 flying bombs! A racecourse was then the one place where one hardly heard a reference to Hitler's V-1s . . .' The bloody things were crashing over one's head, but one kept it down, studied the form and talked of what would win the next race; and this illusory oblivion, this aid to everyday courage, was the service that the sport performed for the nation. Indeed, those who abhorred the idea of racing in wartime had it absolutely the wrong way around. It is *precisely* at that time that sport is necessary. One can easily argue that it is made too important in peacetime; but during a war, as football teams from the Balkans surely have shown, sport comes into its own and fulfils its true function.

So those people who were criticised for going to watch the 1940 Cambridgeshire on the July Course – both legs of it, as 54 horses had been entered and the race had to be split in two – were only doing what their instincts had told them. 'Apparently,' sneered a local newspaper, 'racegoers had saved their petrol coupons for this special occasion.' Yes, yes, and they had probably saved their sanity at the same time.

Newmarket, meanwhile, as it had done in the First World War, was carrying on as best it could, training its dwindling number of horses (1,000 of them in 1939, far fewer a year later), again with the help of septuagenarians and women. At the same time, it was sharing the Heath with the RAF. How this was managed, one can only try and imagine, for the absurdity of the situation must have been frequently made apparent; especially when, at the start of the war, Wellingtons landing on the Heath were greeted by the sight of Cecil Marriott, Clerk of the Course, waving his stick and shouting that permission had not been given by the Jockey Club.

The Jockey Club, as ever, abided by its own arcane set of rules. In 1944, a caretaker of the building on the High Street[8] was reported for breaking the blackout, when six ground-floor windows were seen blazing with light in the middle of the night. A policeman went in and switched them off, but they were back on again half an hour later. 'I don't care,' said the caretaker, 'I'm independent of the police.' He failed to appear in court and received a £3 fine *in absentia*. Earlier, back in 1940, the threat had loomed of trenches being dug on the gallops; the Jockey Club burst into action, in that stately way which could be so ruthlessly effective. Representations were made to local Army chiefs ('now, Toppy, old chap . . .'). 'The officer in charge of the excavator was spoken to on the telephone and it was found that his instrument of destruction

---

[8] This, the same building that now stands, had been reconstructed in 1932–4 in the neo-Georgian style. The façade dates from this time. In 1935 a fire, started by a workman with an errant blow-lamp, destroyed much of what lay behind it, rooms that the Jockey Club had occupied for over a hundred years.

was booked for at least a year. The Newmarket gallops continued to be the training centre for racing . . .'[9]

Relationships between the racing establishment and the temporary service units were therefore not always easy, but they must have eventually got used to each other. They had to: the Rowley Mile course had been requisitioned by the government, right at the start of the war, and contemporary commentators actually expressed the fear that this would be a permanent arrangement, and Newmarket would be reduced to the July Course only. Of course this rumour had no substance, and indeed it is hard to see why the government would have wanted the Rowley Mile in peacetime; but it is easy to forget, when one has a comfortable knowledge that the war will come to an end in 1945, that in 1939 the future must have seemed horribly up for grabs.

As it was, the RAF left on the last day of 1947, although the Rowley Mile land was back in use by 1944, when the aircrews were most helpful to the Jockey Club in keeping trespassers off the Heath. But Newmarket remained an active airfield throughout the war. In 1917, a couple of night-flying training squadrons had been stationed there; this, though, was quite different. It was a real presence, an occupation. Photographs from the time show a soldier standing guard over the 'entrance' to Racecourse Side; tangles of barbed wire over the Rowley Mile, which had been painted with imitation hedges to make it resemble fields from the air; men smoking cheerfully on the racecourse grandstand steps; and clusters of Stirlings parked on the Heath. These were on dangerous missions, but before they could get a shot at the enemy they were, on occasion, brought down closer to home. A number of these aircraft are recorded as having 'cr. Devil's Ditch'. On black and windy nights, when the earthwork could not be seen, planes would strike into it; in a perverse way it was still doing the job for which it had been built.

Aircrews were sleeping in the Rowley Mile grandstand (which had, incidentally, been refurbished in 1925), with beds set up on the covered steps and in the Long Bar. Nissen huts and so forth were not constructed until 1943. Meals were

---

[9] From *East Anglia 1940* by R. Douglas Brown.

also taken in the grandstand. The saddling rooms were part of Station Headquarters, and the armourers' workshop was in the Jockey Club bar. Members of 161 Squadron, which had been formed at Newmarket and took part in clandestine operations, lived at Sefton Lodge, in the stable lads' quarters above the horse boxes. In the house itself were the WAAFs, where no doubt the ghost of the dear old Duchess of Montrose urged its valiant encouragement.

Of course, all this RAF activity made Newmarket a target for bombs, and these did indeed land. Those that fell in 1940 were mostly in open fields. In January 1941, two high explosives were dropped on the July Course (by someone who did not know when the racing season started, presumably). But it was the following month that saw the greatest disaster, when a bomb landed on to the High Street and scored a direct hit on the White Hart hotel. Twenty-seven people were killed, 248 injured. It seemed to have been intended as an attack on a convoy of military vehicles. Nevertheless, there was a rumour of an important meeting of high command, taking place at that time in the King Edward VII Memorial Hall (whose façade is still dented with little holes, left by bits of shrapnel). Had the building not been set back from the road, it would certainly have been struck, so maybe the rumour was correct.

Yet, disdaining fear, shrugging off disapproval, something approaching 30,000 people crammed themselves on to the July Course (which feels very full with a crowd of 10,000) for the 1941 Derby. The congestion caused by the 4,000 cars brought criticism in the House of Commons, which with Germany marching upon Russia surely had more important things to worry about. Always good to have a more manageable hate figure, though. In the cinemas, a newsreel item about a transatlantic tanker crew contained this bitchy piece of voiceover: 'That ought to be enough petrol to take quite a few racegoers to Newmarket.' But the sport ploughed on, giving its shred of comfort to the wicked, and in 1942 its persistence in the face of attack was rewarded. Out of this least likely of situations came one of the best horses of the century: and she ran, God bless her, in the colours of King George VI.

* * *

Sun Chariot, a daughter of Hyperion, was the sixth filly to win the female Triple Crown, and she is ranked with Sceptre and Pretty Polly. Strong, beautiful and delicate as a piece of Sèvres, she was a terrible madam – 'I've a few grey hairs and she gave them to me,' said her jockey, Gordon Richards – and a truly brilliant racer. A contemporary report on the St Leger read: 'Sun Chariot was last until the straight but then came away to win in a canter by three lengths and five.' She had done it as she liked, and behind her, helpless in her breathtaking wake, was the Derby winner, Watling Street. 'She was probably the greatest racehorse I've ever been across,' said Richards, who sat on plenty in 26 seasons as champion jockey.[10] He was clearly bedazzled by the very feminine form that her magnificence took. 'You never knew what she would do. In the Oaks she let them go a furlong at the start, then decided to go after them and won in a canter. In the St Leger she made a hack of the Derby winner.'

The implication was that she could have won that too. Had she done so, it would have given all five classics to the King, whose colt, Big Game, a son of Bahram, had won the Two Thousand Guineas (and the Champion Stakes) although he disappointed in the Derby. It was an extraordinary collection of successes, notwithstanding the fact that the King's two classic horses had been leased from the National Stud, Minoru-style: ever dutiful, he had reduced his breeding stock in accordance with war etiquette.

The royal relationship with racing had continued after the death of Edward VII – indeed, George V was considered by Richard Marsh a far better judge of a horse than his besotted father – although the high pitch of intensity, as reached in 1909, was not sustained, for that was not really George V's style. But he had a huge fondness for Newmarket, especially the July Course: 'He asked nothing better than to be able to wander without formality or fuss about the paddocks, where he felt like a landlord among his faithful tenants, and where he would smile to the poor people'[11] (sometimes one wonders

---

[10] Gordon Richards was knighted by the new Queen in 1953, five days before he beat her horse, Aureole, in his only Derby win, on Pinza. 'Gordon is the first man to be knighted for his equestrian performances since the Middle Ages,' said Lord Derby.

[11] From *Royal Newmarket* by R.C. Lyle.

if Manny Shinwell didn't have a point). As his father's had been, George's horses were trained at Egerton, where a staircase from the old Newmarket palace was installed. 'I wonder how many times Nell Gwyn climbed that,' the King remarked.

Edward VIII had little interest in the sport, or indeed in anything much except himself and his dreary love affairs, and rather oddly tried to sell Sandringham stud to his own brother. But George VI made his commitment to racing clear from the first. He was not a real *aficionado*, but he understood the sport's symbolic importance, and was greatly touched by the present of a pair of race-glasses, given to him by the Newmarket stable lads who had contributed sixpence each to the purchase. He supported Egerton House and Richard Marsh's successor, Willie Jarvis, although by 1942 Jarvis was near to death, and Sun Chariot and Big Game were trained by Fred Darling at Beckhampton. There the present Queen would identify them on the gallops for her father (after running her hands over Big Game's 'dark sherry-brown coat',[12] it was said that she didn't wash them for a week). When Jarvis died in 1943, the position of official royal trainer went to Cecil Boyd-Rochfort at Freemason Lodge.

The fact of the King's *annus mirabilis* in 1942 seems to have given some sort of official sanction to wartime racing: after all, it was impossible to be more respectable than George VI. Even had he not been King, he would never – the feeling surely went – have done peculiar deals with petrol coupons in order to get himself to the races. The sight of him, in RAF uniform, leading in Sun Chariot to the Newmarket winners' enclosure, had something deeply reassuring about it.

What with the King and Lord Derby (owner of Watling Street)[13] winning the five classics between them, the sport rediscovered some of its pre-war lustre and *la grande illusion*,

---

[12] Ibid.

[13] Lord Derby was, however, ambivalent about Big Game's defeat of his horse in the Guineas. '. . . it is certainly a good thing for racing that he should win,' he wrote to George Lambton. But 'I am afraid it will mean that Bahram will be head of the stallion list this year. Of course the worst of it is, however good a stallion he is, the Aga will have no compunction whatever about selling him and to any country whether enemy or not which wants to buy him. As you know I have a very poor opinion of the Aga's patriotism.' This is a little strange, though, bearing in mind that Bahram had *already* been sold.

of which people were more in need than ever, began to weave its spell again. In keeping with this was the presence of Lord Rosebery, a very dashing chap in his top hat, the son of the former prime minister. His horses were in training with Jack Jarvis (brother to Willie) at Park Lodge, and three of them sketched, with some poignancy, a history of wartime racing. In 1944, Ocean Swell won the Derby, after which Lord Rosebery was unable to get a seat on the train back to London and spent the journey in the guard's van. Five years earlier, a few weeks before war broke out, he had won the race with Ocean Swell's sire, Blue Peter. This horse may well have been the best of his generation; he had won the Guineas, but he was balked in his shot at the Triple Crown when, for the only time in its 223-year history, the St Leger was abandoned. Remarkably, this was the sole example, in either war, of a great horse being cheated of his 'destiny'; although Blue Peter did acquire for himself a different kind of legend. And his bad luck, if it can be called that, was nothing compared to that of Ribbon, a dear little filly on the Hyperion scale, who was entered in all three legs of the Triple Crown. The One Thousand Guineas she lost by a neck; the Oaks by a neck again; and the St Leger by a short head. 'I still feel sore about the St Leger,' said Jack Jarvis afterwards. 'Poor little Ribbon had a terribly rough passage and was bumped and knocked all over the place. She would not be denied, though, and putting her head down she battled on like the little heroine she was. I have no doubt in my mind that she won by a neck . . .' Lord Rosebery, trying to let the filly go out on the success that she, probably more than any other horse, deserved, entered her for the Jockey Club Cup. On her way to the course she was frightened by a passing jeep, reared up and fell on her side, then galloped off into the town. It was too late to withdraw her; she ran the last, and worst, race of her life.

Ribbon was one kind of heroine. Sun Chariot – the glamorous, the stellar, the capricious – was another, and *Royal Newmarket* simply oozes as it relates the arrival of the King and Queen to watch her. 'To say that the crowds cheered is a poor description. Those cheers were but the outward and audible signs of a feeling that touched the hardest of hearts. War was in progress; bombers were flying overhead, either going on their deadly missions or coming safely home, the King and Queen were with their people, sharing their pleasures as they shared their perils. They had been inspecting the Fens and the Queen had worn tweeds and stout shoes. To please her people on her first appearance at Newmarket' (as Queen, presumably) 'she had, between times, changed, and appeared on the racecourse in a mauve crêpe dress, a long mauve coat of the same material and a mauve straw hat with a feather, and a handbag to match. Few women would have gone to all this trouble to please their husbands. The Queen did it to please her people, and pleased they were.' Put that in your pipe and smoke it, Mr Herbert Morrison.

Newmarket racing was not exactly an escape; it was a defiance, as it was a defiance for the occupied French to run the Prix de l'Arc de Triomphe. An escape it could hardly be, not when, in 1943, there were 1,000-plus planes flying day and night out of East Anglia, sometimes hundreds of them at a time, constantly filling the sky like a mass of evil birds. Nor when, in May of that year, an RAF plane crashed on to the July Course, killing its occupants and causing the Guineas races to be postponed for a week. And yet, despite the shards of wreckage still embedded in the turf, when the Derby came around four weeks later the crowd was vaster than ever. People cycled there; people were queuing at Liverpool Street station from 6.45 in the morning (1,200 packed themselves on to a train that seated 700); people arrived the night before the race and spent the night in the open, or paid residents £2 to let them sit for a few hours in an armchair. Who could deny the power of this? Again, the only parallel is with a big football match nowadays. And no football match could ever come up with someone like the Hon. Dorothy Paget, who won the 1943 Derby with Straight Deal; for this was a woman on the Duchess of Montrose scale. When she died in 1960, she had owned more horses than any other female owner in the history of racing, and had spent around £3 million on the sport. She was, in fact, a figure from an earlier and bolder age. She gambled like a Lord Hastings, trembling with excitement as her horses ran, and had a network of commission agents to get her bets on. She moved her horses around like a Lord Glasgow, although the story is that it once worked the other way and that the Belgian trainer Henri Jelliss, at Beverley House on Exeter Road, gave her a day's notice to take her string away, failing which he would turn it out on to Newmarket High Street. No doubt he was bored with being telephoned at three o'clock in the morning to be asked his opinion about tomorrow's runners (George Bentinck also went in for chats of this kind, droning on at John Kent until the sun came up).

Having once broken down on the way to the races – upon which Dorothy Paget gave £300 for a Baby Austin parked outside a butcher's and took its owner to the course with her – for safety's sake she took two Rolls-Royces to every meeting. But it was her appearance that was truly extraordinary. Despite having ridden in her youth (she was born in 1906), she became the size of a house – Twelve Mile Bottom might have been a fair nickname – and even at Ascot would be dressed in what 'Jennifer' called 'her famous blue tweed coat, which I think must have been air-conditioned or thermostatted, as she wore it summer and winter in all weathers! She never seemed to buy any new clothes, and had a very sweet tooth. I remember someone laughingly saying that they thought she must swop her clothes coupons for sweet coupons!' Hard to know, really, which of these two women was the more splendid.

Meanwhile, as Miss Paget stepped up in her greatcoat to collect her glittering prize, all the other, familiar, wartime tales were playing themselves out in Newmarket. Abortionists were up in court. Servicemen were sent to prison for contracting bigamous marriages. Italian POWs were working on nearby farms (or, in 1944, going on strike; a meeting of the Newmarket Urban District Council was 'critical of their freedom'). Householders were complaining at the Council Offices about having evacuees billeted on them. A local woman's diary from the summer of 1944 explained why:

> Horseracing is in full swing. Stablemen can never earn
> enough to keep families, and so wives are compelled to
> take in racing men, who are lavish with money and

food. One offered my brother 30 shillings the other night for the privilege of spending a night in one of his armchairs. I daresay many are paying 20 shillings for bed and breakfast. If the owners of the little bathless boxes called houses in Newmarket can get 20 shillings for a very temporary inconvenience, they will hardly take the bread from their children's mouths because the government have not made fairer and more adequate provision for evacuees.

The same patronage, taking a different form. And what would happen to it, when the war was over? In 1945, George Lambton and Steve Donoghue died, following Lord Lonsdale the year before and the Duke of Portland in 1943. Lord Derby's Sun Stream – his last classic horse – won the One Thousand Guineas on V-E Day. Dante, whose name is commemorated in a bar on the July Course, was watched by what is still a record Newmarket crowd of 31,000 – including the King and Queen, Princess Elizabeth in her ATS uniform, women valiantly putting on a smart show and a crowd of demobbed servicemen, sitting like schoolboys on the grass beside the rail – as he won the last wartime Derby of the century. Triumph, unlikely as this had sometimes seemed, had been pulled from disaster. Now Newmarket was out on its own again: fighting its corner in the peacetime world.

10 Survival

'All Men who Love the Horse' – 1946–1999

T HIS WAS NEVER GOING to be easy. Racing was now set on a collision course with the twentieth century. As the world changed, as it began to fall in love with different ways of amusing itself and, above all, with the notion of 'choice', so the sport would start to panic. My God – what if they don't choose us? Which of course some of them did not. Which meant that, within racing, the desire for 'change' began to take a hold. This proved a dangerous urge, not least because the degree to which racing was able to change, without completely destroying itself, was very limited – something that its most loyal patron, the monarchy, was later to discover for itself.

Nevertheless the Jockey Club – in sombre, hairshirt-wearing mood – published a report in 1943 which urged 'alterations', as a means of attracting 'the increased attendances which we seek'. These alterations were left carefully unspecified. The report then went on to warn that they 'would constitute drastic innovations in a country tenacious of its traditions and essentially conservative in its outlook'. Quite obviously the Jockey Club itself was one of those conservative traditions, and no doubt it shuddered at the implications of its own suggestions. But, as has been said, it is an adaptable institution. It subscribed to the notion of 'change', just like the dukes with the dodgem rides in their back gardens: just as it had always done, in its way.

Yet the changes that had been made in the early years of the sport had been obvious, concrete, practical. After the war the idea of 'change' became a bit vague, because it now implied something to do with the image and perception of racing. Not that there were no concrete changes to be made on that score. At Newmarket, for example, it was very obvious indeed that something would have to be done about the Private Stand. This was loosely equivalent to the Members' enclosure today, but whereas now one can pay to get in, until the 1950s one needed a member of the stand to sign a voucher (as with Royal Ascot), plus the backing of a member of the Jockey Club (whose yearning for 'increased attendances' no doubt left it pretty sharpish at this point). This was ridiculous, of course; which is not to say that Members' nowadays – stuffed to the gills, on big race days, with people who have paid £20 to enter and then spend ten times as much on booze – is an improvement. Those who want a bit of peace are simply forced to create their own *de facto* Private Stand, by paying for annual membership, a view of the racing and a bar that is not strewn with drunks. The hierarchies within the racecourse are not so easily got rid of as all that – as the tiers of privilege within Newmarket's admirable new grandstand make very clear.

But this grandstand is a necessary change. Anyone who ever struggled their way through the subterranean warren of bars in the old stand, stumbling over champagne bottles as they went, would surely agree. Enough fiddling about had been done over the years: a refurbishment in 1925 and 1967, a bit stuck on here, a bit pulled down there ('They frequently seem to rebuild and alter their stands, sometimes for the worse!' wrote 'Jennifer', which can be taken as the last word on the subject), a new Tote building here, a moved parade ring there. The time had come to do the job properly.

All too often, though, the sport has managed not to do whatever needed to be done. It has put restaurants or marching bands or pop concerts on racecourses, when what the average racegoer would frankly die for is somewhere to sit in simple comfort and have a drink and an edible sandwich. And – the worst indictment of all – it has performed a *danse macabre* around the central question that the sport has faced, ever since the legalisation of betting shops in 1961: how do we get more money out of these bookmaking bastards? If racing had any idea whatsoever (no

– it has *ideas*,[1] but they never seem to leap into life) about how to get its hands on a larger chunk of the £4,000 million or so that is gambled on the sport every year in betting shops, of which (as of 1999) around 1.2 per cent is currently returned in the form of the Levy, then almost every one of its 'problems' would melt miraculously away. And 'increased attendances' could go hang.

Like most institutions, racing prefers solving perceived problems to real ones. It is easier. And the awful irony here, of course, is that a terrible, irredeemable old snob like Lord George Bentinck would have waded in and *got things done*, got everyone a tea table, got the bookmakers to pay more, for the simple reason that he would not have been worried about being careful and consensual and 'moving with the times'. All this lip service paid to 'change' comes down to nothing more than post-war embarrassment about having ever been so unashamedly patrician. It is like the Conservative party, post-1997, all over again. It is stunningly irrelevant. It simply means that people who love racing have to fight their way through a load of drunks, women with their hats falling off and squawking children, none of whom will probably ever go to a racecourse again, in order to stand on tiptoe and see a few ears flickering around the paddock. Meanwhile, what has changed? The sport is still full of nobs, the thoroughbred is still the ultimate nob, and no one who cares about racing could care less. The real racegoer abides by a different code, the one laid down by the horse himself: and objects to one thing only, which is the swamping of the sport by people – be they nobs or louts – who have no feeling for this code.

And so they object, yes, to the process whereby this self-conscious, pseudo-egalitarian, marketing-managerial era of ours has, in recent years, done its best to turn the sport into a series of open-air theme parks with, for those who feel the chill, hermetically sealed hospitality capsules lined with

[1] A gleam of hope showed itself at the start of the new century, however. Twelve of Britain's most prestigious racecourses – including, need one say it, Newmarket – closed a proper deal at last, giving them £200 million plus for television rights over the next ten years. More importantly, perhaps, the deal opened the way for the possibility of interactive betting, bypassing the Levy, which could direct more of the vast sums gambled on racing back into the sport itself. The question remains as to how these new riches might be spent.

television screens. In Newmarket, of course, racing could never be just an 'entertainment' – what with it being the essence of the place, and all that – and so Newmarket has remained, in its heart, proudly aloof from these shenanigans. But it has suffered for its pride, all the same: for being a sport, an industry, a part of the leisure world, a familiar modern concept to which none of the known rules seemed to apply.

It would start to be castigated, in fact, for the crime of being what it was. This is from Roger Mortimer's book about the Jockey Club, published in 1958:

> Newmarket is badly situated geographically ... Some people find the bleak austerity of the Heath repellent, others took a rooted dislike to Newmarket in the days when admission to the Private Stand was made as difficult as possible ... Race after race on a straight course is tedious, and the early part of the running of long-distance races at Newmarket is almost entirely concealed from view. It is difficult to pick the leaders in the Cesarewitch until two-thirds of the race is over and spectators of that event have been described as 'hanging about in Suffolk for a race that is run in Cambridgeshire'. Old-fashioned individuals, who dislike the idea of a round course, point to the vast crowds that come to the Cesarewitch every year, but the crowds are drawn not by the attraction of the race as a spectacle, but chiefly because of the amount of ante-post betting ... Taking it all in all, there is ample reason for Newmarket's comparative lack of popularity today ...

It did not, in other words, dance to the moderniser's tune: a discordant little ditty, preferring trills and twiddles to true melody, insubstantial after a few listenings.

And this 'lack of popularity', however much it may have been bubbling under, was not evident in the immediate post-war years. Far from it. In fact things looked to be just the same as ever, only better.

In 1946, for example, despite the fact that Newmarket horses were no longer on home territory for the classics, they won them all anyway. Airborne, who took the Derby and St Leger, was a hugely popular animal, one of those flat race horses who arouse a tremulous sentimentality more usually associated with National Hunt. Trained at Beaufort Cottage (now an equine veterinary practice) between St Mary's Church and the High Street, Airborne was a grey, always so much easier to anthropomorphise, because the eye is so much clearer against the pale head. He was owned by an 'ordinary' person, a plastics manufacturer from Godalming; he was 50/1 and barely known when he came flying past Lord Derby's horse in the Epsom straight; but his name had ensured that plenty of returning RAF men had had their money on. And so he was popular in a way that perhaps no classic winner had been since little Hyperion. Both horses created an illusion of accessibility, and this was something that the public increasingly sought, as it became increasingly unwilling to lose itself in something beyond itself.

Meanwhile, Newmarket was even acquiring a certain – good lord – glamour, which was just what it needed after years of austerity, khaki and blue tweed coats. Two of the young things who had watched Dante win the Derby now brought a new gloss to the sport and the town. Since the days of mad George Baird, Newmarket had created the impression of being almost entirely occupied by people born at the age of fifty-five. Edward VII's circle had given off that staid, shall-I-ever-get-up-from-the-dinner-table-again? image; Lord Derby and the Aga Khan were both as stout as washerwomen; George VI always looked very careworn; George Lambton and Cecil Boyd-Rochfort both conformed to Clive James' description of Sir Oswald Mosley, 'simultaneously ageless and out of date, like some Art Deco metal sculpture recently discovered in its original wrappings'. Of course the wars had stripped Newmarket – as indeed everywhere else – of its youth. Now it came high-stepping back to the place.

Prince Aly Khan, son of the demonised Aga, was indeed perhaps the most dashing owner of post-war racing. Photographs do not, one assumes, convey his irresistibility (in them he looks more like wicked Nancy Mitford's nickname for him, Jungle Jim), yet this was apparently total. He simply danced with a woman, pressed himself up against her, and that was that. As with the crushes on Fred Archer, there was probably a certain contagiousness about this. If one woman had slept with the prince, then the others wanted to do so as well. Nevertheless it must be said that these 'others' included the Duchess of Argyll, Thelma Furness, Pamela Harriman, Gene Tierney and Rita Hayworth (who, lucky girl, stayed at Gilltown stud with him), all of whom were a cut above your average Saturday night pull.

But racing was a true passion with Aly Khan who, like many people who have been brought up in Ireland, acquired an intimate feel for the thoroughbred. He also had horses in France and, gathering up his retinue in thrillingly impulsive style, would fly across the Channel and back in an afternoon to watch a race. In Newmarket, his treatment of trainers was not wholly gentlemanly: in 1950, he had made decisions about a couple of his father's horses over the head of Frank Butters; and in 1953 he left Butters' successor, Marcus Marsh, in the lurch by moving the family string away from Fitzroy House, despite the fact that Marsh had just trained the Aga Khan's Tulyar to a Derby–St Leger double. The horses were sent to Noel Murless at Warren Place, the yard that would later be taken over by Murless' son-in-law, Henry Cecil,[2] and where, in 1955, Lester Piggott would become stable jockey. Two years after that the Aga Khan died. Perhaps understandably, he had decided to overlook his son as his successor; his grandson, Karim, inherited his title, and has in his turn bred a seemly procession of extremely stylish racehorses.

It was the Murless–Piggott partnership (which would become as legendary as Dawson–Archer) that had charge of Aly Khan's greatest horse, Petite Étoile: fittingly enough a filly, a blissful grey creature, elegant as a Dior, winner of the One Thousand Guineas, Oaks and Champion Stakes of 1959. 'Hers is a woman's face and a woman's character,' said Murless. She was a madam on the Sun Chariot scale, who refused to follow a lead horse on the gallops unless it, too, was grey. Once she had been visited in her box by Aly Khan's racing manager, who had prodded her in the neck and told

---

[2] Henry Cecil married his first wife, Julie Murless, in 1966 and his second wife, Natalie, in 1991.

her she was 'getting a bit fat'; doing what any woman would wish to do in the circumstances, Petite Étoile picked the man up in her teeth by the lapels of his coat. How Aly Khan must have adored her, recognised her. Just a year after she won the Guineas for him, he was killed, aged forty-eight, in a car crash outside Paris; beside him was a model known simply as Bettina.

This was all a long way from the home life of our own dear Queen; but she, too, was bringing a fresh gleam to Newmarket, where her horses were trained by the lordly Cecil Boyd-Rochfort (step-father to Henry Cecil). The Queen's love and understanding of racing were – are – profound, perhaps more so than with any other monarch. Just to see her nowadays on a racecourse makes this completely clear; her loss of self, her engrossed relaxation, her appearance of being absolutely *chez soi* are all, somehow, both endearing and reassuring. Although the snobs and the class warriors interpret the Queen's presence within racing according to their own idiotic ideas ('God bless you, ma'am!' or *'Vive la Revolution!'*), she herself is abiding by that other, stronger, more arcane code.

Of course (or so the theory goes) she is no longer allowed to own any ostentatiously good horses, lest their successes cause the republican movement to burst its banks; but in the 1950s she was no more or less than a pretty young goddess in Norman Hartnell, and the thought of Derby victory in her coronation year brought genuine pleasure. 'How are preparations going?' the new Queen was asked, not long before the ceremony was due to take place at Westminster Abbey. 'Yes. Aureole is working very well, thank you,' she replied (it is also said, rather more nastily, that when a dinner party conversation turned to the writer of *The Divine Comedy*, she believed it to be referring to the winner of the 1945 Derby at Newmarket).

Aureole finished second to Pinza in 1953, but he was a tremendous horse, and the following year, when the Queen was leading owner on the first of two occasions, he won the Coronation Cup at Epsom and the King George at Ascot. At the same time he was what is known as a 'flashy chestnut', handsome as you like, but there are those within racing who distrust that flaming red look and indeed – although it is hard to see, frankly, how this can have had anything to do with his colour – Aureole was a very temperamental horse. (Perhaps this was attractive to the Queen, in the way that Petite Étoile would have been for Aly Khan.) Indeed he was so fiery that Boyd-Rochfort brought in a neurologist to lay his soothing hands on him; a charming idea, although not an unqualified success. Despite his quirks Aureole was a wonderful stallion, champion sire of 1960–1. He died in 1974 and was buried in his stud paddock; the man who had looked after him was given a holiday at this time.

Aureole was a product of the Royal Stud. So too was Pall Mall who, despite a pair of very dodgy forelegs, and rather to the surprise of both the Queen and her trainer, won the Two Thousand Guineas in 1958. The Queen was still breeding some very nice horses indeed.[3] Of course she did not, at this time, pay tax, the terrible weight of which was doing no favours at all to the other private owner-breeders. As Peter Willett, whose knowledge of this subject is unparalleled, put it in his book *The Thoroughbred*:

> The great owner-breeders – like Lord Falmouth and the Dukes of Westminster and Portland in the nineteenth century and Lords Derby, Astor and Rosebery in the period between the two World Wars – have played the chief parts in sustaining the reputation of the British thoroughbred as a classic performer. Yet taxation, death duties and economic factors generally have eroded the position of the once powerful private studs to a point at which, in the second half of the twentieth century, few of them were still operating and fewer still were capable of producing top-class horses with any regularity.

The new Lord Derby, for example, did his best to carry on, but it was entirely impossible that he should have the success

---

[3] The symbolic 'end' of the Queen's reign as an important breeder came in 1982, when she sold a mare named Height of Fashion to Sheikh Hamdan al Maktoum for over £1 million. This mare threw Unfuwain, winner of the Princess of Wales' Stakes and second in the King George at Ascot, and Nashwan, in 1989 the last horse to date to win the Guineas and the Derby (as well as the Eclipse and the King George). Both horses are highly successful sires.

of his father. Indeed, his finest horse was probably one that he inherited, Alycidon, who won a legendary Gold Cup victory in 1949 (although Teleprompter, bred at Woodland Stud, won America's rather more lucrative Arlington Million in 1985). Times had changed too much for an English member of the *ancien régime* ever again to win twenty classics in his lifetime. The 18th earl may have been a different sort of man from his father, with a less imposing personality (Nancy Mitford describes, in a letter to Evelyn Waugh, meeting the Derbys at a house party in France: 'Low horse power & no great effort to please. Diana says to me out loud come on let's get away from these bores'). But even the bore's[4] father would have found the conquest of racing too great a challenge in the years after the war. In 1963, Lord Derby was obliged to turn Stanley House into a public yard and lease it to his trainer, Bernard van Cutsem. In 1976, after van Cutsem's death, the yard was sold to his replacement, Gavin Pritchard-Gordon; and a 73-year occupancy, unlike any other in the history of Newmarket, came to an end.

The scale of the breeding problem was such that, in the twenty years after the war, thirty of the hundred classics run were won by foreign-bred animals. Back in the 1950s, it was the French, especially, who were coming over and putting our poor old classics at their mercy: not only did they have better prize money and better clothes to wear at the races, they had better horses. Even when the owner was as sparkly and chic as Madame Suzy Volterra, whose Phil Drake took the 1955 Derby,[5] it was hard to be gracious about it. If this was glamour – and it was – then you could keep it. The following year, the French finished first *and* second in the Derby. Fortunately, or perhaps not, the two countries were at the time in an alliance over Suez, otherwise unforgivable things might have been said, along the lines of how the people who had won the war had come out of it worse than those who had sat there, being occupied.

---

[4] In 1969, Lord Derby became the chairman of a Soho-based theatrical agency, which actually sounds rather exciting; he had also had the singer Billy Fury as a guest in his box at Epsom, when Fury had the Derby fourth in 1964.

[5] Mme Volterra's husband, owned the 1949 Derby second, Amour Drake, who lost by a head. Leon Volterra was desperately ill and his wife told him that his horse had won the race; he rallied briefly at this, but died soon after.

But the French dominance, dazzling though it had been, did not last; really it lived and died with the influence of one clever man, Marcel Boussac. English breeding, breathlessly recovering from the shock of losing its old patrons, pulled itself together. Crepello's Guineas–Derby double in 1957 was given the headline in the *Daily Telegraph*: 'French Colts Eclipsed'.

Since then France has produced what might be called a lesser 'average' horse but a steady succession of staggering champions: from the one that some consider the best post-war horse of the lot, Sea Bird, who won the 1965 Epsom Derby in a contemptuous canter, through to Montjeu, who pulled off the French–Irish Derby double in 1999 (of course both horses took the Arc as well). Racing is not so profoundly rooted in the French culture as the English. It is typical that Chantilly, the *centre d'entrainement* set inside a forest and beside a château, should have only 250 acres of training gallops as opposed to Newmarket's forty miles, but should be a place of incomparable beauty and ineffable style. And, as with most things, the French do the job far more efficiently than their shrugging, nonchalant attitude would make it appear.

They also have one huge advantage over this country, the foundations of which were laid in 1891. This was the year that bookmaking was banned. Instead of betting shops France has those dinky little PMU cafes, where one can have a *fine* and a bet, and all the money wagered on this nationalised *pari-mutuel* Tote system goes through the State. Sometimes a bit of government control is just what is needed in a sport whose market is so very free: the French Tote revenue returns to racing in chunks of a size that Britain can only dream of, contributing prize money that covers, on average, half of an owner's costs, compared with less than a quarter in this country. Despite the fact that France's 200-plus racecourses are almost empty and Britain's 59 sometimes so full that there isn't room to swing a jockey, France is awash with money and Britain starved of it.

For this, the Jockey Club must take its share of the blame. The Tote might have achieved a monopoly in this country in 1960, when the new Betting and Gaming Act (which legalised betting shops and posited the Levy) came into force, but the

Jockey Club – Lord Rosebery in particular – had withdrawn its support for the idea four years earlier, on the grounds that it would not have public support. Really, one could cry. It is, of course, true that there is a tremendous gambling sub-culture in this country. People love all the bobbing and weaving and dancing around looking for a price, the feeling that they are doing something terribly shrewd and daring, above all the sense that they are in personal, head-to-head combat with the bookmaker. Yet, as with most everything connected with racing, since gambling became an industry it has lost much of its sporting flavour. There are not many bookmakers nowadays who would take bets on the Lord Hastings scale, and betting shops just come right out and refuse to pay anyone who wins too much money. So the argument that a big bet on the Tote is negated, by the effect that it has upon the price, thereby loses some of its strength. Ah . . . but the *atmosphere* of bookmaking is what people love, goes the cry. It is true, again, that bookmakers do generate a theatrical buzz at a racecourse – theatrical being the operative word, no one really dresses like that – although the same could hardly be said of betting shops, especially now that they are so respectable. And the strange thing is that when one goes racing in France one never gives the missing 'atmosphere' a second thought. It is all a bit of a con, really; for racing, a very destructive one.

It was at Newmarket's July Course that the Tote was first introduced in 1929, where it was regarded with some bafflement and where panicking bookmakers sent their prices up into the skies: a horse of Lord Rosebery's, The Bastard, won at 100/1. The first ever Tote dividend, of 80 shillings sixpence to a two shilling stake, was also pretty handsome. Really this was a day to go gambling; one need never have worked again.

It was not then thought that the Tote – the 'robot bookie', as it was inaccurately called – would ever achieve a monopoly. Yet the fact that the opportunity was not taken when it came along has been disastrous. It was probably the single worst decision made, or fudged, by the sport this century. For the Tote is on racing's side: it was introduced – and this, to be fair, was also a Jockey Club initiative, the result of a 1919 report into funding new racecourse facilities – for the express purpose of giving more money back to the sport. But the bookmakers are on their own side. They work for themselves and, nowadays, for their shareholders. They use the product of racing and, because no one can say what they 'owe' for that usage, they naturally enough give as little as they can get away with. Their contribution to the sport's financial problems, however, has been generous in the extreme.

That string of French victories back in the 1950s may not have lasted very long, but it had made its point: one which had been illustrated, in different form, when the Aga Khan sold his Derby winners to America, and would be made again when the six Derby winners from the 1990s (plus Dancing Brave, Pentire, Pilsudski and co.) would leave for Japan. The point was brutally simple. It said that everything was up for grabs. At any time, another country could march upon the world of English racing, the home of the thoroughbred, pitch up its tents and run off with the spoils.

As money drained steadily out of the sport, so this became easier to do. Even the Maktoums sold Lammtarra – the perfect, the immaculate, the son of a Derby winner and an Oaks winner – before they knew whether he would be any good or not as a sire, presumably because they were unable to resist that $30 million offered by the abundantly wealthy Japanese racing industry (Tote monopoly, wouldn't you know). Because prize money and thus yearling prices and thus stud fees are all so high in Japan, $30 million – although a gamble – is a reasonable gamble. In Newmarket, a stallion is simply not worth that much; nor should he be, one might say, except that with the commercial pressures of the global market those have become the new rules. And even the *richissime* have to concede these pressures, which is why Lammtarra was sold. After all, the Maktoums are already underwriting the sport to an alarming extent, filling in the wells from which the betting shop revenue has been drained. Enough is sometimes enough.

And the paradox, now, is that in order to compete in a wider field, in the 'global market' where other countries have so much more spending muscle, horses have to be sold overseas in order that there should be enough money to produce more of them. Of course if too many of them are sold then there will be nothing left to make any new ones – a scenario which did begin to cross people's minds, trailing a good deal of panic in its wake, when Lammtarra became the biggest prize yet captured by Japan. But, to date, the world is still spinning – sometimes slowly, sometimes frighteningly fast – on its axis: the sales ring at Tattersalls.

After the war, Tattersalls transferred its operations completely to Newmarket, and its pre-eminence as a bloodstock auction house became confirmed beyond question. As Peter Willett wrote in his history of the firm: 'Between 1949 and 1984, 38 individual winners of 41 British classic races were sold by Tattersalls as either foals or yearlings; and although horses bought for high prices at the principal North American yearling sales have bitten deeply into the British classic cake since the late 1960s, horses sold by Tattersalls like To-Agori-Mou, Circus Plume and Commanche Run were still winning British classic races in the 1980s.' Circus Plume, incidentally, who won the Oaks, was bought for 98,000 guineas as a *foal*, but this was 1981, when the bloodstock market was revving up towards the height of its madness. All the same, the St Leger-winning Commanche Run was a rather better bargain at 9,000 guineas. This is the ludicrous nature of the whole sales game. Yet it goes on: a romantic folly, underpinned by the reassurance of pseudo-science, masquerading as a business.

Tattersalls, which had of course begun at Hyde Park Corner, moved its London premises to Knightsbridge Green in 1865. When these were bomb-damaged, however, plans were made to set up the whole shooting match at Parks Paddocks off The Avenue, where the Newmarket July Sales had been held since 1870. Compared with Knightsbridge – which had been as smart as its SW1 setting would imply, with stately mahogany yard doors that were polished every day, and 'Jennifer' as a regular visitor – Park Paddocks was extremely basic and scruffy. An aerial photograph taken in 1943 shows nothing but an expanse of land. The sales ring seems to have looked like an oversized DIY pagoda that never got finished: wooden, makeshift and, on that raised ground with the wind coming straight from the Urals, incredibly cold. 'In their search for protection from the biting weather, the gathering resembled a tramps' convention, rather than the élite of the racing world enjoying one of the highlights of the year,' was how the Italian breeder, Mario Incisa, described it. *Caro*, welcome to Newmarket.

But gradually the premises evolved into what we know today: the vastly extended paddocks, the magnificent octagonal sales ring which stands high above the road and, from it, looks like a neo-classical circus tent. Formally opened in 1965, the ring had been designed by Sir Albert Richardson, architect of the 1934 Jockey Club building, and a President of the Royal Academy. 'You've made it much too big,' was the comment of Lord Rosebery (now eighty-three), but in fact it needed to be just as big as it was and, when packed with an audience, feels as intimate as any theatre-in-the-round can do, if the performance is good enough.

Richardson – who died the year before the ring opened – also supervised the transportation to Newmarket of the Fox: a totem which had stood at Tattersalls since the 1780s. It is a highly singular piece of statuary, consisting of a stone cupola – topped with a bust of George IV, who was a good customer and had to be flattered – supported by four Ionic columns, within which sits a bright-eyed fox, one paw raised, on an ornate plinth. It symbolises the origins of Tattersalls, which go back to 1766, when hunters and hounds rather than racehorses were sold at Hyde Park Corner.

It was inconceivable that this should not go to Newmarket, just as it was unthinkable that the arch, which had also stood at Hyde Park Corner, would not now stand at the entrance to Tattersalls. At first, though, things had looked bad for the pro-fox lobby. 'Oh, that old thing,' said one of the firm's partners. 'We'll throw it on the rubbish dump.' And it was, indeed, no easy job to get the Fox to its place in the Lower Sales Paddocks. 'It will be necessary to cut the cupola into sections to transport it to Newmarket,' wrote Sir Albert Richardson. 'There is only one man in England who can do the job. He will arrive here with his tools at eight o'clock in the morning and will work till midday, when he will go off to a pub for lunch and you will not see him again until the next morning. The whole operation will cost you £700.' But it was done, all the same.

Tattersalls now stages a fixed programme of sales in Newmarket: the July Sales, the Houghton, the October, the Autumn and the December, at which yearlings, horses in training, foals and breeding stock are variously sold. It was at the 1967 December sale that the two-year-old, Vaguely Noble – whose reputation went before him, by at least the seven lengths of his most recent victory – entered the ring, followed by a surging crowd who pressed against the rope separating them from the horse. An excited commotion ensued, as if people were in the presence of a film star. 'This is ridiculous in this ring – someone will get hurt,' said the auctioneer. The bidding started at 80,000 guineas, which was already nearly double the Tattersalls record;[6] briskly it rose to 125,000; then, by tantalising thousand guinea degrees, it crept up to 136,000; at which point, two minutes and twelve seconds after bidding had begun, Vaguely Noble was knocked down to a Californian plastic surgeon who, dealer as he was in the construction of dreams, was no doubt unsurprised when his purchase won the 1968 Prix de l'Arc de Triomphe. The horse later became a fine stallion in Kentucky. This time, the gamble had worked.

But it is to the Houghton Yearling Sales that the greatest prestige has, since the 1960s, accrued. Ten years after the sale of Vaguely Noble, the aggregate price for the Houghton was nearly seven million guineas; by 1983, three horses from the sale reached over one million guineas apiece; in 1998 – as the people around the ring applauded, scepticism willingly overcome by awe – a sole yearling was knocked down to Sheikh Mohammed for three million guineas.

The money helps to create the atmosphere at the Houghton, but the money is just the graspable element in the magic. There is no spell quite so potent as the one woven by what have been adjudged the most glamorous, the most desirable yearlings in the country, as they circle the parade ring, the sky blackening and chilling around them, heads jerking against restraint, whinnies catching sharply against

---

[6] Solario, winner of the 1925 St Leger, who got caught in the starting tapes for the Derby, was sold for 47,000 guineas as a ten-year-old stallion in 1932.

the air which, even outdoors, feels thick and full and electric. This is theatre, watched by people whose eyes flick acutely from horse to catalogue, catalogue to horse; but it is also real, and rigorous, and almost frightening in the close, taut beauty of what it shows.

Rightly or wrongly, these yearlings represent the ideal towards which the sport constantly gravitates – they are at the beginning of their journey, but they are also the end of the road. Sometimes this paradox seems ridiculous. Sometimes the point of the whole thing – racing horses – seems lost. A great baby of a colt, his coat turned into shot silk by the uncertain shimmer of youth, enters the ring and the auction-eer tells his audience that here, before them, is a horse so beautifully bred that he is a stallion in the making. Where, one wants to ask, is pleasure in the present to be found, when it is squeezed so tight between past and future? And yet these yearlings would not give off the atmosphere they do if they did not carry past and future around with them, if they were not perceived to be the most privileged scions of the great family, whose duty first and foremost is to carry on the line.

What is being bought inside the Houghton sales ring is not just a horse but a symbol; and before it racing is, as it has always been, helpless. It knows, in a part of itself, how irrational this is. Sheikh Mohammed, crouching on the steps above the ring in jeans and baseball cap, knows that the glorious yearling beneath him will almost certainly never earn back what is being bid, knows that in all likelihood the yearling will never even win a Group race. For heaven's sake, the man has won them all already. He owns Dalham Hall stud just up the road, where he can breed horses of his own at least as desirable and glamorous as the one now stalking the ring. Yet, when it is down there in front of him, all that pedigree and possibility on the stage, under the hot and liquid light – he cannot resist. At the Houghton Sales the ideal is made flesh, the hope that it eternally inspires is made flesh, the sweet, drowning helplessness in the face of that hope is made flesh. And while Newmarket can still produce a show like this every year, it will still be irresistible to people who, nowadays, have the choice to go elsewhere.

Because even now, with this great big international racing world of ours, nothing can quite compare with Newmarket:

the remorseless allure of the Heath, the three-hundred-plus years of history stuffed casually up alleyways, behind shop fronts, under the ground. While the connection between past and present – brought to gleaming life by the Houghton yearlings – remains intact, and while there are people who still value this connection, Newmarket will remain fundamentally safe, untouched, unchanged.

Which is not to deny the change going on all around it: the collision course with the twentieth century. The world outside racing – which is what it has become once more – has values that are so inimical to those of Newmarket it is a wonder the place is still allowed to exist. Good lord, does the government know that women with pushchairs are obliged every morning to make way for strings of horses? That young men are forced to starve themselves systematically in order to make a living? That an average of five loose horses every day on the Heath could constitute a major traffic hazard? That racehorse owners throw hundreds of thousands of pounds away every year and do not ask for financial counselling? That trainers work 16-hour days without paternity leave? What the hell *is* this town?

Élitist, remote, self-regarding, badly behaved, over-sexed: not just the thoroughbred stallion, but the popular image of Newmarket. And what, one might wonder, could be more enthralling? If only it were true! It is fascinating that people should, in an apparently more informed and knowing world, subscribe to this notion. Yet they do, and to an extent that makes one wonder whether 'knowingness' is not a very poor substitute for sophistication, and whether an obsession with the images of things has left people incapable of understanding anything that is real.

Take, for example, the famous myth that Newmarket – and the racing world in general – is amazingly highly sexed. This gets trotted out regularly in newspapers and so forth, so much so that perfectly intelligent people will start nudging and winking on hearing the word 'stallion'. It says very little for metropolitan sex lives that those who lead them are so easily galvanised. Perhaps they should try living in country villages, where people enter into extra-marital affairs with a free and easy proficiency that would be almost French, if the clothes were not so arboreal. Newmarket is a provincial town, but the racing set within it forms a closed community, like a village, and what would be really surprising is if there were *no* affairs within it.

In 1999, the highly infamous scandal broke in which Henry Cecil sacked his stable rider, Kieren Fallon. Cecil's wife admitted an affair in the newspapers with a 'top jockey', and the implication was there for everyone to perceive. The excitement in the newspapers was truly orgiastic. It was incredible. Even if it were true that Natalie Cecil slept with Kieren Fallon in a racecourse shower – and Fallon has always denied this, to the extent of suing for wrongful dismissal – so what? What could be more usual, more predictable? What could be more commonplace than the fact that there is sex among stable workers, or the occasional affair between a stable girl and a trainer? Were it not for the fact that rumour is the stuff of life in Newmarket, rushing across the gallops faster than any horse ever went, no one would ever bother to speculate about human beings: but the habit of gossip is hard to break. And were it not for the newspapers, rumour is what it would remain: strong, yet somehow inconsequential.

From the outside, however, the idea of sex within the world of racing is apparently irresistible. It seems to trigger something primal, rather as miscegenation does, although it is no longer particularly acceptable to say so, whereas anything can be said about something as wickedly élitist as racing. Of course the élitism is part of the fascination. Racing is now seen as a world that dares to do what other worlds do not: politically incorrect to a degree that is truly erotic. The idea of a jockey sleeping with the master's wife conjures the dead spectre of feudalism. The idea of race-riding before sex conjures the near-dead notion of genuine knackering physicality – hey, this is sex as it was *meant* to be! Whips as well! There is a kind of envy, then, behind this mythologising of Newmarket as a hotbed of hot beds; although whether the protagonists in the Cecil–Fallon drama were greatly consoled by that, as their intimate lives were splurged dirtily across newspaper headlines, is debatable.

As in the time of William Palmer, whose murder trial caused a crush at the Old Bailey in 1855, British society is rather bored with itself at present, fiddling about with the keys on its Compaq and creating a compulsive disorder out of going to the shops every day. Therefore racing, which is interested in something *outside of itself*, is vastly intriguing. Any scandal is magnified to the power of ten if it was generated by someone on a horse. This was true for poor Lester Piggott, the greatest jockey by a furlong of post-war years – 'No, you can't call him great, he's too good for that,' said one of his colleagues – who became a figure of appalled fascination (not that he would have cared) when jailed for three years in 1987. It was not so much what Piggott had done: the £3.25 million tax fraud; the £1.36 million account filled with money from bets placed for him by owners; the secret retainer deal with Henry Cecil; the seventeen bank accounts and bloodstock dealings handled by companies in the Cayman Islands, the Bahamas and Panama; the refusal on three occasions to declare his tax situation to the Inland Revenue. This was grimly interesting, of course (though the idea that someone should go to prison for financial crimes always smacks of vengefulness). But it was the racing connection that put the paprika into the sauce. The world unto itself had come up against the law of the land; and the crunch was very satisfying indeed.

The class thing, of course, is at the heart of it. Élitism exists in all sorts of places – how can it be otherwise? – but still the pretence must be kept up that it does not, and with racing that pretence is not possible. It is simply a lie to say that anyone can own a horse. It is also a lie to say that anyone can afford a season ticket to Manchester United, but that is different.

Snobbery is perceived to be the culprit within racing, but commercial pressures have been just as guilty of keeping the sport exclusive – it was easier to own a horse before Robert Sangster & Co. made them 'worth' millions, and even easier before Bookmakers PLC helped to prevent prize money from keeping up with costs. Again, though, this is not the conventional line. The line is that the modern world is put off racing because it is a symbol of the old order. People may be curious about it, but only from a distance and never when the football is on.

This trivialising of the class issue has helped to obscure the real, hard truths about racing. The fact is that, except for a tiny number of phenomenally rich people – and, with this sport, the rich you will always have with you – it is not a privileged world at all. This is the necessary illusion that it creates, the illusion created by the thoroughbred horse. But the life is actually tough beyond belief, and frighteningly unforgiving. There are sixty or so trainers in Newmarket, out of which a small percentage are assured, so far as anyone can be, of their future: Henry Cecil at Warren Place and Sir Michael Stoute at Freemason Lodge (and Beech Hurst) are the two most obvious examples. Beneath this top stratum is another percentage of smaller yards, kept buoyant by a combination of work, intelligence, support and the occasional superior horse. And then there are the others, the ones who, in the familiar way, are unable to resist the lure of Newmarket but who, without one strong shaft of luck every season or so, simply go under. In the 1990s, 44 new trainers set up in Newmarket, to replace the 43 who gave up. The terrible, relentless hope that underpins this sport . . .

In 1999, a smashing, courageous two-year-old filly named Torgau won the Cherry Hinton Stakes at the July meeting, after which her trainer, a young man named Giles Bravery, stood in front of the Channel 4 television cameras and articulated, with charming simplicity, the truth that never gets said: that for the smaller trainers life is damn near impossible, a hole into which they are sucked ever deeper, and that, had this filly not won, financial pressures would have forced him out of Newmarket at the end of the season. This one race – and, subsequently, a second place in the Cheveley Park Stakes – had given him a three-year reprieve. 'Our job in life,' said Bravery, 'is to get a Torgau, win a race, flog her and keep going.' And if she had not won? If she had lost a shoe, or stumbled, or needed an extra furlong? And among the horses behind her, were there those whose victory would have saved another trainer from impending disaster? Again, the impossibility of running racing as a business – something predictable, assimilable – is made alarmingly clear. But what is even more alarming, in a sense, is the sport's dependence upon the willingness of people, like Giles

Bravery, like almost every racehorse owner, to take these mad risks in the name of hope. The risk is the same as it has always been, ever since the first person lost his shirt on a horse, but the context in which it is taken could hardly be more different.

Oh, well, they don't *have* to do it! would no doubt be the response. Who's forcing them? Nobody, of course. That is not the point. The point is that the sport would crumble if they did not. Racing talks the language of commerce and is kept going by an army of virtual volunteers.

None more so, incidentally, than the forgotten people at its heart, the body of workers who keep the whole bloody thing up and running. When those horses appear at racecourses, for the modern audience to ignore as it makes its way to the bar, someone has woken at five o'clock in the morning to clean their box, to feed them, to groom them, to keep them calm and happy, to get them into a horse-box, to make sure they arrive at the course in one piece, to plait their mane, to whisper reassurance into their twitching ears, to saddle them up, to walk them for long minutes around a pre-parade ring and the paddock; and then, when they lose – as the chances are they will, over and over again – to treat them with the same patient kindness as if they had won, to wash them down, to take them home again, to feed them again, to walk them up and down and make sure that they are sound . . . Heavens, if these people are having unusually good sex lives then they really deserve them. The odd one amongst them might be a tricky character, on the look-out for information and a fuller wallet (again, who can blame them?) but mostly they are motivated very simply: by love. Without them – without this whole sub-structure of knowledge and experience and willingness, in stables and in studs – there would be nothing: no theatre, no spectacle, no chance for everyone else to make and lose all that lovely money.

Occasionally, this precarious edifice has collapsed under the strain. In 1975, around a third of Newmarket's 600 or so stable lads (there are now closer to 2,000 of them) went on strike over demands for an extra £1.47 a week – how pathetic it sounds, a cup of coffee in the new grandstand – and tried to disrupt the Guineas meeting. On One Thousand Guineas day, the jockey Willie Carson was pulled from his horse by demonstrators, who then got into a fight with some racegoers who had run down to defend Carson (or perhaps, in a few cases, to enjoy a bit of a punch-up).

The racing finally took place; but the next morning, Two Thousand Guineas day, a dozen craters were dug out of the course – the matchless Rowley Mile – and although these were filled in, the lads staged a sit-down protest in front of the starting stalls. In the end, the Guineas had to be started in the old, Bentinck way, by a man with a flag. The lads were eventually removed by the police, but one hopes very much that it did not distress the horses. Some of what happened certainly alienated any sympathy with the strikers: flying pickets descended on Newmarket looking for trouble and a barn was set on fire at Palace House, which thankfully only burned 90 tons of hay. Some lads cheered as the flames blazed. It sounds horrible, yet it is hard not to feel sorry for these grimly underpaid workers.

Newmarket was in a very depressed state in the 1970s. It could not, like everyone else, do a three-day week, because horses always do a seven-day one, but it was naturally affected by the prevailing malaise.

Once again, the classics were falling to foreign horses. Bolkonski, who won the 1975 Two Thousand Guineas (ridden by Frankie Dettori's father), was Italian-owned, as was the Derby winner, Grundy – which was fine, however, because both horses were trained in England and had been sold through Tattersalls. More worrying was that in 1974, the French horse Nonoalco had won the Two Thousand Guineas; in 1976, Empery won the Derby and Pawneese the King George, again for France, and so on. The English classics simply could not afford for this to happen, not at so dark a time. But what English owner could possibly compete, with top rate tax at 98p in the pound and the threat of petrol at a pound a gallon? It was only when the oil money itself came to pour itself on Newmarket's troubled waters that the town would start to float again; and the life of the stable lad would become a little more certain.

Some pressures, though, do not change. Back in 1956, *The Times* had reported: 'Miss Rachel Mary Parsons, aged seventy-one, was found dead with head injuries at her home,

Landsdowne House, Falmouth Avenue, Newmarket, yester-day afternoon. Last night Newmarket police said that a local stableman had been arrested and charged with her murder. He will appear in court today.'

Rachel Parsons, the first woman to take a mechanical science tripos at Cambridge, was the daughter of Sir Charles Parsons, who had invented the marine steam turbine: 'The companionship of his daughter was the delight of his most active days,' reads his biography. 'From 1922 to 1925 she served as a Member of the London County Council. Miss Parsons has the distinction of being one of the three women members of the Institution of Naval Architects ...' The family traced its lineage back to Edward III, and Rachel Parsons had owned, before the war, a house in Belgrave Square that once belonged to the Duke of Kent. With the £840,000 left to her by her father, she had bought a vast 3,000-acre establishment near Newmarket, named Branches Park, in which she set up a stud. She also took over the training of her horses at Landsdowne House (a large and slightly haphazard building, in which Jack Watts – son of the man who rode Persimmon to Derby victory – had trained in the 1920s. After Rachel Parsons' death, it would be renamed Holland House yard, and is now a nursing home).

This was not, in short, the sort of person whom one expects to find beneath sacks in her larder, battered to death with an iron bar: privilege would seem to have protected her from that. But her eccentricity in old age had become wearisome. Having been a celebrated hostess before the war, at Branches House – where some of the ground floor rooms were used for storing oats – she would give guests a boiled egg for dinner. Somehow she bred fourteen winners at the stud. At Landsdowne, she had problems with staff, who could not cope with her demands, and two months before her death a stableman named Dennis Pratt, aged twenty-six, walked out on her over a dispute about holiday pay. He was subsequently warned by the police not to return to the stable.

Soon after this, Pratt very stupidly strolled into a jeweller's in Cambridge and, giving a false name, tried to sell some racing glasses. When the police arrived, summoned by the suspicious proprietor, Pratt was found to have more goods in an attaché case. He seems to have cracked very quickly when these were found. 'This will be a shock to you,' he said. 'I have done her in.' The story that he told was of having turned up at Landsdowne House, again asking for his money; of Rachel Parsons hitting him with her handbag; and of losing his temper and picking up 'a big bar of iron from the ground'. The police entered the house through the cellar and found the body. They also found hundreds of egg shells in the bedrooms, the bath choked with tea leaves, thousands of house keys everywhere and a general state of terrible neglect.

It sounds like a kind of hell, and, in his summing-up, the judge made reference to 'an eccentric, quarrelsome, unpleasant old woman, dirty in her habits and uncontrolled in her language'. She had, said Pratt's defence counsel, the future Lord Justice Havers, called him a guttersnipe and struck him repeatedly when he asked for his money. Whether or not this was the truth, it convinced the jury. Pratt was convicted of manslaughter, and jailed for ten years. Rachel Parsons, who died intestate, left over £600,000 as well as her properties and bloodstock. Branches Park, reported *The Times*, was sold 'by private negotiation, after it had failed to reach the reserve price at an auction in Newmarket'. Meanwhile 'fillies out of training, unbroken fillies and a brood mare, offered by order of the administrators of the estate of the late Miss R.M. Parsons, were the first lots to be auctioned at yesterday's session of Tattersalls second October sales at Park Paddocks . . .' There were 63 horses in all, which realised a total of £53,145: a hell of a lot of holiday pay.

Dennis Pratt emerges from this a good deal more sympathetically than William O'Brien was to do, 38 years later, when one evening he picked up a shotgun, walked up to the Newmarket trainer, Alex Scott, and fired once, fatally, into his chest. Scott, aged thirty-four, a married man with three children, died at his Glebe stud home in Cheveley. His Oak House yard, which is now called Gainsborough, was at the time the home of the two-year-old Lammtarra. The 33/1 ante-post Derby bet on the horse, made by Scott a couple of months before his death, after Lammtarra's sole run in 1994, was honoured by Ladbrokes and paid to his widow, Julia.

O'Brien, aged fifty-seven, was Scott's stud groom. He seems to have resented the younger man simply for what he was – an assured, well-connected, handsome old Etonian – and, thus, for the authority that he had over him. O'Brien had worked at the stud before the arrival of the Scotts and perhaps had it in his head that his position was being usurped. 'I just flipped,' was his explanation for picking up the gun. Alex Scott, he said, had treated him 'like a slave . . . Everything I worked for had gone. It had all just fallen at my feet'. But O'Brien's attempt at self-mitigation was dismissed and he was sent to jail for life, for murder.

In this story, the victim is a popular man with what looked to be an assured future (Lammtarra's Derby win was unbearably poignant in this regard; after the race, his jockey Walter Swinburn spoke of coming down the hill round Tattenham Corner: 'I said "Please God, please Alex, give me daylight," and it was like Moses and the Red Sea opening up . . .'). Compared with Rachel Parsons, he is an extremely attractive character. Conversely, William O'Brien comes across as a pig, a boor, a man who was said to have used a pitchfork on both stable workers and horses; whereas Dennis Pratt, whom *The Times* called 'a man of below average intelligence', simply seems pitiful. Of course these can only be impressions, although the juries in each case seem to have shared them. What is almost certain is that, in both cases, which in terms of the personalities appear to be quite different, the motivation would have been the same: a resentment so unbearable – of real or perceived privilege, of arrogance, of injustice – that it turned to madness.

There was to be another murder in Newmarket, this time of a quite different kind although again, in its way, a product of the age. The pretty, rustic July Course was probably the least likely setting in the country for such an incident. After racing on 6 August 1988, a drunken brawl took place which resulted in the death of a twenty-four-year-old man. Having been violently assaulted by several members of a coach party, he had choked on his own vomit.

Those involved had been thrown out of the racecourse while the meeting (attended, incidentally, by Princess Anne) was still going on. These men had no interest in racing, of course; they might just as well have been anywhere; a week later, let us be honest, they would probably have been at a football match. But *The Times* was absolutely right, nonetheless, when it called the incident 'the culmination of deteriorating crowd behaviour, much of it drink-related, that is clouding the sport'. There was talk, immediately afterwards, of banning alcohol at certain big race meetings. Naturally, this did not happen, and would have been pretty tough on all those normal racegoers who treasure a glass of fizz. Nor did any lasting improvements in crowd behaviour happen either. There were no more murders, and stewarding gradually became more visible, but the drunken element remained to make life intermittent hell.

As was made clear by the nasty little racecourses that came to brief life in the mid-nineteenth century, behaviour of this kind was not invented by the modern age. The difference, though, is that whereas in the 1840s racecourse drunks were regarded as an aberration, and the tracks at which they flourished were eventually legislated out of existence, nowadays these abysmal nuisances are likely to be lording it in the Members' enclosure. They are, in a passive way, *encouraged*. At the 1998 Guineas meeting, the last in the old Rowley Mile stand, people in Members' were literally collapsing with drink, like dominoes that had been touched with a finger. They were not going to go off and murder anyone, but they still constituted a considerable bore for those people who wanted to wade past them, without being verbally assaulted in some idiotic way, and go and watch some racing. One of them was even more of a bore to a horse, when he cracked a plastic glass close to the winners' enclosure and caused the animal to rear in terror. Pat Eddery, who had been about to dismount, looked as though he would have liked to kill the man, but how could such an incident have been prevented? And it was nothing, really. Yet in that moment, the whole teetering structure of racegoing seemed to tremble. One realised just how much it was founded upon trust, and how easily that trust could be broken: in an instant, and for ever.

But who is to blame the sport for letting this happen, when it is so fearful of falling attendances, of not being loose and cool and *laissez-faire*, of offending the people who do not really love it but who just might, one day, grow to do so, of not competing for the leisure pound (which is already being spent on racing, in the betting shops)? It is not an easy situation. And yet it should be so simple. The joke, in the end, is that a place like Newmarket – *Newmarket* – should believe for one moment that what it offers is not enough. That it has to bribe people with booze, for God's sake. That its three hundred years of strange, rich, majestic history cannot hold their own against the modern mantra of Accessibility, Equality, Conformity. That the unchanged magic can no longer weave its spell, because the world beyond the Heath no longer wants to believe in it.

Yet the magic *is* unchanged, and this is not its weakness but its strength. The anxious shifting backdrop of the post-war years seems to fade into nothing more than an insignificant series of tantrums when set against the calm of the Heath. In that time, it has seen some of the great races of the sport's history. There is the grey Abernant, not quite getting home in the 1949 Two Thousand Guineas, going on to win two July Cups with a voluptuous ease: 'He would give a great big sigh,' said his jockey, Gordon Richards, 'prop himself lazily on three legs and have a look round ...' There is Petite Étoile, skipping prettily to her Guineas victory in 1959 as Prince Aly Khan applauded his favourite girl. There is Nijinsky, again with Piggott up, pulling away casually in the final furlong to win the first leg of his 1970 Triple Crown; and Nijinsky back again on the Rowley Mile at the end of his career, after his narrow defeat in the Arc, back so that he could go out on a high in the Champion Stakes. The biggest crowd since Dante's Derby – more than 20,000 – came to watch the horse in all his fiery glamour: ' ... one was reminded time and time again,' wrote *The Times*, 'that many will still shun their television sets in order to see good racing and good horses in a good environment. And this was racing on the Rowley Mile course at its best ... Nijinsky was the magnet, of course, and it was sad to see him beaten for the second time in a fortnight. The sight of him in the paddock beforehand was reassuring, but during the parade he was restive and, in the opinion of one seasoned trainer of my acquaintance, a bundle of nerves. Unbeknown even to those closest to him, the devil had gone out of him . . .'

Nijinsky lost the Champion Stakes by a length and a half to Lorenzaccio and, after the race, Piggott said: 'He is still the best horse I have ever ridden.' Lorenzaccio, he later wrote in his autobiography, was 'a good horse but one that Nijinsky in his prime could have picked up and carried'. In fact the beautiful bay nearly won two Triple Crowns: the old Guineas–Derby–Leger one, and the new Derby–King–George–Arc one that his son, Lammtarra, was to achieve twenty-five years later. No animal before or since had come so close to such a feat. It exhausted him; he was a horse who lived very much on his aristocratic nerves – 'a bit more zip than was good for his peace of mind,' said his trainer, Vincent O'Brien – and, on Champion Stakes day, he was dancing in distress away from the attentions of the crowd and the cameras.

And so the story had the wrong ending. Racing does not deal in fairytales, except incidentally. But it had all been worth trying, because he had been so truly magnificent. 'Oh, he's trotted up!' said Peter O'Sullevan, almost laughing with delight as Nijinsky pulled joyfully clear of the 1969 Derby winner in his King George win at Ascot; 'What a horse this is.'

He was, in fact, the herald of another little golden age: three horses who, between them, lost five times in forty-five races and whose names, ever since, have become the totems of the post-war era. As Nijinsky went to begin his amazingly successful stallion career in America, so Brigadier Gerard ran against Mill Reef for the only time and beat him by three lengths in the Two Thousand Guineas. Mill Reef never lost again. Brigadier Gerard, who was one of that dying stalwart species, the English home-bred, lost once in a career of eighteen starts. His owner-breeders, Mr and Mrs John Hislop, were rumoured to have turned down an offer of £250,000 for him before the Guineas: 'He was never really for sale,' said Hislop. He was worth an estimated £1 million, and was still not for sale, when he won the Champion Stakes of 1971 in horrible wet ground. The following year he was back, after the shock of his defeat – at the hands of the Derby winner, no less, but a sad silence had still fallen, because by that time he had seemed invincible – in the Gold Cup at York. And in the 1972 Champion Stakes, the Brigadier did what Nijinsky no longer had the energy to do: stuck out for the fairytale ending.

The statue of Brigadier Gerard – a calm, gentlemanly looking piece of work, very much like the horse himself – stands in the centre of the pre-parade ring on the Rowley Mile. Both he and Mill Reef went to stud in Newmarket; both horses are buried there. The Brigadier, who stood at Egerton, lies in the grounds of Swynford Paddocks on the Six Mile Bottom road into the town. Mill Reef is in the little graveyard of the National Stud, where a woman brings a yellow wreath of flowers for him every year on his birthday. His own statue, by Skeaping, stands wonderfully alive in the grounds of the stud. On its plinth is inscribed a poem by his owner, Paul Mellon, an American of vast wealth and even greater style, whose words prove – if proof were necessary – that sentiment about the horse is a noble emotion: 'Swift as a bird I flew down many a course/Princes, lords, commoners, all sang my praise/In victory or defeat I played my part/Remember me, all men who love the Horse/If hearts and spirits flag in other days/Though small, I gave my all, I gave my heart.'

For these three horses were not just admired, they were loved. Nijinsky, who created drama by his mere presence; Mill Reef, 'the sweetest little horse' since Hyperion, who received get-well cards from all over the country when he broke his leg in 1972; Brigadier Gerard, whose one defeat only served to emphasise the majestic completeness of his career. When racegoers thronged the Rowley Mile course for the Champion Stakes in 1970 and 1972, they were not there for a booze-up or a whoop-up – at least, if individuals amongst them were, the crowd as a whole was not. They were there to see stories of incomparable romance act out their final scene; to see – or so they hoped – greatness avenge defeat; to see a fleeting moment, a quickening like an intake of breath, which would be absorbed into the immensity of the Heath, but of which they themselves had nevertheless, on one brief afternoon, been a part.

What changed so much, in the last thirty years of the century, that this mysterious collaboration between racing and its audience was no longer deemed possible? 'Ah, they don't make horses like that any more.'

Now it is true that, for example, a Triple Crown winner like Nijinsky has become a lost ideal; and for a very simple reason, which is that breeding has become so specialised, so speed-obsessed (the American influence, this), that horses who win a Guineas nowadays are rarely Derby horses, and St Leger horses are often despised as nothing but ploddy old 'stayers' – this despite the fact that, if it is popularity that the sport wants, ploddy old stayers are the name of the game. But the notion that the thoroughbred is defined by its classic ability, by its capacity to triumph over the classic distance of eight to fourteen furlongs, is a dead one. It exists in name, but not in fact. That is why the races that comprise what one might call the 'new' Triple Crown are all over the same distance; and why the greatest three-year-olds of the 1990s – Generous, Lammtarra, Helissio, Peintre Célèbre, Mark of Esteem – have all tended to run over the distance at which they were supreme, over and over again.

And then, it is said that they do not run often enough: they are faceless, unknowable, whisked off to stud before there is a chance to form a rapport with them. Again, it is true that horses nowadays tend to have shorter careers. For example, the last Guineas winners of the twentieth century seemed to be overcome, subsequently, by the strain of victory. Pennekamp (1995) injured himself in the Derby and never ran again; Mark of Esteem (1996) had two superb victories after the Guineas, but it took him until late summer to recover; Entrepreneur (1997), who had been tearing across the gallops for Michael Stoute – as quickly, said his trainer, as Shergar had once done – never ran a decent race afterwards; King of Kings (1998) ran in the Derby and was retired hurt to stud; Island Sands (1999) has not, to date, been heard of since Guineas day. With the fillies, the story is not very different. Only *la divine* Bosra Sham – who, with her poor hurt foot, won the 1996 Guineas with sublime ease effectively on three legs – went on to further conquests: of hearts and of Halling, no less.

Now there is nothing 'wrong' with those other animals, in the sense of being inferior to Guineas winners of the past.

Mark of Esteem was quite obviously the equal of any great miler, and even Island Sands did well on the day – of course he did. But something is out of joint, all the same. It may be that both the Guineas and the Epsom classics now come too early in a long season, and in some years are won by horses who have a fitness advantage at the time and thereafter collapse. It may be, more seriously, that the mania for speed – and Guineas horses nowadays tend to be speed animals, some of them barely even getting a mile – has caused too much stamina to be sacrificed. These horses, it sometimes seems, are not 'what they were' because they lack the constitution to support their ability. They break as easily as bone china; their muscles fray like ripped silk; they tire quickly, as if their engine had run down with alarming suddenness.

Because breeding has become a big business, breeders need to sell what makes money, and speed horses in the making – who will win a Guineas, rather than keeping everyone hanging around for half a season or more – are where the money lies. Entrepreneur, for example, made 600,000 guineas at the 1995 Houghton Sales. He now stands at Coolmore Stud in Ireland; one of his foals went for no less than 220,000 guineas at the December sales in 1999; Guineas horses are expensive because they are expensive. Meanwhile any weaknesses that they may have, any fragility that they may pass on to their offspring, is outweighed by the hope that they will also pass on speed. And so the cycle continues, having started up when it became clear, to men like Robert Sangster, that it made better business sense to let a horse have sex than to let it run. Once again, the laws of commerce are helping to depredate the commodity in which they deal.

Yet the story is not quite so simple. Nor is it anything like as gloomy as it seems. For there was another little golden age at the end of the twentieth century, twenty-five years after the first, and this time it was created by a breed that seemed to have vanished: the older horse, in all his stalwart strength, rose from his bed of straw and brought the century to a beautiful, surprising and extremely moving end.

For this, racing is indebted to that other old stalwart: the patron, the symbol of élitism, the owner who prefers sport, racing, the thing itself, to a buck in the bank and a stallion in the covering barn. And so, thanks to Lord Weinstock[7] and the Godolphin operation, horses like Pilsudski, Singspiel, Swain and Daylami were allowed to stay in training at the age of four, five, six. They had been good horses at three – good enough to retire to stud – but they were sound, free of the disease of fragility, and so why not keep going? Give them as long as it took to grow into greatness. And the sight of these animals, returning to every season with more assurance and self-knowledge, their heads higher, their necks more proudly arched, their eyes more serenely disdainful of competition, was satisfying beyond words. Not just for they themselves, but because they denied every one of the dreary new 'truths' about racing, and brought back thoughts of an earlier, freer, bolder age.

Cut, then, to Champions' Day, 1997: the best afternoon's racing at Newmarket since the day, exactly twenty-five years earlier, when Brigadier Gerard brought his story to that exquisitely triumphant, elegaic end. In 1997, the French two-year-old, Xaar, shot away with the Dewhurst Stakes – also won by Hyperion, Nijinsky, Mill Reef, Generous, Pennekamp, you name them – bounding down the Rowley Mile with the incomparable exuberance of youth. But it was the old campaigners who gave to the afternoon its soft, sweet, symphonic pleasures. Singspiel galloped. Bosra Sham paraded, her full chestnut haunches swaying with the usual slow grace. Pilsudski won the Champion Stakes as he won almost everything else, without fuss or show, with honesty and heart. It was the last time that racegoers in this country would see any of these horses, who had become as familiar as friends. And it was clear as never before that here, within this crowd, was an unbridgeable gap between those who were profoundly engaged, lost in the spectacle, and those who were fundamentally indifferent, lost only in the part that they themselves were playing. It hurt to see the return of Pilsudski to the winners' enclosure, after yet another display of heartbreaking heroism, and to feel the small steel chill of

[7] It was Lord Weinstock's late son who bred Pilsudski (who, like Singspiel, was trained by Michael Stoute). He died before the horse became the gallant, indefatigable winner of the Eclipse Stakes, Champion Stakes, Irish Champion Stakes, Japan Cup and Breeders' Cup Turf.

apathy beneath the warmth of his reception. It hurt to see eyes turned away from Bosra Sham, pretty as a Boucher as she made her calm circuit of the paddock. And no, the horses do not know – they are not asking for approval – which somehow makes it all the more ridiculous, this mad desire within racing to find favour amongst those who engage with the world so very differently. For the fact is that it doesn't get any better than Champions' Day, 1997. That is as good as it can ever be, or ever was. There is nothing more to offer. Leave it there, then, with Pilsudski in the winners' enclosure, dank, exhausted, fêted, having given to his audience all that he had – except his thoroughbred mystery, so infinite, so boundless, that it seemed to reduce the world of his sport to the taut little circle trodden by his shifting hooves.

On the Heath, past and future are the same: a succession of mornings, some dim-lit, some flooded with sun, and a succession of galloping horses. There should be so many ghosts: of the Town Plate runners from the years of Restoration, breathing steam into the air as they were rubbed down between heats, ridden by grooms in coloured taffeta or by the King in his long black wig, laughing at his own determination to meet this peculiar challenge; the competitors in the match races of the eighteenth century, their flanks ripped by spurs, their lungs bursting into flames; Flying Childers and Eclipse, white feet flashing across the Beacon Course; Escape, losing and winning as the mounted spectators looked on and wondered; those early unknown Guineas winners with their odd, remote names – Hephestion, Cwrw, Nectar, Zeal, Whizgig; Hermit pouring blood from his nose on the gallops; the robust races of the Autumn double, followed by the stoical gamblers on their hacks; the horses of the golden age – Isinglass, Ormonde, St Simon, La Flèche, Persimmon, Diamond Jubilee; the consoling, defiantly glamorous victories of wartime – Gainsborough, Sun Chariot, Dante; little Hyperion twinkling across Lord Derby's gallops; Aureole watched by the Queen, oblivious to thoughts of her coronation; Petite Étoile dazzling, Crepello eclipsing the French, Nijinsky boiling over, Brigadier Gerard keeping his cool, Dancing Brave dominating, Nashwan barely seeming to touch the ground, Rodrigo de Triano giving Piggott his last classic victory; Fred Archer on his pale grey hack . . .

And yet, and this is the most mysterious thing, there are no ghosts at all. Memory is so dense that it is absorbed into the turf. It just seems to be waiting, with all the power of passivity, for more memories to come. Past and future are the same; and here, on the Heath, is where they meet.

For the town, change makes itself a little plainer, of course. The High Street takes the same shape, but the horses have been gradually marginalised. They no longer, as they once did, emerge from Palace House, Beaufort, Lowther, Kingston, Primrose and the rest, to clip-clop amongst the shoppers every morning. The real world, if that is what it is, has asserted its territorial rights to that extent, at least. It wanted more, of course. In 1977, the Jockey Club won a symbolic battle when Park Lodge, just behind the High Street, was threatened with demolition by the local council. It was, said the planners, a hazard, an anomaly, which should be replaced by fifty dwelling units.

And yes, it is easy to mock the bureaucratic enemy, but in a reasonable world it would have right on its side. In fact at the time the council was alarmed by predictions of a sudden increase in Newmarket's population, which stood – and still stands – at around 18,000. Such predictions are a dangerous science, yet it is easy enough to see that, for those who live in Newmarket but are not – like the 3,500 connected with the racing industry – in the *heart* of Newmarket, the thought that people would not be housed seemed more pressing than the thought that horses would not be housed.

But the laws of the world outside did not prevail. The Jockey Club won its case against the council. It had to do so, else the tremulous footing upon which Newmarket stands, the knowledge, resolutely denied, that it is indeed an anomaly, might have toppled into the seas of normality, banality, conformity, where the thoroughbred does not rule.

He still rules in Newmarket, but he has been sent to lord it over the relative hinterlands: the roads east of the Clock Tower – Bury, Fordham, Snailwell, Moulton – and Hamilton Road, the Jockey Club-owned land which runs down beside the Racecourse Side gallops and which, from the late 1960s onwards, has been developed into modern training establishments. This is where Lester Piggott built Eve Lodge, when he gave up riding for the first time; where Henry Cecil briefly trained, at Marriott stables, before moving to Warren House; where Alex Scott ran Oak House, now Gainsborough; where Giles Bravery trained Torgau. These are the yards that change hands most often, that tend to lay empty until some brave soul decides to give it their best shot. They are the younger Newmarket, without the beauty of the central yards like Fitzroy House and Park Lodge, or the solidity of Freemason and Warren Place. But they are no different, really, from the others; only that the hope and disappointment show more clearly.

Meanwhile the High Street remains that of a bustling, provincial town, incidentally surrounded by a history unlike any other. Roads named after Fred Archer, Noel Murless, Nat Flatman, Lord Falmouth, the Dukes of Portland and Queensberry, Admiral Rous, William Crockford, Bahram. Paintings of old champions in every pub. Two defunct palaces, built by monarchs who fell in helpless thrall to the place. A graveyard full of dead jockeys and trainers. Dead yards behind every inch of the High Street. And dead horses: in the little graveyards of every stud; the 1793 Derby winner, Waxy, beneath the ground in front of All Saints' Church; Albert – who died in a match race in 1831 – beneath the garden of the Edward VII Memorial Hall; Chamossaire, who won the 1945 St Leger, in a magnificent statue that vibrates with life at the empty end of the Snailwell Road; Brigadier Gerard; Eclipse; Mill Reef – in the town, yes, there are ghosts.

How is it possible, one wonders, looking along the length of that little High Street? How can it continue to hold this magic at its heart? There, at the end of the street before the Clock Tower, the curve of Fred Archer Way takes in the Rookery shopping centre, where the court of Charles II once lodged itself, and where Ellesmere House and Primrose Cottage once stood. Further down, the bright, ephemeral façades of Warehouse Clearance Shops, of Thing-Me-Bobs, of Blockbuster Video, lie firmly stamped across the past.

And from his plinth outside the Jockey Club, Hyperion looks on.

Index

leads Jockey Club 147
Rous Memorial cottages 183
Rowley Mile 5, 9, 12–13, 41, 289, 318
Royal Air Force 288–290, 294
Royal Lodge stud 94
Royal Stud 22, 25–26, 147, 244, 304
Rubens, Peter Paul 22
Rugeley Poisoner (William Palmer) 145
Running Rein (horse) 139–141
Runyon, Damon 256
Rush (horse) 132–133
Rye House Plot 52

Sackville House Stables 120
saddling 137
Salman, Princes Fahd and Ahmed 270
Salvanos (horse) 206
Samwell, William 31
Sandown racecourse 172, 173
Sangster, Robert 269–271
Sansovino (horse) 273, 274
Sartorius, John Nost 87, 96
Sassoon, Sir Victor 271
Savernake, Lord Billy 196
Sceptre (horse) 232, 257–261, 271
Scott, Alex 320–321, 331
Sea Bird (horse) 306
Sefton Lodge 188, 290
Sefton stud 189
Severus, Septimius, Roman emperor 18
sex, and the racing world 313–314
Sex Discrimination Act (1975) 267
Seymour, James 87
Shadwell, Thomas 36–37
Shalfleet yard 190
Shilelagh (horse) 117
Shinwell, Emmanuel 285–286
Sievier, Robert 257–261, 271
Sims, Willie 254
Singspiel (horse) 328
Sir Peter Teazle (horse) 78
Six Mile Bottom stud 104
Sloan, Tod 254–256
Solario (horse) 311n
Soltykoff, Dmitri 187
Sporting Duchess, The (musical comedy) 189
Sporting Kalendar (1751) 55, 68, 72, 266
St Agnes church 189
St Frusquin (horse) 33, 208, 236, 242
St Gatien (horse) 179
St Leger, Colonel Anthony 105
St Leger classic 110, 130
  wartime 262, 293

St Mirin (horse) 228
St Simon (horse) 127, 208, 234–236
stable hands 317–318
Stanley House 189, 268, 272–274, 276, 279, 305
starting 137
  starting gates 255
starvation and jockeys 210–212
Stiff Dick (horse) 60
Stirling-Crawfurd 188–189
Stockbridge House 185
Stoute, Michael 316
Straight Deal (horse) 294
strike action 317–318
Stuart, Frances 41
Stubbs, George 88–90, 91, 96, 103, 113
Subscription Rooms 138, 170n
Sue, Eugène 71
Suffolk, 3rd Earl of 31
Sullivan, Sir Arthur 185
Sun Chariot (horse) 291, 293
Sun Stream (horse) 280, 296
Surplice (horse) 143, 179
Swain (horse) 328
Swinburn, Walter 212, 321
Sykes, Sir Tatton 244–245

Tattersall, Richard 58, 110, 131–132, 145
Tattersall, Somerville 257–258
Tattersalls 56, 67, 98, 256–257
  Houghton Yearling Sales 311–312
  Subscription Rooms 138
  transfer to Newmarket 309–311
  World War I 265
Taylor, Alec 189, 260
Terrace House stables 185
Thomond, Earl of 30, 38
Thormanby 127, 129, 170, 187, 218
Thornhill, Thomas 117
Thoroughbred Breeders' Association 265
thoroughbreds 69, 91, 97–98, 232–233
Tillemans, Peter 3
Tillyard, Stella 84
Tiresias (horse) 127
Top Cees (horse) 105n, 179
Torgau (horse) 316, 331
Tote 299n, 306–308
  French system 306
touts, early 120
Town Plate 27–29, 84
Townshend, Thomas, 1st Viscount Sydney 80
trainers:
  early 118–123